A Spiritual Strategy

FOR COUNSELING
AND PSYCHOTHERAPY

A SPIRITUAL STRATEGY

FOR
COUNSELING
AND
PSYCHOTHERAPY

P. SCOTT RICHARDS
AND
ALLEN E. BERGIN

AMERICAN PSYCHOLOGICAL ASSOCIATION
Washington, DC

Forth printing February 2002

Published by
American Psychological Association
750 First Street, NE
Washington, DC 20002

Copies may be ordered from
APA Order Department
P.O. Box 92984
Washington, DC 20090-2984

In the United Kingdom, Europe, Africa, and the Middle East, copies may be ordered from
American Psychological Association
3 Henrietta Street
Covent Garden
London WC2E 8LU
England

Typeset in Goudy by Maryland Composition Company, Inc., Glen Burnie, MD

Printer: Port City Press, Inc., Baltimore, MD
Cover Designer: Minker Design, Bethesda, MD
Technical/production editor: Olin J. Nettles

Library of Congress Cataloging-in-Publication Data
Richards, P. Scott.
    A spiritual strategy for counseling and psychotherapy / P. Scott Richards, Allen E.
    Bergin.
        p.   cm.
    Includes bibliographical references and index.
    ISBN 1-55798-434-4 (acid-free paper)
    1. Psychotherapy—Religious aspects.   2. Mental health counseling—Religious
aspects.   3. Psychotherapy patients–Religious life.   4. Spirituality.   I. Bergin,
Allen E., 1934– .   II. Title.
RC489.R46R53   1997
6I6.89—dc21   97-8297
                                                                                         CIP

British Library Cataloging-in-Publication Data
A CIP record is available from the British Library.

Printed in the United States of America

Dedicated to
Sir John Marks Templeton
whose ideals and philanthropy have
ushered in a new era of faithful
scholarship in science and religion

CONTENTS

PART III: PSYCHOTHERAPY PROCESS AND METHODS

PART IV: RESEARCH AND FUTURE DIRECTIONS

PREFACE

I have had the good fortune of being influenced and mentored by Allen Bergin for 18 years; almost my entire academic career. I first met Allen in 1979 when I was an undergraduate psychology student at Brigham Young University (BYU), not long after his landmark "Psychotherapy and Religious Values" article had been accepted for publication in the *Journal of Consulting and Clinical Psychology* (Bergin, 1980a). Allen was a guest speaker in one of my classes and spoke about this article. I was immediately captivated and not long after volunteered to assist him with some of his research. Later, during my master's degree program, he hired me to work as one of his graduate assistants. This provided me with further opportunities for mentoring from him. As I worked on my PhD at the University of Minnesota, I remained in touch with Allen and continued to keep abreast of his work. I was delighted at his continuing success at bringing a spiritual perspective into mainstream psychology and psychotherapy. I was in the audience in Boston in 1990 when he delivered the American Psychological Association (APA) Distinguished Professional Contribution to Knowledge Award Address, titled "Values and Religious Issues in Psychotherapy and Mental Health," and I was pleased to see it published the following year in the *American Psychologist* (Bergin, 1991).

Allen continued to encourage me while I was at Minnesota to pursue my interests in religious and spiritual issues in mental health and psychotherapy. When I returned to Brigham Young University in 1990 as a faculty member, we renewed our friendship and collaborative efforts. Three years ago, when I encouraged him to write this book, I was very happy that he invited me to coauthor it with him. He unselfishly asked me to be first author on the book and to take the lead in writing it. Allen's writings over the past two decades provided the conceptual and research foundation for this book. His encouragement, support, and mentoring gave me the confidence and direction I needed to complete my portion of the manuscript. Collaborating with him on this work has been the high point of my career.

I feel very deeply about bringing a spiritual perspective and strategy into mainstream psychology and psychotherapy. A spiritual strategy will greatly enhance our capacity to understand and effectively assist the human family. In my view, the deepest, most profound, lasting psychological change occurs when spiritual healing also occurs. I know that such healing is possible, because I have experienced it and I have observed clients experience it. It is my hope that our book will assist psychotherapists in their efforts to help their clients grow and fulfill their great potential. If it does, our purpose in writing it will have been realized.

P. Scott Richards

When Scott Richards proposed that we synthesize my work on religion and mental health and publish it as a book, I was pleased by this idea and by the fact that Scott had the energy and talent to make the concept into reality. I had admired him many years earlier when he served as my research assistant. He had gone on to obtain his PhD and then do some teaching in the University of Minnesota system and later was a faculty member at Central Washington University. I was impressed that his Minnesota doctoral dissertation won the annual dissertation prize from Division 5 (Evaluation, Measurement, and Statistics) of APA, and so I was pleased when he returned to BYU and then became director of the doctoral program in counseling psychology. This book would not have been published nor conceptualized so well without him. Indeed, the project became much more than a synthesis of my work, but rather an integration of it with Scott's own burgeoning and influential research, along with the ideas, data, and techniques of many excellent scholars in this field. As such, it is a much better product than it would otherwise have been.

I insisted, at the beginning of our contract with APA, that Scott be senior author. This proved to be wise because Scott ultimately did most of the work, even though it rests on foundations I laid over a 15-year period.

I am particularly happy that APA Books chose to print this volume and am pleased that we could work with such an astute, able, and supportive editor as Peggy Schlegel. As my career is approaching its closing years, I am gratified that my crusade to bring religion within the mainstream of clinical psychology is finally succeeding. There has been a host of competent and original colleagues who have brought about this dramatic shift in conceptual and clinical orientation. It is an achievement worth celebrating!

What we celebrate and what this book symbolizes is that the human spirit, under God, is vital to understanding personality and therapeutic change. If we omit such spiritual realities from our account of human behavior, it won't matter much what else we keep in, because we will have omitted the most fundamental aspect of human nature. With this dimension included, our ability to advance psychological science, professional practice, and human welfare can truly soar.

We hope that you, the reader, will approach the study of this volume with a meditative, prayerful mind-set and open your being to the possibilities described therein. With a mental and emotional openness to the spirit of truth, a person can discern what is trustworthy and most valuable. One can also bring to the reading experience added inspirations that may provide additional insights above and beyond what is already in print. We hope this may be particularly true for students as they search for original pathways in the course of their own writing, research, and clinical projects.

Allen E. Bergin

ACKNOWLEDGMENTS

We are grateful to Peggy Schlegel, our acquisitions editor at APA, for encouragement to assume the formidable task of formulating an approach to spiritual psychology that would appeal to a broad spectrum of psychologically informed and interested readers. Her support and her advice were absolutely crucial.

We were also aided immeasurably by the suggestions and critiques of students and colleagues, especially professors Lane Fischer, Roger R. Keller, Spencer J. Palmer, I. Reed Payne, Brent A. Slife, and James R. Young; and graduate students Ronald B. Chamberlain, Lisa Ducommun McGrath, Alan Hansen, David T. Morgan, Randy K. Moss, Jan Peterson, Richard W. Potts, and John R. Rector.

Thanks are also due to several outstanding therapists and experts who have influenced our clinical thinking, particularly Barbara Swain and the late Alan R. Anderson and Albert Bandura and the late Carl R. Rogers. In addition, the work of many spirituality researchers influenced and inspired us. They are referred to in the book and the reference list, but we acknowledge in particular the following: Gary R. Collins, Stanton L. Jones, Eugene W. Kelly, Jr., David B. Larson, Robert J. Lovinger, H. Newton Malony, John E. Martin, William R. Miller, Melvin Morse, L. Rebecca Propst, Edward P. Shafranske, Bernard Spilka, Alan C. Tjeltveit, and Everett L. Worthington.

We also greatly appreciate those who contributed to the book by writing case reports for chapter 11: Robert J. Lovinger, Lisa Miller, Carolyn A. Rayburn, Clifford H. Swenson, Edward P. Shafranske, Alan C. Tjeltveit, and Wendy L. Ulrich.

Finally, we are deeply grateful to our wives, Marian Bergin and Marcia Richards. Their continuing love and support are sources of inspiration, joy, and strength.

I

INTRODUCTION

PROLOGUE

No single volume can do justice to the range and depth of human faith in and devotion to religious and spiritual phenomena; nor can the possibilities for healing that derive therefrom be described in full. We have been humbled by the greatness of this subject and by our inadequacy truly to comprehend and explain it. We are deeply conscious of our limitations and of the biases inherent in exploring from our own cultural context a world of spiritual experience that is universal, and more varied and complex, than anyone can grasp.

We know that our theistic perspective will touch only a portion of the world's people; nevertheless, we have begun a task that has proved to be deeply rewarding. It has brought us in touch with a literature and a variegated group of perceptive thinkers and practitioners who have stretched our boundaries and enriched our lives. We believe that this work has taken us a step beyond existing writings and that it is creating a synergy with the work of similarly motivated colleagues. A momentum has clearly been created, and a critical mass of intellectual and clinical effort is leading us in new directions that are promising and hopeful. Our own ability to help other people has been strengthened, and we believe that the synergy being created will lead to clinical innovations of profound significance.

Fundamental to all of this is a renewed and deepened appreciation for the diversity of human spirituality. It is a multiform manifestation of inwardly real experiences that are not readily categorizable in the standard

3

languages of social science. Despite diversity there is much commonality. We have tried hard to reach for those threads of common humanity that bind us together as a human family existing in one world under a divine order that people perceive dimly but fervently. The potential of the commonalities to improve the human condition by blessing each other in multiple ways seems endless, and are, we think, pleasing to God.

On the other hand, we are also deeply pained by the way cultural traditions and categorizations have led to divisions, intolerance, discrimination, coercion, and even warfare. We see such themes justified by ideologies and played out clinically in the social–emotional abuses that occur in relationships and families. To derive hatred and violence from spiritual conviction is high tragedy. Such are alien to the spirit of God, even if rationalized by religious precepts. Many modern world problems grow out of deeply held but erroneous beliefs. Sadly, most traditions carry a measure of conceptual baggage that lends itself to unrealities, limitations on human possibilities, and, ultimately, the undermining of people's sense of worth and motivation for growth. We cannot begin to propose solutions for all of these problems, but they do stand as a warning that the labels *spiritual* or *religious* do not automatically identify something good. The same is true when the label *psychotherapy* is applied to a technique. Not all psychotherapy is therapeutic!

Despite such problems, we are encouraged by the fact that there is a large group of spiritually dedicated, intelligent people of good will who stand together on behalf of human welfare. Drawing upon this benevolent base, our perspective begins with a theistic position and accompanying assumptions. We state these as openly and clearly as we can so they can be evaluated further by us and by others. Such evaluations can be both empirical and spiritual, objective and subjective, and qualitative and quantitative. By defining a viewpoint and being open to evaluation, we hope that new theoretical and clinical integrations of the spiritual domain will occur within professional mental health approaches.

Although we adhere to a tradition within the Judeo–Christian framework, we are sincerely and emotionally committed to an ecumenical perspective of respect and appreciation for the varied world cultures of belief, including spiritual humanism and individualized religiosity. Also, despite a tendency among Western intellectuals to ignore or demean Oriental, African, Native American, and other traditions, we believe it is essential to embrace the ennobling graces of these spiritual schemes in an ecumenically sophisticated psychology of religious therapeutics. We pursue these goals in this book and in our next book on religious diversity and psychotherapy.

1

THE NEED FOR A SPIRITUAL STRATEGY

We are not human beings having a spiritual experience;
We are spiritual beings having a human experience.

—Teilhard deChardin

In recent years, there has been a resurgence of spiritual interest and faith within the American population and an explosion of popular and professional literature on the subject. For example, the leading mainstream newsmagazines and newspapers such as *Time, Newsweek,* and *U.S. News and World Report* have featured cover stories on these issues (e.g., Gibbs & Chua-Eoan, 1993; Kantrowitz et al., 1994; Kaplan, 1996; Ostling, 1992; Wallis, 1996; Woodward & Underwood, 1993). Numerous popular books have been written on it (e.g., Borysenko, 1988, 1993; Peck, 1978, 1983, 1993; Redfield, 1993; Rodegast & Stanton, 1985). Many TV specials also have been aired, including Hugh Hewitt's Public Broadcasting System (PBS) series "Searching for God in America" and Bill Moyers's PBS series "Genesis." Moyers (1996) stated that

> something is happening in America that as a journalist I can't ignore. Religion is breaking out everywhere. Millions of Americans have taken public their search for a clearer understanding of the core principles of belief and how they can be applied to the daily experience of life. (p. 4)

5

This spiritual energy has created a powerful cultural demand for psychotherapists to be more aware of and sensitive to religious and spiritual issues. Unfortunately, relatively few psychotherapists are adequately trained or prepared to deal effectively with such issues. Because of the alienation that has existed historically between the behavioral sciences and religion, the religious faith and spiritual concerns of clients have long been neglected in the psychotherapy profession (Bergin, 1980a, 1983, 1991; Collins, 1977; Henning & Tirrell, 1982; Jones, 1994).

It is time for this to change. The recent professional literature suggests that many clients can be successfully treated only if their spiritual issues are addressed sensitively and capably (Bergin, 1991; Kelly, 1995; Shafranske, 1996; Worthington, Kurusu, McCullough, & Sanders, 1996). Just as therapists need to seek training to help them enhance their skills and sensitivity with respect to issues of gender, race, and other aspects of diversity, they also have an ethical obligation to increase their skills and sensitivity with clients who are religious and spiritually oriented (American Psychological Association, 1992; Shafranske, 1996; Tan, 1993). Consider the following illustrative cases.

Case 1: Kristen

Kristen[1] was a 32-year-old married White woman with three children. She was an active member of the Lutheran church who presented for treatment at a private practice psychotherapy office in the mid-Atlantic region of the United States after being referred by her pastor. Kristen had struggled with anxiety and some agoraphobic symptoms since the age of 17. In recent years, her symptoms had worsened, and, at the time she presented for treatment, she was experiencing obsessions, compulsions, agoraphobic symptoms, phobias, and extremely high anxiety. Kristen was also very fearful of God's wrath and tried to follow all of God's laws, including rules from all religions just to be sure she did not leave any out.

Case 2: Odessa

Odessa was a 50-year-old married Black woman with four children. She was a devout member of the Seventh-Day Adventist faith who presented for treatment at a private practice office in a cosmopolitan eastern city in the United States. During her childhood and adolescence, Odessa's father and two older brothers physically abused her and attempted to abuse her sexually. They also sexually abused her older and younger sisters. At the time she began treatment, Odessa was struggling with deep feelings of shame, guilt, self-hatred, and depression. She was also very angry at her father and brothers and at her husband for his passivity and lack of support. Odessa also felt very guilty and "unchristian" whenever she felt intense anger toward her father, brothers, and husband because of her religious beliefs that she should love and respect

---

[1] Names and identifying characteristics have been changed in all cases reported in this book.

her parents and siblings and support and give deference to her husband in his role as the head of the household.

Case 3: Helen

Helen was a White woman in her early 40s. She was recently widowed and had two children. Helen was a devout member of The Church of Jesus Christ of Latter-day Saints (Mormon). Helen presented for treatment at a private practice office in the midwestern United States after being referred by her religious leader (bishop). When Helen began treatment, she was extremely depressed, quietly desperate, and suicidal. She was also troubled by a variety of obsessive thoughts and some compulsive behavior. She was extremely anxious in any social setting, to the point of having difficulty speaking at all in a group. Of greatest concern to Helen, however, was her belief that she was unspiritual and unrighteous. Helen was convinced that she was spiritually defective, unworthy in God's eyes, and that salvation was impossible for her.

Case 4: Sheila

Sheila was a 38-year-old married Hispanic woman with two children. Although raised in a devout Roman Catholic family, she now described herself as a born-again Christian and as an active participant in a free-standing evangelical church. Sheila presented for treatment at a private practice office in a suburb of a major city in the southwestern United States. When she began treatment, Sheila expressed concerns about sexual difficulties and conflict in her current (second) marriage over these difficulties. She was also struggling with depression (dysthymia) and anxiety related to physical intimacy. Because of her religious upbringing and beliefs, sexuality was a taboo subject for her, and sexual relations had always been rife with conflict, guilt, and shame.

The psychotherapy clients just described are not unusual. Their presenting problems are commonly reported by clients (e.g., anxiety, panic, depression, stress, and marital conflict). These clients are not unusual in another way: They are all religious, as are the vast majority of people in the United States.[2] There is one other way that these clients are not unusual. As will become apparent later in this book, in the complete case reports provided by their therapists, each person had spiritual issues that were inextricably intertwined with their presenting problems. Their treatment could not have been completely successful if their therapists had not appropriately addressed these beliefs and issues.

---

[2] Gallup Organization polls have revealed that the level of religious belief in the United States has remained steady and high during the past several decades, with approximately 95% of the population professing a belief in God, approximately 70% professing membership in a church or synagogue (Gallup & Castelli, 1989; Greeley, 1989; Hoge, 1996; Princeton Religious Research Center, 1990; Report on Trends, 1993), and about 60% being identified in congregational membership rolls (Jacquet & Jones, 1991; see also Table 1.1 for demographic statistics for all religions in the United States.)

TABLE 1.1
Religious Adherents in the United States of America, mid-1995

Adherents	Number	%
Christians	224,457,000	85.3
Professing Christians	224,457,000	85.3
Unaffiliated Christians	43,963,000	16.7
Affiliated Christians	180,494,000	68.6
Roman Catholics	55,259,000	21.0
Protestants	80,678,000	30.6
Evangelicals	72,363,000	27.5
Anglicans	2,350,000	0.9
Orthodox	5,631,000	2.1
Black Christians	25,261,000	9.6
Black Evangelicals	18,420,000	7.0
Catholics (non-Roman)	526,000	0.2
Other Christians	10,789,000	4.1
Non-Christians	38,791,000	14.7
Atheists	870,000	0.3
Baha'is	300,000	0.1
Buddhists	780,000	0.3
Chinese folk religionists	76,000	0.0
Hindus	910,000	0.3
Jews	5,602,000	2.1
Muslims	5,100,000	1.9
Black Muslims	1,400,000	0.5
New-Religionists	947,000	0.4
Nonreligious	22,928,000	8.7
Sikhs	190,000	0.1
Tribal religionists	38,000	0.0
Other religionists	1,050,000	0.4
Total population	263,248,000	100.0

Notes. This table was adapted from Barrett (1996), p. 298. with permission from *Britannica Book of the Year, 1996.* 1996, Encyclopedia Britannica, Inc.

Methodology: This table depicts the United States, the country with the largest number of adherents to Christianity, which is the world's largest religion. *Structure:* Vertically the table lists 27 major religious categories. The 12 major religions (including nonreligion) in the U.S. are listed alphabetically, except for the largest (Christians), which is listed first. Indented names of groups in the "Adherents" column are subcategories of the groups above them and are also counted in these unindented totals, so they are not added into the column total. *Christians:* Professing Christians are all persons who profess publicly (in censuses or polls) to follow Jesus Christ as Lord and Saviour. This category is subdivided into *affiliated Christians* (church members) and *unaffiliated (nominal) Christians* (professing Christians not affiliated with any church). *Evangelicals:* Churches, agencies, and individuals that call themselves by this term usually emphasize five or more fundamental doctrines (salvation by faith, personal acceptance, verbal inspiration of Scripture, depravity of man, Virgin Birth, miracles of Christ, atonement, evangelism, Second Advent). *Black Christians:* Members of denominations initiated by African Americans. *Other Christians:* This term here denotes members of denominations and churches that regard themselves as outside mainline Protestant/Catholic/Orthodox Christianity. *Non-Christians:* Followers of non-Christian religions or of no religion; the 12 largest such varieties are listed. *Jews:* Core Jewish population relating to Judaism, excluding Jewish persons professing a different religion but including immigrants from the former U.S.S.R., Eastern Europe, Israel, and other areas. *Other categories:* Definitions as given in Table 4.1 in this book.

Empirical research has shown convincingly that religious devoutness and commitment are usually positively associated with healthy physical, emotional, and social functioning (Bergin, 1991; see also chap. 5 in this book for a review of this research). These findings have contributed to a reevaluation by many mainstream mental health professionals regarding the role of religion and spirituality in mental health and psychotherapy (Ellis, 1996; Jensen & Bergin, 1988; Worthington et al., 1996). Religious and spiritual beliefs can no longer be viewed simply as neuroses or irrationalities to be treated and cured. To the contrary, many therapists now consider spiritual beliefs and behaviors as possibly powerful resources for promoting therapeutic change (Bergin, 1991; W. R. Miller & Martin, 1988; P. S. Richards & Potts, 1995a; Shafranske, 1996).

During the past 15 years, a broad-based, ecumenical, interdisciplinary effort has been under way to develop a spiritual orientation for psychotherapy and psychology. Efforts have been made to articulate spiritual views of human nature and personality and to propose moral and religious frames of reference for therapy. Considerable effort also has been made by psychotherapists to develop and implement religious and spiritual interventions in their therapeutic work. Thus, there is now a substantial body of professional literature in this domain, and formal training opportunities are beginning to be made available for therapists (e.g., Bergin, 1991; Jones, 1994; Kelly, 1995; Larson, Lu, & Swyers, 1996; Lovinger, 1984; W. R. Miller & Martin, 1988; P. S. Richards & Potts, 1995a; Shafranske, 1996; Spero, 1985; Tan, 1996; Worthington, Kurusu, McCullough, & Sanders, 1996).

Despite the impressive amount of work that has been done to develop a spiritual strategy for psychotherapy, this body of theory, research, and clinical techniques is currently somewhat fragmented and incoherent. As a result, this approach does not have a prominent place of equality alongside other major therapeutic approaches. Many therapists would like to incorporate spiritual perspectives and interventions into their work, but they do not understand how to do so. The purpose of our book is to describe a spiritual strategy that we hope will help bring some improved coherence to this domain, thereby making it more accessible to mainstream mental health professionals. The book is intended for practitioners; graduate students; and academicians in mainstream clinical and counseling psychology, psychiatry, clinical social work, and marriage and family therapy. We hope that the concepts, approaches, and interventions that we describe will help mental health professionals become more attuned to the religious and spiritual issues in the lives of their clients so that they can assist them more effectively.

BACKGROUND AND OVERVIEW

Introducing spiritual content into mainstream theory, research, and practice is a formidable task. Strong forces of historical inertia resist this effort, but worldwide cultural and intellectual trends that are affecting modern thought propel it forward. For good reasons, the leading minds in the development of science, including psychology, deliberately excluded spiritual content from their theories, laws, principles, and technical procedures. Some of these leading thinkers were simultaneously religiously devout, whereas others were neutral or antagonistic; however, there was a general acquiescence to excluding theological ideas and denominational biases for the sake of becoming a science. Also, for many (e.g., Isaac Newton), the scientific project in itself was a way of revealing the designs of God in nature. Excluding the spiritual was thus a practical decision rooted in the methodological and conceptual assumption that things that cannot be observed, measured, or reliably described pertain to a different realm than science.

Assertions concerning faith in the existence of God, the Spirit of God, Divine Intelligence, the Spiritual Essence of humans, the possibility of spiritual regulators of behavior, or the influence of God on the mind or body were thus ruled out of scientific discourse. Faith in science became an alternative to traditional faith. Theologians and, to a degree, philosophers lost the prominent place they once held in the world of scholarship.

The movement broadly defined as "scientific modernism" gained momentum and eventual ascendancy. The choice to become objective, empirical, and, when possible, experimental and quantitative succeeded beyond the expectations of even the most gifted scholars' visions of the future. The marvels of the modern world and the pace of new development in science and technology stand as a testament to the insight of the originators and promoters of modern science. These successes have been most evident in the physical and biological fields, but the power of scientific approaches to knowledge and application have spread broadly and influenced nearly all fields of inquiry, including the behavioral sciences.

We have substantial admiration for this way of comprehending and managing the world, including its use in many areas of basic psychological science. However, as students of personality and therapeutic change, we have regularly confronted obstacles to applying this way of thinking in an efficacious way to the clinical phenomena at hand. This frustrating circumstance is nothing new, and it is the reason that so many individuals and groups have split off from mainstream psychological science over the years. Dozens of great people have grappled with the gap between modernist psychological scientific models or methods and the need to understand the personal and clinical phenomena with which they were dealing. Some of these efforts were valiant in keeping the less tangible aspects of humanity close to standard scientific procedures, whereas others broke entirely from the mold in which they were trained, taught, and had faith. This long, hard trail of history is marked by some of the great names in the field: Gordon Allport, Robert Coles, Erik Erikson, Viktor Frankl, William James,

Carl Jung, George Kelly, Rollo May, Abraham Maslow, Hobart Mowrer, M. Scott Peck, Carl Rogers, Joseph Rychlak, and Irvin Yalom.

In the spirit of what these pioneers were attempting, we propose an alternative perspective, influenced by but departing in degrees from them. The humanistic, existential, cognitive, agentive, and spiritual themes they espoused touched on and opened the door for considering a theistic dimension within the psychological domain. Our effort goes a step further and is built on the works of insightful and courageous creators of a theistic, spiritual perspective in human personality and psychotherapy. Some of them have been only marginally noted in the mainstream psychology literature because much of their work has been disparate from that literature. Some of the prominent contributors include Peter Benson, Gary R. Collins, James W. Fowler, Richard L. Gorsuch, Ralph W. Hood, Stanton L. Jones, Eugene Kelly, David B. Larson, Jeffery Levin, Robert J. Lovinger, H. Newton Malony, John Martin, William R. Miller, David Myers, Bruce Narramore, Kenneth Pargament, L. Rebecca Propst, Edward P. Shafranske, Melvin Spero, Bernard Spilka, Merton B. Strommen, Sing Yan Tan, and Everett L. Worthington. Although our thought has been influenced by everyone from Gordon Allport to Everett Worthington, this book is our personal synthesis and program.

A Theistic, Spiritual Strategy

The spiritual strategy we are proposing for mainstream psychology and psychotherapy is based on a theistic, spiritual view of human nature and of the world. We describe the theistic worldview in considerable detail in chapter 4, but here we want to simply emphasize that the most important assumptions of the spiritual strategy we are proposing "are that God exists, that human beings are the creations of God, and that there are unseen spiritual processes by which the link between God and humanity is maintained" (Bergin, 1980a, p. 99). We base our strategy on the theistic worldview for several reasons. First, the theistic view of human nature and of the world has profound implications for personality theory, psychotherapy, and the processes of healing and change (Bergin, 1988, 1991). This perspective contributes uniquely to psychology and psychotherapy by providing (a) a spiritual conception of human nature and personality (see chaps. 4 and 5); (b) a moral frame of reference for guiding and evaluating psychotherapy (see chaps. 6 and 7); and (c) a body of spiritual techniques and interventions (see chaps. 8–11). It also provides a spiritual view of scientific discovery and the research process (see chap. 12).

Second, most psychotherapists are much more likely to encounter clients who approach life with a theistic worldview than other worldviews. There are five major theistic religions in the world: Judaism, Christianity, Islam, Sikhism, and Zoroastrianism. In North America more than 88% of the population professes belief in, adherence to, or affiliation with one of the theistic world religions, and in Europe more than 80% of the population does (Barrett, 1996; Hoge, 1996). Thus, from the standpoint of numbers only, the need for a theistic spiritual strategy for mainstream psychotherapy is more pressing than it is for other spiritual approaches.

Third, we are believers in the theistic worldview, and, as a result, we know much more about it and can comprehend and articulate more clearly its potential for enriching mainstream psychotherapy. Although our book is based on a theistic worldview, we do nevertheless believe that it also will be helpful to therapists who believe in Eastern spiritual traditions and humanistic and transpersonal spirituality and to those who are agnostic or atheistic. There is much that is ecumenical about the strategy we describe, and we hope to build bridges wherever we can with psychotherapists and clients who approach life with differing worldviews. Regardless of a therapist's personal views, the contents of our book should assist her or him in working more sensitively and effectively with clients of diverse religious and spiritual backgrounds and orientations.

In basing our spiritual strategy on a theistic worldview, we are not endorsing all theistic religions or their practices. We recognize that there has been, and still is, much harm done in the name of religion. For example, the oppression of minority groups and women, acts of violence, and war have been waged in the name of religion (Ellis, 1986; Meadow, 1982; Shrock, 1984). We deplore the use of religion for such destructive purposes. We endorse in the theistic world religions only that which is healthy and beneficial to all of humankind. In chapter 5 we discuss in some detail our views about how theistic, spiritual beliefs and institutions can contribute powerfully to healthy personality development, mental health, and harmonious social relations.

We also recognize that there is an entire scholarly-clinical tradition that is nontheistically spiritual that has much value and appeal. Because we think there is merit to humanistic spirituality and transpersonal psychology, we include references when pertinent, but our primary focus is on that type of spirituality that is combined with theistic beliefs and experiences. We refer readers who would like to learn more about nontheistic humanistic and transpersonal psychology to Chandler, Holden, and Kolander (1992) for an outline and to Elkins (1995) and Vaughan, Wittine, and Walsh (1996).

Definitions of Religious and Spiritual

As we approach this topic, it may be helpful to define what we mean by the words *religious* and *spiritual* even though we expand on their meanings throughout this book. The *American Heritage Dictionary of the English Language* (1992) defines *spiritual* as "of, concerned with, or affecting the soul" and "of, from, or relating to God" (p. 1738). These definitions are a good beginning, but by themselves they are not adequate to convey our understanding of the word *spiritual*. By spiritual, we also mean those experiences, beliefs, and phenomena that pertain to the transcendent and existential aspects of life (i.e., God or a Higher Power, the purpose and meaning of life, suffering, good and evil, death, etc.). The Murray et al. (as cited in Peterson & Nelson, 1987) definition of spiritual is also helpful. They referred to spiritual as "the transcendental relationship between the person and a Higher Being, a quality that goes beyond a specific religious affiliation, that strives for reverence, awe, and inspiration, and that gives answers about the infinite" (p. 35).

The *American Heritage Dictionary of the English Language* (1992) defines *religious* as "having or showing belief in and reverence for God or a deity" and "of, concerned with, or teaching religion" (p. 1525). These definitions are helpful, but they do not fully convey our understanding of the word *religious*, nor do they make clear the distinctions between *religious* and *spiritual*. We view religious as a subset of the spiritual. Religious has to do with theistic beliefs, practices, and feelings that are often, but not always, expressed institutionally and denominationally as well as personally. Thus, the terms *religious* and *spiritual* are interrelated, but they can be distinguished from each other along several dimensions. Religious expressions tend to be denominational, external, cognitive, behavioral, ritualistic, and public. Spiritual experiences tend to be universal, ecumenical, internal, affective, spontaneous, and private. It is possible to be religious without being spiritual and spiritual without being religious.

We assume that spiritual is its own unique domain and cannot be subsumed by other domains such as cognitions, emotions, social systems, and so on. The spiritual is a different realm, a different reality, and one that has not been articulated well in behavioral science and practice. We have made it our task to be part of the beginning and development of that articulation as we try to bring to bear that which is ineffable, yet powerful, on the practical realities of emotional distress and its resolution.

Characteristics of a Viable Spiritual Strategy

To be viable in the mainstream mental health professions, we assume that a theistic, spiritual strategy for psychotherapy needs to be empirical, eclectic, and ecumenical (Bergin & Payne, 1991). A viable spiritual strategy also will accommodate and facilitate denominationally specific applications (Bergin & Payne, 1991). When we say that a viable spiritual strategy must be *empirical*, we mean that those contributing to it should rigorously evaluate their claims regarding human nature, the change process, and treatment effectiveness with careful research. It is widely recognized that psychotherapy is not simply an applied technology but is also an intuitive, artistic enterprise. Nevertheless, there is a commitment within the mental health professions to the belief that the field of psychotherapy must examine its practices and claims with empirical research to advance as a field and maintain its credibility (Bergin & Garfield, 1994).

The practices and claims of a spiritual strategy must also be submitted to such scrutiny. Without a reasonable degree of harmony with the findings of other researchers, we doubt that a spiritual strategy will advance or be taken seriously by mainstream mental health professionals. This is not to say that we endorse a narrow view of what science should be. Rather, we support the notion of "methodological pluralism," which has been identified by Kazdin (1994) and is referred to by several authors in the recent *Handbook of Psychotherapy and Behavior Change* (Bergin & Garfield, 1994). Thus, we value traditional experimental and quantitative research paradigms, but we also believe that qualitative, phenomenological, and experiential approaches can contribute much to the understanding of human personality and psychotherapy (see chap. 12 in this book).

When we say that a viable spiritual strategy must be *eclectic*, we mean that therapists who use a spiritual strategy should not use spiritual interventions exclusively or in a "cookbook" fashion, but as part of a flexible, multidimensional, integrative treatment approach that includes mainstream secular perspectives and interventions. During the past two decades, there has been a widespread movement in the psychotherapy field away from allegiance to a single school of thought and toward a multidimensional approach (Garfield & Bergin, 1986; Norcross, 1986; Norcross & Goldfried, 1992; Stricker & Gold, 1993). The majority of psychotherapists now use an eclectic, integrative approach (Jensen, Bergin, & Greaves, 1990) through which they seek to tailor their treatment approach and interventions to match the unique characteristics and needs of each client. Even those who advocate careful outcome studies on single approaches have also acknowledged that ordinary practice is an art in which multiple approaches are almost always integrated cumulatively as the therapist proceeds to adapt strategies to the client. Thus, the homogeneous manual-guided treatments of major outcome studies are not the ordinary practice (Mental health: Does therapy help?, 1995; Seligman, 1995).

In keeping with this movement, a spiritual strategy needs to be eclectic so that psychotherapists can integrate spiritual perspectives and interventions into their existing therapeutic approaches. We do not believe that a spiritual strategy supercedes the need for psychodynamic, behavioral, cognitive, humanistic, and systemic perspectives or for medication or hospitalization when necessary. Rather, it should complement these other enduring therapeutic traditions and uniquely enrich understanding of human personality and therapeutic change (Bergin, 1988, 1991). An eclectic spiritual strategy also will give therapists the freedom to flexibly choose the religious and spiritual interventions that seem to best match the needs of a given client rather than applying such interventions invariably to all clients. We consider this type of approach a means by which to access clients more fully, thereby tapping into the resources of a spiritual dimension that may be a major aspect of their lives (Bergin, 1988, 1991).

This does not, however, imply that we have resolved the many theoretical and technical inconsistencies across strategies that therapists may wish to combine. We are also aware of the argument that such inconsistencies may reflect a theoretical incoherence and technique incompatibility that limits the efficacy of therapies so combined (Slife & Williams, 1995). Our point is that given the lack of a comprehensive theory of change, psychotherapists need to be open to all possible resources in the change process. Therefore, we endorse experimentation with and evaluation of efforts to use spiritual approaches, singly and in combination with other orientations, with which clinicians are familiar and comfortable. Obviously, this will be easier with some combinations than others.

When we say a viable spiritual strategy must be *ecumenical*, we mean that as much as possible, the philosophical and spiritual assumptions of the strategy need to be reasonably accommodating to the worldviews of the major religious and spiritual traditions that modern therapists are likely to encounter. An ecumenical approach will enable psychotherapists from a variety of backgrounds to use its theoretical perspectives, clinical guidelines, and therapeutic interventions. By identifying the common ground that undergirds the spirituality of clients, an ecumenical approach will help therapists avoid getting tangled in the many theological conflicts that exist among divergent belief systems. Thus, an ecumenical approach will help therapists intervene sensitively and effectively in the religious and spiritual dimensions of their clients' lives regardless of their clients' religious affiliation and spiritual beliefs.

Without an ecumenical approach, the best that can be hoped for are a variety of denominationally specific spiritual approaches to therapy (e.g., for Catholics, Protestants, Jews, Muslims, etc.). Although denominationally specific perspectives and interventions are needed, without a unifying ecumenical spiritual strategy, the fragmentation and incoherence that currently characterizes this domain of psychotherapy will continue, and spiritual perspectives and interventions will not adequately affect mainstream psychotherapy practice.

When we say that a viable spiritual strategy will accommodate and facilitate *denominationally specific* applications, we mean that it must be flexible and contain guidelines that will help therapists understand how to use denominationally specific concepts and interventions sensitively and effectively. Bergin and Payne (1991) pointed out that clients from different religious traditions "present different needs embedded in languages and life styles that demand technical content adapted to their needs" (p. 208). A spiritual strategy should help therapists honor and fully use the unique religious beliefs and spiritual resources available to clients who belong to a particular religious denomination or spiritual tradition (Kelly, 1995; Lovinger, 1984). Given a general spiritual understanding, it is appropriate for therapists to grow into a broader range of skills and to use denominationally specific perspectives and interventions with clients from their own background or religious traditions of which they have acquired an in-depth understanding. Thus, a spiritual strategy should help psychotherapists "learn how to function both in the broader ecumenical world and in the fine texture" (Bergin & Payne, 1991, p. 208) of one or more specific religious traditions.

In this book we describe a spiritual strategy for counseling and psychotherapy that partakes of the four characteristics described earlier. We recognize that some of our perspectives and recommendations will be perceived as controversial by some behavioral scientists and psychotherapists. The fact that our strategy is based on the belief that there is a Supreme Being who guides and influences human beings will certainly be objectionable to some professionals. We address this concern at various points throughout the book, but particularly in chapters 2–5. Our view that it is possible, even desirable, for therapists and clients to seek guidance and inspiration from the divine source to assist them in the healing process might also seem controversial. So might our recommendation that therapists use various spiritual interventions, such as praying for their clients, using imagery with spiritual content, and encouraging clients to seek blessings and spiritual guidance from their religious leaders.

We hope that professionals who find such perspectives and recommendations objectionable will not "throw the baby out with the bath water" and conclude that there is nothing of value for them in this book. Those who feel negatively about a specific perspective or intervention can certainly disregard it. They may still find considerable value in the overall strategy we describe, and it should assist them in working more sensitively and effectively with their theistic clients. We recognize that we are embarking on much new ground. Some of our ideas have not been tested empirically, so there is much room for discussion, debate, and revision in the years ahead. We do not present our ideas dogmatically but openly and with a hope that they will prove helpful to researchers and practitioners of diverse theoretical and spiritual perspectives.

Plan of the Book

In chapters 2–5 we present the historical, philosophical, and theoretical foundations of a theistic, spiritual strategy. Practitioners who prefer to jump right into the clinical applications of the strategy should go to chapter 6, where we begin our discussion of psychotherapy process and methods. We hope that readers will then return to chapters 2–5 because the rationale and justification for a spiritual strategy presented in these chapters is essential.

In chapter 2 we briefly discuss the fact that religious and spiritual issues have been neglected historically in the mainstream mental health professions. We assert that in attempting to establish their theories as "scientific," the early leaders of psychology and psychiatry adopted many of the philosophical assumptions of 19th-century Newtonian and Darwinian science. These philosophical assumptions are defined briefly, and we discuss why their influence excluded spiritual perspectives for so long from mainstream psychotherapy.

In chapter 3 we discuss the fact that a new zeitgeist has arisen within the behavioral sciences, including the field of psychotherapy, that is much more consistent with religious and spiritual worldviews. We discuss the major influences outside and within the field of psychotherapy that have contributed to the development of this spiritual zeitgeist.

In chapter 4 we discuss the importance of a *weltanschauung*, or worldview, in personality development, mental health, and psychotherapy. We describe and contrast three major metaphysical worldviews: the worldviews of the Western or theistic world religions (i.e., Christianity, Islam, Judaism, Sikhism, and Zoroastrianism), the eastern spiritual traditions (i.e., Hinduism, Buddhism, Jainism, Shintoism, Confucianism, and Taoism), and modern-day science.

In chapter 5 we briefly discuss some of the major assumptions of a theistic, spiritual view of human personality, including the views that God exists, that human beings have a spirit or soul, that human beings are able to communicate with God through spiritual means, and that by living in harmony with universal principles people can grow and develop in a healthy manner and fulfill their divine potential. We review empirical research that provides evidence that religious and spiritual influences are positively related to physical and mental health, and we discuss qualitative evidence that there are spiritual realities, including a discussion of reports of near-death experiences and parting visions.

In chapters 6–11 we describe the clinical application of a spiritual strategy. In chapter 6 we discuss the implications of a theistic worldview for the understanding of psychotherapy. We begin by discussing the major goals of a spiritual strategy. We discuss the major roles and tasks of therapists who implement a spiritual approach in their work, including relationship establishment, assessment, and intervention from a spiritual perspective. We also discuss, from a theistic perspective, the client's role in therapy.

In chapter 7 we consider ethical questions and dangers that therapists should be sensitive to when they use a spiritual strategy. These include (a) dual relationships, or blurring boundaries between professional and religious roles; (b) displacing or usurping religious authority; (c) imposing religious values on clients or being insensitive to their values; (d) violating work setting (church–state) boundaries; and (e) practicing outside the boundaries of professional competence.

In chapter 8 we describe a rationale and approach for conducting a religious and spiritual assessment. We describe clinically important religious and spiritual dimensions that therapists should assess. We then describe a multilevel, multidimensional assessment strategy that includes consideration of all major systems in clients' lives (e.g., physical, social, behavioral, cognitive, educational-occupational, psychological-emotional, and religious-spiritual).

In chapter 9 we describe a variety of enduring religious and spiritual practices that have been practiced for centuries by members of the world's great religious traditions (e.g., prayer, meditation or contemplation, reading Scriptures or sacred writings). We discuss and cite research that supports the potential healing properties of these spiritual practices, and we offer suggestions for using them in therapy.

In chapter 10 we review research that documents the wide variety of spiritual interventions that contemporary psychotherapists have used to date and briefly define and describe many of these interventions. We describe several spiritual–secular treatment package approaches that have been reported in the literature and discuss the use of spiritual interventions in marital and family therapy and with children and adolescents. We also identify contraindications for spiritual interventions and conclude by offering general process suggestions regarding their use.

In chapter 11 we present several case studies written by therapists from around the country who have integrated spiritual perspectives and interventions into their therapeutic approach. These cases describe clients from a variety of religious faiths, illustrate how religious and spiritual issues can be intertwined with a variety of presenting problems, and show how spiritual interventions can be used along with secular methods to enhance the processes and outcomes of therapy.

Chapters 12 and 13 cover a variety of topics pertinent to the future of a spiritual strategy. In chapter 12 we discuss the implications of the theistic worldview for our understanding of scientific discovery and the research process. We describe a theistic view of epistemology and scientific discovery and discuss the role of intuition and inspiration in the scientific discovery process. We also briefly describe some of the major quantitative and qualitative research designs or strategies that have potential for contributing to the advancement of a spiritual strategy in personality theory and psychotherapy.

In chapter 13 we outline some of the needs and directions for the future in regard to the advancement of a spiritual strategy for psychotherapy. In particular, we discuss needs and directions in the areas of theory and research, education and clinical training, and several professional practice domains, including psychotherapy, medicine, health psychology, public health education, pastoral counseling, and religious institutions.

II

HISTORICAL, THEORETICAL, AND PHILOSOPHICAL FOUNDATIONS

2

THE ALIENATION BETWEEN RELIGION AND PSYCHOLOGY

Many worlds of consciousness exist . . . which have a meaning for our life . . . the total expression of human experience . . . invincibly urges me beyond the narrow "scientific" bounds. Assuredly, the real world is of a different temperament—more intricately built than physical science allows.

—*William James*

During the past few decades, many writers have discussed the fact that religious and spiritual issues have traditionally been neglected in the mainstream mental health professions (e.g., Bergin, 1980a, 1980b; Campbell, 1975; Collins, 1977; Lovinger, 1984; Strommen, 1984). For example, Collins (1977), a clinical psychologist, pointed out that

during the course of its history, psychology has never shown much interest in religion. General psychology books tend to give the topic scant if any attention. Apart from a few classic studies like those of James, Freud, and Allport (James, 1902/1936; Freud, 1927; Allport, 1950), the topic of religious behavior has been largely ignored by psychological writers. (p. 95)

A survey of introductory psychology texts by Spilka and colleagues clearly documents this situation (Spilka, Comp, & Goldsmith, 1981;

Spilka, Hood, & Gorsuch, 1985). Spilka et al. (1981) found that about 40% of introductory psychology texts published in the 1950s included something about religion. This number dropped to only 27.5% for texts published in the 1970s. Citations were mostly to well-known figures such as Freud, James, and Jung and to philosophers and theologians. Research in the psychology of religion generally was ignored (Spilka et al., 1985).

Strommen, a psychology of religion expert and editor of *Research on Religious Development: A Comprehensive Handbook* (Strommen, 1971), observed that religion has also been neglected in psychological research.

> Let me begin by drawing your attention to a most ironic situation—one that seems strange for a discipline that prides itself on its objectivity. For the past one-half century, the dimension of life—a religious faith—that occasioned the name *psychology* has been ignored systematically as an important variable in the pursuit of understanding human behavior. This, in spite of the fact that religious beliefs and values [we have found] are among the best predictors of what people will say or do. (Strommen, 1984, p. 151)

Thus, theoretical areas of literature and research have revealed a paucity of information about religion and spirituality as a dimension of human experience and basic existence. Bergin (1983) pointed out that religious and spiritual issues also have been neglected in graduate training programs:

> Training in the clinical professions is almost bereft of content that would engender an appreciation of religious variables in psychological functioning. Race, gender, and ethnic origin now receive deserved attention, but religion is still an orphan in academia. (p. 171)

Given that religious and spiritual issues have been neglected in psychological and clinical theory, research, and training, it is not surprising that psychotherapists also have tended to neglect religious and spiritual issues as they work with clients (Bergin, 1980a, 1983; Collins, 1977; Henning & Tirrell, 1982). In a national survey of psychotherapists, Jensen and Bergin (1988) found that only 29% of the therapists believed that religious matters are important for treatment efforts with all or many of their clients. Henning and Tirrell (1982) observed that

> there has traditionally been much counselor resistance on professional and personal grounds to examining spiritual concerns. . . . Most counselors feel free to openly examine occupational, family, sexual and interpersonal issues. . . . Religious issues, however, are frequently viewed with apprehension. (p. 92)

Why is it that religious and spiritual concerns have so long been excluded from the mainstream mental health professions? There is not a simple answer to this. The relationships among religion, psychological thought, and psychotherapy are long and complex. Historical, philosophical, and theoretical influences all seem to have contributed to this alienation from spirituality during the past century (Appleyard, 1992; Barbour, 1990; Beit-Hallahmi, 1974; Bergin, 1980a; Collins, 1977; Fuller, 1986; Hearnshaw, 1987; Karier, 1986; Lovinger, 1984; Lundin, 1985; Murray, 1988; Strunk, 1970). It is beyond the scope of this book to provide a chronological history of these influences (see Vande Kemp, 1996). Instead, we briefly describe the historical context within which modern-day behavioral science developed. We then define and discuss the philosophical assumptions of 19th-century science and why they alienated mainstream psychology and psychotherapy from religion.

THE AGE OF SCIENCE

Although the Middle Ages (approximately 500 A.D. to 1300 A.D.) of Western civilization were significantly influenced by Islamic civilization, they were characterized mainly by centuries of intellectual domination and control by medieval Christianity. In Europe, the Middle Ages were followed by the Renaissance in the early modern period of Western history (approximately 1300 A.D. to 1600 A.D.). This was a time when the domination and control by medieval Christianity was being challenged philosophically (e.g., humanism), theologically (e.g., the Protestant Reformation), and scientifically (e.g., Copernicus's and Galileo's heliocentric [sun-centered] universe). The early beginnings of psychological and clinical thought can be traced to religious and philosophical ideas of the early modern period of Western civilization's history, to the Age of Reason (1700s to 1800s), which followed, and to the rise of modern science (1600 to the present; Hearnshaw, 1987; Murray, 1988; Ronan, 1982). The modern period of Western civilization, or the Age of Science, has been a culmination of these historical trends. It was during this time that what is now often referred to as *modern* or *modernistic science* (e.g., Bertens, 1995; Griffin, 1989; Griffin, Cobb, Ford, Gunter, & Ochs, 1993) rose to unprecedented influence.

Modern-day psychology and psychiatry developed during the late 19th and early 20th centuries, which was a time when modern science was successfully challenging religious authority and tradition as the dominant worldview and source of truth (Appleyard, 1992; Barbour, 1990; Bergin, 1980a; E. M. Burns & Ralph, 1974; Collins, 1977; Hearnshaw, 1987; Karier, 1986; Lucas, 1985). The Newtonian "clocklike" view of the physical universe dominated the scientific world at this time, giving rise to deterministic and mechanistic thought (Appleyard, 1992; Barbour, 1990; Hearnshaw, 1987; Lucas, 1985; Slife, 1993). Many scientists "believed that humanity was . . . a part of the all-encompassing world machine, whose operation could be explained without reference to God. Such a materialistic world held no place for consciousness or inwardness except as subjective illusions" (Barbour, 1990, p. 220). Charles Darwin's theory of evolution was also rapidly gaining scientific acceptance as an explanation regarding the origin of life (Appleyard, 1992; Barbour, 1990; Lucas, 1985; Mason, 1962). The prestige and technological successes of science, combined with the lack of persuasive response from religious institutions, contributed to the decline in status and influence of religious explanations regarding the origins and nature of the universe and human beings (Appleyard, 1992; Lucas, 1985). Many people at this time believed that it would be science, not religion, that unlocked all the mysteries of the universe.

To escape religious contamination and establish psychology and psychiatry as respected sciences, Sigmund Freud, along with early founders of the behavioral tradition (i.e., Watson, Thorndike, Skinner) and other early leaders of the behavioral sciences, accepted the prevailing scientific philosophies of the day (Karier, 1986; Wertheimer, 1970). Naturalism, determinism, universalism, reductionism, atomism, materialism, mechanism, ethical relativism, ethical hedonism, classical realism, positivism, and empiricism were dominating the scientific world at this time and were adopted as the philosophical foundations for the behavioral sciences.

However, what exactly were these philosophies and why did they create such an enduring rift between psychology and religion? In the remainder of this chapter, we attempt to answer these questions. We first briefly define and describe the assumptions of 19th-century modernistic science. We then briefly discuss their adoption by the early leaders of psychology and point out how they conflicted with the views of the world's religious and spiritual traditions. Because the psychoanalytic and behavioral theories had such a major influence on the fields of psychology and psychotherapy as they developed during the first half of the 20th century (Bergin & Garfield, 1994; Karier, 1986; Matarazzo, 1985), we use them as illustrative cases.

Assumptions of 19th-Century (Modernistic) Science

Metaphysical Assumptions

Metaphysics is the branch of philosophy that is concerned with the nature of reality and with "the origin and nature of space and time, the nature of change and causality, the nature of the human person, freedom and determinism, the existence of God, and the problem of evil" (Percesepe, 1991, p. 20). *Naturalism* is the metaphysical belief that human beings and the universe can be understood and eventually explained without including "God" or a "Supreme Being" in scientific theories. Naturalism posits that "the universe is self-sufficient, without supernatural cause or control, and that in all probability the interpretation of the world given by the sciences is the only satisfactory explanation of reality" (Honer & Hunt, 1987, p. 225). *Atheism* is similar to the philosophy of naturalism and is the "positive belief that God does not exist" (Percesepe, 1991, p. 469). *Agnosticism* is also closely related to the philosophy of naturalism and is the belief that it "is not possible to know whether there is a God or a Supreme Being" (Honer & Hunt, 1987, p. 97).

Although not all scientists are atheistic or agnostic, most scientists during the past century have adopted naturalism as the primary underlying assumption of their theories and research. Naturalism is "the oldest and deepest of science's substantive commitments" (Leahey, 1991, p. 378), for without the belief that the happenings of the universe can be explained in natural terms, it was feared that science would become obsolete. Scientific explanations of the universe would be no more tenable than religious, mystical, and superstitious ones. As stated by Leahey (1991), naturalism is "science's central dogma, without which it could not function" (p. 379).

Determinism is the belief that "every event in the universe is completely dependent on and conditioned by its cause or causes" (Honer & Hunt, 1987, p. 219). According to Percesepe (1991), hard determinism is the belief that "every event has a sufficient natural cause; nothing is left to chance. The same laws of causality that govern nature govern human actions as well" (p. 403). *Universalism* is the "notion that natural laws—because they are lawful—do not change in time or space. . . . A law should work universally; otherwise, it only applies to one point in time and space and thus is not lawful (or truthful)" (Slife, Hope, & Nebeker, 1996, p. 11).

Reductionism is the belief that "a whole can be completely understood by an analysis of its parts" (Honer & Hunt, 1987, p. 216). Closely related to reductionism are the philosophies of atomism, mechanism, and materialism. *Atomism* is "the notion that the material objects of our observation and knowledge can themselves be separated and divided into variables, constructs, and laws that are smaller and presumably more basic than their larger counterparts" (Slife et al., 1996, pp. 12–13). *Mechanism* is the belief that human beings, the world, and the universe are "like a machine, that is, . . . composed of smaller pieces working smoothly together, the working of the whole being lawfully determined and necessary" (Slife & Williams, 1995, pp. 134–135). *Materialism* "is the view that matter is the fundamental reality in the world, and whatever else exists is dependent upon matter. In its most extreme form, materialism holds that whatever exists is physical" (Percesepe, 1991, p. 316).

Axiological (Ethical) Assumptions

Axiology is the "branch of philosophy that deals with value theory" (Percesepe, 1991, p. 20). Ethics is the discipline within axiology "that attempts to establish rational grounds for right conduct" (Percesepe, 1991, p. 21) and that "attempts to determine what is good for people and what is right for them to do" (Honer & Hunt, 1987, p. 221). *Ethical relativism* is the axiological belief that "there are no universally valid principles, since all moral principles are valid relative to cultural or individual choice" (Percesepe, 1991, p. 572). In other words, "whatever a culture or society [or individual] holds to be right *is* therefore right or, at least, 'right for them'" (Solomon, 1990, p. 235). *Ethical hedonism* is the belief that "we always ought to seek our own pleasure and that the highest good for us is the most pleasure together with the least pain" (Honer & Hunt, 1987, p. 222).

Epistemological Assumptions

Epistemology is the "branch of philosophy that studies the nature, sources, validity, and limits of knowledge" (Percesepe, 1991, p. 18). Science embraces *positivism*, which is the belief that "knowledge is limited to observable facts and their interrelations and, hence, that the sciences provide the only reliable knowledge" (Honer & Hunt, 1987, p. 226). According to positivism, scientific theories can be "shown to be true on the basis of evidence" (Bechtel, 1988, p. 18). Positivism is associated with a belief in classical (or naive) realism. *Classical realism* posits that the universe is real, existing independently of human consciousness, and through experience with it, it eventually can be accurately perceived and understood by human beings (Barbour, 1990; Lincoln & Guba, 1985).

Positivism is also associated with a companion belief in empiricism. *Empiricism* is the epistemological belief "that our sense experience—seeing, touching, hearing, smelling, tasting—provides us with reliable knowledge of the world" (Percesepe, 1991, p. 19). Empiricism assumes that "knowledge has its source and derives all its content from experience. Nothing is regarded as true save what is given by sense experience or by inductive reasoning from sense experience" (Honer & Hunt, 1987, p. 220). Thus, positivists believe that it is possible for scientists to be objective, value-free observers and that through empirical observation the verification of scientific facts and theories will provide a complete understanding of reality.

Psychology's Adoption of Modernistic Assumptions: An Alternative Faith

Although it was not always done explicitly or even deliberately, the early leaders of the psychoanalytic and behavioral theories, and other early leaders in experimental psychology, built their theories on faith in the modernistic philosophical assumptions described earlier (Karier, 1986; Leahey, 1991). As was true of other scientists, the foundational axiom of faith that these early leaders adopted was that human behavior could be explained naturalistically (i.e., without resorting to spiritual or transcendent explanations). At least some of these leaders were also atheistic (Karier, 1986). For example, both Freud and Watson rejected the religious faiths of their parents and replaced those beliefs with their own naturalistic, atheistic psychological faith (Karier, 1986). This was also true of numerous other leaders in the field, such as Skinner, Hull, Wolpe, Bandura, and Rogers.

Perhaps because of their personal beliefs about religion, and perhaps because science in the late 19th and early 20th centuries was vigorously challenging religious authority and tradition, psychoanalytic and behavioral theories were not only naturalistic, but they also portrayed religious beliefs and behaviors in negative ways. For example, in the *Future of an Illusion*, Freud stated that religious ideas "are illusions, fulfillments of the oldest, strongest and most urgent wishes of mankind" (Freud, 1927/1961, p. 30). He also said that religion is "the universal obsessional neurosis of humanity" (Freud, 1927/1961, p. 43). Freud also compared religious beliefs to a "sleeping draught" and said that "the effect of religious consolations may be likened to that of a narcotic" (Freud, 1927/1961, p. 29).

Watson basically ignored spiritual behavior, but when he did mention it his writings revealed his bias against religion. For example, in his book *Psychology From the Standpoint of a Behaviorist*, Watson said that "psychology, up to very recent times, has been held so rigidly under the dominance both of traditional religion and of philosophy—the two great bulwarks of medievalism—that it has never been able to free itself and become a natural science" (Watson, 1924/1983, p. 1). This clearly reflects the aim of early psychologists to situate psychology firmly within the sharp lines of science and as far away from the "fuzzy" areas of religion and philosophy as possible.

In arguing why psychology should not concern itself with studying consciousness, Watson said that "'states of consciousness,' like the so-called phenomena of spiritualism, are not objectively verifiable and for that reason can never become data for science" (Watson, 1924/1983, p. 1). According to Leahey (1991), Watson "linked introspective psychology to religion and railed against both" (p. 239). Karier (1986) observed that "Watson . . . made the quantum leap between the animal and human kingdoms" and then went further and "quickly proceeded to deny soul, mind, consciousness, or any unique status for man or his mental or spiritual experiences" (p. 129).

The early leaders of psychology also adopted as underlying assumptions deterministic, reductionistic, atomistic, materialistic, and mechanistic views of human beings. Freud theorized that human behavior is determined by unconscious intrapsychic instincts and drives and by psychosexual events that occur during the first 5 or 6 years of life (Hillner, 1984; Lundin, 1985). Freud's theory was deterministic, reductionistic, atomistic, and mechanistic in the sense that Freud believed that early childhood psychosexual events and intrapsychic forces explain and control human motivations (especially pathological ones) and behavior (Hillner, 1984; Lundin, 1985). Early behaviorists (e.g., Watson) believed that behavior is determined by environmental influences (Hillner, 1984; Lundin, 1985; Watson, 1924/1983). The early behavioral theory was also reductionistic, atomistic, materialistic, and mechanistic in the sense that it was believed that human behavior could be explained and reduced to stimulus–response connections and that only observable behavior was considered real (Hillner, 1984; Lundin, 1985; Watson, 1924/1983). Human beings were a materialistic "machine" that was completely controlled by environmental influences (Krasner, 1962).

The early leaders of psychology also adopted the assumptions of ethical relativism and ethical hedonism. The influence of Darwin's theory of evolution led Freud and the early behavioral leaders to theorize that human beings by nature are highly similar to the rest of the animal kingdom (Hillner, 1984; Lundin, 1985; Watson, 1924/1983). That is, they theorized that humans are basically hedonistic or reward seeking, also advocating that human beings should be more accepting of these tendencies (Hillner, 1984; Lundin, 1985; Watson, 1924/1983). They rejected the notion that there are transcendent moral and ethical universals that can or should optimize human behavior and social relations.

The early psychologists also adopted the assumptions of classical realism, positivism, empiricism, and universalism. They believed that they were establishing respectable scientific theories of human behavior by following the lead of physical and biological science (Hillner, 1984; Lundin, 1985; Watson, 1924/1983). They believed that their theories and research were describing and verifying universal laws of human behavior and functioning. They claimed that their theories were grounded in empirical observations and would be proved true on the basis of empirical evidence (Hillner, 1984; Lundin, 1985; Watson, 1924/1983). As stated by Karier (1986), "While Freud considered himself a scientist akin to Darwin, he also saw himself as the creator of a new science, one that would effect the crossover from the world of the poetic artist to that of the empirical scientist" (p. 214). Watson (1924/1983) stated that "for the behaviorist, psychology is that division of natural science which takes human behavior—the doings and sayings, both learned and unlearned, of people as its subject matter" (p. 4). "Behavioristic psychology attempts to formulate, through systematic observation and experimentation, the generalizations, laws and principles which underly man's behavior" (Watson, 1924/1983, p. 5).

CONFLICTS OF MODERNISTIC ASSUMPTIONS WITH THE WORLD'S RELIGIOUS TRADITIONS

It is easy to see how the naturalistic view of Freud that religiosity is an illusion or an obsessional neurosis, and the behavioral view that religious behavior is simply a conditioned response, conflict starkly with a spiritual conception of the world. The theistic world religions teach that there is a

Supreme Being who was involved in the creation of the world and who continues to influence the lives of human beings. They also describe religious and spiritual beliefs and behaviors as being essential for optimal human growth and fulfillment (Bergin, 1980a). The deterministic, reductionistic, atomistic, mechanistic, and materialistic views of human behavior also conflict with the views of both the Western and Eastern world religions because they assert that human beings are responsible agents and inherently different from the conception of humans as machines. The world religions also affirm that there are nonmaterial, spiritual realities; not everything that is real is physical or material. The world religions also view human beings as being more multidimensional, both spiritually and holistically, therefore disagreeing with reductionistic and atomistic beliefs that the behavior and emotions of human beings are simply the product of primitive biological drives or environmental stimuli and responses.

Several writers have pointed out that the philosophies of ethical relativism and hedonism also conflict with the teachings of the major world religious traditions (e.g., Bergin, 1980a, 1980b; Campbell, 1975), most of which describe human beings as being more ethical and spiritually advanced than other living organisms. These religions teach that human beings can choose to control and transcend their hedonistic tendencies in order to experience spiritual fulfillment. They also can transcend self-interest and altruistically promote the welfare of others. They also each teach that there are moral universals that God has revealed, or that are built into the universe, that should guide human behavior and social relations (Smart, 1983).

Although many religious traditions of the world do not reject empirical ways of knowing, or even the possibility that scientific theories might be supported by empirical evidence, they do reject the belief that empirical knowledge is the only valid source of truth or that empiricism alone can lead to a completely accurate knowledge of the universe. They also teach that there are some experiences that are contextual, invisible, and private (i.e., spiritual and transcendent ones) that cannot necessarily be empirically observed, replicated, or publicly verified (Slife et al., 1996). The world religions also teach that there are spiritual ways for human beings to learn and know truth about the realities of the universe (e.g., inspiration, enlightenment, mystical harmony, and revelation). In Table 2.1 we summarize and contrast the major philosophical assumptions of modernistic science and psychology with those of the major world religious traditions. One can see that the philosophical assumptions adopted by early psychologists and psychiatrists were in most ways incompatible with those of the spiritual traditions.

Some Caveats

The foregoing analysis highlights the strong influence of naturalistic, deterministic, reductionistic, mechanistic, and positivistic assumptions in

TABLE 2.1

Conflicting Philosophical Assumptions of Modernistic Science and
Psychology and the Theistic Religious Traditions

Modernistic science and psychology	Theistic religious traditions
Naturalism and atheism: There is no Supreme Being or transcendent spiritual influences.	*Theism:* There is a Supreme Being and transcendent spiritual influences.
Determinism: Human behavior is completely caused by forces outside of human control.	*Free will:* Human beings have agency and the capacity to choose and regulate their behavior, although biological and environmental influences may set some limits.
Universalism: Natural laws, including laws of human behavior, are context free; they apply across time, space, and persons. A phenomenon is not real if it is not generalizable and repeatable.	*Contextuality:* Although there are natural laws that may be context free, there may also be some that are context bound (i.e., they apply in some contexts but not in others). There are real phenomena that are contextual, invisible, and private. They are not empirically observable, generalizable, or repeatable (e.g., transcendent spiritual experiences).
Reductionism and atomism: All of human behavior can be reduced or divided into smaller parts or units.	*Holism:* Humans are more than the sum of their parts. They cannot be adequately understood by reducing or dividing them into smaller units.
Materialism and mechanism: Human beings are like machines composed of material or biological parts working together.	*Transcendent spirit and soul:* Humans are composed of a spirit or soul and physical body; they cannot be reduced simply to physiology or biology.
Ethical relativism: There are no universal or absolute moral or ethical principles. Values are culture bound. What is right and good varies across social and individual situations.	*Universals and absolutes:* There are universal moral and ethical principles that regulate healthy psychological and spiritual development. Some values are more healthy and moral than others.
Ethical hedonism: Human beings always seek rewards (pleasure) and avoid punishments (pain). This is the basic valuing process built into human behavior.	*Altruism:* Human beings often forego their own rewards (pleasure) for the welfare of others. Responsibility, self-sacrifice, suffering, love, and altruistic service are valued above personal gratification.

TABLE 2.1 *(cont.)*

Modernistic science and psychology	Theistic religious traditions
Classical realism and positivism: The universe is real and can be accurately perceived and understood by human beings. Science provides the only valid knowledge. Scientific theories can be proved true on the basis of empirical evidence.	*Theistic realism:* God is the ultimate creative and controlling force in the universe and the ultimate reality. God and the universe can only be partially and imperfectly understood by human beings. Scientific methods can approximate some aspects of reality but must be transcended by spiritual ways of knowing in many realms.
Empiricism: Sensory experience provides human beings with the only reliable source of knowledge. Nothing is true or real except that which is observable through sensory experience or measuring instruments.	*Epistemological pluralism:* Human beings can learn truth in a variety of ways, including authority, reason, sensory experience, and intuition and inspiration. Inspiration from God is a valid source of knowledge and truth.

the history of psychology that were derived from 19th-century natural science. For many years, these assumptions greatly influenced the content of text-books, the criteria by which submitted journal articles were judged, the nature of graduate education, and the types of recognition provided by professional societies (Bergin, 1980a, 1980b; Slife & Williams, 1995). It would, however, be incorrect to imply that these assumptions were so dominant as to be mono-lithic and completely overpowering in the behavioral sciences.

During this period of strong "scientism," there was a continuing, but not entirely effective, opposition by another movement called *humanistic-existential psychology* (Maslow, 1971; May, Angel, & Ellenberger, 1958; Rogers, 1951, 1961; Yalom, 1980). Although it was also based on the assumption of naturalism, it was opposed to the deterministic, reductionistic, and mechanistic views that prevailed. This movement gave hope to those who viewed human behavior as being more complex and potentially agentive, as being a reflection of the potential for actualization that had some similarities to the aspirations of idealistic religions. This movement opened the way for alternative conceptions of human functioning, yet it partook of the naturalistic and relativistic themes of the dominant scientific tradition.

Similarly, the cognitive movement in psychology also grew up in paral-lel to the more deterministic trends but did not break through as a substantial influence until the late 1960s. It, too, created a space for serious discussion of agency and self-control, as opposed to control by biology or environment, yet it suffers to a degree from lingering reductionistic and mechanistic influences that led to machine or computer models of intelligent functioning that, with "inputs" and "outputs," resembled scientism in many ways (see Gardner, 1985, for a historical and philosophical analysis of the rise of science and the emergence of the cognitive revolution).

At the same time there was the third continuing counterculture consisting of writers who wrote frankly about religion; these included James (1902/1936) in the early 20th century and psychoanalysts such as Jung (1938), social psychologists such as Allport (1950), psychiatrists such as Frankl (1959), and the continuously developing pastoral counseling movement. However, this "religiously open" counterculture did not begin to significantly influence the mainstream behavioral sciences until the 1970s and 1980s, as we discuss in more detail in chapter 3.

In addition to the humanistic-existential, cognitive, and spiritual trends that challenged the dominant psychodynamic and behavioral traditions over these years, there also was considerable variety within the behavioral and psychodynamic traditions that yielded considerable debate and richness. Not only did Jung oppose classical psychoanalysis but Adler, Fromm, Horney, Sullivan, Erikson, Winnicott, and others contributed to ego psychology and social interactionism in human dynamics that provided for controversy and latitude in thinking about human behavior (C. S. Hall & Lindzey, 1957). These trends were particularly important in the clinical fields, in which the change process noted by clinicians often evidenced many phenomena that could not be construed within the classical mechanistic perspective. In addition, the behavioral movement was laced with criticisms and oppositions such as those by Tolman and other early cognitive behaviorists, a trend documented powerfully by Koch (1959–1963). This trend also was greatly accentuated and enlarged by Bandura (1969, 1986) and others who followed his work.

It is interesting that despite the opposing trends and the potential for latitude in thought and practice that were provided thereby, even some of the most radically dissenting psychologists had difficulty avoiding the dominating influence of the naturalistic and mechanistic worldview. For instance, Carl Rogers, who was one of the strongest advocates of human agency and potential, independent of conditioning and unconscious processes, found himself writing and speaking in somewhat deterministic ways (e.g., Rogers, 1957, 1959). Even though Rogers tried to apply the dominant paradigm to the clinical phenomena he dealt with, he ultimately was frustrated by this attempt and went in new directions (Coulson & Rogers, 1968; Rogers, 1980). In these efforts, Rogers, as others like him, adopted radically different views of what science is, what knowledge is, and how truth should be sought (Koch, 1981).

CONCLUSION

Psychoanalytic and behavioral theories have had a major and long-lasting impact on mainstream psychology and psychotherapy (Bergin &

Garfield, 1994; Matarazzo, 1985). The philosophical and theoretical biases against spiritual perspectives adopted by the early psychoanalytic and behavioral leaders, and other leaders, became deeply embedded in psychological and clinical thought during the first half of the 20th century. The continuing influence of these assumptions is perhaps the major reason why religious and spiritual perspectives have not yet been more fully integrated into the modern-day, mainstream professions of psychology and psychotherapy. However, as we discuss in chapter 3, a new spiritual zeitgeist has arrived.

3

THE NEW ZEITGEIST

The beginning possibility of unification of religion and science is the most significant and exciting happening in our intellectual life today.
—*M. Scott Peck*

Although the naturalistic faith adopted by the early leaders of psychology and psychiatry had a long and powerful impact on the mental health professions, during the second half of the 20th century the influence of this belief system has gradually weakened. Discoveries in physics, changes in the philosophy of science, research on the brain and consciousness, renewed societal interest in spiritual phenomena, and research on religion and mental health are some of the major influences outside the profession of psychotherapy that have contributed to an erosion of the early assumptions.

Challenges to these assumptions also came from within the profession of psychotherapy. The development of alternative psychotherapy traditions such as the humanistic-existential and cognitive approaches, the movement toward eclecticism, the multicultural counseling movement, a recognition of the importance of values in psychotherapy, and the articulation of spiritual views of human nature have influenced modern-day therapy perspectives. The purpose of this chapter is to briefly describe these trends and to discuss how they have contributed to a theoretical zeitgeist[1] within the natural and behavioral sciences that is more in harmony with a spiritual worldview than the zeitgeist of the 19th and early 20th centuries (Barbour, 1990; Bergin, 1980a, 1991; Jones, 1994).

INFLUENCES FROM OUTSIDE
THE PSYCHOTHERAPY PROFESSION

Changes in Physics

At the end of the 19th century, the view of the universe provided by Newtonian science was realistic, positivistic (objective), deterministic, mechanistic, linear, and reductionistic (Slife, 1993). However, the 19th-century Newtonian view of the universe as "an elaborate clockwork mechanism, utterly logical and predictable in its operations" began to crumble in the early 20th century (Lucas, 1985, p. 166) as Albert Einstein's theory of relativity, Max Planck's quantum theory, and other scientific discoveries and theories came to the forefront (Paul, 1992). Theories that directly challenged the clockwork precision view of the world, such as Heisenberg's uncertainty principle, Bohr's complementarity principle, and Bell's theorem, revolutionized the view of the universe (Appleyard, 1992; Barbour, 1990; Lucas, 1985; Paul, 1992).

Instead of realism and positivism, the findings of modern-day physics suggest that scientific theories and observations are only "partial representations of limited aspects of the world as it interacts with us" (Barbour, 1990, p. 99). The process of observation itself may alter the nature and properties of the object being observed, and the ability to perceive or observe reality accurately may be fundamentally limited (Barbour, 1990; Lucas, 1985; Mason, 1962). Instead of a deterministic universe, the findings of modern-day physics suggest that "there is a complex combination of law and chance. . . . Nature is characterized by both structure and openness. The future cannot be predicted in detail from the past" (Barbour, 1990, p. 220). Instead of mechanism and reductionism, modern-day physics suggests that "nature . . . is relational, ecological, and interdependent. Reality is constituted by events and relationships rather than by separate substances or separate particles. . . . Distinctive holistic concepts are used to explain the higher-level activities of systems, from organisms to ecosystems" (Barbour, 1990, p. 221). Templeton and Herrmann (1994), citing the physicist Paul Davies, further documented the notion of a nonmechanical, creative universe that is nonlinear and not subject to reductionism (cf. Davies, 1988, 1992).

---

[1] *Zeitgeist* is a German term popularized in psychology by Boring (1950), meaning "spirit of the times" or "habits of thought that pertain to a culture."

The findings of 20th-century physics have not only called into question the assumptions of determinism, mechanism, reductionism, classical realism, and positivism, but they also have reopened the door to the possibility that spiritual realities exist in the universe (Templeton & Herrmann, 1994). At the end of the 19th century, many scientists believed that religious and spiritual views of the universe were doomed to extinction. However, during the past decade several physicists and scientists have acknowledged that the view of the universe provided by modern physics is surprisingly compatible with religious and spiritual views of reality (Appleyard, 1992; Barbour, 1990; Brush, 1988; Capra, 1983; Lucas, 1985; Polkinghorne, 1990; Templeton & Herrmann, 1994; Tipler, 1994; Weidlich, 1990). Thus, current research in physics has not ruled out the possibility that God and spiritual realities exist, but it has left such beliefs well within the realm of rational plausibility.

Changes in the Philosophy of Science

During the late 19th and early 20th centuries, classical realism, positivism, and empiricism were the most widely accepted and influential epistemological assumptions in the philosophy of science (Edwards, 1967). However, during the second half of the 20th century, studies in both the history and philosophy of science led to a reappraisal and decline of these premises (e.g., Hesse, 1980; Kuhn, 1970; Laudan, 1984; Lincoln & Guba, 1985; Polanyi, 1962; Toulmin, 1962). This examination and reevaluation by mainstream historians and philosophers of science regarding the nature of the scientific enterprise has stimulated, and been stimulated by, an intellectual movement called *postmodernism*.

Postmodernism is a family of perspectives and philosophies that contend that "there are no metaphysical absolutes; no fundamental and abstract truths, laws, or principles that determine what the world is like and what happens in it" (Slife & Williams, 1995, p. 54). Postmodern philosophers have challenged, or attempted to deconstruct, the deterministic, reductionistic, mechanistic, and positivistic assumptions of mainstream science and psychology (Faulconer & Williams, 1985; Gergen, 1982, 1985; Messer, Sass, & Woolfolk, 1988; Packer, 1985; Slife, 1993; Slife & Williams, 1995).

Postmodernists favor a worldview that centers on the person's involvement with the world. Human behavior is seen as meaningful only within the contexts or relationships in which it occurs. Human behavior is contextual; it cannot be "objectified" by artificially removing it from that which gives it significance. Postmodern theory holds that all meaning comes from the relationships between individuals and their world, their culture, their language, and each other. This renders concepts of knowledge and truth to be the interpretive creations of a set of people who share a common language, culture, and view of the world. Postmodernists therefore reject positivistic science and "empiricism and rationalism as universal ways of knowing that supposedly apply to all or most situations" (Slife & Williams, 1995, p. 77). According to postmodernists, all knowledge and "our interpretations of our world, are socially constructed" (Slife & Williams, 1995, p. 80).

The foregoing historical and philosophical critiques of science have competed with and to some extent undermined 19th- and early 20th-century views of science. Instead of the belief that the universe can be perceived by human beings objectively and accurately, there is now considerable agreement that people's ability to accurately perceive reality is limited. *Critical realism*, the belief that the universe exists independently of people's observations but that it cannot be completely or accurately perceived by human beings, is now more widely accepted than classical realism (Barbour, 1990; Manicas & Secord, 1983). People thus are always approximating reality or truth rather than having a completely accurate picture thereof. Some philosophers and scientists have also pointed out that their observations themselves may influence and change the nature of that which is observed (e.g., Heisenberg's "uncertainty principle"; Barbour, 1990; Fennema & Paul, 1990). This may be especially so in the behavioral sciences.

In contrast to the belief that scientists are objective, value-free observers, it is now widely recognized within science and psychology that all scientists have values and biases that influence and limit their observations (Howard, 1985; Jones, 1994). Scientific observations are viewed as value and theory laden, and it is understood that scientific theories cannot be proved true in an absolute sense, nor can they be easily falsified (Brush, 1988; Kuhn, 1970; Lakatos & Musgrave, 1970; Polanyi, 1962). Science is now understood by many philosophers of science as a "social activity in which disciplines develop their own rules of practice" and where "knowledge is a social and historical product" (Manicas & Secord, 1983, p. 401). Again, these limitations are thought to be more pronounced in the social and behavioral sciences than in the natural sciences.

In contrast to the positivistic belief that the only way to gain knowledge and understanding of the world is through rigorous application of traditional quantitative and experimental empirical methodologies, many scholars now endorse epistemological and methodological pluralism (e.g., Denzin & Lincoln, 1994; Greenberg, Elliott, & Lietaer, 1994; Kirk & Miller, 1986; Reichardt & Cook, 1979). Rational and intuitive ways of knowing are being reconsidered, and more subjective, exploratory, and qualitative methodologies have been advocated and used (Denzin & Lincoln, 1994; Lincoln & Guba, 1985).

Although many of these trends are controversial, and we do not agree with the relativistic extremes they sometimes go to, this broadening of our ideas about the nature of science has helped break down some of the boundaries, distinctions, and alienation between science and religion. It is now more widely recognized that science and religion are more epistemologically compatible than was once thought (Barbour, 1990; Jones, 1994). As summarized by Barbour (1990),

> there are many parallels between science and religion; the interaction of data and theory (or experience and interpretation); the historical character of the interpretative community; the use of models; and the influence of paradigms or programs. In both fields there are no proofs, but there can be good reasons for the judgments rendered by the paradigm community. There are also important differences between science and religion, but some of them turn out to be differences in emphasis or degree rather than the absolute contrasts sometimes imagined. We have traced a number of polarities in which the first term was more prominent in science and the second in religion, but both were found to be present in both fields: objectivity and subjectivity; rationality and personal judgment; universality and historical conditioning; criticism and tradition; and tentativeness and commitment. (p. 65)

The recognition of this greater epistemological compatibility has opened the door to a consideration of the ways in which religious and spiritual perspectives may validly contribute to the understanding of the scientific process, human beings, and the universe.

Research on the Brain, Cognition, and Consciousness

In the late 19th and early 20th centuries, relatively little was known about the human brain in relation to cognition and consciousness. Early attempts to study these relationships proved unfruitful, and interest in studying mental phenomena was declining because of the scathing criticisms of early leaders of the behavioral psychology movement (e.g., Watson, 1924/1983). The reductionistic view that all mental phenomena are fully caused and controlled by chemical and electrical events within the brain also preempted researchers' interest in mental events (R. W. Sperry, 1988). Thus, cognition and consciousness were viewed as inappropriate subject matter for hard-nosed (i.e., respectable) behavioral scientists.

During the 1960s and 1970s, dissatisfaction with anti-mentalist perspectives, the rising interest in computers and artificial intelligence, and the development of new technologies for studying the human brain contributed to a renewed interest in the study of the biology of the brain, cognition, and consciousness (Karier, 1986; R. W. Sperry, 1988). This revolution led to impressive advances in the understanding of consciousness and the human brain. As described by R. W. Sperry (1988),

> by the mid-1970s, mainstream psychology had also revised its earlier views concerning consciousness and the subjective, replacing long dom-

inant behaviorist theory with a new mentalist or cognitive paradigm. This changeover, impelled by a large complex of cognitive, linguistic, computer, and related theoretic and sociologic developments . . . has now legitimized the contents of inner experience, such as sensations, percepts, mental images, thoughts, feelings, and the like, as ineliminable causal constructs in the scientific explanation of brain function and behavior. (p. 607)

R. W. Sperry and other leading brain researchers (e.g., Eccles & Robinson, 1984; Popper, 1972; Popper & Eccles, 1977) also have argued that "conscious mental states . . . interact functionally at their own level and also exert downward causal control over brain physiology in a supervenient sense . . . subjective mental qualities of inner experience . . . play an active, causal control role in conscious behavior and evolution" (R. W. Sperry, 1988, p. 607). Although not all of these researchers believe in God or in transcendent spiritual phenomena (e.g., R. W. Sperry, 1988, 1995), they are in agreement that such understandings of human consciousness and the brain are more in harmony with spiritual views of human nature than were the earlier anti-mentalist, reductionistic views (e.g., Eccles & Robinson, 1984; Popper & Eccles, 1977; R. W. Sperry, 1988, 1995).

Eccles and Robinson (1984) did believe in transcendent spirituality and, after rigorously discussing research on brain functioning and physiology, they concluded that

since materialist solutions fail to account for our experienced uniqueness, we are constrained to attribute the uniqueness of the psyche or soul to a supernatural spiritual creation. To give the explanation in theological terms: Each soul is a Divine creation, which is "attached" to the growing fetus at some time between conception and birth. It is the certainty of the inner core of unique individuality that necessitates the "Divine creation." We submit that no other explanation is tenable; neither the genetic uniqueness with its fantastically impossible lottery nor the environmental differentiations, which do not determine one's uniqueness but merely modify it. (p. 43)

Renewed Societal Interest in Spiritual Phenomena

At the dawn of the 20th century, it was widely believed in society that religious and spiritual beliefs were completely separate from, even inferior to, scientific thought (e.g., Freud, 1927/1961). The triumphs of science over medieval religious doctrines and traditions led many to place their faith in science. Science was viewed as the new hope for humanity with its impressive discoveries and technological successes. During this period it appeared as if a strong belief in religion and spirituality was on the decline. A variety of studies seemed to support this trend, and some observers confidently predicted that the influence of religion would continue to decline even to its extinction (e.g., Beckwith, 1985).

However, it appears now that these conclusions were wrong. To the contrary, a renewed interest in religion and spirituality has been evident in the world, particularly in North America (e.g., Antoun & Hegland, 1987; Kantrowitz et al., 1994; Shine, 1996; Taylor, 1994). There are many manifestations in popular culture of this spiritual renewal, such as in the print, audio, and visual media (e.g., Kantrowitz et al., 1994; Moyers, 1996; Taylor, 1994). The signs of change also are evident in the surge of religious music, the growth of religious revivalism in the public and on college campuses (Shine, 1996), the search for new moral guidelines, and increases in religious orthodoxy. There has also been an increase in moral and value-oriented literature and a preoccupation with spiritual phenomena (e.g., near-death experiences, angelic visitations, other visions, etc.; Antoun & Hegland, 1987; Kantrowitz et al., 1994; Taylor, 1994). Thus, in the popular culture, dissatisfaction with the back-seat role of spirituality has become pervasive.

Many factors have contributed to this increased interest in spirituality. For example, many people have lost faith in science's ability to provide solutions to all of humanity's problems (Bergin, 1980a). Many people experience anxiety and fear as they observe and contemplate street violence, crime, war, family disintegration, and social upheaval, all of which test people's sense of meaning and coherence in the world today. Whatever the reasons may be, society's renewed interest in spiritual issues has influenced the field of psychology and seems to have contributed to a greater openness to the consideration of religious and spiritual perspectives in mainstream psychology and psychotherapy.

Research on Religion and Mental Health

Although more than 70 years have passed since religious beliefs were first widely regarded in mainstream psychiatry and psychology as unhealthy and unproductive, this viewpoint, or versions of it, has persisted in mainstream psychology and psychotherapy until recent years (Bergin, 1980a, 1980b, 1983, 1991; Ellis, 1980; Jensen & Bergin, 1988). For example, in 1980, Albert Ellis, one of the most influential of contemporary psychologists, stated that "religiosity . . . is in many respects equivalent to irrational thinking and emotional disturbance. . . . The elegant therapeutic solution to emotional problems is to be quite unreligious and have no degree of dogmatic faith that is unfounded or unfoundable in fact" (p. 637). Such views persisted in mainstream psychology (Bergin, 1980a) despite the fact that research investigating the relationship between religion and mental health was surprisingly sparse, and perhaps because early reviews of what research there was were more negative and partook of the older anti-religious zeitgeist (Dittes, 1971; Sanua, 1969).

During the past decade, however, this view has changed. In response to Ellis (1980), Bergin (1983) reviewed the limited research literature up to that time that had investigated the relationship between religiosity and mental health. He found that when religiosity was correlated with traditional paper-and-pencil measures of mental health (e.g., the Minnesota Multiphasic Personality Inventory, manifest anxiety, neuroticism, self-esteem, irrational beliefs, ego strength, and psychic adequacy), of the 30 effects found, "only 7, or 23%, manifested the negative relationship between religion and mental health assumed by Ellis and others. Forty-seven percent indicated a positive relationship and 30% a zero relationship. Thus 77% of the obtained results are contrary to the negative effect of religion theory" (p. 176).

Since Bergin's (1983) review, many additional studies have examined the relationship between religiousness and emotional or social functioning. Overall, the findings have not supported the "religiosity-neurosis/emotional disturbance" hypothesis, but, to the contrary, have provided evidence that religious beliefs and behaviors are positively related to many indicators of emotional and social adjustment (Batson, Schoenrode, & Ventis, 1993; Gartner, Larson, & Allen, 1991; Payne, Bergin, Bielema, & Jenkins, 1991).

Research on religion and mental health has contributed to a reevaluation by many mainstream mental health professionals regarding the role of religious and spiritual beliefs in psychotherapy, a reevaluation that was clearly manifested in a national survey of four professional groups of therapists (Jensen & Bergin, 1988). Even Ellis (1996) has revised his views in this regard. Religious beliefs and behavior can no longer be viewed simply as a neurosis or irrelevant response to be ignored or extinguished. To the contrary, a majority of mainstream psychotherapists now consider such beliefs and behaviors to be resources for promoting therapeutic change (Bergin, 1991; P. S. Richards & Potts, 1995a; Shafranske, 1996).

CHANGES WITHIN THE PSYCHOTHERAPY PROFESSION

Alternative Therapeutic Traditions

Even as psychoanalysis and behavioral psychology rose to prominence during the early 20th century, dissenters began to criticize and challenge the assumptions of these theories. Several of Freud's early followers eventually broke from the tenets of psychoanalytic theory to establish their own approaches. For example, Adler and Jung rejected Freud's reductionistic views of human nature (Kaufmann, 1989; Mosak, 1989). As noted in Bandura's (1986) review, behavioral psychology also quickly attracted critics, especially for its dogmatic denial of both mental processes and consciousness, and its rigid adherence to strict empiricism and positivism. Although behavior therapy was built on the philosophical foundations of early behavioral psychology, the attempt to design a behavioral technology has been essentially displaced by the cognitive–behavioral movement, which is more agentive in perspective (see Bandura, 1969, 1986).

During the 1950s and 1960s, major alternatives to psychoanalysis and behaviorism arose (Leahey, 1991). One of these became the "third force" in psychology: the humanistic-existential tradition (May, Angel, & Ellenberger, 1958; Leahey, 1991). Rogers (1961, 1980) and Maslow (1968, 1970, 1971), two leaders of humanistic-existential thought, challenged the deterministic and reductionistic views of human beings promoted by the psychoanalytic and behavioral traditions. They argued that human beings cannot be reduced to simple biological drives or environmental stimulus–response connections and that humans have the capacity to transcend their circumstances, thus actualizing their innate human potential through positive choices. Rogers, Maslow, and others challenged psychology's commitment to strict experimental empiricism and positivism by virtue of their phenomenological emphasis and willingness to describe emotions, purpose, values, and other nonobservable phenomena (see Rychlak, 1981).

The cognitive and systemic philosophies were also developing during the 1950s and 1960s, although it was not until the 1970s that these two traditions emerged as major influences within the field. The leaders of the cognitive psychotherapy tradition challenged deterministic and reductionistic views of human beings with their emphasis on the interdependence of cognition, affect, and behavior and their belief that human beings can change the way they feel and behave by changing their thinking (Beck, 1976; Burns, 1980; Ellis, 1973; Meichenbaum, 1977). The leaders of the systemic tradition also challenged deterministic and reductionistic views of human beings with their emphasis on complex systemic influences on human behavior. Such theorists assume that human beings are not simply passive recipients of systemic influences but agents who have the capacity to actively modify their family systems to bring about change (Gurman & Kniskern, 1981). Both the cognitive and systemic traditions contributed to an increased appreciation of the complexity of human behavior and emotions, thereby raising further doubts about the positivistic claim that human behavior can be understood completely and predicted through empirical observation and linear causality.

Thus, during the first 75 years of the 20th century, five major therapeutic traditions rose to prominence in mainstream psychotherapy: the psychoanalytic, behavioral, humanistic-existential, cognitive, and systemic strategies (Matarazzo, 1985). The assumptions of determinism, reductionism, classical realism, and positivism were rejected or questioned to some degree by the early leaders of the humanistic, cognitive, and systemic traditions. By the 1970s and early 1980s, even leaders within the psychodynamic and behavior therapy traditions were beginning to lay aside these assumptions. Contemporary psychoanalytic thinking is more open to the legitimacy of the spiritual domain and is much less reductionistic (e.g., Spero, 1992), and behavioral therapy even acquired the new designation of "cognitive–behavioral" (Beck, 1976; Garfield & Bergin, 1986; Meichenbaum, 1977).[2]

The Movement Toward Eclecticism

During the past 15 years, a new movement has risen to prominence: the eclectic, integrative approach (Bergin & Garfield, 1994; Norcross, 1986; Norcross & Goldfried, 1992). According to a national survey by Jensen, Bergin, and Greaves (1990), a majority of psychotherapists are now using eclectic and multidimensional philosophies in their approach to psychotherapy. Perhaps not surprisingly, the techniques used most often are a combination of the psychodynamic, behavioral, cognitive, humanistic-existential, and systemic traditions (Jensen et al., 1990). Thus, the five major therapeutic traditions continue to remain, in an eclectic fashion, the most influential in mainstream psychotherapy. Spiritual techniques are also beginning to find their way into this broad clinical perspective (Payne, Bergin, & Loftus, 1992).

With its emphasis on treatment tailoring, client and therapist choice, holism, and integration, the eclectic, integrative tradition has further contributed to a rejection by psychotherapists of the assumptions of determinism and reductionism. The eclectic tradition's acknowledgment of the great complexity of human personality and therapeutic change also seems to have further highlighted for many the limitations of strictly empirical and positivistic epistemological claims.[3]

The Multicultural Counseling Movement

During the first half of the 20th century, the majority of influential contributors to theory, research, and practice in mainstream psychology

---

[2] Slife and Williams (1995) argued that although the humanistic, cognitive, and systemic traditions appear to reject determinism, reductionism, and positivism in some regards, at another level such philosophies remain implicitly embedded in their theories. Slife and Williams might have been correct, but, if so, we would argue that this has remained hidden from most behavioral scientists. Perhaps the humanistic, cognitive, and systemic traditions do implicitly and unknowingly partake of deterministic, reductionistic, and positivistic philosophies; however, in explicitly questioning and challenging them, these traditions have reduced their plausibility in the minds of many behavioral scientists.
[3] Slife and Williams (1995) argued that eclecticism also partakes of the same hidden assumptions that are embedded in the theories of the five major psychotherapy traditions. We question whether this is necessarily so and also would argue that in the minds of most behavioral scientists, eclecticism has served to reduce the plausibility of determinism, reductionism, and positivism.

and psychotherapy were White, middle- to upper-class men. Little attention was given to the issues and concerns of women or minority group members (D. W. Sue, 1981; D. W. Sue & Sue, 1990). When women and minority group members were included in psychological theories or research, they were often portrayed as deficient or pathological (Gilligan, 1982; Sue & Sue, 1990). Most psychotherapists seemed to believe that their therapeutic approaches could be applied equally effectively to all clients, regardless of the client's gender, race, religion, or lifestyle.

During the turbulent decades of the 1960s and 1970s, culturally encapsulated views of women and minority groups received widespread criticism (D. W. Sue & Sue, 1990). The civil rights and feminist movements challenged and began to break down many of the prevailing stereotypes. Within the psychotherapy profession, the cross-cultural or multicultural movement gained momentum and became a major force. During the 1980s and 1990s, numerous articles and books discussing the importance of multicultural sensitivity were published (e.g., Ibrahim, 1985, 1991; Ponterotto, Casas, Suzuki, & Alexander, 1995; Ponterotto, Suzuki & Moller, 1996; D. W. Sue, 1981; D. W. Sue & Sue, 1990; S. Sue, Zane, & Young, 1994). Many professional associations incorporated guidelines regarding respect for diversity and multicultural sensitivity into their ethical and training standards (e.g., American Counseling Association, 1995; American Psychological Association, 1981, 1992).

The multicultural movement has helped mainstream mental health professionals become more aware and tolerant of the great diversity that exists in the world, including religious and spiritual diversity. Fourteen years ago, Bergin (1983) pointed out that religious diversity had not yet been given sufficient attention by mainstream psychology and psychotherapy. However, this is beginning to change as evidenced by the publication of this book and others on religious and spiritual issues by mainstream professional organizations (e.g., Kelly, 1995; Shafranske, 1996) and by the explicit inclusion of religion as a type of diversity in the American Psychological Association's (1992) most recent ethical guidelines. Thus, the multicultural movement, and the growing awareness of and tolerance toward religious and spiritual diversity, has helped prepare the way for a spiritual strategy in psychology and psychotherapy.

Recognition of the Importance of Values

As psychology and psychotherapy developed, early leaders believed that values could be kept out of psychological theory, research, and practice (Patterson, 1958). These leaders assumed that therapists could be a "blank slate"; objective, scientific technicians; or nonjudgmental, nonevaluative listeners. Yet, as early as the late 1940s and continuing into the 1960s and 1970s, the belief that values could be kept out of psychotherapy was challenged theoretically and empirically (Beutler, 1972; Kessell & McBrearty, 1967; Patterson, 1958). Several writers have argued persuasively that psychotherapy is a value-laden process (Bergin, 1980a, 1980b; 1980c; Campbell, 1975; R. F. Kitchener, 1980a, 1980b; London, 1964, 1986; Lowe, 1976). It is now widely accepted in mainstream psychotherapy that it is impossible for therapists to remain value free as they work with their clients and that psychotherapy research also is influenced by the researcher's values (Bergin & Garfield, 1994).

Ethical relativism and ethical hedonism continue to remain influential within the profession of psychotherapy (e.g., Ellis, 1980). However, even these assumptions have been challenged by behavioral scientists and psychotherapists in recent years (e.g., Barbour, 1990; Bergin, 1980a, 1980b, 1983, 1985, 1991; Collins, 1977; Doherty, 1995; Jones, 1994). Several writers specifically have criticized psychology's and psychiatry's long-standing promotion of ethical hedonism. For example, in his 1975 presidential address to the American Psychological Association, Campbell said that

> a major thesis of this address is that present-day psychology and psychiatry in all their major forms are more hostile to the inhibitory messages of traditional religious moralizing than is scientifically justified. . . . The religions of all ancient urban civilizations . . . taught that many aspects of human nature need to be curbed if optimal social coordination is to be achieved, for example, selfishness, pride, greed, dishonesty, covetousness, lust, wrath. Psychology and psychiatry, on the other hand, not only describe man as selfishly motivated, but implicitly teach that he ought to be so. They tend to see repression and inhibition of individual impulse as undesirable, and see all guilt as a dysfunctional neurotic blight created by cruel child rearing and a needlessly repressive society. They further recommend that we accept our biological and psychological impulses as good and seek pleasure rather than enchain ourselves with duty. (pp. 1103–1104)

Campbell (1975) further commented that "on these issues, psychology and psychiatry cannot yet claim to be truly scientific and thus have special reasons for modesty and caution in undermining traditional beliefs systems" (p. 1103).

Several writers have also criticized psychology and psychiatry in terms of their promotion of ethical relativism (Bergin, 1980c, 1985; Doherty, 1995; R. F. Kitchener, 1980a). For example, R. F. Kitchener (1980a) offered the following:

> Why has relativism been so influential and popular among social and behavioral scientists? Why has it seemed to be a logical conclusion that inevitably had to be drawn? I could give several reasons, but an obvious one is the following. In looking around at different individuals and

cultures, one of the most striking features is the obvious fact that people value different things [cultural relativism]. . . . Even if this were true (and there are reasons to think it is not), it would not show that psychological relativism and cultural relativism are true. It does not follow that what ought to be valued differs from individual to individual (ethical relativism). (pp. 5–6)

Commenting on R. F. Kitchener's article, Bergin (1980c) stated that

Kitchener (1980[a]) properly identifies inconsistencies in the philosophies and between the philosophies and actions of behavior therapists. This state of the art is not, however, confined to the behavioral position, but is true of most approaches to therapy and to applied behavioral science in general. It is interesting to observe professional change agents who believe in a relativistic philosophy and simultaneously assert dogmatically the virtue of the therapeutic goals they promote. . . . Kitchener correctly identifies such inconsistency [ethical relativism] as a dilemma for therapists who wish to logically justify the positions they take with respect to therapeutic goals. (p. 11)

There is now evidence that the majority of therapists do believe that certain values promote mental health and that these values should be endorsed and used to guide therapy (Jensen & Bergin, 1988). Although there are still questions and debate about what specific values therapists should use to guide and evaluate psychotherapy, the majority of therapists (with notable exceptions, such as Ellis, 1980) no longer seem to concur with relativistic or hedonistic moral philosophies. Instead, many endorse personal responsibility, family commitment, humility before God, self-control, self-sacrifice, forgiveness, and honesty (Doherty, 1995; Jensen & Bergin, 1988; see also chaps. 5 and 6 in this book). Thus, current perspectives within the psychotherapy profession concerning values are more in harmony with religious and spiritual worldviews than were the value-free, ethically relativistic, and hedonistic beliefs of the early leaders of psychiatry and psychotherapy (Bergin, Payne, & Richards, 1996).

The Restoration of Spiritual Perspectives

The scientific, philosophical, and social influences we have discussed in this chapter have eroded the credibility and influence of the philosophies of determinism, reductionism, empiricism, classical realism, positivism, ethical relativism, and ethical hedonism. The changes in the philosophical and theoretical climate that have occurred during recent decades have laid the foundation for a reconsideration of naturalism, psychology's and psychiatry's most deeply and rigidly held philosophical assumption.

A number of mental health professionals have called for the restoration of spiritual, theistic perspectives in the profession of psychotherapy (e.g., Bergin, 1980a, 1988, 1991; Collins, 1977; Jones, 1994). For example, Jones (1994), citing the philosopher Alvin Plantinga (1984; Plantinga & Wolterstorff, 1983), recently argued that

> there is no compelling reason for individuals who believe in God not to include the existence of God among the fundamental worldview assumptions brought to the scholarly, scientific task. . . . Albert Ellis and B. F. Skinner, among others, have explicitly made naturalism . . . a part of the fundamental commitments they bring to the scientific task. If disbelief in the supernatural can suitably be among the control beliefs of some scientists, it would seem that belief in God and related beliefs about human persons could be allowable for others as part of their control beliefs. (p. 195)

Consistent with this idea, Bergin (1980a) stated that

> other alternatives are . . . needed. . . . The alternative I wish to put forward is a spiritual one. It might be called theistic realism. . . . The first and most important axiom [of theistic realism] is that God exists, that human beings are the creations of God, and that there are unseen spiritual processes by which the link between God and humanity is maintained. (p. 99)

Because of the changes in philosophical and theoretical climate that have occurred in science, philosophy, and psychology during recent decades, such spiritual, theistic perspectives are being seriously considered and accepted by many mainstream personality theorists and psychotherapists (Shafranske, 1996; Worthington et al., 1996). The zeitgeist is now ripe for the integration of a spiritual strategy into mainstream psychotherapy theory and practice.

4

WESTERN AND EASTERN SPIRITUAL WORLDVIEWS

There is something strikingly new in modern spirituality. . . . The world's diversity of religious traditions . . . has come home to us in a quite literal way . . . the . . . presence of so many people of once-alien traditions . . . is . . . requiring a degree of accommodation and respect that was earlier unknown . . .

—David Wulff

Although the major purpose of our book is to describe a spiritual strategy for mainstream psychotherapy that is based on a Western, theistic worldview, we also describe in this chapter two other major worldviews that influence humanity and that clinicians will encounter: the Eastern spiritual tradition and the naturalistic, scientific worldview. We describe the history, demographics, and core metaphysical beliefs (e.g., their views of deity, human nature, purpose of life, spirituality, morality, and life after death) of the five Western and six Eastern world religious traditions. We also compare and contrast the Western, Eastern, and scientific worldviews.

We have done this with the hope that it will help psychotherapists and mental health professionals better understand and appreciate each of these important perspectives. We also show that the theistic worldview is in harmony with the beliefs of a large proportion of the world's population, including the majority of psychotherapy clients. Although we do not expect all psychotherapists and mental health professionals to agree with this view, we argue that it is important for them to make efforts to understand and appreciate it more fully, given that many of their clients approach life with this perspective.

THE IMPORTANCE OF A WELTANSCHAUUNG

During the past few decades, a number of writers have pointed out how important it is for psychotherapists and mental health professionals to understand their clients' worldviews. For example, Ibrahim (1985) stated that a

> lack of understanding of one's own and one's clients' world views results in frustration and anxiety for both the helper and the client. Goals and processes considered appropriate by the helper may be antithetical and meaningless for the client. In such an instance, the appropriate course for the helper is to establish clearly how the client views the world. (pp. 629–630)

A weltanschauung, or worldview, according to Wilhelm Dilthey, a German philosopher and pioneering contributor to the understanding of worldviews (Dilthey, 1978), is composed of beliefs a person holds about the universe and the nature of reality that attempt "to resolve the enigma of life" (Kluback & Weinbaum, 1957, p. 25). Worldviews "furnish answers to the largest questions that human beings can ask about their condition" (Wagar, 1977, p. 4).

The deepest questions human beings can ask about the nature of reality and their existence are metaphysical and existential questions. For example, how did the universe and the Earth come to exist? How did life, particularly human life, come to exist? Is there a Supreme Being or Creator? What is the purpose of life? How should people live their lives in order to find happiness, peace, and wisdom? What is good, moral, and ethical? What is undesirable, evil, and immoral? How do people live with the realities of suffering, grief, pain, and death? Is there life after death, and, if so, what is the nature of the afterlife? Such questions have concerned religious leaders, artists, philosophers, writers, and scientists throughout the history of humankind (Kluback & Weinbaum, 1957).

During the past few decades, several scholars have written about the importance of worldviews and have pointed out that worldviews have a major impact on human relationships, societies, and cultures (e.g., Horner & Vandersluis, 1981; Kluback & Weinbaum, 1957; C. Kluckhohn, 1951, 1956; F. R. Kluckhohn & Strodtbeck, 1961; Sarason, 1981; Sire, 1976, Wagar, 1977). For example, Sarason (1981), a clinical psychologist, stated that "one's view of the universe is interwoven with one's view of people. However one conceives of the universe, it is connected to how one sees oneself in relation to other people, the social world" (pp. 47–48). Wagar (1977) asserted that the "cultural life of all societies takes form and direction from . . . [their] world views" (p. 4).

A person's worldview also has a significant influence on physical and mental health and interpersonal relationships. As illustrated in Figure 4.1, a person's metaphysical worldview influences values and goals, which in turn influence lifestyle and behavior, which influence physical and mental health and, in turn, interpersonal relationships.

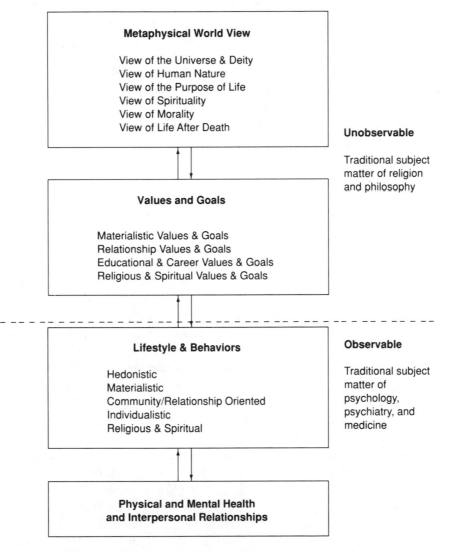

Figure 4.1. The influence and importance of one's metaphysical worldview.

The following example helps clarify this point. John is a devout Mormon who believes in God and believes that God has revealed a health code that emphasizes care of the physical body as the "temple of one's spirit." Those who follow this code are promised both health and wisdom. This is part of John's metaphysical worldview. In keeping with this principle, John sets a goal early in life to abide by its admonition against alcohol and tobacco. John's goals and values influence his lifestyle and behavior, and he avoids drinking parties and bars and refuses cigarettes when they are offered to him. Because of his religious beliefs, John remains abstinent from alcohol and tobacco throughout his life and avoids the negative effects of tobacco use and the potential of alcohol abuse. His physical and mental health and interpersonal relationships are free of the damaging effects of these substances. Perhaps his mental processes are also clearer and his judgment wiser than they otherwise might have been.

If John's metaphysical worldview did not include a belief that God had commanded him to abstain from tobacco and alcohol, he may not have set a goal to abstain, and he may have decided he enjoyed and valued drinking and smoking. Smoking and drinking may have become part of his lifestyle, and, ultimately, he would have suffered the health consequences of such behaviors, including, for example, the possibility of cancer or alcoholism and all of the emotional and relationship problems associated with them.

There is not, of course, a one-to-one relationship between people's worldviews and their physical and mental health and interpersonal relationships. People's values and goals are not always consistent with their worldviews, nor are their lifestyles and behaviors always consistent with their values and goals. In addition, many other factors potentially affect a person's physical and mental health and relationships, such as genetic vulnerabilities, disease, aging, and accidents. Nevertheless, a worldview is one important influence on physical and mental health and relationships. Traditionally, psychologists and psychiatrists have tended to ignore worldviews and values and have limited their research, theory, and practice to a consideration of what is observable: behaviors, relationships, and physical and mental health. Fortunately, this has begun to change in recent years.

Multicultural writers in the psychotherapy and mental health professions have, in recent years, drawn attention to the ways that people from various races and cultures differ in their worldviews (e.g., Horner & Vandersluis, 1981; Ibrahim, 1985, 1991; Speight, Myers, Cox, & Highlen, 1991; D. W. Sue, 1978; D. W. Sue & Sue, 1990). For example, D. W. Sue (1978; see also D. W. Sue & Sue, 1990) proposed a two-dimensional locus of control–locus of responsibility model that he believed would be helpful for understanding how minority- and majority-group clients differ in their worldviews. Building on the value orientation theory of Kluckhohn (1951,

1956; F. R. Kluckhohn & Strodtbeck, 1961), Ibrahim (1985) proposed a five-dimensional (i.e., human nature, person and nature, time sense, activity, and social relations) value-orientations model and illustrated how this model could help therapists understand how clients from different cultural and racial backgrounds differ in their worldviews.

The contributions of multicultural scholars have made an important contribution to the understanding of worldviews and have illustrated how important it is for psychotherapists to understand each client's unique perspective. However, as valuable as these worldview models have been, they have been somewhat limited in scope and have not provided an adequate understanding of the spiritual dimension in the major metaphysical perspectives of humankind.

THREE MAJOR METAPHYSICAL WORLDVIEWS

According to Wilhelm Dilthey, although there is a great variety of philosophical and religious belief systems in the world, there are only three major types of metaphysical worldviews: naturalism, idealism of freedom, and objective idealism (Ermarth, 1978; Kluback & Weinbaum, 1957; Rickman, 1976, 1979).[1] In discussing Dilthey's typology of worldviews, Wagar (1977) described the core differences between them concisely:

> naturalism, apprehends reality as a physical system accessible to sense experience. . . . Idealism of freedom, takes a subjective view of reality, discovering in man a will independent of nature and grounded in a transcendental spiritual realm. . . . Objective idealism, shrinks from the dualism implicit in the second. It proclaims the unity and divinity of all being. . . . The naturalist . . . defines the good life as the pursuit of happiness or power, the subjective idealist . . . defines it as obedience to conscience or divine will, and the objective idealist . . . sees it as a midpoint between the two extremes. . . . The naturalist . . . tends to subscribe to a mechanistic determinism that undercuts freedom of will, whereas the subjective idealist . . . upholds moral freedom, and the objective idealist . . . unites determinism and indeterminism. (pp. 5–6)

Examples of philosophies or worldview subtypes that can be classified within Dilthey's *naturalistic worldview* are rationalism, positivism, Marxism, existentialism, and secular humanism (Wagar, 1977). The Western, or

---

[1] The Russian American sociologist Sorokin (1957) proposed a similar typology as the basis for a theory of comparative world cultures.

monotheistic, world religions (i.e., Judaism, Christianity, Islam, Zoroastrianism, and Sikhism) are major examples of the *idealism of freedom, or subjective idealistic, worldview*. The Eastern world religious traditions (i.e., Buddhism, Hinduism, Jainism, Shintoism, Confucianism, and Taoism) are major examples of the *objective idealistic worldview*. According to Dilthey, these three major types of worldviews have coexisted during the past several millennia and have rivaled each other by providing alternate answers to the major metaphysical and existential questions of life (Ermarth, 1978; Kluback & Weinbaum, 1957; Rickman, 1976, 1979, Wagar, 1977). Of course, we emphasize that although most worldviews ultimately may be classifiable into one of Dilthey's three types, there is much individual variation in specific worldviews. Many people undoubtedly combine elements from all three worldview types and others "may also elaborate idiosyncratic world views [sic] that draw upon the reigning orthodoxies and in some measure transcend them" (Wagar, 1977, p. 4).

As we discussed in chapter 2, the naturalistic worldview has dominated the psychotherapy and mental health professions during the past century, and religious and spiritual perspectives have been excluded from theory, research, and practice deliberately. As a result, most psychotherapists and mental health professionals are well acquainted with the naturalistic worldview, but they have less understanding and appreciation of the two major religious and spiritual worldviews: the Western, or monotheistic, worldview and the Eastern (polytheistic or pantheistic) spiritual worldview.

The Western, or Monotheistic, World Religions

There are five major monotheistic religious traditions in the world: Judaism, Christianity, Islam, Zoroastrianism, and Sikhism (Palmer & Keller, 1989). As can be seen in Table 4.1, approximately one half of the world's people belong to one of the monotheistic world religions. Judaism, Christianity, and Islam are the major monotheistic religions of the Western world (Smart, 1994). Zoroastrianism and Sikhism are monotheistic religions whose majority of followers live in India. These religions all believe in *theism*, that is, the belief that "God exists transcendent to the world as the Creator who gives to the world its original existence and sustains it in existence" (Honer & Hunt, 1987, p. 231). They also believe in *monotheism*, that is, the belief that there is one Supreme Being or Supreme God (Honer & Hunt, 1987).

The roots of Judaism can be traced to the early patriarchs of the ancient Middle East—Abraham, Isaac, and Jacob—in the 2nd millenium B.C. (Nielsen et al., 1988; Palmer & Keller, 1989; Smart, 1994). Many scholars and Jewish people view the prophet Moses and his brother Aaron as the founders of Judaism (Palmer & Keller, 1989; Smart, 1994). In approximately 1300 B.C., Moses led the Israelites in an exodus from their bondage in Egypt to Mount Sinai. During the period in Sinai, Moses communicated with God on Mount Sinai and was called to be a leader and prophet to his people. Today, Moses is still considered the prophetic basis of Jewish law and practice.

After wandering in the wilderness for 40 years, the Jewish people settled in their Promised Land (the land of Canaan and the city of Jerusalem). Eventually, the Jewish people were exiled from the Promised Land and scattered throughout the Middle East, North Africa, Europe, and other parts of the world (Palmer & Keller, 1989). After centuries of exile, the State of Israel was founded in 1948, and many Jewish people began gathering again in their ancient Promised Land.

Today there are approximately 14 million Jewish people in the world: about 6 million in North America, 4.3 million in Asia, and 2.5 million in Europe (Barrett, 1996). There are now numerous divisions within Judaism; however, the major divisions are Reformed Judaism, Conservative Judaism, and Orthodox Judaism (Palmer & Keller, 1989; Smart, 1994).

The roots of Christianity are embedded clearly in Judaism, but Christianity emerged as a new world faith because of the life and teaching of Jesus of Nazareth (Nielsen et al., 1988; Palmer & Keller, 1989; Smart, 1994). Jesus was born in Bethlehem of Judea sometime between 6 B.C. and A.D. 6 (Nielsen et al., 1988). Jesus was raised in the Jewish faith. At the age of about 30, he was baptized by his cousin (John the Baptist) and began his public ministry. Jesus taught about the Kingdom of God and preached a message of love, peace, service, and forgiveness. In addition, he claimed to be the Son of God, the Messiah, or the Anointed One and bore witness that he had been sent to Earth by God, his Father. In approximately A.D. 33, Jesus was crucified. According to early Christian writings (the New Testament in the Bible), 3 days after his death, Jesus was resurrected from the dead and appeared to his followers. Jesus commissioned his followers (apostles) and told them to go into all of the world preaching his message.

There are approximately 1.9 billion Christians in the world today (approximately one third of the world's population; Barrett, 1996). The majority of Christians live in the Western world (i.e., North and South America and Europe); however, Christians can be found throughout the world. There are approximately 250 million Christians in North America (more than 85% of the population). There are numerous divisions within Christianity today. The largest denomination is the Roman Catholic church, which makes up nearly one half of the world's Christians (Barrett, 1996). Eastern and Oriental Orthodox churches number about 217 million (Barrett, 1996). Another major division in Christianity is Protestantism, which had its beginnings in the Reformation. There is a myriad of denominations that fall within Protestantism, including the Episcopalian, Methodist, Lutheran, Presbyterian, Congregational, Mennonite, Unitarian, and Baptist denominations (Palmer & Keller, 1989). There also are a

TABLE 4.1
Adherents of All Religions by Continental Areas in Mid-1995

	Africa	Asia	Europe	Latin America	Northern America	Oceania	World	%	Number of Countries
Christians	348,176,000	306,762,000	551,892,000	448,006,000	249,277,000	23,840,000	1,927,953,000	33.7	260
Roman Catholics	122,108,000	90,041,000	270,677,000	402,691,000	74,243,000	8,265,000	968,025,000	16.9	249
Protestants	109,726,000	42,836,000	80,000,000	31,684,000	123,257,000	8,364,000	395,867,000	6.9	236
Orthodox	29,645,000	14,881,000	165,795,000	481,000	6,480,000	666,000	217,948,000	3.8	105
Anglicans	25,362,000	707,000	30,625,000	1,153,000	6,819,000	5,864,000	70,530,000	1.2	158
Other Christians	61,335,000	158,297,000	4,795,000	11,997,000	38,478,000	681,000	275,583,000	4.8	118
Atheists	427,000	174,174,000	40,085,000	2,977,000	1,670,000	592,000	219,925,000	3.8	139
Baha'is	1,851,000	3,010,000	93,000	719,000	356,000	75,000	6,104,000	0.1	210
Buddhists	36,000	320,691,000	1,478,000	569,000	920,000	200,000	323,894,000	5.7	92
Chinese folk religionists	12,000	224,828,000	116,000	66,000	98,000	17,000	225,137,000	3.9	60
Confucians	1,000	5,220,000	4,000	2,000	26,000	1,000	5,254,000	0.1	12
Ethnic religionists	72,777,000	36,579,000	1,200,000	1,061,000	47,000	113,000	111,777,000	2.0	104
Hindus	1,535,000	775,252,000	1,522,000	748,000	1,185,000	305,000	780,547,000	13.7	94
Jains	58,000	4,804,000	15,000	4,000	4,000	1,000	4,886,000	0.1	11
Jews	163,000	4,294,000	2,529,000	1,098,000	5,942,000	91,000	14,117,000	0.2	134

								Countries
Mandeans	0	44,000	0	0	0	44,000	0.0	2
Muslims	300,317,000	760,181,000	31,975,000	1,329,000	5,450,000	382,000	1,099,634,000	19.2	184
New-Religionists	19,000	118,591,000	808,000	913,000	956,000	10,000	121,297,000	2.1	27
Nonreligious	2,573,000	701,175,000	94,330,000	15,551,000	25,050,000	2,870,000	841,549,000	14.7	226
Parsees	1,000	184,000	1,000	1,000	1,000	1,000	189,000	0.0	3
Sikhs	36,000	18,130,000	490,000	8,000	490,000	7,000	19,161,000	0.3	21
Shintoists	0	2,840,000	1,000	1,000	1,000	1,000	2,844,000	0.0	4
Spiritists	4,000	1,100,000	17,000	8,768,000	300,000	1,000	10,190,000	0.2	30
Other religionists	88,000	98,000	443,000	184,000	1,068,000	42,000	1,923,000	0.0	182
Non-Christians	379,898,000	3,151,195,000	175,107,000	33,999,000	43,564,000	4,709,000	3,788,472,000	66.3	262
Total population	728,074,000	3,457,957,000	726,999,000	482,005,000	292,841,000	28,549,000	5,716,425,000	100.0	262

Note. Reprinted with permission from Encyclopedia Britannica Book of the Year, 1996 © 1996. Encyclopedia Britannica. Inc. These statistics are approximations and are less accurate than, say, the U.S. Census which is itself subject to many inaccuracies. Our review of diverse sources of religious affiliation statistics suggests that (a) numbers in larger groups tend to be overestimated while numbers in smaller groups may be underestimated, and (b) the influence of religion is exaggerated by such numbers because they include a large proportion of only nominally affiliated persons whose beliefs and lifestyles are only minimally influenced by the religious tradition they are classified with. *Continents*: These follow current UN demographic practice, which divides the world into the 6 major areas shown above and 21 regions. *Countries*: The last column enumerates sovereign and nonsovereign countries in which each religion or religious grouping has a numerically significant following. *Rows*: The list of non-Christian religions is arranged in alphabetical order. *Christians*: Followers of Jesus Christ affiliated with churches (Church members, including children: 1,791,227,000) plus persons professing in censuses or polls though not so affiliated. *Other Christians*: This term in the above table denoted Catholics (non-Roman): marginal Protestants, crypto-Christians, and adherents of African, Asian, black, and Latin-American indigenous churches. *Atheists*: Persons professing atheism, skepticism, disbelief, or irreligion, including antireligious (opposed to all religion). *Buddhists*: 56% Mahayana. 38% Theravada (Hinayana). 6% Tantrayana (Lamaism). *Chinese folk religionists*: Followers of the traditional Chinese religion (local deities, ancestor veneration. Confucian ethics. Taoism, universism, divination, some Buddhist elements). *Confucians*: Non-Chinese followers of Confucius and Confucianism, mostly Koreans in Korea. *Hindus*: 70% Vaishnavites. 25% Shaivites. 2% neo-Hindus and reform Hindus. *Jews*: Adherents of Judaism. *Muslims*: 83% Sunnites, 16% Shi'ites, 1% other schools. Up to 1990 the ethnic Muslims in the former U.S.S.R. who had embraced communism were not included as Muslims in this table. *New-Religionists*: Followers of Asian 20th-century New Religions, New Religious movements, radical new crisis religions, and non-Christian syncretistic mass religions, all founded since 1800 and most since 1945. *Nonreligious*: Persons professing no religion, nonbelievers, agnostics, freethinkers, dereligionized secularists indifferent to all religion. *Other religionists*: Including 70 minor world religions and a large number of spiritist religions. New Age religions, quasi religions, pseudo religions, parareligions, religious or mystic systems, and religious and semireligious brotherhoods of numerous varieties. *Total population*: UN medium variant figures for mid-1995.

number of other newer denominations who consider themselves Christian but who are not always accepted as part of mainstream Christianity, including Mormons, Jehovah's Witnesses, and Seventh-Day Adventists.

The roots of Islam can be traced to Abraham, but Islam originated as a new world faith because of the life and teachings of the prophet Muhammad (Farah, 1994; Nielsen et al., 1988; Palmer & Keller, 1989; Smart, 1994). Muhammad was born in A.D. 570 in Mecca. In A.D. 610, according to tradition, Muhammad was praying and engaging in religious devotions in the hills above Mecca when he had a vision of the angel Gabriel (Farah, 1994; Nielsen et al., 1988; Palmer & Keller, 1989; Smart, 1994). Muhammad had other revelatory experiences that started him on his mission as a messenger of God (Allah). Muslims also believe that God's eternal speech and words were revealed to the prophet Muhammad and are recorded in the Qur'an, the Muslim holy book. Although Muhammad's message at first found little acceptance in Mecca, after establishing a following elsewhere (the city of Medina), Muhammad eventually returned to Mecca and became its leader (Farah, 1994; Nielsen et al., 1988; Palmer & Keller, 1989; Smart, 1994).

There are approximately 1.1 billion Muslims in the world (Barrett, 1996). The major population centers of Islam are in North Africa (e.g., Morocco, Algeria, Libya, Egypt), Asia (e.g., Turkey, Iran, Iraq, Jordan, Kuwait, Saudi Arabia, Pakistan), and Indonesia (Palmer & Keller, 1989; Smart, 1994). There also are approximately 5.4 million Muslims in North America (Barrett, 1996). There are numerous divisions or traditions within Islam; however, the two major traditions today are orthodox or Sunni Islam and Shi'ah or Shi'ite Islam (Farah, 1994; Nielsen et al., 1988).

Zoroastrianism originated in ancient Persia, the geographical area today known as Iran (Nigosian, 1994). Zarathustra, also known by his Greek name Zoroaster, was the prophet founder of Zoroastrianism. Zarathustra was born, it is believed, sometime before 600 B.C. According to tradition, Zarathustra had a vision in which he was met by a supernatural messenger who led him into the presence of the Supreme God where he was given a commission to preach his message for the benefit of all humankind (Boyce, 1979, 1984).

Today there are only about 115,000 Zoroastrians (Palmer & Keller, 1989). Zoroastrianism is practically unknown in the world outside of India—only approximately 7,000 live in North America (Palmer & Keller, 1989). Although Zoroastrianism is a small religion in terms of numbers, it is an important world religion in the sense that, according to some scholars, in ancient times it influenced the beliefs and worldviews of the religions of Judaism, Christianity, and Islam (Boyce, 1979; Palmer & Keller, 1989; Smart, 1994).

Sikhism was founded in northern India not far from present-day Lahore, Pakistan, in the 15th century A.D. by Guru Nanak. At the age of 30,

TABLE 4.2
Metaphysical Beliefs of the Major Western (Monotheistic) Religious Traditions

Worldview dimension	Judaism	Christianity	Islam	Zoroastrianism	Sikhism
View of deity	There is one Supreme Being. God, also called Elohim or Jehovah, is the creator of all things. God is eternal, all-powerful, and all-knowing. Most modern Jews believe God does not have a physical body, but they believe God is real. God revealed himself and his law through Moses, which is recorded in the Torah (the Pentateuch or first five books of the Old Testament).	Most Christians believe in the Holy Trinity: God the Father, God the Son, and God the Holy Ghost. Some Christians believe that the Holy Trinity is one in essence, but other Christians believe they are one in purpose but not in essence. God is a personal God. He is the creator of all things. God is eternal, all-powerful, all-knowing, and all-loving. God has revealed himself and his words in Jesus Christ, of whom the Bible bears witness as the Son of God.	God, also called Allah, is the only true God or Supreme Being. Allah is the creator of the universe and of human beings. God is all-powerful, all-seeing, all-hearing, all-speaking, and all-knowing. God does not have a body, but is real. God is eternal. God has revealed his eternal speech and words to human beings in the Qur'an (the holy book of scripture).	There is one supreme God, also called Ahura Mazda. There are also six lesser immortal beings who work in concert with God. In the view of some, Ahura Mazda is an anthropomorphic God. God is just and benevolent. God has revealed himself to human beings in the Avesta (sacred books of Zoroastrianism).	There is one God, also called 1 Oankar or Satnam. God is the creator and sustainer of all things. God is formless, but is a personal God. God is immanent in his creations and transcendent. God is eternal. God has revealed himself through the 10 gurus in the Guru Granth Sahib (a body of sacred scriptures that are viewed as an "embodiment of God").
View of human nature	Human beings are made in God's image; humans are the high point of God's creations. Human beings have a spiritual soul that is immortal. People have free will and have the agency to obey God's laws.	Human beings were created by God. Humans have a body and an immortal spirit or soul. Most Christians believe that human beings have free will—the power to choose good over evil. Many Christians believe that there is something basically evil in human nature because of the fall of Adam and Eve, which can be corrected only by God's grace, and that people's own self-effort cannot free them from sin.	Human beings are God's creations. People have both a body and an immortal soul. Some controversy exists in Islam over the question of free will. Some believe God determines human actions, whereas others say that humans have agency to choose, particularly those actions on which they are judged.	Human beings are the creations of God. They have a body and an immortal spirit. Human beings have the power to choose between good and evil.	Human beings are the creations of God. They have an immortal spirit. Human beings are free to choose between good and evil and to show devotion to God.

(table continues)

TABLE 4.2 *(cont.)*

Worldview dimension	Judaism	Christianity	Islam	Zoroastrianism	Sikhism
Purpose of life	The Jewish people are God's chosen people and have a mission to help make the world a better place morally and spiritually. Individually, each person needs to obey God's commandments to develop morally and to qualify to live in a place of peace and eternal progress in the world to come.	God wishes to have a relationship with human beings. God created people to enjoy his divine presence forever. Human beings are to glorify God by having faith in Jesus Christ and by repenting their sins and following the teachings of Jesus. Those who do so will receive God's grace, be forgiven, and be welcomed into God's presence (Heaven) in the hereafter.	Human beings must learn to submit to God's will, obey his law, and do good. They must give up worldly things and overcome their vices. Those who do so will be rewarded in the hereafter (Heaven).	Human beings may have lived in a spiritual existence before mortal life. They must learn to choose between good and evil and to obey and serve God. The faithful must cooperate in defeating the powers of evil. The righteous will be rewarded with peace, happiness, and immortality.	The ultimate purpose of life is to obtain spiritual liberation from the cycle of rebirth and to achieve union with God and to receive spiritual insight in this life. People must learn to choose good over evil and develop love, faith, and humility.
View of spirituality	Obedience to God's laws and worshipping him leads to character development (acquisition of qualities such as goodness, humility, and holiness). Humans can communicate with God through prayer and worship. God responds to people reaching out to him.	Accepting Jesus Christ as Savior will lead one to good works, a moral life, and devotion and worship. This will allow one to receive the influence of the Holy Spirit and partake of other fruits of the spirit (e.g., love). Through prayer and the influence of the Holy Spirit human beings can communicate with God and receive God's help, influence, and grace.	Obeying God's law as revealed in the Qur'an and "giving up" worldly things allows people to grow spiritually. The path of spiritual growth involves overcoming vices such as arrogance, greed, and dishonesty. This leads to higher levels of religious experience and union with God. Humans can communicate with God through prayer, meditation, and repetition of set phrases or the name of God.	Choosing good over evil, prayer, and meditation will help people on the pathway to spiritual growth. Human beings can communicate with God through prayer.	Through dependence on God, human beings can overcome their ego and pride and achieve spiritual liberation and growth and a mystical union with God. Spiritual growth leads one to the qualities of love, faith, mercy, and humility. Humans can communicate with and worship God, particularly through prayer and singing.

View of morality	God revealed his law at Sinai. There are 613 commandments or religious duties (Mitzvat). Charity, good deeds, respect for human dignity, humility, truthfulness, controlling one's anger, and not being envious are examples of other morally good behaviors and qualities.	There are both good and evil in the world. Human beings must learn to choose good over evil. Accepting Jesus as Savior and following his teachings is the path to righteousness and morality. Morality includes behaviors and qualities such as love, service, honesty, family devotion, and abstinence from behaviors such as drunkenness, adultery, and fornication.	God has revealed his law in the Qur'an. Those who worship Allah and obey his laws are good. There are five classes of moral actions: those that are obligatory, recommended, prohibited, disapproved, and indifferent. Examples of prohibited behaviors include drinking of alcohol and immodesty of dress. Fasting and prayer, payment of alms, and devotion to the family are examples of morally good behaviors.	There are two basic powers in the world: truth versus the lie. There is an adversary (a "Hostile Spirit"). Having children is good, but practices such as adultery and prostitution are evil.	There are five evil passions: lust, anger, covetousness, attachment to worldly things, and pride. From these five passions comes all violence and falsehood. A number of behaviors are considered immoral (e.g., gambling, theft, smoking, cutting one's hair, marital infidelity).
View of life after death	The soul of human beings lives on after mortal death in a spirit world. Eventually the bodies of the dead will be resurrected, although many Jews believe only in the immortality of the soul. There will also be a judgment in which people will be judged for what they did with their lives. The righteous will go to a place of peace, where they will continue to progress and enjoy a nearness to God. Those who were evil will not enjoy this state.	The spirit or soul of human beings continues to exist after mortal death. Someday there will be a judgment and a resurrection of the body and spirit (or at least a spiritual resurrection). Those who have accepted and followed Jesus will be accepted into God's presence to enjoy him forever. Those who have done evil and who have not accepted Jesus will be banished to hell, outer darkness, or extinction.	The soul of human beings does not cease to exist at mortal death. There will be a judgment at the final hour of the world. The dead will be resurrected. The wicked will be punished by God by being sent to hell and the good rewarded in heaven.	The spirits of those who die hover near their earthly body for 3 days and nights before passing to an initial individual judgment. The spirit and the body will be joined at the time of the resurrection, or "Final Renovation." Good people will be rewarded with immortality. The spirits of the wicked have no such assurance.	Followers believe in reincarnation. Devotion to God leads to spiritual liberation and a release from the cycle of birth and rebirth. Such a release allows human beings to enter into a realm of infinite and eternal bliss and union with God. Those who are evil obtain adverse karma, which endlessly protracts the cycle of reincarnation.

Note. Sources consulted in preparing this table were Palmer and Keller (1989), Nielsen et al (1988), Smart (1994), Carmody and Carmody (1989), Boyce (1984), Jacobs (1984), Nigosian (1994), and Farah (1994).

Nanak experienced a life-changing vision in which he reported that he was carried up to God's presence and told that there was "neither the Hindu nor Muslim" (R. R. Keller, personal communication, May 8, 1996; Nielsen et al., 1988; Palmer & Keller, 1989). At this point Nanak became a guru (i.e., one who drives away darkness and preaches enlightenment; Nielsen et al., 1988). The religious teachings of Sikhism parallel the Sant tradition within Hinduism. Sikhism has significant similarities with Islam. Guru Nanak rejected many of the teachings of popular Hinduism and "urged his followers to meditate, worship God, and to sing hymns" (Nielsen et al., 1988, p. 362).

Today there are approximately 20 million Sikhs (Barrett, 1996) in the world. About 85–90% of Sikhs live in the Indian state of Punjab in Asia. There also are large groups of Sikhs who live in Delhi and other parts of India. Approximately 490,000 Sikhs live in Europe, and approximately 490,000 live in North America (Barrett, 1996).

In Table 4.2 we summarize the core metaphysical beliefs of each of the major monotheistic world religions. Although there is a great deal of variation between (and within) the monotheistic world religions about specific religious doctrines and practices, it can be seen in Table 4.2 that, at a more general level, there is surprising harmony among them concerning their global weltanschauung.

In general, the worldview of all of the major monotheistic world religions includes the belief that there is a God, a Supreme Being, who created the world and the human race. Human beings were placed on the Earth by the Creator and are here for a divine purpose. Human beings have a spiritual essence or soul and can communicate spiritually with God through prayer, meditation, and other spiritual practices. Human beings also can receive spiritual guidance and strength from God.

Although there is much that is evil, materialistic, and spiritually destructive on the Earth, human beings have agency and can choose to overcome and transcend these influences. God has revealed moral truths and principles to human beings to guide their personal behavior and social relations. Spiritual growth and progression are both desirable and possible and lead to enlightenment and fulfillment. The human soul and personality do not cease to exist on death of the mortal body but continue to live in some type of an afterlife. Human beings will someday be judged by God for how they lived their mortal lives. The reward or position human beings will receive in the afterlife is influenced by their obedience to God's teachings and by their spiritual growth and progression in this life.

The Eastern Spiritual Traditions

There are six major Eastern world religious traditions: Hinduism, Buddhism, Jainism, Shintoism, Confucianism, and Taoism (Palmer & Keller,

1989; Smart, 1993). Approximately one quarter of the world's population adheres to one of the Eastern world religious traditions (Barrett, 1996). For the most part, the Eastern religious traditions believe in either polytheism or pantheism, although some are atheistic or agnostic. *Polytheism* is the belief that "there is a multitude of personal gods, each responsible for a different sphere of life" (Percesepe, 1991, p. 469). *Pantheism* is the belief that "God is identical with nature; all is God, and God is all. . . . Everything exists ultimately in God" (Percesepe, 1991, p. 469).

The roots of Hinduism can be traced back to the 2nd millenium B.C. to the arrival of a cultural group named the Aryans in India and their mingling with the Dravidians, the prehistoric inhabitants of India (Nielsen et al., 1988; Palmer & Keller, 1989). The religious beliefs of these two groups of people became intermingled and contributed to the formation of classical Hinduism (Nielsen et al., 1988; Palmer & Keller, 1989). Hinduism has no personal founder, and it does not have a central authority or structured organization. The beliefs and practices of individual Hindus tend to be highly diverse because Hinduism has assimilated much from other religions in the world (Palmer & Keller, 1989). For example, some Hindus believe in many deities, including nature deities such as Indra (the atmospheric god) and Agni (the god of fire), whereas other Hindus believe in only one God. Ultimately, most Hindus believe that there is one absolute reality, or Brahman-Atman (i.e., that "everything in the universe is one," Nigosian, 1994, p. 85).

Despite this diversity in belief, or perhaps because of it, Hinduism "has provided a framework for the life of most Indians for well over two thousand years. . . . Hinduism continues to be the dominant religious tradition of India" (Nielsen et al., 1988, p. 132). There are approximately 780 million Hindu people in the world today (Barrett, 1996). Approximately 80% of the people in India consider themselves to be Hindus. A substantial minority of the people in Bangladesh are Hindu. There are approximately 1.2 million Hindus in North America and approximately 1.5 million in Europe (Barrett, 1996).

Buddhism originated in India in the 5th century B.C. Its founder was Siddhartha Gautama, who was born, it is believed, in 563 B.C. in Lumbini, India. According to Buddhist tradition, Siddhartha Gautama achieved enlightenment and became the Buddha (the Awakened One). In so doing, Buddha rejected the Hindu gods and preached a doctrine of enlightened equality. Buddha did not consider his message to be a divine revelation, nor did he advocate dependence on the gods or a Supreme Being (Nielsen et al., 1988; Palmer & Keller, 1989).

There are approximately 323 million Buddhists in the world (Barrett, 1996), with the majority of them living in Asia. In North America there are approximately 920,000 Buddhists and in Europe approximately 1.5 million

(Barrett, 1996). There are three main schools of Buddhism: Theravada Buddhism (meaning "Way of the Elders"), Mahayana Buddhism (meaning "The Greater Vehicle"), and Vajrayana Buddhism (meaning "Vehicle of the Thunderbolt") (Nielsen et al., 1988; Palmer & Keller, 1989). Theravada Buddhism is today the dominant religion in Ceylon (Sri Lanka) and much of mainland Southeast Asia (Nielsen et al., 1988). Mahayana Buddhism is found chiefly in China, as well as Taiwan, Korea, Vietnam, and Japan (Nielsen et al., 1988). Vajrayana Buddhism, "which can be treated as an aspect of Mahayana" (Palmer & Keller, 1989, p. 53), is "found mainly in Tibet and Mongolia, but also in Japan, where it is known as Shingon" (Nielsen et al., 1988, p. 203).

The different schools of Buddhism differ somewhat in their understanding of concepts such as the existence of deities and the nature of nirvana (one's release from mortal existence). For example, Theravada Buddhism is functionally atheistic because, although it accepts that some "gods may exist, they cannot help others gain the release from the wheel of rebirth" (Palmer & Keller, 1989, p. 54). Mahayana Buddhism teaches that there are a large number of deities and helping beings to worship and adore (Palmer & Keller, 1989). However, most Buddhists in Eastern countries practice their religion within the context of native beliefs, folklores, and superstitions that existed long before Buddhist teachings (Palmer & Keller, 1989). Therefore, there is a difference between Buddhist philosophy and popular Eastern Buddhism. Several schools of Buddhism also have spread to North America, including Zen Buddhism and Nyingma Tibetan Buddhism (Palmer & Keller, 1989).

Jainism originated in the 5th century B.C. in northeastern India. Its founder was Vardhamana Mahavira (Nielsen et al., 1988; Nigosian, 1994; Palmer & Keller, 1989). Mahavira, according to legends and traditions, spent his youth in luxury and then left his home at age 30 to seek salvation through self-denial. At the age of 42, after wandering as a naked ascetic, he found full enlightenment and became a "conqueror" (a *jina*; Nielsen et al., 1988; Nigosian, 1994; Palmer & Keller, 1989). Mahavira did not believe in a Supreme Being or other deities; he believed that the universe is eternal and uncreated (Nielsen et al., 1988). Jainism has not spread beyond the boundaries of India. There are approximately 5 million Jains in the world (Barrett, 1996). Most Jains are "concentrated in the northern states of Rajasthan, Gujarat, and Maharashtra, and in central India" (Palmer & Keller, 1989, p. 35). There are approximately 4,000 Jains in North America and about 15,000 in Europe (Barrett, 1996).

Shinto is the native religion of the people of Japan. The origins of Shinto are unknown. Shinto has no known founder. It is believed that the formative years of Shinto were during the 3rd–6th centuries A.D. Shinto has been the religion of the common people and has been passed on in their daily lives. There is no Supreme Being or transcendent deities, although there are a variety of deities that are not omnipotent or transcendent. There are many different Shinto groups, including Shrine Shinto, Sectarian Shinto, Pure Shinto, Confucian Shinto, Mountain Shinto, Purification Shinto, Redemptive Shinto, and Folk (Popular) Shinto (Nigosian, 1994). Many of these Shinto groups are composed of subgroups. There are approximately 2.9 million Shintoists in the world, with the majority of them living in Asia (Barrett, 1996). Shinto today has more adherents in Japan than does any other religion (Nigosian, 1994). There are approximately 1,000 Shintoists in North America and about 1,000 in Europe (Barrett, 1996).

Confucianism originated in the 5th century B.C. (Nielsen et al., 1988; Nigosian, 1994; Palmer & Keller, 1989). Its founder, Confucius, was born in the present-day Shantung peninsula of China. Confucius sought political office for many years but never achieved this goal. Later in life, Confucius resumed teaching, studying, writing, and editing. He died at the age of 72. Before his death, the number of his followers had grown steadily and continued to grow after his death. Confucius thought of himself as a devoted student of antiquity and a transmitter of the wisdom of the past. Confucius was generally not interested in metaphysical questions, and his writings did not contain teachings about a Supreme Being or other deities, although there is evidence that he believed in a personal heaven (Palmer & Keller, 1989). Confucianism is primarily a social and political philosophy, although it does have some moral and religious dimensions, in that it states that human beings need to learn to live with inner virtue and proper conduct. For the past 2,000 years, "the teachings of Confucius have had a great influence on the thought, government institutions, literature, arts, and social customs of China" (Nielsen et al., 1988, p. 272). Confucianism has also been influential in Japan, Korea, and Vietnam (Nielsen et al., 1988; Nigosian, 1994; Palmer & Keller, 1989). There are approximately 5.2 million Confucians in the world today, with the majority of them living in Asia (Barrett, 1996). There are approximately 26,000 Confucians in North America and about 4,000 in Europe (Barrett, 1996).

Taoism originated in the 5th century B.C. in China (Nielsen et al., 1988; Nigosian, 1994; Palmer & Keller, 1989). Its founder was Lao Tzu. Tzu, it is said, worked in government circles in Loyang, the Chinese imperial capital. Eventually, Tzu became disillusioned with political and government service and left it. Before leaving Loyang, Tzu wrote a book titled the *Tao Te Ching* (meaning "The Way of the Tao" or "The Wisdom of Tao"; Palmer & Keller, 1989). According to some scholars, Tzu was a contemporary of Confucius and disagreed with him about a number of beliefs. Tzu did not believe in a Supreme Being or deities of any kind, although he believed in the Tao, or "Way" (an impersonal principle that gives order and harmony to the universe; Nigosian, 1994; Palmer & Keller, 1989). Religious Taoism came into existence sometime around the 2nd or 1st century B.C. and moved away from a purely philosophical belief system and became a "widely accepted cult whose members practiced divination, exorcism, healing and sorcery" and who believe in some deities and in immortality (Palmer & Keller, 1989, p. 71).

In Table 4.3 we summarize the core metaphysical beliefs of each of the major Eastern world religions. In examining Table 4.3, one can see that there is much diversity in belief among these six religious traditions, more so than among the five monotheistic world religions. Because of this diversity, it is difficult to find commonalities between the Eastern religions. Nevertheless, some broad generalizations are possible. First, for the most part, the Eastern religions do not teach that there is a transcendent or Supreme God or Creator. Instead, Hinduism, Mahayana Buddhism, Jainism, Shinto, and Religious Taoism teach that there are many gods or deities (polytheism) that, along with all of nature and humanity, are all ultimately One. These religions do concern themselves with metaphysical and mystical questions. Confucianism and philosophical Taoism do not concern themselves with gods or deities and could be perhaps be thought of as atheistic or agnostic. All the Eastern religious traditions, either explicitly or implicitly, affirm that human beings have free will and the capacity to choose how to live their lives. All these religions also reject ethically hedonistic philosophies. Instead, they teach that there are moral paths, or ways of living one's life, that are desirable, ethical, moral, and honorable and that following these paths will lead to enlightenment, peace, happiness, honor, and ideal relationships.

The major purpose of life, according to the polytheistic Eastern traditions, is to gain freedom from the constraints of the flesh and society and to achieve harmony and union with the divine (S. J. Palmer, personal communication, June 5, 1996). Another major purpose of life is to learn to live in harmony with the moral or ethical path or way. Although most of the Eastern religions reject the idea that spiritual assistance and communication with a transcendent God is possible, the polytheistic ones do believe that assistance from deities or helping beings is available. Most of the Eastern religions also reject the idea that personal identity continues in an afterlife, but they do teach that individual identity eventually ceases either in extinction or in some type of spiritual enlightenment or unity with the impersonal and eternal divine essence, or One.

The Spiritual Worldviews and Contemporary Scientific Naturalism

In Table 4.4 we compare and contrast the core metaphysical beliefs of the two major spiritual worldviews with the contemporary naturalistic, scientific worldview. In such a brief table, it is necessary, of course, to oversimplify the metaphysical beliefs of each of these major worldviews. Nevertheless, Table 4.4 does provide some insight into the similarities and differences between them. The Western spiritual worldview and naturalistic, scientific worldviews differ the most dramatically. Their metaphysical beliefs across all six worldview dimensions are almost diametrically opposed, although there is some agreement about the notions that pursuing truth, harmonious relationships, and the betterment of humanity is desirable and that there are some moral or ethical principles that, if followed, can promote healthy social and interpersonal relations. The Western and Eastern spiritual worldviews have more similarities, including the general notions that (a) some sort of harmony with an eternal principle or essence (with God or an impersonal One) is possible; (b) human beings have free will; (c) there are moral or ethical principles or laws with which human beings should seek to live in harmony; and (d) there are paths or ways that lead to personal and social harmony, enlightenment, growth, peace, and happiness.

The discrepancies between the Eastern spiritual worldview and the naturalistic, scientific worldview are less dramatic than are the differences between the Western spiritual worldview and the naturalistic, scientific worldview. The Eastern and naturalistic worldviews tend to be in agreement that there is no transcendent God or Supreme Being, although the naturalistic worldview rejects the idea of polytheism. The Eastern notion that there is some type of mystical eternal One is not totally compatible with the naturalistic worldview, although this notion is easier to reconcile with the naturalistic worldview than the monotheistic belief in a transcendent Supreme Being.

Because the Eastern spiritual traditions (particularly Theravada Buddhism, Shinto, Confucianism, and Philosophical Taoism) say less about questions regarding the "world to come," such as whether there is an immortal soul, a final judgment, and an afterlife, than do the monotheistic religious traditions, the naturalistic worldview conflicts less with the Eastern worldview than with the Western view. Of course, an exception to this is the Buddhist, Hindu, and Jain beliefs in reincarnation, which are incompatible with the naturalistic worldview. The emphasis of the Eastern traditions on living in harmony with the universe and following an 'ethical path that promotes good social relations seems compatible with some of the humanistic currents within the contemporary naturalistic, scientific worldview.

CONCLUSION

The naturalistic (scientific), subjective idealist (Western or monotheistic), and objective idealistic (Eastern) worldviews continue to compete for the cognitive and emotional allegiance of human beings throughout the world. Adherents to each of these three major perspectives can be found

TABLE 4.3
Metaphysical Beliefs of the Major Eastern Religious Traditions

Worldview dimension	Hinduism	Buddhism	Jainism	Shinto	Confucianism	Taoism
View of deity	There are many deities, including nature deities such as Indra (the atmospheric god) and Agni (the god of fire). Three predominant gods are Brahma (the creator), Shiva (a god of destruction), and Vishnu (a god of benevolence and love). Ultimately, there is one Absolute Reality, or Brahman-Atman (i.e., all deities, human beings, and everything in the universe are one, "they are identical"; (Nigosian, 1994, p. 85). There are a large number of sacred Hindu writings, including the Vades, Upanishads, and others.	There is no Supreme Being. Theravada Buddhism (TB) is functionally nontheistic. Although some "gods may exist, they cannot help others gain release from the wheel of rebirth since they themselves are subject to death and rebirth" (Palmer & Keller, 1989, p. 54). Mahayana Buddhism (MB) teaches that there are a large number of deities and helping beings to worship and adore. There are a large number of sacred Buddhist writings or scriptures, including the Tripitaka (TB scriptures) and the Mahavastu, and Lalita Vistara (MB scriptures).	There is no God, Supreme Being or Creator. Nor, according to Mahavira, are there any other deities. The universe is eternal, infinite, and uncreated and "operates in accordance with its own inherent principles" (Nigosian, 1994, p. 163). There are two canons of Jain scripture: the Svetambora and Diambara. The Jain canon is thought to contain Mahavira's basic teachings and those of his followers.	There is no supreme God or transcendent deity. There are a variety of "kamis" (gods or spirits), but these deities are not omnipotent or transcendent. Kami "also refers to the spirit of human beings and to spirits in the universe—in animals, plants, seas, mountains, and so on. Anyone, or anything, or any force that possesses superior power" is considered a kami" (Nigosian, 1994, p. 218). There are no holy scriptures in Shinto; there is an ancient text called the K'jiki (Record of Ancient Matters) that contains myths and stories about the creation, gods, men, customs, and ceremonies (Whiting, 1983).	There is no Supreme Being. Confucious believed there is a heaven that he believed is "an impersonal, ethical force, a cosmic counterpart of the ethical sense in a man" (Palmer & Keller, 1989, p. 76). There is evidence that Confucious also came to view heaven in a more personal way (as "the Lord of human beings") and that he believed "heaven had entrusted him with a sacred mission as a champion of the good and true in China's culture" (Palmer & Keller, 1989, p. 76). The C'hing is a classic Confucian text (Smart, 1993).	According to philosophical Taoism, there is no Supreme Being or deities of any sort. There is a "Tao" or "Way" that is the mystical essence that is "the underlying principle that gives order and harmony to the universe" (Palmer & Keller, 1989, p. 70). "Tao . . . is the primordial, undivided state underlying both being and nonbeing. In short, Tao is the inherent, purposeless, impersonal Cosmic Principle" (Nigoslan, 1994, p. 188). Religious Taoists believe in a variety of gods. Taoist texts include the Tae-te Ching (the Classic of the Way and its Virtue) and the Book of Chuang-tzu (Whiting, 1983).

View of human nature	Human beings have an innermost and unseen force, or self, called Atman. Atman is identical to Brahman, which is "the whole external world, as well as the whole inner being" of the universe (Nigosian, 1994, p. 84). Thus, the individual "self" and the universal "self" are identical in essence. Human beings are divine. Human beings have free will or the capacity to follow one of the "three paths" to salvation.	There are no clear doctrines regarding how human beings came to exist. Humans do have free will. People have the power to be loving and compassionate and to achieve enlightenment and nirvana. According to TB, people do not have an eternal soul. Nirvana is the extinction of the soul. MB implies that there is some type of eternal existence and that nirvana is a state of ego-free peace.	Human beings have an eternal soul that moves up or down the levels of existence depending on how much karma the soul carries. Human beings have free will and can achieve enlightenment and self-salvation through their own efforts.	Human beings are inherently good. Human beings do have a "kami," or spirit.	There is no precise or explicit doctrine regarding how human beings came into existence or whether people have a soul or spirit. Human beings do have free will and can learn to behave with inner virtue and proper conduct.	Human beings do not have a soul but may become immortal in Religious Taoism. Human beings have free will; they can learn to live in harmony with the Tao.
Purpose of life	The purpose of life is to attain salvation by following one of the three paths: the Way of Works, the Way of Knowledge, or the Way of Worship. By following one of these three paths, people can acquire good karma (action or work) and move up the ladder of existence each time they are reincarnated. Eventually, people can escape the rounds of rebirth by experiencing a total oneness with Brahman-Atman.	The world is a place of suffering. The purpose of life is to learn how to get off the treadmill of endless birth and rebirth by realizing nirvana (which, according to TB, is extinction or, according to MB, a state of "supreme," ego-free peace" (Palmer & Keller, 1989, p. 6).	The purpose of life is to free people's soul (jiva) from matter (ajiva) and the eternal round of birth, death, and rebirth so that their soul can enter the heavenly realm and enjoy peace and bliss.	The purpose of life is to value and enjoy beauty and nature, observe rituals and taboos, and show allegiance to one's family, group, community and to the kami of the area in which one is born, or the kami worshipped by one's ancestors.	Human beings need to learn to live with inner virtue and with right conduct. People should seek to cultivate ideal relationships with other people and "a sense of dignity toward human life" (Palmer & Keller, 1989, p. 77).	Human beings need to learn to live in harmony with the Tao, or the "Way." "The pinnacle of peace, human happiness, and wisdom is achieved when a person adjusts himself to the motion and movement of the universe" (Palmer & Keller, 1989, p. 70).

(table continues)

TABLE 4.3 *(cont.)*

Worldview dimension	Hinduism	Buddhism	Jainism	Shinto	Confucianism	Taoism
View of spirituality	Spirituality is achieved through good works, knowledge, and worship and devotion (one of the three paths to salvation). Ultimately, spiritual growth leads to a realization of the oneness of all things (Brahman-Atman) and to a release from the rounds of rebirth. People can communicate with the deities and receive assistance from them.	In TB, spiritual enlightenment and eventual nirvana come from renouncing the world, believing in the four Noble Truths, and following the Eightfold Middle Path. In MB, loving service, faith, and compassion (not merely celibacy or asceticism) are seen as the keys to spiritual growth and enlightenment. MBs may worship helping beings.	Spiritual enlightenment is viewed as pure omniscient consciousness or infinite knowledge. Release from karma matter and spiritual enlightenment is gained through overcoming attachment to worldly things (asceticism), faith in the Jain saints, right knowledge, right conduct (e.g., ahisma or nonviolence), and meditation.	Spirituality is perhaps best thought of as feelings of appreciation and closeness to nature and enjoyment of life. Human beings can worship the kamis (deities) to "secure their continued favor" (Palmer & Keller, 1989, p. 87).	There are no teachings about spiritual communication with deity or about transcendent spiritual enlightenment. Confucius did describe what he believed are the characteristics of a "superior man" or "true gentleman." These qualities included "li (the code of moral, social conduct), jen (virtue, compassion, love), yi (righteousness), and te (virtue)" (Nigosian, 1994, p. 200).	Living in harmony with the Tao is the pathway to inner harmony and peace. An important principle of the Tao is we-wei; that is, the principle of nonaction. We-wei is "a call to passive action. . . . One should not resist, confront, or defy. One should not lay down . . . rules, or requirements. . . . Only sincere humility, minimal desires, and pure spontaneity can enable one to find the Way" (Palmer & Keller, 1989, p. 70).
View of morality	The three paths to salvation each provide alternate perspectives of morality. Doing one's duty, seeking knowledge and wisdom, and worship and devotion of a deity all represent different moral paths and can determine the nature of one's next incarnation. There are also guides for proper conduct associated with each caste (social class).	Morality for TBs consists of following the Eightfold Middle Path, which consists of many teachings about what constitutes moral behavior and thought (e.g., not being cruel, abstaining from lying, violence, stealing, unlawful sexual relations). MBs believe that compassion and loving service are the hallmarks of morality.	Jains believe in a variety of moral values and behaviors, including charity, meditation, and ahisma (respect for all of life). Jains believe lying or giving false evidence, stealing, committing adultery, gambling, eating meat, and drinking liquor are wrong. Extreme asceticism is viewed as fundamental and essential for annihilating karma matter.	There is no binding moral code or list of commandments in Shinto. There is no sin, but one should avoid pollution or uncleanliness. Loyalty and fulfilling one's duty to family, ancestors, and tradition are viewed as important. Gratitude, courage, justice, truthfulness, politeness, reserve, and honor are valued.	Inner virtue and proper conduct is the way to personal and social harmony. There are five basic qualities of inner virtue, including "uprightness or integrity, righteousness, conscientiousness toward others or loyalty, altruism or reciprocity, and most important, benevolence or jen" (Palmer & Keller, 1989, p. 77).	Taoism does not proscribe rules, laws, or moral constraints. People need to submit to the natural order of things and live in harmony with the Tao. "Judgments of what is right and wrong are relative to one's personal stance, situation, and needs" (Nigosian, 1994, p. 189).

View of life after death	Human beings and other creatures experience a potentially endless cycle of birth, death, and rebirth. If people achieve good karma, they move up to higher levels of existence when they are reborn. Eventually, people can receive salvation by escaping the rounds of birth, death, and rebirth by experiencing a total identification "of one's individual self with the universal 'Self' (Brahman-Atman)" (Nigosian, 1994, p. 88).	According to TB, there is no life after death, only nirvana or extinction. Some schools of MB believe people can experience rebirth into the presence of Amitabha, the Lord of the Western Paradise.	At death, the souls of human beings float (go up or down) to another level of existence depending on the amount of karma matter they have collected in their previous life (doing evil collects karma matter). When all karma matter is annihilated, people's souls are liberated and ascend to the top of the universe, where all released souls (siddhas) dwell in a state of bliss. Released souls have no individuality and are omniscient.	There is no doctrine in Shinto regarding the nature of life after death. Shinto believers can appeal to the teachings of other religions, such as Buddhism, regarding such questions.	There is no explicit or precise doctrines regarding what happens at death. Confucius believed that people are better off focusing their energies on living right in this life rather than concerning themselves with speculations about life after death.	The founder of philosophical Taoism did not believe in immortality; when a person dies he or she "passes into Nonbeing and individuality is dissolved" (McCasland, Cairns, & Yu, 1969). Religious Taoists believe in immortality. Those who become immortal "were thought to dwell on a paradisiacal island called P'eng-lai" (Palmer & Keller, 1989, p. 71).

Note. Sources consulted in preparing this table included Nielsen et al. (1988), Palmer and Keller (1989), Nigosian (1994), McCasland, Cairns, and Yu (1969), and Smart (1993).

TABLE 4.4
Comparison of the Western and Eastern Spiritual Worldviews With the Naturalistic, Scientific Worldview

Worldview	View of deity	View of human nature	Purpose of life	View of spirituality	View of morality	View of life after death
Western (monotheistic)	There is a God, a Supreme Being, who created the universe, the Earth, and human beings. God is eternal, omnipotent, and all-knowing. God loves and assists human beings.	Human beings are creations of God. Human beings have an eternal soul or spirit. Human beings have free will and the capacity to choose good over evil and to obey God's commandments.	There is a transcendent, divine purpose to life. Human beings are here on Earth to learn to be obedient to God's will, to choose good over evil, and to prepare to live in a joyful and peaceful afterlife.	Human beings can communicate with God through prayer and meditation. People grow spiritually as they obey God's will, worship him, and love and serve their fellow human beings.	God has revealed laws and commandments to guide human behavior. Obedience to God's laws promotes spiritual growth, harmonious social relations, personal happiness, and prepares people for rewards in the afterlife.	The spirit or soul of human beings continues to exist after mortal death. There is an afterlife of peace and joy for those who live righteously in mortal life. The wicked are punished or suffer for their sins in the afterlife.
Eastern	There is no Supreme Being or God. There may be nature deities or helping beings, but they are not all-powerful and all-knowing. There may be an eternal, impersonal, universal essence, or One.	Human beings may or may not have an eternal soul. Individual identity eventually ends either in extinction or in mystical unity with the eternal, universal One. Human beings do have free will and the capacity to choose a path that leads to enlightenment and harmonious relationships.	The purpose of life is to learn to follow a path to enlightenment and harmony, to live an ethical and moral life so that one can obtain release from endless rounds of rebirth, or at least so that one can enjoy honor, peace, and ideal relationships in this life.	Spiritual enlightenment comes from living in harmony with the ethical path and through meditation and self-denial. Enlightenment leads to insight into the true nature of the universe and of reality.	A variety of notions exist about what is moral and desirable behavior. There tends to be agreement that a moral path or way does exist and that following it leads to enlightenment and personal and social harmony.	Considerable variety regarding beliefs about the afterlife, ranging from a belief that people cease to exist at death, to the belief that they are immortal but no longer have individual identity and are part of the universal One, to the belief that some type of individual soul persists after death.

Naturalistic, scientific	There is no God or Supreme Being, nor are there any supernatural gods or transcendent forces of any kind. The universe was produced and is maintained by natural forces, processes, and laws (e.g., the big bang theory, organic evolution).	Human beings are the end product of millions of years of evolutionary processes, as theorized by Charles Darwin and evolutionary scientists. Life originated on this Earth through natural processes; there was no God or transcendent force involved in the creation of life. Human beings do not have an immortal spirit or soul. Human consciousness can be completely accounted for with biological and physiological explanations. Human beings may or may not have free will depending on the particular naturalistic theory.	There is no transcendent purpose or meaning in life. The only purpose or meaning in life is that which human beings construct or invent for themselves. Pursuing truth and knowledge and contributing to the betterment and welfare of humanity is seen as a meaningful purpose for science.	Spirituality is just another word for naturalistic phenomena (i.e., psychological, physiological, and cognitive processes). There are no transcendent spiritual realities. Human beings cannot communicate with a God because there is no God to communicate with.	There are no moral absolutes or universals. Societies and groups may construct moral and ethical guidelines to help regulate social functioning and protect the welfare of individuals, but such moral and ethical guidelines are relativistic and may be suitable for that particular society or group.	There is no life after death. When human beings die, they cease to exist.

among intelligent, rational, good people throughout the world. In our global society, where communication and cultural barriers are rapidly breaking down, these views conflict more frequently and more directly than in past centuries. Unfortunately, these clashes of cultures and worldviews create anxiety, tension, and intrapsychic and interpersonal conflict for many people. Distrust, suspicion, and violent confrontations between people of different races, cultures, and religions is widespread in the world and can be attributed, in part at least, to differences in beliefs. We hope that understanding and tolerance of conflicting worldviews will increase so that peace and harmony will eventually prevail in the world.

We believe that both the Western and Eastern spiritual worldviews have much of value to contribute to mainstream psychotherapy. For too long, the naturalistic worldview has dominated. At the least, a better understanding and appreciation of the Western and Eastern spiritual perspectives should help psychotherapists and mental health professionals work more sensitively with clients who approach life with these belief systems. These two spiritual worldviews can also enrich the understanding of human personality, psychotherapy, and the processes of healing and change.

In the next chapter, we discuss some of the major implications of a theistic, spiritual worldview for personality theory. In subsequent chapters, we describe in as much detail as possible a strategy for psychotherapy that we believe is consistent with the theistic worldview. When possible, we point out how our strategy might be suitable for psychotherapists and clients who do not believe in this view. There is much that is ecumenical about the strategy we describe and hope to build bridges wherever we can with psychotherapists and clients with diverse perspectives.

5

A THEISTIC, SPIRITUAL VIEW OF PERSONALITY AND MENTAL HEALTH

I do believe there is some kind of transcendent organizing influence in the universe which operates in man as well . . . My present, very tentative, view is that perhaps there is an essential person which persists through time, or even through eternity.

—*Carl R. Rogers*

A theistic, spiritual perspective has direct implications for how clinicians conceptualize human personality and the change processes that characterize growth, development, and healing. Integrating such content into mainstream clinical theory, research, and practice is a formidable task. The reasons for proceeding have been outlined in the overview of history and new trends provided in the previous four chapters. In this transitional chapter, we set forth additional concepts and observations that establish the scholarly rationale for the clinical applications that will follow in the succeeding chapters. This rationale is rooted in standard, modernist methods and results as well as newer trends in theory and research. Beyond this, and fundamental to our purpose, we attempt to integrate these with spiritual traditions and literature. Although our spiritual perspective is theistic, we acknowledge the importance of other spiritual traditions, such as spiritual humanism, transpersonal psychologies, and the nontheistic religions mentioned previously.

SOME BASIC ASSUMPTIONS
OF A THEISTIC, SPIRITUAL STRATEGY

The resurgence of humanistic-existential thought, the emergence of the cognitive revolution, and the postmodern movements in support of hermeneutics, narratives, qualitative research, and social constructivism have created a logical space for a spiritual strategy. We agree with the changes in philosophy of science associated with these movements that are supportive of human agency versus determinism, humanism versus naturalism, and probability versus mechanism (Neimeyer & Mahoney, 1995). However, we build on these trends by adding explicitly religious and spiritual content.

The qualitative study of personal experience, phenomenology, constructive alternativism, and the use of hermeneutic interpretations are critical, but the relativism inherent in the postmodern notion that all science is subjective we think is unfortunate. No matter how "new" the philosophy or how pluralistic research methodologies become, it would be a mistake to give up the quest for procedures that establish the reliability of observation and thus a clear means for checking one's perceptions against those of other observers. If behavioral scholarship focuses exclusively on postmodern methods, the time-tested sources of knowledge are lost. Thus, we affirm that our task is to develop spiritual models of humans that are harmonious with both phenomenological and qualitative descriptions and "objective" methods.

At the same time, we acknowledge that modern and postmodern strategies are currently based on opposing assumptions about human nature and the procedures for ascertaining knowledge about that nature (Slife & Williams, 1995; Wann, 1964). No one has theoretically reconciled these incompatibilities, but we prefer not to reject one or the other. While the debate continues, we think there are advantages to supporting both of these "ways of knowing" in the pluralistic quest to understand human experiences or phenomena.

We also acknowledge that all modes of inquiry and theory building are based on faith and "biases," including our own. All scientific and scholarly modes are culture bound, rooted in unprovable assumptions, and expressible only within contexts and by selected invented languages. The choice of how to proceed and the criteria for judging results are personal ones. We therefore invite readers to "come and see" whether our perspective seems promising and fruitful.

Our general assumptions may be posed in broad terms that could prove useful to an ecumenical array of theistically oriented clinicians. First, God exists; is humankind's Creator; embodies love, goodness, and truth; and acts on people's behalf and for their sakes. Second, human beings are beings of body and spirit, both temporal and spiritual. They are the offspring of

God, created in the image of God, and carry within them the germ or seed of divinity. Third, human existence is sustained through the power of God. Fourth, human beings are able to communicate with God by spiritual means, such as prayer, and this inspired communication can positively influence their lives. Fifth, there is spiritual evil that opposes God and human welfare. Humans also can communicate with and be influenced by evil to their detriment and destruction. Sixth, good and evil can be discerned by the "Spirit of Truth." Seventh, humans have agency and are responsible to both God and humanity for the choices they make and the consequences thereof. Eighth, because theistic, spiritual influences exist, their application in people's lives should be beneficial to their well-being. Ninth, God's plan for people is to use the experiences of this life to choose good, no matter how painful life may be, to learn wisdom and develop their potential to become more like God, and, ultimately, harmonious with the spirit of God.

What we mean by the word *spiritual* are invisible phenomena associated with thoughts and feelings of enlightenment, vision, harmony with truth, transcendence, peak experiences, and oneness with God, nature, or the universe (cf. James, 1902/1936). These have often been correlated with but are not synonymous with objective visible mental, emotional, and biological measures (Chadwick, 1993; Hood, 1995; Larson & Larson, 1994; Levin, 1995; Matthews et al., in press). We define *spirituality* as attunement with God, the Spirit of Truth, or the Divine Intelligence that governs or harmonizes the universe. In our discussion, we use the term *Spirit of Truth* as the generic label for what we mean because it facilitates communication across diverse perspectives. We assume that human nature includes spiritual capacities (i.e., ways of responding to, harmonizing with, or acting on the promptings, enlightenment, or sense of integration that may be associated with the Spirit of Truth). Commonly used terms such as *inspiration*, *conscience*, and *revelation* also are embraced within this concept. This perspective is readily accessible in the world's religious, spiritual, poetic, and mystical literature. For instance, we find the following in the Biblical Book of Job: "There is a spirit in man [humans]: and the inspiration of the Almighty giveth them understanding" (Job 32:7).

In addition to these premises, religious literature, history, and scripture identify other conceptual themes and bipolar behavioral themes that lay the basis for the beginnings of a new theory of personality that are discussed at the end of this chapter. First, however, we must consider the empirical reasons for building a conceptual and clinical structure on our basic assumptions.

We believe that spiritual phenomena or experiences, although difficult to describe and measure, can be inferred through observable means, often quantitative or qualitative self-reports. These reports can be reliably structured such as in standardized questionnaires, content analysis systems for interviews, and so on. In principle, these phenomena can be studied in ways similar to the examination of other "private" events such as cognitions and feelings (e.g., attitudes, beliefs, love). In addition to standardized measures, qualitative and hermeneutic approaches are essential to understanding such phenomena.

There is now substantial evidence that spirituality can be defined and described in consensually acceptable ways and that these descriptions bear significant and sometimes powerful relations with other phenomena. The literature on religious orientation (Batson, Schoenrade, & Ventis, 1993), meditation (H. Benson, 1993), conversion (Malony & Southard, 1992), prayer (L. B. Brown, 1994; Dossey, 1993), forgiveness (Freedman & Enright, 1996; McCullough & Worthington, 1994a, 1994b), and mystical experiences (Hood, 1995) are examples; however, physical health may be the most solidly established example that shows links between spiritual self-reports and more objective measures (see the section on physical health).

SPIRITUAL AND RELIGIOUS FACTORS AND HEALTH

The following review of research literature and related conceptual content provides a substantive basis for the expanded theoretical content and clinical implications discussed later in this chapter. Note, however, that little of this literature is based on phenomenological and qualitative studies. We anticipate that when such studies are done, the picture of these phenomena will be even more enlightening and convincing than the portrayal we now have mainly through traditional "objective" measures and statistics. Our basic assumptions imply that theistic, spiritual influences exist and should have beneficial influences on people's mental and physical well-being.

Mental Health

The relationship between religion and positive mental health or adjustment is not a uniform phenomenon. There are diverse, broadly defined measures of both religiousness and mental functioning. When so many inconsistently defined indexes of religion and pathology are correlated in different studies, they have yielded different results. The proportion of positive, negative, and zero correlations between religion and pathology from a cross-section of generic studies is about the same (Bergin, 1983). No broad, general conclusions can be drawn from such inconsistent findings, but clarity increases markedly when both religion and positive mental health are differentiated into subcategories and defined precisely. Several major reviews of the literature confirm this perspective (Batson et al., 1993; Bergin, 1983, 1991; Gartner, Larson, & Allen, 1991; Judd, 1985; Larson & Larson, 1994;

Lea, 1982; Matthews, Larson, & Barry, 1993–1995; Pargament & Park, 1995; Payne, Bergin, Bielema, & Jenkins, 1991).

Although the studies examined vary greatly in scope and quality, the accumulating evidence from several hundred sets of findings show that

> religious affiliation is not damaging to mental health, nor is it entirely predictive of better mental health. The more useful question to ask is *how* a person is religious rather than *whether* a person is religious. Specific measures of religiosity, such as intrinsic and extrinsic orientation, level of commitment, and activity level provide more informative findings than rougher estimates like affiliation. (Payne et al., 1991, pp. 11–12)

In addition, correlations between religion and mental health are stronger when mental health is also carefully defined and described. There are several ways to achieve this differentiating task, and the choice of how to do it requires tentativity and balance to avoid the prejudices that so easily distort interpretations of evidence.

Types of Religiosity and Categories of Mental Health

We differentiate religiousness in terms of *intrinsic* and *extrinsic* orientation and categorize mental health into three groups of data under the following headings: *psychological adjustment, pathological social conduct,* and *mental illness.* Although there are many problems with these categories, there are more problems with other divisions. Also, as we show, the empirical literature is most easily arranged and distributed among these categories (cf. Payne et al., 1991).

Payne et al. (1991) noted that Allport and Ross's (1967) concept of intrinsic and extrinsic religiosity has proved to be particularly useful:

> Definitions of intrinsic versus extrinsic religiosity typically refer to ends versus means, unselfish versus selfish, and committed versus utilitarian. Intrinsic people internalize their beliefs and live them regardless of consequences, while extrinsic people use religion as a means of obtaining status, security, self-justification, and sociability. Baker and Gorsuch (1982) noted that anxiety has correlated both positively and negatively with religion in past research. The reason suggested is that global undifferentiated measures were used. Their research [showed] intrinsicness . . . to be associated with higher ego strength, more integrated social behavior, less paranoia or insecurity, and less anxiety, while extrinsicness was associated in the opposite direction. It was suggested that if research samples contain more extrinsics than intrinsics, the positive correlation of religiosity and anxiety will be found with general measures of religiousness but the correlation will be negative if more intrinsics are found in the population. Bergin, Masters, and Richards (1987) studied Mormon students in psychology classes at Brigham Young University. They found that intrinsic religiosity is negatively

correlated with anxiety and positively correlated with self-control and better personality functioning as measured by the California Psychological Inventory. The opposite was true of extrinsic religiosity. (pp. 19–21)

In Table 5.1 we see distinctly different patterns of correlations between religion and adjustment depending on whether religion is defined and measured as intrinsic or extrinsic. Batson et al. (1993) summarized 173 findings on the intrinsic and extrinsic dimensions relative to seven definitions of mental health. As in the Bergin et al. (1987) study, the array of findings shown in Table 5.2, although only crudely quantitative, shows a dramatically different pattern of relationships depending on which type of religious orientation is being evaluated. It is clear from such findings that these two ways of being religious have different implications for mental health. It is no wonder, then, that generic studies of religion that do not make such distinctions consistently yield ambiguous implications for health because they lump together different individuals under the same label of "religious." For instance, Table 5.3 summarizes results from 115 empirical findings where religiousness was defined broadly and ambiguously in terms of affiliation, attendance, orthodoxy, and so forth. The pattern of results is thus less clear.

There are several other ways of dimensionalizing religiosity that continue to be the subject of research (Batson et al., 1993; Hood, Spilka, Hunsberger, & Gorsuch, 1996), including a possible curvilinear relationship between the intrinsic and extrinsic dimensions and the division of "extrinsic" into subscales, but they are beyond the scope of this summary chapter.

Types of Mental Health

Batson et al. (1993) used seven definitions of mental health in their analysis, which is better than a singular criterion, but there are significant flaws in their system, which may have contributed to the shifting pattern of results that appear in both Tables 5.2 and 5.3. For instance, three of their categories (i.e., personal competence and control, self-acceptance and self-actualization, and open-mindedness and flexibility) sound good as positive definitions of mental health, but the studies listed under these rubrics frequently used questionnaires containing items that are biased against religious individuals. For example, "Everything is turning out just like the prophets of the Bible said it would" counts against personal competence and control as measured by Barron's Ego Strength Scale; "I am orthodoxly religious" counts against self-acceptance and self-actualization as measured by the Personal Orientation Inventory; and "The wild sex life of the old Greeks and Romans was tame compared to some of the goings on in this country" counts against open-mindedness and flexibility as measured by the Authoritarianism Scale. These reflect the relativism of modernism and the Enlightenment notion of maturity, in which *maturity* means the most "open-

TABLE 5.1
Pearson Correlations of the Religious Orientation Scale With the Manifest Anxiety Scale, Self-Control Schedule, California Psychological Inventory, Irrational Beliefs Test, and Beck Depression Inventory

Personality Scale	Intrinsic	Extrinsic
Psychology classes		
Manifest Anxiety Scale ($n = 61$)	−.27*	.27*
Self-Control Schedule ($n = 33$)	.38**	−.19
California Psychological Inventory ($n = 78$)		
Dominance	.16	−.11
Capacity for Status	.13	−.19*
Sociability	.30***	−.21*
Social Presence	.07	−.21*
Self-Acceptance	.03	−.03
Sense of Well-Being	.34***	−.24**
Responsibility	.44***	−.23*
Socialization	.24*	−.08
Self-Control	.32***	−.13
Tolerance	.35***	−.24*
Good Impression	.34***	−.26**
Communality	.03	.04
Achievement by Conformance	.34***	−.22*
Achievement by Independence	.17	−.23*
Intellectual Efficiency	.29***	−.38***
Psychological-Mindedness	.17	−.17
Flexibility	.06	−.14
Femininity	.08	.12
Religion class		
Irrational Beliefs Test ($n = 32$)	−.03	.15
Total score of subscales[a]		
1. Approval need	.03	−.04
2. Competency need	−.07	.16
3. Blameworthiness	.16	−.02
4. Catastrophizing	−.07	−.10
5. Externalizing	−.17	.36*
6. Obsessing	−.02	.14
7. Avoidance	−.08	.07
8. Dependency	.20	.02
9. Determinism	−.37*	.20
10. Perfectionism	.23	.08
Beck Depression Inventory ($n = 32$)	.05	−.02

Note. Reprinted from Bergin, A. E., Masters, K. S., & Richards, P. S. (1987). Religiousness and mental health reconsidered: A study of an intrinsically religious sample. Journal of Counseling Psychology, 34, 197–204. Copyright 1987. Used by permission of the American Psychological Association.
[a] The names are our abbreviations.
*$p < .05$. **$p < .01$. ***$p < .005$.

TABLE 5.2
Line Score on Research Examining the Relationship Between Mental Health and Two Dimensions of Individual Religion

Conception of Mental Health	Individual Religion Dimension					
	Extrinsic (means)			Intrinsic (end)		
	+	?	−	+	?	−
Absence of illness	1	7	11	11	7	1
Appropriate social behavior	0	1	4	5	0	1
Freedom from worry and guilt	0	7	15	15	5	4
Personal competence and control	0	4	9	11	4	3
Self-acceptance and self-actualization	0	5	3	1	8	3
Unification and organization	0	3	0	5	0	0
Open-mindedness and flexibility	0	4	6	1	6	2
Total	1	31	48	49	30	14

Note. The three columns under each dimension of individual religion indicate the number of reports of a positive relationship with each conception of mental health (+), the number of reports of no clear relationship (?), and the number of reports of a negative relationship (−). Adapted from *Religion and the individual: A social psychological perspective* by C.D. Batson, P. Schoenrade, & W. C. Ventis. Copyright © 1993 by C.D. Batson, P. Schoenrade, & W. C. Ventis. Used by permission of Oxford University Press, Inc. (A third dimension, called *quest*, is omitted here because it is not discussed in this book.)

TABLE 5.3
Line Score on Research Examining the Relationship Between Seven Conceptions of Mental Health and Amount of Religious Involvement

Conception of Mental Health	Relationship With Amount of Religious Involvement			
	+	None	−	Total
Absence of illness	17	12	4	33
Appropriate social behavior	12	4	5	21
Freedom from worry and guilt	4	3	5	12
Personal competence and control	2	2	11	15
Self-acceptance and self-actualization	2	6	11	19
Unification and organization	0	1	0	1
Open-mindedness and flexibility	0	3	11	14
Total	37	31	47	115

Note. From *Religion and the individual*: A *social psychological perspective* by C.D. Batson, P. Schoenrade, & W.C. Ventis. Copyright © 1993 by C.D. Batson, P. Schoenrade, & W.C. Ventis. Used by permission of Oxford University Press, Inc.

minded." It is doubtful that anyone is open-minded in this sense. We agree with the postmodern notion that everyone, including the psychology of religion researcher, is biased by context. We thus prefer the notion that bias is always there and that is it best to know one's biases and their alternatives. That is why we seek to be open about our biases here and elsewhere in this book. It seems safer to know our biases than to pretend that we have none and are thus neutral or "objective." For such reasons, we have set aside the three foregoing categories from the Batson et al. reviews until better data and rationales are available.

In our analysis, based on that of Payne et al. (1991), we determined that the pathology dimension in several studies was best classified under psychological adjustment and life satisfaction among normal and mildly disturbed individuals. These studies were generally like, or the same as, studies classified by Batson et al. (1993) under their absence of illness definition (a low-to-high mental illness dimension), but most of the studies that they reported and that we also reviewed had little to do with mental illness in the clinical sense of the term. The studies subsumed under their definition dealt with several ways of identifying more-or-less healthiness in nonclinical populations.

Our overall conclusion concerning adjustment and life-satisfaction, based on our extensive review, is that religious commitment and participation, especially intrinsicness, related positively, compared with the less religious, nonreligious or extrinsics, in all of the following comparisons: well-being versus dysphoria, self-esteem versus self-doubt and feelings of inadequacy, marital satisfaction versus discord and divorce, family cohesion versus conflict, life satisfaction versus dissatisfaction, ability to cope with stress and manage crises versus disorganization and malaise, positive mood versus mild-to-moderate depression, and confidence versus fear or mild-to-moderate anxiety. Clearly, religious commitment shows a pattern of positive correlations with various aspects of adjustment and satisfaction (see Payne et al., 1991, for more detail).

We have a second large set of findings categorized under *pathological social conduct* (see Payne et al., 1991). Batson et al. (1993) listed these results under appropriate social behavior. These areas all show "beneficial" correlations with religiousness, especially the intrinsic kind (i.e., rates were lower for the religious subsamples compared with others with respect to alcohol abuse, drug abuse, premarital sex, teen pregnancy, suicide, and crime and delinquency). These often appear under the headings of mental health or mental illness, but they actually constitute a different category of phenomena: social conduct. Some of them are discussed elsewhere in this chapter.

Note that religious conversion also has been associated with major transformations in pathological social conduct. Some of these have received considerable publicity in the media, such as Charles Colson of Watergate fame, Eldridge Cleaver of the Black Panthers, and Malcolm X of the Nation of Islam. Others are less known, such as the high school and college students studied by David Rosenhan at Stanford University (personal communication, April 28, 1989), who were shown to have changed positively and sometimes dramatically as a result of religious conversion. Chadwick (1993) has also documented the finding of lower rates of social misconduct by adolescents who had private religious experiences than those who were also religious but did not report such experiences. Such findings are further elaborated in this chapter (see the section on Eternal Identity Versus Mortal Overlay).

The third major category is *mental illness,* as defined by the categories in the fourth edition of the *Diagnostic and Statistical Manual of Mental Disorders* (*DSM–IV*) of the American Psychiatric Association (1994). Examples include mood and anxiety disorders, developmental disorders, somatoform disorders, personality disorders, eating disorders, paraphilias, sexual and gender identity disorders, schizophrenia and other psychotic disorders, and dissociative disorders.

Empirical evidence on the relationship of spiritual and religious variables to these truly clinical disorders is dramatically less abundant than on the other categories of human functioning because most studies have been done on cross-sections of college students. Some findings do show that people with psychosis (Stark, 1971) and depression (Spendlove, West, & Danish, 1984) are less likely to be involved in religion, but this could be because their disorders preclude activity in many of life's social dimensions. Similarly, studies showing more religiously active people to be less depressed does not necessarily mean that religiousness is causing them to be less depressed, although it certainly may be beneficial. In general, there are few comparisons of truly pathological versus nonpathological groups, nor are there sufficient assessments of the rates of occurrence of specific clinical disturbances within random samples of particular religious and nonreligious groupings. Judd's (1985) accumulation of Minnesota Multiphasic Personality Inventory data from studies of many religious groups showed normal mean profiles and no differences across mainstream denominations in the United States. Because of the ambiguous evidence to date, no firm conclusions can be drawn about religion and serious clinical disorders, although there are sufficient observations to warrant guarded optimism that careful research will yield findings comparable to those in the areas of adjustment and social conduct.

Some Caveats

Although many studies show positive relationships between intrinsic religion and a variety of mental health indexes (except serious mental illnesses), there are several important reservations to be noted about these findings: (a) Most of the data are correlational, partly because researchers cannot manipulate experimentally a person's spirituality; (b) most researchers do not control for additional variables that may contaminate religion and mental health correlations (e.g., marital status is related to both religiousness and mental health); and (c) the definition and measurement of spiritual or religious variables are not well refined, which leads to large error variances and frequent small correlations.

Countercritique

Despite the foregoing, research on religious variables is not worse than that which is done on other personal and social variables. The trend in numerous studies shows a pattern of findings favorable to religious involvement that has not previously been identified with such consistency. This observation is particularly relevant to practice because about one third of the U.S. population identifies religion as the most important factor in their lives, whereas another one third considers it to be among the more important influences (see Bergin, Payne, & Richards, 1996, p. 304). "Furthermore, it would seem that healthy religious involvement is better than no religious involvement as far as adjustment and well-being are concerned" (Payne et al., 1991, p. 33). Yet, practitioners often ignore this potentially important source of health benefits.

As summarized by Payne et al. (1991),

> Theories of pathology and psychotherapy are secular and do not lead naturally to thinking of religion as a health promoting agent. In fact, early research and theory portrayed religion as anti-health (Bergin, 1983). Although it is true that certain religious orientations (e.g., extrinsic) are often associated with counterproductive aspects of life, religiosity that is internalized, committed, mature, and unselfish will generally be found on the side of mental health. Even so, the picture is more complex than a summary can indicate.
>
> It remains for researchers studying religion and mental health to further explicate the dimensions of religiosity and their interaction across populations and across situations. Specificity, careful sampling, control of variables, appropriate designs and replications, building on the extensive work already done, will undoubtedly yield interesting and useful results. Religious beliefs and practices are powerful forces in our society, as yet only partially understood. (p. 34)

Further speculations regarding the positive trends would include these points (Payne et al., 1991):

1. Strong religious values may correlate positively with mental health in part because both reflect the optimum socialized behaviors of the culture.

2. Mental health values might overlap with religious values. (Even so, we must be careful not to equate viable religion with mental health.)
3. Some forms of religiosity are likely congruent with personal growth, achievement, stability, avoidance of a harmful lifestyle, family cohesion and self-actualization.
4. There may be religiously encouraged developmental patterns that are basically prosocial and extend over the life span.
5. A sense of direction, destiny, purpose, and transcendent meaning can be helpful in providing consistency and guidance across time and situations.
6. The survival of religion may say something about its utility and adaptability. (p. 33)

Physical Health

There is an abundant, even larger literature on physical health than on mental health, which is even more positive than the literature on mental health (Koenig, 1997). It is not feasible to summarize this large literature extensively, so we simply note that it is a frequently replicated finding that actively religious people have lower rates of many physical disorders. The National Institute for Health Care Research (NIHR) in Rockville, Maryland (a private institute), has been able to accumulate a huge amount of information on religion and physical health (Matthews et al., in press). Headed by David B. Larson, NIHR is advancing knowledge of the relations between theistic, spiritual perspectives and the prevention and treatment of disease. A vast array of illnesses ranging from cancer to heart disease show lower rates for religiously active people. Mortality rates are lower. Coping with death and other forms of stress is better. Recovery rates for almost everything, including surgery, are better for the religiously active individuals (Larson & Larson, 1994; Matthews et al., in press).

The fall 1996 newsletter of the National Institute for Health Care Research, *Faith and Medicine Connection*, states the following:

Patients Want Doctors to Address Spirituality

In two recent national surveys by *Time*/CNN (June, 1996) and *USA Weekend* (February, 1996), over 70% of patients polled believe that spiritual faith and prayer can aid in recovery from illness; 64% of those surveyed believe that physicians should talk to patients about spiritual issues as part of their care and pray with patients if they request it.

Studies Show Religion is Good for Your Health

Medical students without a religious affiliation are four times more likely to develop alcoholism (Moore, R. D., Mead, L., Pearson, T. "Youthful

Precursors of Alcohol Abuse in Physicians." American Journal of Medicine 1990; 88:332–6).

One of the strongest predictors of survival after heart surgery is the degree to which patients draw strength and comfort from their religion, and the more religious they are, the greater their protection from death (Oxman, T. E., Freeman, D. H., and Manheimer, E. D. (1995). "Lack of Social Participation or Religious Strength or Comfort as Risk Factors for Death After Cardiac Surgery in the Elderly." Psychosomatic Medicine, 57:5–15, 95.4 (1)).

Weekly church attendees have been found to have 50% fewer deaths from coronary artery disease, 56% fewer deaths from emphysema, 74% fewer deaths from cirrhosis and 53% fewer suicides (Comstock, G. W., Partridge, K. B. "Church Attendance and Health," Journal of Chronic Diseases 1972; 25:665–672). (pp. 1–2)

Martin and Carlson (1988) similarly documented a wide array of health benefits from religious experience and activity in their provocative review of spiritual dimensions in health psychology. Their cognitive–behavioral orientation has been stretched to embrace the meditative, loving, and social support aspects of religion as factors in both prevention and recovery.

Although the accumulating evidence for mental and physical health benefits of some features of religiousness and spirituality has become massive, we recognize that the picture is not always positive. Clinical practitioners who are treating disturbed individuals often see some of the worst aspects of religion, and we address such issues in the clinical chapters. Another counterpoint to the statistical data is that all these results could be interpreted spiritually or naturalistically; they do not have to be interpreted spiritually.

Some possible interpretations have been summarized by Levin (1995), a social scientist at the Eastern Virginia Medical School in Norfolk, Virginia. We have used his outline and rephrased it according to our understanding of the issues. First, religious belief and affiliation provide a person with a secure sense of identity, which lowers one's average anxiety level and facilitates resiliency under stress. Second, religious conviction may provide a sense of purpose and meaning that allows for rational interpretations of life's problems, including death. Third, positive emotions of hope, faith, optimism, and catharsis emerge from beliefs and rituals, including the process of forgiveness and the hope of healing and redemption. Fourth, religious affiliation provides a link with a network or community of believers—large and small—that provides a feeling of belonging, family, and social support in times of need as well as a steady flow of opportunities to serve other people. Fifth, religion through prayer, ritual, worship, and so forth provides inner experiences of communion between the individual and the "Higher Power" that may yield insight or peace even if there is not a Higher Power. Sixth, many beliefs lead to a lifestyle that includes behavioral habits and an inner sense of responsibility and self-control that are healthy in and of themselves. For example, Mormons and Seventh-Day Adventists show positive health indicators because they do not smoke or drink and eat meat only moderately.

Actually, all of these "natural" explanations imply that religion, as a sociocultural factor, can be a powerful, beneficial force even without invoking the influence of God; however, our conclusion is that none of these influences would be enduring or powerful if the influence of God were not present. There is another possible alternative interpretation, also proffered by Levin (1995): There is a superempirical healing energy activated by religion that is, in effect, a divine blessing on the human bioenergetic system. In other words, "God blesses us."

Consider an example from biobehavioral research that supports the divine blessing concept. Larson et al. (1989) conducted a multifactorial study of blood pressure levels among 407 rural White men. Those men who smoked were split into subgroups for whom religion was of high or low importance and who attended church frequently or not frequently. Blood pressure levels were adjusted for age, socioeconomic status, and height-to-weight ratio. Those smokers for whom religion was very important had significantly lower blood pressure levels than smokers for whom religion was unimportant. Several other findings also suggested a protective effect of religion on abnormal blood pressure but were statistically weaker. Because smokers who were more religious had less risk of hypertension than smokers who were less religious, religion may have had health benefits beyond merely those attributable to lifestyle. Thus, the Larson et al. (1989) study is consistent with Levin's (1995) notion of a superempirical healing energy, although it provides only preliminary evidence and also needs replication where other lifestyle factors are controlled.

Regardless of how it is interpreted, the religion and health area is the one that now shows the most substantial statistical data favoring a spiritual perspective on human functioning. Despite the documented successes in finding statistical correlations between various spirituality measures and diverse indexes of physical and mental health, it has been argued by Slife, Hope, and Nebeker (1996) that this field of inquiry is laced with inconsistencies and incompatibilities in its definitions, methodologies, and theoretical concepts. Improving the coherence and efficacy of this work clearly is a prime objective for the immediate future, and doing so could enhance the strength of the findings.

THEISTIC REALISM: THEISTICALLY BASED SPIRITUAL REALITIES

The previous account of objective research provides an ample basis for a scholarly spiritual perspective. Compared with the dearth of academic substance for such a view that existed 40 years ago, the extent and quality of the current empirical findings are stunning. We consider these data to be valuable and important; however, a spiritual worldview goes far beyond such ordinary empirical findings and has profound implications for understanding human personality and functioning. Although standard empirical results are an important building block, they are not the main foundation of a spiritual perspective. We emphasize that the following content breaks with traditional empirical philosophy and method. It provides a serious introduction to spiritual ways of knowing that we consider to be valid and of great importance. This approach depends on careful study of individual cases using qualitative procedures that aspire to "subjective proof." Some of these small-N studies also include parallel quantitative procedures (e.g., Bergin et al., 1994). Our effort to establish "spiritual validity" thus goes beyond the merely anecdotal. It should therefore be noted that many of the case vignettes that appear here and elsewhere in the book are used illustratively, but they arise from a context of broader, in-depth empirical study.

The accumulated careful research in the religious and spiritual domain by behavioral scientists is now amenable to articulation with the worldwide findings from descriptive ethnographic studies by comparative religionists and cultural anthropologists (see chap. 4). The overarching conclusion we draw from all of this work is that the variegated human family has in common the belief that there is another world than the one directly perceivable by people's biological senses or by scientific instruments that aid people's senses. Equal in importance and universality to the worldwide cultural existence of family, kinship, and economic and political structures, this equally universal belief in "something more" or "something beyond" is no longer easily trivialized by naturalistic scientific interpretations or the waning "secularization hypothesis" of sociology (Hoge, 1996). Therefore, among all divisions of inquiry—behavioral, natural, and cultural—there is an openness to spiritual perspectives that is unique in this century.

In keeping with the themes argued in chapters 1–3 of this book, we reject the "classical realism" that reflects strong, if not singular, commitment to a naturalistic and materialistic view of the universe. Critical realism and postmodernism have opened scholarly pathways in directions that make our task easier, but we do not fully endorse either one. We prefer *theistic realism* as a working title for our in-process research and theorizing, a terminology we have alluded to briefly in chapters 2, 3, and elsewhere (Bergin, 1980a) and that we describe in more detail in chapter 12.

This notion that God, in person, in spirit, and in intelligence is behind, part of, or sustaining of all existence is fundamental. We want to be clear that our references to spiritual realities are not occult, pantheistic, or part of numerous popular spiritualistic modern movements. Our view is distinctly theistic and generally in the Western tradition that dominates in

North American culture; however, we embrace some aspects of spiritual humanism and Eastern spirituality that seem to be consistent with newer developments in philosophy and science and that can also be in harmony with theism. We are also eclectic or integrative in that we assume that honest and flexible searches for truth and understanding, whether in philosophy, the sciences, humanities, arts, or theologies—which are disciplined and subjected to critique—have something significant to offer our picture of how and why the Creator works and what our part is in the grander scheme.

In their provocative review of trends in the biological and physical sciences as they relate to the major existential questions, Templeton and Herrmann (1994) pointed to mind-stretching possibilities. They concluded their chapter on the search for reality with the following statements that reflected their perception of prominent themes in the work of many of the best thinkers and researchers in the natural sciences.

> Here is a world in which novelty and order are intertwined . . . [God's] action can be mediated both through the interaction of law and chance . . . through . . . new form and direction at the infinity of starting points and branching points in nonlinear chaotic processes.
>
> All that we have said seems to shout for a God of marvelous creativity who mediates in a world in dynamic flux, a world moving in the direction of ever more complex, more highly integrated form—form set free to dance. . . .
>
> Molecules, organisms, species are not fixed states of being, but rather stages of becoming. The current perspectives on reality of both science and theology seem to grasp dimly the edges of this grand paradigm of becoming. Perhaps in the end it is only God who expresses this ceaseless progression toward the highest integration and the greatest complexity. Perhaps in the end the only reality is God. (Templeton & Herrmann, 1994, pp. 162–163)

Theirs is a way of expressing theistic realism in a way that we like; however, there is more to the story than metaphors from biology and physics can embrace. We intend to go further and show how the power of God is manifested in human existence, in personal spirituality, and in positive change processes.

We have already made a substantial presentation of empirical findings that there are mental and physical health benefits of many (but not all) kinds of religious and spiritual commitments. We have also noted the possibility of a superempirical healing energy. Not only are many competent academicians attracted to these new findings and theories (see Templeton & Herrmann's 1994 review), they are also consonant with the existential and religious worldviews of the vast majority of human beings, from the Native American cultures of North and South America, through the prominent nations of occidental civilization, to the wisdom of the people of the Orient. All of these, both empirical and philosophical, constitute an overwhelming assemblage of witnesses that there is a spiritual reality. Even to the occidental skeptics this has become easier to accept now that biology and physics have unveiled so many hidden realities behind observable phenomena, such as the fluctuating particles of nuclear mystery that are now captured in poetic metaphors like "quarks," "charm," and the "dance" of electrons.

For clinicians, the important point is that most people whom they will be paid to treat believe in this reality and that they are personally part of it (i.e., they believe they have an internal spiritual existence in addition to and correlated with any other spiritual energy, reality, or God "out there"). Most people also believe strongly (Shafranske, 1996) that their identity, spirit, or personality will persist after death. We believe that they are right. We have had our own ineffable spiritual experiences of encounter with the eternal that undergird our personal lives and professional work. The following account illustrates our view at a very personal level. It is taken from a collection of student narratives we gathered at Brigham Young University (BYU). This is an account by a young female college student:

> I was 16 and enduring the worst year and deepest depression of my life. My sister was really popular and it seemed I could never do anything better than she. . . . I felt so useless that for a whole year I wanted nothing more than to simply stop existing. One evening I was reading and listening to the radio and a song came on that I liked. . . . It had a weird effect upon me. . . . I suddenly felt a sense of understanding, and when I looked up toward the radio in surprise it seemed like I could see through the walls, so thin were the physical limits of my fragile world. A new insight transcended my previous understanding, and I suddenly felt what I was really like, as a pure, everlasting spirit. I was neither young nor old, just there. I was neither good nor bad, just a steward over certain things God had seen fit to give me. I owned nothing, I needed nothing, and the problems which I felt were so exclusively and painfully mine really had no bearing on me except what I might learn from them. It was a feeling of comfort, of peace, and a kind of relief to know so positively that I had always been loved in an everlasting, fundamental way. I understood more then than I ever had before or since the wealth of meaning Jesus employed in the simple, I AM. In that moment I knew that He is, that I am, and that I always will be.

When a person thus assumes that what he or she is transcends the ordinary collection of emotions, actions, and cognitions that appear visibly in therapy, then the "game" of treatment, the dance of therapeutic encounter, takes on a new dimension and becomes a spiritual encounter as well. When Rogers (1973) said that he believed in "other" realities, he had the courage to act on the assumption, as he did with so many of his other insights. He came to believe, as we do, that the spirit of the therapist can perceive, respond to, and help heal the spirit of the client (C. Rogers, personal communication, June 9, 1986). We return to this topic later when we discuss "meta-empathy." For now, our point is that our speculations concerning science, philosophy, and religion ultimately have a clinically practical result.

The Spirit or Soul: Qualitative Reports of Visions and Near-Death Experiences

To understand more deeply the dynamics and importance of the spiritual perspective, we turn now to the profound modern observation, through parting visions and near-death experiences, of the ancient view that humans have a spirit or soul. Sacred texts attest to this notion, and theologians and scholars have wrestled with it for centuries (Elkins, 1995).

That there could be a spiritual energy source integrated with the mind and body of human beings is a challenge to mainstream, traditional theories. It is also an appealing invitation to reach beyond the visible, material world to those invisible realities that may be more powerful and lasting than the things people can observe using their senses. Visions and near-death experiences provide such a challenge and invitation to clinicians. Although this territory of inquiry can bring clinicians close to the region of pure speculation and wishful fantasy, if they are careful in their inquiries and reporting methods, they may also come closer to God and to the spiritual realities that regulate the universe.

Numerous books and articles have been written on this subject, some of which are enlightening (Chandler, Holden, & Kolander, 1992; Helminiak, 1996), and others are far from scholarly. We now turn to one of the more reliable and substantial, a systematic accumulation of narratives compiled and interpreted by Melvin Morse, a clinical professor at the University of Washington Medical School. He is a practicing pediatric physician and an agnostic Jewish[1] individual who has gradually changed his opinion about several of these spiritual phenomena because of personal experiences and observations he has gathered over the years that seem to have better documentation than common anecdotes. We describe a few excerpts from his

---

[1] Since this was written, one of us met with Morse and learned that he has given up his agnostic view and is now a religious and spiritual theist. Note also that the narratives reported by Morse and by us were given at the urging of investigators and are not self-promoting on the part of the experiencers. They hold their experiences as private, or even sacred, but have permitted researchers to summarize them for the sake of science.

book *Parting Visions* (M. Morse, 1994a), which generally concerns death-related visions, including but not limited to near-death experiences. Of particular interest is that many of the excerpts were reported by physicians, nurses, and other professionals and not simply by the lay public alone, although many such stories are included there as well.

The first example concerns Lizabeth Sumner, a veteran nurse in San Diego, California, who observed and assisted many individuals into and through the process of death. After many years of experience, she had a peculiarly vivid death-related vision that cannot be discounted easily as a grief-induced hallucination. In this case, Lizabeth was caring for a young boy named Jimmy who was dying slowly, and she was assisting him in letting go and being as comfortable as possible. He died surrounded by his family, his doctor, and Lizabeth. On her way home,

> as she drove down the freeway, the windshield was suddenly filled with a vision so vivid that she had to pull off to the side of the road. In this vision she saw Jimmy, happy and animated, holding a man's hand. . . . He looked adoringly toward the man's face and had a look of great peace. The vision was as real as a moving picture and continued for as long as one minute. No words were spoken by the boy, but his eyes said it all as far as Lizabeth was concerned. "The life was back in his bright blue eyes and he was very comfortable" . . . I could hear him say, "I'm all right now," without him moving his lips (M. Morse, 1994a, p. xii)

Lizabeth attended Jimmy's funeral and, while standing outside of the cemetery next to Jimmy's mother, Lizabeth decided to tell the mother what she had seen: "The woman immediately burst into tears. 'That's exactly what my husband saw. . . . Right after Jimmy died, my husband saw the same thing' " (M. Morse, 1994a, p. xii). Such additional witnesses of these visions of the spirit make such cases more reliable than when there is only one person's self-report. Corroboration by others strengthens the testimony.

Another excerpt in the book involved a female ski instructor whose husband was a physicist. They professed no religious beliefs. They lived in Seattle and, with their two sons, were involved in an accident in which their car skidded off a bridge and fell to the bottom of a river. The mother broke out of the vehicle, got to the surface, and screamed for help. One child got out of the car and floated downriver. The younger child, unconscious, was soon pulled out of the car by a bystander, but the husband drowned. The mother reported, "When I reached the surface of the water, I sensed that my husband was sitting on the rocks watching the rescue below. . . . [He] seemed perfectly content. . . . I was angry . . . [and] began to scream at him . . . [and] he disappeared" (M. Morse, 1994a, pp. 5–6).

This was strange because she knew he was still trapped in the car under water. Soon after the accident, she had other visions of his visiting her at home, especially when she was sleeping. She said she did not want it to happen, it just happened. In addition, she claims to have seen her deceased husband at least two other times. On one of these occasions, she was wide awake and sitting in her living room. "At first, she denied these visions were anything but 'a crazy widow-thing'" (M. Morse, 1994a, p. 6). Then, about 3 weeks after the accident, Chris, the younger boy, told of how, while trapped underwater in the car, he had died and gone to heaven and that he had gone through something like a huge noodle or a tunnel and that there was a rainbow in it. He also said that he saw his grandmother, who had died years earlier, and had heard loud music that stuck with him. It was 3 weeks after the accident that Chris told his mother about these experiences.

The mother was amazed, and the effect on her was immediate:

> Suddenly it all came together for me. . . . Before hearing his story, I could only sleep for a few minutes without waking up in fear and terror. After hearing Chris' story, I slept six hours and awoke fully rested. "Why?" I asked. Because of Chris's experience, I believed that my husband was letting me know that he was okay . . . not that he was going to live, but that it was okay that he had died." [She then] accepted the visions of her husband as real events, not made-up dreams. In short, Chris's experience validated her own. She now believes in God and an after-life, just as she accepted her husband's message to her that "everything was going to be all right". . . . "My experience was as real as the one Chris had," said Patti, "and they have both given us such peace. How could I ever deny that they are real?. . . We lost a lot in that accident, but the visions gave us depth, meaning, and the strength to carry on." (M. Morse, 1994a, p. 7)

Again, the report of spiritual experiences was corroborated by the experience of another witness.

A related area of study is the subject of premonitions of a child's death by parents whose child died of sudden infant death syndrome (SIDS). Thirty-one of 174 families who responded to this study had strong premonitions that their child would die. Twenty-one percent of those whose babies died had strong premonitions, sometimes including visions, before the death. Three control groups, consisting of parents whose babies did not die were studied. In each of these groups, only 3% had premonitions or thought that something harmful might happen to their child. This is a remarkable degree of difference between the two groups. A specific example from the many reported in the book is given by a woman named Judy. She was 7 months' pregnant and told the following story:

> I suddenly found myself floating out of my body to the ceiling of the bedroom [while she was resting on her bed in the afternoon, fully

awake]. I hovered in the air, looking down at myself. Suddenly I realized that there was a lady floating in the air next to me. She glowed with a soft, white light.

The lady and I looked down at my body. It was as though that person on the bed was someone else. The lady began to talk about the person on the bed as though it wasn't me. "You know," she said with great love and compassion, "she can't keep the baby. It going to die." I wasn't angry, instead I felt great love and compassion when she said that, as if this baby's death was part of a greater purpose and plan. (M. Morse, 1994a, pp. 48–49)

Less than a year later Judy's child died of SIDS. These examples illustrate the scores of accounts documented by M. Morse and analyzed qualitatively, and sometimes quantitatively, by him. In addition, he has reviewed and synthesized the history and controversy over findings in this area of inquiry (M. Morse, 1994b). Although such reports are wrenching to traditional empirical philosophies, they continue to accumulate and often come from surprisingly reliable witnesses. Although we have long-standing spiritual convictions, even we have been somewhat startled by the evidence we have reviewed and have had to stretch our conceptual boundaries as well. Some of this evidence has emerged close to home.

Besides the reports compiled by M. Morse, we have several colleagues who have shared with us similar important experiences when they understood our interests and willingness to treat them with the respect that such personally sacred experiences deserve. We describe them here in narrative form. One of these was reported to one of us by Ray Harding, a Utah fourth district judge. His experience came unbidden and was a surprise (R. M. Harding, personal communication, March 13, 1996). Several years ago, while he was sleeping, he was awakened by a voice that spoke to him the following words: "What about your sister?" He said that he sat up in bed and looked around to see if there was someone in the room because of the vividness of the communication, whereupon these same words were repeated to him quite clearly as he sat in a completely awakened state: "What about your sister?" He thought about this for a couple of hours and went back to sleep. In the morning he discussed it with his wife. As he reflected on the experience, at first he was puzzled because he had no sister. Then, after pondering, he recalled that he did have an older half-sister who was born and died several years before his birth. This sister had died shortly after birth, and he had not thought about her for a long, long time. Thus, his surprise in response to the communication by the voice. He and his wife concluded that it would be important for them to do sacred church ceremonies on behalf of this sister, which they did.

It turns out that he and his wife also had a daughter who had died of leukemia at an early age. Some years after the experience of hearing a voice concerning his sister, he had a vivid dream (vision) in which he saw his deceased daughter and his sister together in spiritual bodily form. His daughter's arm was around the sister's shoulder in an act of comfort or of loving association. The meaning of the dream (vision) to him was that both his sister and his daughter were okay, that they were happy and at peace, and that he and his wife had done all that could be done on their behalf. We share this story because of the vividness of the various connections over the period of years that were involved and because Harding is a distinguished jurist and respected public figure known for his objectivity and reliability.

Just as the accounts in M. Morse's (1994a) book, we have the testimony of an intelligent, well-educated professional sharing a vivid spiritual experience that he was convinced came from the invisible world of spiritual reality. We are aware, of course, of the various naturalistic explanations that have been offered in an attempt to account for near-death experiences, parting visions, and other spiritual experiences, such as oxygen deprivation to the brain, chemically induced hallucinations, psychological defenses protecting the individual from the emotional trauma of near death, and so on (e.g., Groth-Marnet, 1989; Ring, 1980; R. K. Siegel, 1980). However, those who try to explain all such experiences in naturalistic terms seem more incredulous than those who are willing to stretch their theoretical boundaries to take in evidence from the invisible, spiritual, but real world. William James, perhaps the greatest American psychologist of all time, was willing to do this (James, 1902/1936), but the majority of psychologists have forgotten his great example. We consider ourselves to be directly in the Jamesian tradition. We respect him and his work and wish to restore his insightful perspectives of a century ago to our modern research.

Next, we describe an experience shared with one of us by David Haymond, who worked for many years as a general practitioner of medicine and then received training as a psychiatrist (D. Haymond, personal communication, March 13, 1996). A few years ago, he experienced ventricular fibrillation during a coronary arteriogram, during which he was temporarily dead and attempts were made to revive him. During this time, he had an experience that many others have reported of near-death experiences, in which it seems that their spirits had left their bodies. He had such an experience and felt his spirit move into another sphere, where he met individuals whom he knew, whom he loved; he also felt a great feeling of peace and warmth and light. This continued for a short time, whereupon he was dramatically brought back to temporal reality with his spirit present in his body, concurrently with the action of electrodes on his chest. He indicated that he could not remember the specific individuals in his visionary experience but that they were people he knew and cared about. The experience remains somewhat vague in its details, but its essence was powerful and dramatic for him.

Here, again, we have a respected publicly known individual, who had the best secular academic and professional training, attesting to an experience of the unseen world of the spirit. His report is consistent with the massive evidence accumulated concerning near-death experiences in which people recount leaving their physical bodies yet finding themselves transported in a spiritual body that has heightened capacities of intellect, perception, and action.

Both of the preceding reports came from members of The Church of Jesus Christ of Latter-day Saints (Mormon). A third account was reported to one of us by a female university (PhD) faculty member who was denominationally unaffiliated. Her father was Jewish, her mother Catholic (I. Klein, personal communication, October 17, 1996). She was struck by a car in an intersection and thrown from her vehicle into the street, where she bounced twice at high speed while still conscious. The second bounce crashed the back of her head against a curb, and she lost consciousness. Before losing consciousness, her entire life flashed before her as though on film, but there was no sense of time and the entire review occurred in about one second of ordinary time.

While her body laid motionless in the street, she felt herself floating through a tunnel at about a 45° angle, as though a magnet was drawing her upward. There was an opaque membrane at the "end" of the tunnel with a light behind it that seemed to guide her toward it. There was a grayish color inside the tunnel and a rush of something like bubbles going in the same direction she was. She heard something that sounded like music but not anything like earthly music. She also heard a voice as she approached the light, although it was not a voice like anything she had ever heard before. She was asked whether she wanted to proceed on through the membrane of light, and she said no. She was then sucked back through the tunnel rapidly, as if in a vacuum hose, and in a second or so began to feel her physical body again.

She opened her eyes and saw an elderly man with a cane looking down at her and shaking her. She remembered seeing him on the sidewalk just before the crash. He said, "Thank goodness, Miss—you're not dead!" There was a crowd of people around, and two emergency technicians from a nearby hospital were standing over her, talking. She was taken to the hospital for examination and radiological assessment, but was released in about 90 min. She had an occipital contusion on the right side but no fractures or internal injuries.

She reported this experience to have been the most beautiful moment of her life. The sense of harmony, peace, and total love and warmth were indescribable. She felt free of all worry despite the many problems in her life. She became spiritual and serene despite having been indifferent or antagonistic toward religious or spiritual matters. Her life gradually became much different. She became more mature and resilient to stress, improved her relationships, changed priorities regarding what was important in life, and became fearless about death.

The International Association for Near-Death Studies and its international journal have become rich resources for careful research on these unusual phenomena. Although such research tends to get pushed by mainstream scholars into the category of the scientific fringe, we believe that such stereotyping is unfair and misleading. We were skeptical, beginning with the publication in 1975 of Moody's book, *Life After Life*, but we have changed our view because of the accumulating, large amount of careful research that has been done since then. Although the popular near-death literature is rife with popularized accounts of visions and transportation to other worlds, we believe that the scholarly literature is good and we agree with our colleague, David Haymond, that something real is happening here and that the happenings are consistent with themes in major world religions and native belief systems.

Some of the best summaries and most carefully conducted research has been done by Kenneth Ring of the University of Connecticut (Ring, 1980). Interestingly, he is another agnostic Jewish scholar, which, in a sense, strengthens his credentials as an observer because of his lack of favorable religious "bias" toward such spiritual content. The most recent work by his research group concerns out-of-body experiences of blind individuals. Reports were given of *visual* observation of persons, places, and events that require "seeing." Although the "vision" of blind people is somewhat different from that of a person who has always had sight, there are strong preliminary evidences from these respondents that support the previous large accumulation of visual perceptions by sighted people who were thought to be dead but who were able to see via spiritual "eyes" physical objects they knew previously only through their other senses (Ring, 1995).

Without further arguing the extensive evidence, we add our names to the growing list of traditional scholars (see chap. 1 in this book) who have concluded that there is a spirit or soul capable of perception and action that is normally integrated with the physical body but that constitutes the lasting or eternal identity of the individual. It is apparently through the human spirit that the spirit of God most readily has its influence on people's thoughts, feelings, actions, and well-being. Given the foregoing, we assume that the spirit interacts with other aspects of the person to produce what is normally referred to as personality and behavior. The related epistemology of religious experience has a long history in philosophical scholarship, which we cannot review here, but Alston (1991) provided an excellent review and a modern rationale for the perceptual knowledge of God. The foregoing material is only a small sample of the qualitative reports that have been accumulated that indicate the existence of spiritual realities. They are presented in narrative form as stimuli to readers' *spiritual* understanding and way of knowing rather than as "proof" in the logical or scientific sense. This "way of knowing" is essential to a spiritual strategy (James, 1902/ 1936), as we discuss further in chapters 6 and 12 in this book. Of course, many of the reports have no specific reference to God, whereas others do. In either case, the experiences often have a positively transforming effect on those who have experienced them. Interestingly, many experiencers report an increase in spirituality and in faith but a decrease in denominational adherence (Sutherland, 1992). M. Morse (1994a) nicely summed up his observations of an array of findings with the following statements, with which we concur:

> People who have visions of this type enjoy excellent mental health. . . . There is some evidence that they are actually physically changed by their encounter with the light. It may alter the subtle electromagnetic fields that surround our bodies . . . near-death experiences are not the result of brain dysfunction. Similar transformative effects are not seen after hallucinations from oxygen deprivation, narcotics, and acute psychotic events. (p. 160)

> There is strong scientific support for my conclusion that there are physical and spiritual patterns that interconnect all of life. Modern physicists teach us that life is light, of varying wavelengths. . . . Electromagnetic forces unify everything we consider to be real. (pp. 162–163)

> We have a large area of our brain devoted to spiritual visions and psychical abilities . . . the right temporal lobe and surrounding structures. . . . We have a portion of the brain that connects us with the divine. But are these experiences . . . proof of life after death? As far as I am concerned, the answer is yes. (p. 173)

An Integrative, Multisystemic Viewpoint

By introducing a spiritual aspect into personality theory, we do not intend to subsume all other aspects of personality via a single dominating perspective, as some theories have attempted. Our view is more eclectic or integrative. We also endorse some (but not all) major themes of other perspectives, such as psychoanalysis (unconscious dynamics and insight), behaviorism (conditioned emotional reactions and self-regulation), cognitive theories (deficient schemas and rationality), humanistic and experiential views (incongruent experiencing of self and self-actualization), and interpersonal and familial systems theory (triangulation and balance). Spiritual aspects of people's lives may be influenced by any of these and vice versa. We believe that human personality operates according to a complex variety of principles and that an adequate theory of change must be comprehensive and multifaceted.

It is, of course, difficult to embrace within the same frame of reference both mechanistic notions, such as the existence of classically conditioned responses and the idea that people have a mental apparatus with cognitive, agentive, and spiritual aspects. This is made much easier by assuming that the psychobehavioral aspects of organisms are multisystemic, just as the biological aspects are. Our bodies consist of semi-independent circulatory, nervous, muscular, skeletal, and other systems. These depend upon each other, yet they also are entities unto themselves that follow very different laws, for example, the hydraulic laws of the circulatory system and the electrochemical laws of the nervous system. The laws of one system are not necessarily applicable to another system. If this is true for the body, it may also be true for one's psychology. It is conceivable, then, that there is a system that functions according to classical conditioning which coexists alongside other systems having to do with agentive processes and spiritual processes, each having a part to play in the organic whole. Such "systems" are yet to be [fully] identified, differentiated and described, but their possible existence makes it potentially feasible to harmonize seemingly incompatible perspectives on how human beings function. (cited in Bergin, 1988, pp. 24–25)

We believe that there is a spiritual core to human personality. Personality is influenced by a variety of systems and processes, but the eternal spirit is the core essence of identity. Healthy human development occurs as people hearken to the enticings of the Spirit of Truth. The Spirit of Truth helps people understand, value, and regulate their lives in harmony with universal principles that promote human growth and healthy functioning. Personality development and functioning are optimized when people are able to affirm their eternal spiritual identity; follow the influence of the Spirit of Truth; and regulate their behavior, feelings, and thoughts in harmony with universal principles and values.

It is not feasible to fully elaborate a spiritual personality theory here. We have already identified some of the broad assumptions in this position along with specifics, such as the spirit or soul. The detailed dynamics of how these operate and interact with other features of personality are currently under study; however, the outline we provide illustrates how our basic, broad spiritual assumptions articulate with more specific personality domains and how these in turn may apply to counseling and psychotherapy.

SPECIFIC IMPLICATIONS
FOR PERSONALITY THEORY AND CHANGE

Spiritual personality theory, integrated with secular knowledge, may be further outlined in the following themes. The list of bipolar constructs

TABLE 5.4

Psychospiritual Themes in a Spiritually Integrative Personality Theory and Therapeutic Change

I. Eternal identity	vs.	Mortal overlay
II. Free agency	vs.	Inefficacy
III. Inspired integrity	vs.	Deception
IV. Faithful intimacy	vs.	Infidelity
Family kinship	vs.	Alienation and isolation
V. Benevolent power	vs.	Authoritarianism
Communal structure	vs.	Social disintegration
VI. Health and human welfare values	vs.	Relativism and uncertainty
Growth and change	vs.	Stagnation
Good	vs.	Evil

in Table 5.4 was inspired in part by Erikson (1963), but it is also compatible with Gilligan's (1982) notion of women's life cycle and with studies of women's spirituality (Randour, 1987). It derives mainly from studies of religion and mental health, from sacred texts, from studies of religious and spiritual experiences reported by college students we have studied, and from attempts to integrate ideas from these with current secular research, theory, and practice. No attempt is made to sketch a developmental scheme. Rather, the list is hierarchical in the sense of progressing from the core of personality to the complexity of interpersonal and communal interactions. Also note that these opposite poles are endpoints representing continuous dimensions. People may be at various points along the dimension between the polar opposites. Obviously, each of these bipolar topics deserves a chapter unto itself, which will be the focus of a future project.

It may seem that these topics are not obvious derivatives from theistic spiritual traditions, in which one might expect to consider topics such as faith, love, truth, repentance, grace, forgiveness, revelation, reconciliation, redemption, commandments, doctrines, obedience, sacrifice, service, and so on. Actually, such topics are fundamental and are addressed in various ways in our approach; however, this is a psychology, not a theology. Our terms are adaptations of spiritual concepts and integrations thereof with psychological concepts that we consider valuable. The main topics of spiritual literature do emerge, however, in our analysis of the six psychospiritual themes, and they are an important part of it.

Eternal Identity Versus Mortal Overlay

As we discussed earlier, we assume that each person has an eternal, indestructible, personal, spiritual identity that persists through time and eternity (Rogers, cited in Bergin, 1985). As creations of God, eternal identities have noble, infinite potential. This concept is somewhat comparable to some humanistic and psychodynamic theories that emphasize human potential and self-actualization. The potential development of identity can go awry because of imperfect or abusive parenting, social chaos, biological deficiencies, and so on, so that a mortal overlay develops that obscures the person's eternal identity. According to our spiritual view of personality development, when people get in touch with their eternal spiritual core with all of its dignity and power for enhancement, the mortal overlay begins to dissolve and they begin to overcome their pathologies and grow in healthy ways (Ellsworth, 1995). Many therapies do this to a degree, even though it is not explicitly stated in their theories of change. Spiritual counseling helps the person do this with added strength by virtue of spiritual techniques, such as meta-empathy (i.e., the therapist's perceiving and communicating accurate perceptions of the person's spiritual nature), meditation, prayer, illumination, spiritual communion with the revealing spirit of God via acute identity experiences, special blessings, fasting, and other spiritual interventions discussed in chapters 9 and 10 in this book.

The following personal experiences, expressed in narrative form by students we have studied at BYU, illustrate what we mean by getting in touch with and affirming one's eternal spiritual identity. They are similar to Maslow's (1968) accounts of acute identity experiences.

The first is a person who was adopted and whom we call "J." When J. began to attend elementary school, he heard people refer to him as "the adopted one." The pain of this was deepened by the taunting of another young child who talked of him as, "not being one of your own family." He continued to struggle with these doubts about his identity until the age of 15. The following is J.'s account of what happened:

> Then came what I believe to be my acute identity experience. My father was seriously hurt in a farming accident. After he had been taken to the hospital we were told by the doctors that there was a possibility he might not live. My mother and sister emotionally collapsed. It was the first time I had seen both of them in hysterics. I was in a mild state of shock. That night as I lay in the hospital corridor, I began to be afraid as I never had been in my life up to that point. I was so horribly afraid that the only thing I could think to do was to pray. Then I had one of the most spiritual experiences I have ever had. My acute identity experience was the knowledge I carried with me after that night that I was really secure in my family life as a son and a brother. I knew that I had been sealed eternally to my family and that I am secure and have strength and an understanding of my identity that I did not have before this experience.

A female college student experienced the following when she was 8 years old:

I have had several experiences that helped me realize that I am a child of God. I consider one of these to be an acute identity experience. . . . It may seem strange but it occurred through a dream. I dreamed that Jesus Christ was in front of me. He beckoned me to come to him. When I did he opened his arms and took me in. He held me and as he did, it was as if he were speaking to me, telling me that I was completely and totally loved. It was as if he were telling me through his body (every pore) rather than simply vocalizing it through his mouth. I woke up feeling that I belonged in a way I had never felt before. I knew that I was of worth to Christ, that he loves me. In that respect, my identity was established.

These experiences, reported by college students, suggest that there is an underlying reality to one's identity that is often obscured by life experience but that can be penetrated by the spirit and that creates a revelatory perception for the individual of the nature of the eternal self. This carries one's understanding far beyond that of the temporal or empirical world. Such spiritual identity experiences are healing and integrative. They enhance feelings of self-worth and facilitate overcoming emotional problems and unhealthy lifestyle behaviors.

Some specific cases, described next, of change in the identity and behavior of individuals who overcame psychological problems through religious experiences illustrate this spiritually energized change process. These further illustrate the type of powerful phenomena that must be explained and that lead to a much different theory of human nature than now exists in the behavioral sciences. These cases also indicate the unique inspiration and power of healing through the Spirit that comes through religious experience. These cases emerged during a 3-year qualitative and quantitative study that we conducted of religious lifestyles and mental health among a sample of 60 BYU students during the 1980s (Bergin et al., 1994).

The first case involved "E." E. was 24 years old and married in 1984 when first studied. He grew up in a religiously inactive family. Because of the chaos and violence in his family, he became alienated, insecure, and somewhat deviant in his conduct. His school performance was poor. Over the years, he pursued religion on his own and became an active participant. He reported several intense religious experiences that he said helped him compensate for his insecurity and find new direction and fulfillment. His academic performance improved, and he became a leader in school. He served a successful 2-year mission before marriage. Three years later, during a follow-up study we found that his marriage was stable and that he was the father of four children. The instability shown in his early life and adolescence had never reappeared. Indeed, we followed up on him a number of years later and found the same results. Spiritual experience was decisive in bringing him within a nurturing community that provided him with a sense of identity, a role, and satisfying affiliations, including marriage to a strong young woman. His personality seemed to selectively soak up the benevolent features of the religious environment, and he was not plagued by the perfectionism sometimes exhibited by highly religious people (Bergin et al., 1994, pp. 83–84).

Another example is that of "G.," who was also a 24-year-old during the initial study, but he was single and a convert. He had been troubled by various forms of substance abuse, depression, sexual promiscuity, insecurity, and a lack of meaning in his life. G. interpreted his religious conversion as divine intervention in answer to his prayers. An intense religious experience brought a transformation in his lifestyle more dramatic than could be ordinarily attained through professional psychotherapy. G. was able to abstain from drugs and give up his active sex life. His depression lifted; he found new meaning in his existence and went on to serve a successful church mission. At the 3-year follow-up period, G. maintained his new lifestyle and his emotional stability (Bergin et al., 1994, p. 84). The characteristics and changes of both individuals were documented by tests and multiple interviews.

Our outline of eternal identity versus mortal overlay provides an example of how a spiritual perspective complements and expands on the secular understanding of healthy personality development. Of course, identity is only one of many areas in which the phenomenology of religious experience shows evidence of processes that are difficult to describe in ordinary psychological terms but have as profound or more profound effects than any behavior change procedures that we know of in the ordinary professional domain. A full analysis of this and the other topics in Table 5.4 cannot be adequately explained in this chapter and will be the focus of another book. For our purposes here, the following brief accounts will suffice.

Free Agency Versus Inefficacy

We oppose determinism and assert that human beings are personally responsible for their choices and actions. This agentive capacity is a God-given gift. Because of it, people have the opportunity to grow, to refine themselves as eternal beings, and to serve others and transcend ordinary human existence, much as Maslow (1971) suggested was possible. However, because of one's own bad choices (as in addiction), actions by others (as in child abuse), or biological influences (as in brain disorders), agency may be impaired. Psychopathology consists largely of the loss of ability to make rational choices and to enact them. Self-regulative capacities are displaced by loss of internal control or by external control from other sources (Bergin, 1969).

When people's sense of eternal identity is affirmed and their agency strengthened through spiritual experiences, their feelings of responsibility and their self-regulative capacities are enhanced. As they learn to respond to the promptings of the Spirit of Truth, their commitment to healthy lifestyles increases. A major purpose of most therapies is to enhance self-regulatory function and feelings of efficacy (Bandura, 1986) as well as to strengthen feelings of responsibility for choices, actions, and the healthiness of interpersonal relationships.

Such improvements free the person's agency from bondage and opens the person to spiritual guidance in establishing a mentally healthy way of living. In many cases, such enhancement of agency via standard treatment is required before spiritual techniques and discussion of values and lifestyle issues can be effective. In the later phase of therapy, spiritual guidance can assist to establish a lifestyle that will avoid any prior irresponsible or ineffective patterns and maintain the improvements gained through therapy and thus avoid relapse. This philosophy is similar to that in medicine, which helps patients establish a physically healthy lifestyle in order to maintain improvement after treatment or to prevent disease. Sometimes, however, a spiritual focus is needed at the beginning of therapy before the motivation necessary for change can be aroused, such as in the 12-step programs for addiction (see chap. 10 in this book).

Inspired Integrity Versus Deception

Extensive literature now points to the importance of honesty in relationships for the sake of individual and interpersonal health. Authenticity, congruence (Rogers, 1961), openness, and so on are woven into most theories of change. Inauthenticity and deception of self and others have been woven into many theories of psychopathology, beginning with psychoanalysis and extending to family systems theory.

The commandment "thou shalt not bear false witness" is fundamental to most religious traditions. Belief in it is a strengthening factor in the analysis of self and self-in-relationship. Self-deception and the deception of others is at the root of defense mechanisms, interpersonal conflict, and much pathology in general. This is a transparent fact to most clinicians.

Integrity, on the other hand, is a sensitive attunement to the Spirit of Truth. It includes a resilient willingness to face the facts, to "be true," to be nonoffensive, to avoid blaming others, and to accept responsibility for one's defects and bad conduct even when it hurts to do so. Integrity is "egoless" in the senses that the prideful protection or advancement of the ego is given up and that one elects to absorb the painful truths that defenses and deceptions have hidden from oneself and others. This may not be easy, especially in severe cases, but it is essential to real healing. Living a lie is, in the long run, harder than living truthfully (Peck, 1983; Warner, 1986, 1995; Warner & Olson, 1984), and it includes the courage to confront the lies perpetrated by others as well as those within oneself.

The therapeutic solution to deception may be direct, as in group confrontations among addicts and sex offenders, or it may be indirect, as in the sharing of narratives by those who have successfully faced themselves and life with integrity (Warner, 1995). The spiritual dimension is very much at play in the development of integrity, for when people have a strong sense of spiritual identity and affirm their personal responsibility, they are led by the Spirit of Truth to value honesty. As they make the choice (with guidance, example, confrontation, rewards or analysis of defense) to be true to the truth, a spiritual burden of alienation from God is lifted and they are blessed by an infusion of strength and healing, an "integration" as in the classical meaning of the term *integrity*. Then, relationships are healed concurrently with the healing of oneself.

Faithful Intimacy Versus Infidelity

Teachings of the world religions and the conclusions of behavioral science concur in the notion that intimacy, affection, and love are fundamental to human happiness and optimal functioning. They also concur that capriciousness, abuse, exploitation, and faithlessness in such relationships are harmful. A national survey of mental health professionals supports the same view (Jensen & Bergin, 1988).

Studies of marital conflict, divorce, and infidelity support the claim that faithful intimacy is beneficial, as do studies of parent–child relations and therapeutic relationships. Erikson's (1963) notion that the capacity for intimacy grows out of healthy psychosocial development and builds on adaptive identity formation is pertinent, as are the arguments by Gilligan (1982), Mahler, Pine, and Bergman (1975), Bowlby (1969), and numerous others that intimate attachment and love are the fundamental keys to normal human personality development.

Much of the energy of psychotherapy is devoted to instituting or restoring capacities for normal intimacy and the social skills to maintain viable loving relationships. We have said that God is truth, or the Spirit of Truth, but equally valid is the statement that "God is love," and God's love is faithful, stable, and unwavering. As people affirm their spiritual identity and respond to the Spirit of Truth, they are led to value faithful intimacy and love, a process that can be facilitated by a spiritual, theistically oriented therapy. There are many models of both faithfulness and infidelity, in the broad sense of these terms, in the scriptures and in life; therefore, it is not difficult for therapists to find examples to use in helping clients understand this theme and the consequences thereof (cf. V. L. Brown, 1981).

For the religious or spiritually inclined client, it is not difficult to open the client's thoughts to the conviction that there is something universal or transcendent about faithful intimacy that is built into people's nature as human beings. Attaining such conviction is an important therapeutic goal because it often provides the needed motivation to resist temptations to be faithless, exploitative, or abusive. If one has the feeling that the Creator is the author and supporter of faithful love, it can provide courage during moral crises, whether these pertain to intimacy broadly defined as interpersonal goodness or narrowly defined as sexual fidelity.

Erikson (1963) opposed isolation to intimacy, which is a valuable point. Alienation might also be used as an opposing pole, but we find infidelity, as we have defined it, to be the best match for the opposite of real intimacy, and we think that it has more far-reaching consequences for a value-based theory of personality and change.

Family Kinship Versus Alienation and Isolation

Family kinship is a natural subtopic within the intimacy domain because the most powerful intimate relationships, including but not limited to sexual ones, occur worldwide within family structures. The powerful potential of such relationships and social structures is evident in the benevolent consequences of positive family ties and the equally malignant results of disruptive and destructive family relations. Although domestic violence, rape, divorce, open marriage, serial monogamy, various forms of cohabitation, promiscuity, child physical and sexual abuse, and other forms of sex outside marriage have threatened or distorted the long-held meanings of kinship (especially in North America and Europe), the vast majority of world cultures continue to be rooted in familial kinship systems or networks. It is particularly striking that the so-called Third World cultures of Africa, Asia, and Latin America, which are considered to be inferior by some people in economic and intellectual terms, have held firmly to kinship traditions and have defined the family in terms of larger networks of relationships than the nuclear family. Some observers believe, as we do, that this broad sense of family is healthier and provides more opportunity for emotional intimacy and social support than Western traditions (V. L. Brown, 1981; Uzoka, 1979). Street gangs appear to provide substitutes for the loss of family. They exemplify our notion of alienation—from parents, society, and social responsibility that opposes that basic unit of nearly all societies—the legally or custom-sanctioned family kinship system.

From a spiritual viewpoint, we assume that marriage is ordained of God and is good for human beings and that procreation and the care and nurturing of offspring in the context of a moral value system is essential to a good society (Bennett, 1993) and lasting mental health. People who sense the Spirit of Truth will be led to value marriage and family kinship and will show commitment to lifestyles and traditions that support family life. We thus assume that theistic tradition dictates a sociological definition of mental health rather than a merely clinical, individual one. In this sense, behaviors and lifestyles that undermine family kinship and society are pathological even if the individuals engaging in them are not mentally ill in the DSM–IV sense of the term. Therapeutically, our theistic, spiritual perspective is strongly supportive of marriage and family life, particularly when therapies are aimed at the resolution of alienation and the restoration of faithful intimacy within a tradition of sanctioned kinship and benevolent social structure.

Benevolent Power Versus Authoritarianism

On the one hand, power is the ability to control, to decide, to dispense consequences; on the other hand, however, it is the ability to make a difference, to influence, and to collaborate in causing change or maintaining the status quo. Power must be considered here both because of its potential to do harm and its potential for good in human relationships. It stands next to intimacy as a factor in relationships, but it is often orthogonal to it. Power can be used to broaden the potentialities of others and to stimulate their growth, or it can narrow a person's possibilities and be used to degrade or defeat him or her.

Negative correlations between authoritarianism and positive mental health have been well-known since the classic post-World War II study conducted by Adorno, Frenkel-Brunswik, Levinson, and Sanford (1950). The positive benefits of benevolent uses of power are equally evident. This dual potential is evident in marriage relations and those between parent and child, employer and employee, therapist and client, and, of course, the governor and governed.

Gains are to be made in human relations that grant to one another the freedom to grow in identity and relationships. The best uses of power are thus benevolent in that they set limits on intrusions by one person on another and provide stimuli and opportunity for personal growth and individual, collective, and social welfare. A good home and family life thus would provide rules that set limits, a safe and securely regulated structure, and the social-emotional processes that contribute to normal development and self-actualization. In business and industry, there are many developments in ethics, training, and governing that are benevolent (Covey, 1989; Scott & Hart, 1989) changes from earlier authoritarian systems.

Abuses of power are, of course, rampant in modern life. In the family, the failure to share decision making or the misuse of authority to demean, degrade, punish, constrict, or brutalize represents the opposite pole. Religious institutions and the individuals representing them are also known for their abuses of authority. This occurs when being "authoritative" (i.e., using power benevolently) degrades into "authoritarianism" (i.e., using power abusively). Political and family abuses of power are sometimes justified in religious terms: "It is the will of God that you (especially women) submit to me," "Destroy or kill in the name of God," "Giving me sex gratification is ordained of God," and so on. These are dramatic abuses of theistic belief systems, and they are inconsistent with the Spirit of Truth. Institutionalized authoritarian cultures of belief and oppression have no spiritually legitimate claim to spiritual insight, authority, or power; however, helping religious clients, especially women (Rayburn, 1985), reframe perspectives on organizations they belong to can be a delicate and difficult task.

Aware therapists know or are forewarned that the evils of authoritarianism (as defined earlier) may lurk behind seemingly "nice" organizations, families, or religious groups with which clients are affiliated. Sometimes, they must help their clients resist, reform, or flee from such systematic forms of abuse of the human spirit. They also may need to confront clients who use their power in abusive ways (e.g., cases of child and spouse abuse). A spiritual approach can sometimes break down habits of anger and violence and affirm the morality and healthy consequences of benevolent power. Angry, abusive people are often hard to influence. Sometimes, conversion experiences or what W. R. Miller and C'deBaca (1994) referred to as "quantum" change are needed, but these are hard to orchestrate.

People who hearken to the Spirit of Truth value benevolent use of power. They use their authority to serve the needs of people. Thus, instead of people existing for the sake of those in authority (e.g., religious leaders, politicians, parents, teachers, therapists), the authority system exists for the sake of people. Those in authority are thus called on by promptings of the Spirit of Truth to devote their energies and sacrifice their self-interests for the benefit of others. The preferred mode of influence is through information and persuasion in a coaching style rather than a controlling style. This makes communication, communion, and even intimacy possible, whereas authoritarianism destroys all of these.

Communal Structure Versus Social Disintegration

Communal structure is a logical correlate of power and authority issues. The main point is the importance of opportunities for individuals to have group and community identification and support. Erikson's (1963) notion that the case history is embedded in history or that the individual is embedded in the culture is pertinent. Religious communities are often excellent resources for support and healing, including a sense that oneself and one's family are part of a larger coherent whole. Indeed, Erikson argued that identity is never completely formed without this sense of group identification. Perhaps it is this principle that makes ongoing self-help groups, such as Alcoholics Anonymous, so valuable (McCrady & Miller, 1993). The modern decline of communal structures with their points of social identification is a marker of social decay and personal disarray. People who are in harmony with the spirit value their religious and cultural community, and they make efforts to contribute to such communities' cohesion and welfare.

Health and Human Welfare Values Versus Relativism and Uncertainty

All religions, philosophies, spiritual perspectives, and cultures embody systems of value that identify what is important, preferred, acceptable, and worthy of transmission across generations and subgroups. These impose a moral order on personal behavior and social interaction and inculcate internal feelings of worth or of shame and guilt depending on one's conformity to them. There is much literature on this topic in psychology (moral development), anthropology, philosophy, political science, and so on.

Our focus here is on the notion that mental health is sustained by a viable moral belief system that includes mentally healthy values (Bergin, 1985). It is clear that mental health professionals endorse such a view and that they endorse particular values (see chap. 6 in this book) as being favorable to mental health (Bergin & Jensen, 1990; Jensen & Bergin, 1988; Peck, 1978). According to our spiritual view of personality development, as people respond to the Spirit of Truth, they recognize and internalize healthy values and learn to regulate their conduct in harmony with them.

Without an orienting system for assessing the value of one's conduct or that of others, self-effectiveness and self-regulation, the undergirding of civilized and normal behaviors, are undermined (Bandura, 1986). Although the specific ways in which people apply general moral principles may vary, and although individuals often disengage their moral standards for the sake of defenses or gratification (Bandura, 1986), their importance for a mentally healthy and socially constructive lifestyle is clear (Bergin et al., 1996; Jensen & Bergin, 1988). It is also clear that feelings of spiritual conviction give personal value systems the added dimensions of motivation, courage, and endurance despite the temporary pain (facing defenses or resisting impulse gratification) that this may require. The long-term and socially responsible perspective provided by a spiritual worldview encourages the sacrifice of immediate neediness (if contrary to moral commitments) on behalf of higher principles, long-range consequences, and the impact on others, both proximal and distal. Such a perspective has been noted by Fowler (1996) to be the highest level of faith development.

Relativistic morality, on the other hand, is less likely to be enduring because (a) there is less conviction that the moral principles are general and part of the moral nature of humans and the universe and (b) convenience or immediacy in adapting to momentary situations may cloud judgment and lead to self-justification rather than reasoned assessment. Such a philosophy does not recognize sufficiently the enduring contribution of values derived from the tests of time across human history and cultural development (Campbell, 1975).

Growth and Change Versus Stagnation

It is clear from the foregoing analyses that people can understand and regulate their lives through spiritual means. Such change requires both faith and initiative. People who gain a sense of their spiritual, eternal identity and follow the enticings of the Spirit of Truth will want to grow according to the outline provided in Table 5.4. In the process, they will progressively fulfill their divine potential. In doing so, they will develop their capacities and talents and seek to overcome or compensate for deficiencies and disturbances. As they grow, they will also use their abilities and energies in the socially benevolent and constructive ways that have been described. They will give of themselves because they now have more to give, and they will understand that giving of self not only strengthens their interpersonal and social fabric but also strengthens their own personhood.

On the other hand, those who are less in touch with their spiritual identity and the Spirit of Truth are more likely to stagnate and fail to grow in healthy and productive ways. The stresses of life and their own disturbances are likely to influence them in the direction of self-preoccupation, and their ability to adapt and to be an influence for good will shrink. Their motivation and ability to change will be encumbered by a lack of faith and of vision for the future. Personal pathologies and the negative influence of associates may keep them from growing. For such individuals, spiritual awakening may be crucial to curbing downward emotional cycles and self-defeating behaviors. An alliance with a spiritually motivated therapist and, in some cases, a cohesive group can strengthen them and help them alter their course. Then, a combination of spiritual vision that is harmonious with the positive dimensions listed in Table 5.4 and application of effective therapies can make the process of personal change complete.

Good Versus Evil

Reviewing the bipolar themes of this section reveals that our view of personality and mental health is value laden. Certain ways of being and acting are preferable to others. Therefore, human development, parenting, organizational arrangements, and psychotherapy are all seen as means to advance the healthier sides of the various polarities. These valued themes also reflect the classic notion of "good versus evil," although they are applied here to issues of personality and psychotherapy. Just as we believe that there is a spirit of good that comes from God, we also conclude that there also is an opposing spirit of evil (Dickson, 1995; Peck, 1983). The opposition that exists between the good and evil poles provides an abundant array of choices for human beings. We believe that when people follow the influence of the spirit and choose or work on behalf of the positive ends of these dichotomies, pathologies are more likely to be prevented and mental health promoted through therapy or other means. When people choose or are conditioned to accept the negative side, their health and human potential is constrained or undermined. The goals or values of spiritual, theistic therapy thus favor the appropriate development of the good aspects of each dimension: identity, agency, integrity, intimacy, power, and values. How this "therapeutic valuing" of the good may be done in clinical practice is considered more fully in the chapters that follow.

CONCLUSION

In this chapter we have discussed a complex spectrum of topics that are fundamental to a spiritual strategy in personality theory and psychotherapy. A single chapter does not do justice to the extensive literature, the concepts, or the practical implications that flow from them. The strong trends that are altering the flow of professional work in mental health are difficult to condense and to articulate. We expect that we, and many colleagues, will be working on this new frame of reference for a long time.

In the meanwhile, we want to be as clear as possible. We are saying that there is a spiritual reality that is linked with divine intelligence or the Spirit of Truth. This is not "pop psychology." We intend it to be serious—philosophically, empirically, and clinically. It builds on the history of world cultures, a century of behavioral science, and the intense and inspired work of many sophisticated professionals over the past 25 years. It is not new, but its format and style are new.

The assumptions and the bipolar constructs we have presented emerge from a context of multiple influences and authors. We have stated them boldly so that the uniqueness of this perspective will stand out and will give direction to the next steps in research, theory, and practice. We cannot state too emphatically that people are eternal spiritual beings who have the capacity to contact and be influenced by their Creator through spiritual means.

By asserting this new theistic spiritual strategy, we do not intend to denigrate the positive contributions of naturalistic, secular, and humanistic approaches. When possible, they need to be integrated or built together into a more compelling picture of human functioning. Openness to new and different ideas is essential. Similarly, our emphasis on qualitative and narrative inquiries does not mean that standard research and statistical methods should be abandoned. Fortunately, our review of such research has provided substantial hope that there is something to the spiritual phenomena we posit but can only infer from "objective" studies.

Finally, we need to reaffirm that human personality is inherently relational. In this, the social constructionists and postmodernists are correct. The great commandments of the major religions concur in emphases on people's relationships to God and to each other. The human race is a family, and people's kinship flows from a common creation. When identity and agency are optimally functional, their nature and influence shape and are shaped by the basic sociality of humanness as expressed in integrity, intimacy, fidelity, kinship, benevolent power and communal structure, and a commitment to human welfare through personal responsibility.

III

PSYCHOTHERAPY PROCESS
AND METHODS

6

A THEISTIC, SPIRITUAL VIEW OF PSYCHOTHERAPY

Major values in human relations are woven into various religious systems, and they seem to be universally true regardless of what a therapist's attitude toward a Supreme Being might be.

—*Hans H. Strupp*

Each of the major mainstream psychotherapy traditions offers a somewhat unique perspective about the nature of treatment. None of them, however, adequately incorporates a theistic, spiritual view of the world and human personality. In this chapter we discuss some of the important implications of a theistic perspective for psychotherapy. Specifically, we discuss how this perspective affects understanding of (a) the purpose and goals of therapy, (b) the therapist's role in therapy, (c) the client's role in therapy, and (d) the nature of the therapy relationship.

PURPOSE AND GOALS OF THERAPY

As discussed in chapter 5, we endorse a multidimensional view of human nature, personality, and therapeutic change. Biological, emotional, social and systemic, cognitive, behavioral, and spiritual processes affect human functioning. Because of this, no strategy, including a spiritual one, should be used exclusively but as part of a multidimensional, integrative approach. During the assessment phase of treatment, psychotherapists should attempt to understand their clients multidimensionally. Therapy goals should be pragmatically tailored to best meet the unique needs, concerns, symptoms, and preferences of individual clients, and this may or may not include religious and spiritual goals. However, with many clients, such goals may be crucial for success.

We assume that the overall purpose of psychotherapy is to help clients cope with and resolve their presenting problems and concerns and, when possible, to promote their healing, growth, and long-term well-being. This view of the purpose of psychotherapy is not, of course, unique. The unique contribution the theistic, spiritual strategy makes, however, is the view that therapists can help clients cope more effectively with or resolve problems, heal, and grow if they facilitate and strengthen the religious and spiritual resources of their clients' lives. According to this perspective, spiritual beliefs, influences, and behaviors may be especially helpful in establishing value-based lifestyles that will produce lasting change and continuing growth (Larson & Larson, 1994).

Religious and Spiritual Therapeutic Goals

A variety of specific goals that are directly relevant to the religious and spiritual dimensions may be appropriate for therapy depending on the unique concerns and issues of the client. We do not attempt to enumerate all the possibilities, but we do outline five general therapeutic goals of our strategy. Of course, none of these should be imposed on clients who do not wish to pursue them.

1. *Help clients experience and affirm their eternal spiritual identity and live in harmony with the Spirit of Truth.* This is the core therapeutic goal of our theistic, spiritual strategy, and it logically flows from the view of personality and therapeutic change we described in chapter 5. We assume that when therapists succeed at this goal, the healing, change, and growth that clients experience will be more profound, complete, and long-lasting. Clients will grow in their feelings of self-worth, capacity to internalize healthy values, ability to regulate their behavior in healthy and productive ways, and capacity for benevolent and productive contributions to kinship and community.

The goal of affirming a client's spiritual identity and divine worth is appropriate for all clients, but this does not mean that therapists should talk about religion or spirituality with all clients, particularly those who do not believe in God or spiritual realities. For those therapists who view their clients as creations of God having an eternal spiritual identity, however, it is easier to see past the "mortal overlay" of defenses and pain and treat them with special respect, kindness, and unconditional positive regard. Theistic therapists seek to do this valuing of the person regardless of the client's spiritual views or clinical issues. They also encourage clients to follow the promptings of their consciences, or the Spirit of Truth. How therapists can do this is discussed later in this chapter in the section on therapeutic valuing and again in chapter 10 in the section on moral instruction.

2. *Help clients examine and better understand what if any impact their religious and spiritual beliefs have on their presenting problems and their lives in general.* Therapists should pursue this goal with all willing clients. Regardless of what clients' presenting problems and symptoms may be, it is important to determine what role if any their personal, cultural, and spiritual backgrounds and beliefs play in their lives. Without such information, therapists will not adequately understand the clients' worldview, cultural identity, or spiritual influences that could be contributing to or helping them cope with their problems and symptoms. The religious and spiritual beliefs of some clients may be causing or intertwined with their presenting problems and issues in complex ways. With such clients, adequate resolution of their presenting problems may require examining, and perhaps modifying, some of their beliefs, which is a delicate and difficult task.

3. *Help clients identify and use the religious or spiritual resources in their lives to assist them in their efforts to cope, heal, and change.* This goal is most suitable for clients who view their religious affiliation or beliefs as a source of guidance and strength. Tapping into such resources can powerfully assist some clients and should not be overlooked. Therapists do not need to be religious or spiritually oriented themselves to help clients in this way; they only need to be willing to do so (Propst, Ostrom, Watkins, Dean, & Mashburn, 1992). This goal is, of course, inappropriate with clients who are nonreligious or atheistic and should be pursued only with great caution with those who have unresolved issues (e.g., anger, fear, unhealthy dependency) with God or religious authorities, which is not uncommon among clinical patients.

4. *Help clients examine and resolve religious and spiritual concerns that are pertinent to their disorders and make choices about what role religion and spirituality will play in their lives.* This goal is appropriate for clients who explicitly state that they would like the therapist to help them explore (a) religious and spiritual doubts and concerns or (b) questions they have about the role they wish religion and spirituality to play in their lives. Many clients may wish to pursue this goal only with therapists who belong to their own religious denomination. Other clients may wish to discuss their religious and spiritual doubts and concerns only with their religious leaders. Therapists should be sensitive to such preferences and be careful not to coerce clients into examining such doubts, concerns, and questions. Even when clients explicitly say they wish to pursue this goal in therapy, therapists may wish to encourage their clients to also explore their spiritual concerns and questions with religious or spiritual leaders whom they trust.

5. Help clients examine how they feel about their spiritual growth and well-being and, if they desire, help them determine how they can continue their quest for spiritual growth and well-being. This goal is appropriate to pursue with clients who have indicated that their spirituality is important to them and that they wish to explore with the therapist how they can begin, or continue, their efforts to grow spiritually. This is another goal that many clients may wish to pursue only with therapists who belong to their own religious denomination or in collaboration with their religious leaders. Again, therapists should be sensitive to such preferences and pursue this goal only when clients have stated explicitly that they would like to do so with the therapist. Even when clients have done this, therapists may wish to encourage their clients to also discuss their spirituality goals with trusted spiritual leaders.

We want to emphasize that therapists need not necessarily be religious or spiritually oriented themselves to endorse and pursue these goals with clients. Regardless of their own spiritual beliefs, if therapists are willing to expand their multicultural sensitivity and competency into the religious and spiritual domains, we believe that they can, when appropriate, often assist clients with these important goals. Because many therapy techniques are "context free," they can be applied to religious conflicts, questions, and goals just as they are applied to other contents, such as interpersonal relations, anxieties, sex, aggression, and so on (Lovinger, 1984). We recognize that sometimes, despite their best efforts, therapists may still feel uncomfortable pursuing such goals with some clients. In such circumstances, it is appropriate and ethical for therapists to refer these clients to therapists who can work with their issues comfortably and effectively.

THE THERAPIST'S ROLE

Adopt an Ecumenical Stance

The capacity to adopt an ecumenical therapeutic stance is essential for therapists who work with religious and spiritual clients. The word *ecumenical* means "of worldwide scope or applicability" (*American Heritage Dictionary of the English Language*, 1992, p. 584), interdenominational, or open to diverse perspectives. We define an *ecumenical therapeutic stance* as an attitude and approach to therapy that is suitable for clients of diverse religious affiliations and backgrounds. Therapists should use an ecumenical therapeutic approach during the early stages of therapy with all clients and over the entire course of therapy with clients whose religious affiliation or beliefs differ significantly from their own. An ecumenical therapeutic stance is a multicultural approach to therapy that goes beyond contemporary multicultural approaches by emphasizing the specific attitudes and skills that therapists need to understand and sensitively intervene in the spiritual dimensions of their clients' lives. The foundations of an ecumenical therapeutic stance are the attitudes and skills of an effective multicultural therapist.

Multicultural therapeutic attitudes and skills have been described in detail elsewhere (e.g., Ponterotto et al., 1995, 1996; D. W. Sue & Sue, 1977, 1990; D. W. Sue et al., 1982; S. Sue, Zane, & Young, 1994). Briefly, effective multicultural therapists have attitudes and skills such as (a) an awareness of one's own cultural and racial heritage, values, and biases; (b) a respect for and comfort with cultures, races, and values different from one's own; (c) an understanding of how a client's racial and cultural heritage could affect the client's worldview and sense of identity; (d) a sensitivity to circumstances that indicate that a client should be referred to a therapist of his or her own race or culture; (e) specific knowledge about one's clients' particular racial or cultural group; and (f) an awareness of one's own helping style and a recognition of how this style could affect clients from different racial or cultural backgrounds (D. W. Sue & Sue, 1990; D. W. Sue et al., 1982).

Effective ecumenical therapists must be able to generalize these multicultural attitudes and skills to the religious and spiritual domains. Unfortunately, it is not necessarily true that therapists who have developed multicultural attitudes and skills, which enable them to deal sensitively with many human differences, will be able to apply these attitudes and skills in their work with religious and spiritual clients. Despite the admirable efforts that have been made during the past two decades to promote multicultural sensitivity within the psychotherapy profession, religious and spiritual issues have been sorely neglected in training programs and the professional literature (Bergin, 1980a, 1983; Henning & Tirrell, 1982; Tan, 1993). Because of personal biases, lack of knowledge and empathy, and fears about religious and spiritual matters, many therapists remain unprepared to work sensitively with religious and spiritual clients and issues (Bergin, 1991; Henning & Tirrell, 1982).

We think that all therapists, regardless of whether they wish to use spiritual interventions in therapy, should make efforts to increase their sensitivity to religious and spiritual clients and issues. Some of the suggestions that have been offered to help therapists become more aware of issues of diversity also may prove helpful in the religious and spiritual domains. For example, psychotherapists should make efforts to explore and examine their own religious and spiritual heritage, assumptions, biases, and values (cf. Kelly, 1995; Lovinger, 1984). Therapists also should seek to increase their knowledge, understanding, and empathy for religious and spiritual traditions, cultures, and beliefs that are different from their own. Studying books on world religions (e.g., Carmody & Carmody, 1989; Farah, 1994; Jacobs, 1984; Nielsen et al., 1988; Smart, 1994), taking classes on different world religions, and attending religious services of other faiths could all be helpful in this regard. Reading professional literature and taking classes and continuing education seminars in the psychology and sociology of religion and in religious and spiritual issues in mental health and psychotherapy, which are offered at some universities and professional conventions also would be valuable.

In Table 6.1 we summarize some of the foundational attitudes and skills of effective ecumenical therapists. As can be seen, effective ecumenical

TABLE 6.1
Characteristics of Effective Ecumenical Psychotherapists

Characteristic
1. Effective ecumenical therapists are aware of their own religious and spiritual heritage, worldview assumptions, and values and are sensitive to how their own spiritual issues, values, and biases could affect their work with clients from different religious and spiritual traditions.
2. Effective ecumenical therapists seek to understand, respect, and appreciate religious and spiritual traditions, worldviews, and values that are different from their own.
3. Effective ecumenical therapists are capable of communicating interest, understanding, and respect to clients who have religious and spiritual worldviews, beliefs, and values that are different from the therapist.
4. Effective ecumenical therapists seek to understand how a client's religious and spiritual worldview and values affect the client's sense of identity, lifestyle, and emotional and interpersonal functioning, but they are sensitive to how their own religious and spiritual values and beliefs could bias their judgment.
5. Effective ecumenical therapists are sensitive to circumstances (e.g., personal biases, value conflicts, lack of knowledge of the client's religious tradition) that could dictate referral of a religious client to a member of his or her own religious tradition.
6. Effective ecumenical therapists have or seek specific knowledge and information about the religious beliefs and traditions of the religious and spiritual clients with whom they work.
7. Effective ecumenical therapists avoid making assumptions about the beliefs and values of religious and spiritual clients based on religious affiliation alone, but they seek to gain an in-depth understanding of each client's unique spiritual worldview, beliefs, and values.
8. Effective ecumenical therapists understand how to sensitively handle value and belief conflicts that arise during therapy and do so in a manner that preserves the client's autonomy and self-esteem.
9. Effective ecumenical therapists make efforts to establish respectful, trusting relationships with members and leaders in their clients' religious community and seek to draw on these sources of social support to benefit their clients when appropriate.
10. Effective ecumenical therapists seek to understand the religious and spiritual resources in their clients' lives and encourage their clients to use these resources to assist them in their efforts to cope, heal, and change.
11. Effective ecumenical therapists seek to use religious and spiritual interventions that are in harmony with their clients' religious and spiritual beliefs when it appears that such interventions could help their clients cope, heal, and change.

Note. Portions of the ideas in this table were adapted from Sue, D. W., and Sue, D. (1990). *Counseling the culturally different: Theory and practice* (2nd ed., pp. 167–171). New York: Wiley. Adapted with permission of John Wiley & Sons, Inc.

therapists have successfully applied multicultural attitudes and skills to the religious and spiritual domains. As indicated in the Ethical Principles of Psychologists and Code of Conduct of the American Psychological Association (1992), all psychologists, regardless of their religious and spiritual beliefs, have an ethical obligation to seek to acquire these ecumenical attitudes and skills.

Adopting a Denominational Therapeutic Stance

The capacity to adopt a denominational therapeutic stance, when appropriate, also can enhance therapists' effectiveness with some clients. The word *denomination* means "a large group of religious congregations united under a common faith and name and organized under a single administrative and legal hierarchy" (*American Heritage Dictionary of the English Language*, 1992, p. 499). We define a *denominational therapeutic stance* as an approach to therapy that is tailored for clients who are members of a specific religious denomination.

A denominational therapeutic stance builds on the foundation laid earlier in therapy by the therapist's ecumenical stance but differs from the ecumenical stance in that the therapist uses assessment methods and interventions that are tailored more specifically to the client's unique denominational beliefs and practices. When using a denominational approach, therapists also may become more directive, challenging, and educational in their style than they would be when using an ecumenical approach. However, some therapists may never wish to adopt a denominational therapeutic stance with clients. Nonreligious and atheistic therapists, for example, may feel that adopting such a stance would require them to be incongruent with clients or compromise their own beliefs and values. We are not advocating that all psychotherapists should at times adopt a denominational stance, because many therapists will be most helpful to clients if they function only within an ecumenical stance.

Therapists who use a denominational approach should do so only with clients who view them as being able to deeply understand, accept, and respect the client's religious and spiritual culture and beliefs. Such trust and credibility is most likely to occur with clients from the therapist's own religious denomination or from other religious traditions of which the therapist has acquired an in-depth understanding. When such trust and credibility seem to exist, therapists should still not use a denominational approach until a careful assessment of the religious and spiritual beliefs of the client has confirmed that (a) the therapist is confident she or he adequately understands the client's unique beliefs; (b) the client has a positive attitude toward religion and spirituality or is capable of addressing issues of anger, fear, or unhealthy dependency toward religious authorities or God; and (c) the client has stated explicitly that he or she is willing to participate in denominational assessments and interventions.

When it is appropriate, a denominational therapeutic stance can give therapists added leverage to help clients. When therapists have a deep understanding and experiential familiarity with a religious denomination and culture, they are more capable of responding to the fine nuances of a client's religious and spiritual issues. They also are more able to fully appreciate, to honor, and to use the unique religious beliefs and spiritual resources available within the client's religious tradition. Clinical descriptions that illustrate denominational approaches with clients from a number of specific religious denominations have been published (e.g., Kelly, 1995; Koltko, 1990; Lovinger, 1984; Worthington, 1990). These publications provide valuable insight into the complexities and potential benefits of a denominational stance. Throughout the remainder of this book, we discuss various clinical issues (e.g., assessment, ethics, interventions) from both the ecumenical and denominational perspectives to clarify further the differences between these two therapeutic approaches. Tan's (1996) discussion of implicit and explicit integration of religion in clinical practice is also helpful for clarifying our distinction between ecumenical and denominational approaches. An ecumenical therapeutic approach tends to be more implicit in nature, whereas a denominational stance more often involves an explicit use of spiritual resources in therapy.

Build a Spiritually Open and Safe Therapeutic Alliance

Research has consistently shown that regardless of a therapist's theoretical orientation, psychotherapy tends to be the most effective when it occurs in the context of a therapeutic relationship, alliance, or bond. Conditions such as rapport, trust, empathy, warmth, respect, acceptance, and credibility are some of the characteristics of the therapeutic relationship that have been found to be consistently associated with positive therapy outcomes (Lambert & Bergin, 1994). In fact, for many clients it appears that these relationship factors may contribute more powerfully to positive therapy outcomes than do therapy techniques or interventions (Orlinsky, Grawe, & Parks, 1994).

Establishing a trusting therapeutic relationship and a mutual working alliance is crucial whenever a therapist and client wish to explore religious and spiritual issues. Spiritual beliefs and feelings are usually a highly private, even sacred, area of experience for people. If clients do not feel a great deal of trust for their therapists, they are unlikely to freely discuss and work through such sensitive matters. Building a trusting therapeutic alliance with religious and spiritual clients, however, is not always easy. As we discussed in chapter 2, the professions of psychology and psychotherapy historically have been biased against religion and religious believers (Bergin, 1980a).

Many religious and spiritual clients are aware of this bias, and, perhaps not surprisingly, they have fears and suspicions about "secular" psychotherapists and the process of psychotherapy itself (Bergin, 1983; Worthington, 1986).

A letter to the editor from a born-again psychologist published in the Minnesota Psychology Association Newsletter (M. W. H., 1986) illustrates how deeply some religious people distrust psychotherapists and the process of psychotherapy:

> Psychotherapy is one of the most hellish and devastating practices that mankind has contrived. Psychotherapy manipulates, abuses, and destroys those persons who seek help for their problems through it. Psychotherapy makes the "patient" dependent upon the psychotherapist, and I have found psychotherapists to be, for the most part, unspiritual, anti-God, egotistical, and WRONG. Many psychotherapists suffer from the same, or worse, life and personality problems as the persons they pretend to help. (p. 10)

Although such intense suspicions and feelings of distrust undoubtedly represent an extreme view, it nevertheless is the case that a "religiosity gap" exists between many professional psychotherapists and clients (Bergin, 1991). Psychotherapists tend to be less religious than their clients (Bergin & Jensen, 1990), and many people with emotional problems prefer to seek assistance from clergy rather than professional therapists (Chalfant et al., 1990). Worthington and colleagues (Worthington, 1986; Worthington & Scott, 1983) have identified several possible concerns that conservative Christian clients may have about therapists.

> Conservative Christians fear that a secular counselor will (a) ignore spiritual concerns, (b) treat spiritual beliefs and experiences as pathological or merely psychological, (c) fail to comprehend spiritual language and concepts, (d) assume that religious clients share nonreligious cultural norms (e.g., premarital cohabitation, premarital intercourse, divorce), (e) recommend "therapeutic" behaviors that clients consider immoral (e.g., experimentation with homosexuality), or (f) make assumptions, interpretations, and recommendations that discredit revelation as a valid epistemology. (Worthington, 1986, p. 425)

Such concerns about therapists are not uncommon among religious clients from other religious faiths as well, nor are such fears completely unfounded (Bergin, 1980, 1983; Worthington, 1986). Because many clients have such concerns, therapists may need to make added efforts to build trust and establish a therapeutic alliance. In addition, because religious beliefs and spirituality traditionally have not been a domain of clients' experience that psychotherapists have been willing to address (Ganje-Fling & McCarthy, 1991; Henning & Tirrell 1982), clients may not wish, or believe it is appropriate, to discuss such issues in therapy. Thus, therapists may need to communicate explicitly to clients that it is appropriate for them, if they desire, to share and explore their religious and spiritual beliefs and concerns during therapy.

What can psychotherapists do to create a trusting, spiritually safe, and open therapeutic climate? Assuming that they have developed the multicultural attitudes and skills discussed earlier and have successfully generalized these attitudes and skills to the religious and spiritual domains of experience, there are several other specific things they can do. For example, therapists can assess clients' interest in pursuing spiritual issues by using an appropriate intake questionnaire (see chap. 8 in this book). They also should inform clients in their informed consent document that they are willing to discuss and explore religious and spiritual issues in an open, respectful, and sensitive way. Fears that clients have about secular psychotherapists (e.g., that the therapist will view the client's spiritual beliefs as pathological) also could be anticipated and addressed briefly in the informed consent document. Therapists also should inform clients that if it seems appropriate, they may use spiritual interventions, but only after obtaining the client's explicit permission. An example of portions of such an informed consent document is provided in Table 6.2. During therapy sessions, therapists can also, when appropriate, verbally reinforce their openness to the exploration of religious and spiritual issues and respond respectfully to fears their clients may express about psychotherapy.

Therapists also should usually avoid religious symbols, pictures, or dress that "advertises" the therapist's religious affiliation or beliefs. An ecumenical therapeutic stance requires that therapists avoid verbally self-disclosing details about their religious affiliations or beliefs unless clients ask directly for such information, but even then careful exploration of why the question arises may be necessary. Prematurely self-disclosing details about one's affiliation or beliefs may "turn off" clients whose religious affiliation and beliefs differ from those of the therapist. For example, a Christian therapist who prominently displays Christian pictures or symbols in his or her office may, by doing so, make it more difficult to establish rapport and credibility with non-Christian clients. By communicating an openness to exploring religious and spiritual issues without prematurely disclosing specific details about their own religious beliefs, therapists will be more successful at establishing trust and rapport with a wider range of clients.

Psychotherapists also should deal with religious differences and value conflicts that exist between them and their clients in an open, respectful, and tolerant manner. It is inevitable that at times therapists and clients will become aware that they have major differences of opinion with regard to certain beliefs or social values (Corey, Corey, & Callanan, 1993). Differences in religious affiliation and disagreements about specific religious doctrines or moral behaviors (e.g., abortion, premarital and extramarital sex,

TABLE 6.2
Sample Informed Consent Document for a Spiritual Strategy

Information Regarding Counseling Services

Training and Experience

Welcome to the Center for Change. I received my doctorate in counseling psychology in 1988 from the University of Minnesota. Both my doctoral training program and internship training were accredited by the American Psychological Association. I qualified for licensing as a psychologist in the State of Utah by completing additional postdoctoral training and by passing the national psychologist licensing examination. I remain current by attending continuing education workshops and psychological conventions. I also have obtained specialized education and training in working with religious and spiritual issues in counseling by attending professional presentations at conventions, reading professional literature, and consulting with colleagues who have an expertise in spiritual counseling approaches.

My Approach To Counseling

My orientation as a counselor is "eclectic." In selecting treatment methods, therefore, I tend to draw ideas and techniques from a number of the major counseling approaches whose utility have been supported through research (e.g., cognitive therapy, behavioral therapy, client-centered therapy, family systems therapy, and psychodynamic therapy). I also believe that a spiritual perspective is important in counseling, and I am open to exploring any religious or spiritual concerns or issues you might have. I may also suggest that you participate in spiritual practices or interventions that are compatible with your beliefs if I believe they may help in your growth and progress. Of course, you will never be compelled to participate in psychological or spiritual interventions that you do not wish to engage in.

During the early phase of counseling (the first few sessions, generally), I will encourage you to share information with me that will help me understand you and that will help me know more about the nature and history of the concerns that brought you to counseling. As such, I may inquire about a number of aspects of your life (e.g., work, family, church, social relationships, health, spirituality). I also may ask you to take one or more psychological and spiritual assessment tests to help me gain more insight into your concerns.

---

homosexuality) can undermine trust and seriously threaten the therapeutic alliance if they are prematurely or inappropriately addressed or disclosed (Corey et al., 1993; P. S. Richards & Davison, 1989). When such value conflicts become salient during therapy, we believe that it is important for therapists to acknowledge their values openly while also explicitly affirming clients' rights to differ from the therapist without having their intelligence or morality questioned. Therapists should also discuss openly with clients whether the belief or value conflict so threatens the therapeutic alliance that referral is advisable. Handling value conflicts in therapy can be a difficult challenge; further discussion and more specific guidelines regarding this topic are presented later in this chapter in the section on therapeutic valuing and in chapter 7 in the section on ethical issues.

Psychotherapists should also listen carefully and communicate empathy and respect for their clients' belief tradition when clients risk self-disclosing such information. This does not mean that therapists have to agree with their clients' views. However, therapists should remember that for many religious clients, it is anxiety provoking for them to disclose sacred religious and spiritual beliefs because their beliefs may have been discounted, ridiculed, and pathologized (Bergin, 1980a; Worthington, 1986).

The following letter to the editor, which was published in 1989 in the Central Washington University campus newspaper, illustrates an attitude that devoutly religious people often encounter, particularly in professional and academic settings:

> Like most of my contemporaries, religion was force-fed me before I even learned to walk and talk. When I reached age 18, I rebelled by visiting the pastor of my church and telling him that I would discontinue my membership. I stated my reasons: Religion was not derived from common sense, but from superstition resulting from ignorance, fear of the unknown, fear of death. It is based on emotions! . . .
>
> So who do we pray to? Some spirit we invented to help us make it through the day? Sure life is tough. Taking some sort of drug makes it easier. Some turn to alcohol, some to narcotics, some to religion to numb the senses, to soothe, to lull.
>
> Religion has never solved anything. Hitler's SS had "God with us" engraved on their belt buckles. The Jews are convinced of the superiority of their beliefs. So what makes Christians, who claim to be the ones and only, so special?
>
> Ah yes, and the Bible! Every religious cult has its own sacred scriptures. Ours is a historical account of ancient Hebrew tribes, with lots of stone-age level thinking and misinterpretation of natural phenomena mixed in. Also lots of ghost stories and other tales based on imagination rather than fact. As a child I thought it was fascinating. Now I am an adult, and I no longer believe in fairy tales. (E. Pope, 1989, p. 2)

Such attitudes are widespread and are often publicly expressed, even in professional publications (e.g., Ellis, 1980). Because religious people often experience such ridicule, if they do share their spiritual beliefs they often do so apprehensively. Therapists should remember this, and if their clients do disclose some of their beliefs and special experiences, from whatever cultural and family history they may come, therapists should treat this information with as much empathy and respect as they can. It may be useful to acknowledge to clients explicitly, when they have disclosed such information, that it is not always easy to discuss such sensitive, private matters and that they respect the client for having the trust and courage to do so. Letting clients know that they are not viewed as childish, stupid, or deranged for having such beliefs might also be appropriate and necessary on some occasions, even including those in which the beliefs may be dysfunctional from a clinical perspective.

Assess the Religious and Spiritual Dimensions

We endorse a multidimensional, holistic assessment and client conceptualization strategy. Therapists should globally assess how their clients are functioning, including physically, emotionally, socially, cognitively, behaviorally, and spiritually. We are not the first to advocate such an approach, of course. For example, Lazarus (1973, 1976) proposed this in the early 1970s when he described his multimodal behavior therapy. His multimodal assessment approach advocated an examination of each area of a person's BASIC ID: behavior (B), affect (A), sensation (S), imagery (I), cognition (C), interpersonal relationships (I), and drugs or biology (D; Lazarus, 1989). If spiritual (S) were added to this schema, it could become BASIC IDS. Because of the rise in prominence of the eclectic or integrative psychotherapy tradition, many psychotherapists now, to one degree or another, assess and conceptualize their clients in such a multidimensional manner.

A unique contribution a theistic strategy makes to a multidimensional approach is that it provides therapists with a rationale and approach for assessing and conceptualizing the religious and spiritual dimensions of their clients' lives, along with the other dimensions of their functioning. As part of an ecumenical therapeutic stance, during the regular assessment phase of therapy, therapists should globally assess their clients' worldview. That is, to what extent do clients view the world through a Western (monotheistic), Eastern (polytheistic or pantheistic), or naturalistic (scientific) lens? They should also request information about clients' religious and spiritual upbringing, history, current religious affiliation, and beliefs and practices. As they gather this information, along with information about their clients' problems and symptoms, therapists should seek to assess whether their clients' religiosity or spirituality is in some way intertwined with, or contributes to, their clients' problems and disturbance. They should also attempt to determine whether their clients have religious and spiritual resources that could be used in therapy to help promote coping, healing, and change.

Most psychotherapists are not used to routinely gathering information about the religious and spiritual dimensions of their clients' lives, and doing so effectively and sensitively is not necessarily an easy task. Some of this assessment information probably can be obtained fairly quickly through global ecumenical questions on client intake questionnaires or during clinical interviews early in therapy. More specific religious and spiritual assessment information may need to be obtained using denominationally specific questions and assessment measures or by consulting with religious leaders or other experts in their clients' religious tradition. Despite the potential difficulties, we believe that some attention to religious and spiritual issues during assessment is crucial if therapists are to more adequately conceptualize their clients' presenting symptoms and concerns and to better understand how to assist them. In chapter 8, we discuss assessment issues in more depth and offer more detailed rationales and approaches for assessing the religious and spiritual dimensions from ecumenical and denominational therapeutic stances.

Implement Religious and Spiritual Interventions

Therapists should, after carefully assessing and conceptualizing their clients, tailor treatment interventions to fit individual client's unique symptoms and problems. Most therapists now draw on a wide variety of behavioral, cognitive, affective, psychodynamic, and systemic interventions as they seek to tailor their treatments (Jensen & Bergin, 1990). A theistic strategy provides a wide range of explicitly religious and spiritual interventions that most mainstream psychotherapists have not been aware of or systematically used.

The general purposes of these interventions is to help clients affirm their eternal spiritual identity, follow the influence of the Spirit of Truth, and use the spiritual resources and influences in their lives so that they can better cope, heal, grow, and change. Praying for clients, encouraging clients to pray, discussing theological concepts, making reference to scriptures, using spiritual relaxation and imagery techniques, encouraging forgiveness, helping clients live congruently with their spiritual values, self-disclosing spiritual beliefs or experiences, consulting with religious leaders, and using religious bibliotherapy are examples of religious and spiritual interventions that therapists using a theistic, spiritual strategy might use (Ball & Good-year, 1991; Kelly, 1995; P. S. Richards & Potts, 1995a; Worthington, Dupont, Berry, & Duncan, 1988). These interventions and others are discussed in detail in chapters 9 and 10.

Some techniques can be used only by therapists who are religious or spiritually oriented themselves because they require that the therapist believe in God and in spiritual realities (e.g., praying for or with clients, self-disclosing or modeling spiritual experiences or behaviors, sharing one's belief and faith in spiritual realities). However, some interventions can be used by nonreligious therapists because they do not necessarily require that the therapist believe in spiritual realities, but only have a willingness to respect and affirm the client's spiritual beliefs. For example, assessing clients' spiritual worldviews and religious histories, consulting with clients' religious leaders, encouraging clients to use the religious resources in their lives (e.g., prayer, meditation, scripture study, seeking social support from members of their religious community), and analyzing the personality implications of religious doctrine and spiritual concepts are interventions that any therapist could use.

There are several considerations that could influence therapists' decisions about what spiritual interventions, if any, to use with a given client. One major consideration is the severity and nature of the client's disorder.

As illustrated in Figure 6.1, we believe that spiritual interventions and associated social and personal resources are more effective, and can be relied on more heavily, with less disturbed clients (e.g., clients with moderate anxiety and depression, self-esteem problems, interpersonal problems, marriage and family problems, and adjustment disorders). As the severity of the client's disorder increases, the more therapists must rely on technical resources and interventions such as intensive psychotherapy, medication, and hospitalization. This is not to say that spiritual interventions cannot be an important component of treatment with severely and extremely disturbed clients. It just means that, relatively speaking, therapists will need to rely more heavily on technical resources and interventions than on spiritual ones with such clients.

For severe and extreme cases, this is especially true in the early phases of treatment. As the client gets better control of symptoms and cognitive and self-regulatory (ego) processes become more functional, then spiritual, social, and lifestyle factors can be addressed and used more effectively. Thus, when a person's mood disorder is disabling or a person is out of control, discussion of values and spiritual issues could be irrelevant, distracting, or disturbing. After a period of treatment, such interventions may prove very useful, and, near the end of therapy they can help stabilize a lifestyle that will be more resilient and maintaining of the gains made.

Other considerations that could influence a therapist's decision about whether to use a particular spiritual intervention with a client include, for example, the nature of the intervention, the nature of the client's concerns, the client's spiritual status and readiness, and the therapist's comfort with the intervention. We explore these complexities in later chapters.

Therapeutic Valuing

Another contribution the theistic, spiritual strategy makes to one's understanding of the therapist's role is that it provides important insight into how therapists should deal with values in therapy. The theistic world religions make three important assumptions about the nature of morality and values: (a) There are moral absolutes or universals that God has revealed to guide and benefit human beings (Smart, 1983); (b) living one's life in harmony with these moral absolutes or universals is desirable because such principles and commandments promote spiritual growth and harmonious relationships with God and one's fellow human beings; and (c) it is desirable to teach and transmit these values to others (Smart, 1983, 1993). These three theistic assumptions about morality and values have several important implications for psychotherapists and clients.

First, therapists should not adopt an ethically relativistic therapeutic stance. Ethical relativism is questionable (see Bergin, 1980c; R. F. Kitchener, 1980a); all values are not equally valuable and good. Some values are

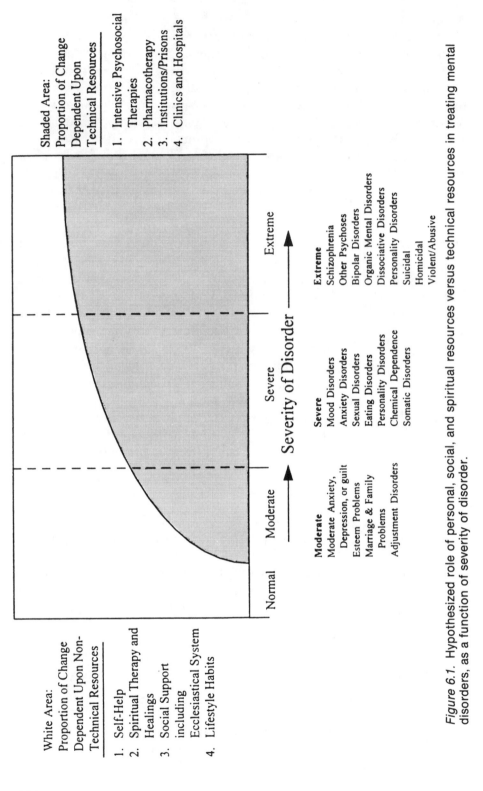

White Area:
Proportion of Change
Dependent Upon Non-
Technical Resources

1. Self-Help
2. Spiritual Therapy and
   Healings
3. Social Support
   including
   Ecclesiastical System
4. Lifestyle Habits

Shaded Area:
Proportion of Change
Dependent Upon
Technical Resources

1. Intensive Psychosocial
   Therapies
2. Pharmacotherapy
3. Institutions/Prisons
4. Clinics and Hospitals

Moderate
Moderate Anxiety,
  Depression, or guilt
Esteem Problems
Marriage & Family
  Problems
Adjustment Disorders

Severe
Mood Disorders
Anxiety Disorders
Sexual Disorders
Eating Disorders
Personality Disorders
Chemical Dependence
Somatic Disorders

Extreme
Schizophrenia
Other Psychoses
Bipolar Disorders
Organic Mental Disorders
Dissociative Disorders
Personality Disorders
Suicidal
Homicidal
Violent/Abusive

Normal   Moderate   Severe   Extreme

Severity of Disorder

Figure 6.1. Hypothesized role of personal, social, and spiritual resources in treating mental disorders, as a function of severity of disorder.

better than others because they do more to promote spirituality, mental health, and harmonious interpersonal and social relations (see chap. 5 in this book; see also Jensen & Bergin, 1988). Second, as we discussed in chapters 4 and 5, metaphysical beliefs and values do affect people's goals, lifestyle, and physical and mental health. Therapists should let clients know that their values do have consequences, and therapists should help clients examine the consequences of their value choices. Third, teaching, endorsing, and modeling healthy moral values is a desirable, ethical, and honorable activity. Therapists should accept that they are value agents and purposely attempt to model and communicate healthy moral and ethical values to their clients (London, 1986; Lowe, 1976). By doing so, they can help clients learn to listen to their conscience, follow the Spirit of Truth, and internalize healthy values that will help optimize their development and growth.

This view of values and therapeutic valuing provides clarity at a time of confusion about values in the psychotherapy profession. Despite the widespread recognition that therapy is a value-laden process (e.g., Bergin, 1980a, 1980b, 1980c; Beutler, 1972; Kessell & McBrearty, 1967; R. F. Kitchener, 1980a; London, 1986; Lowe, 1976; Patterson, 1958), there currently is a great deal of uncertainty and ambiguity in the profession about how therapists should handle values issues (Bergin, Payne, & Richards, 1996). Mixed messages are often sent, and double standards for dealing with values are sometimes adopted by professional organizations. In addition, there currently is a lack of training guidelines and opportunities about how to work ethically with values in therapy. As a result, despite lip service to the notion of not imposing their values on clients, many therapists continue to implicitly advance their value agendas during treatment. There is no reason to believe that the social and cultural "war of values" occurring in the political and public arenas is not also being carried out implicitly in therapy offices with vulnerable, unsuspecting clients.

There are at least four common problematic value styles or approaches in which therapists may be categorized: denyers, implicit minimizers, explicit imposers, and implicit imposers. *Denyers* believe that "maybe some therapists impose their values on clients, but I don't. I am more open-minded and liberal in my views than such therapists. If a client values something, then it must be valuable and okay." Denyers believe that the values of all cultures and clients are equally valuable and good (ethical relativism). They believe there is no right way to believe, a belief that itself is a belief about the right way to believe. Denyers fail to recognize that even their ethically relativistic worldview is value laden and that they do influence their clients with their relativistic values. *Implicit minimizers* believe that "maybe I can't totally keep my values out of therapy, but I can minimize their impact by not sharing them or revealing them to clients." Implicit minimizers do not recognize that failing to be explicit about their values can often be more coercive than being explicit about them.

Explicit imposers believe that "my beliefs and values about various issues (e.g., gender roles, sexual orientation, religion) are correct and that the world will be a better place if I get my clients and society to accept these values. I will be clear and up front with my clients about my value agenda and if they have a problem with this they can look elsewhere for therapy." Explicit imposers zealously and openly proselytize their value agendas with all clients who will listen and, to one degree or another, punish clients who do not agree with them. *Implicit imposers* also believe that "my beliefs and values about various issues are correct and the world will be a better place if I get my clients and society to accept these values." Implicit imposers, however, are not explicit about their value agendas but deliberately, subtly, and covertly attempt to convert clients to their worldview and value agenda. These approaches are problematic because they tend to reduce clients' freedom to grow in their ability to make choices about the direction of their lives.

According to our theistic, spiritual strategy, a moral framework for psychotherapy is possible. By the term *moral framework*, we do not mean a detailed list of moral instructions because this would be contrary to (a) the diversity of clients' orientations even within a theistic orientation and (b) the need for clients to grow by learning to make value choices and accept the consequences thereof. By a moral framework, we mean that there are general moral values or principles available to guide psychotherapy. As discussed earlier, the world religions endorse some common general moral values. Also, as shown in Table 6.3, Jensen and Bergin (1988) found that psychotherapists show high agreement about general values or principles that are important for a mentally healthy lifestyle. Clearly, there is substantial overlap of these value survey results and spiritually based values. Thus, we can appeal both to the psychotherapy profession and to the world's great religious traditions for insight into general healthy values or principles that can be used to guide and evaluate therapy. There is no need to lapse into ethical relativism and the belief that "anything goes."

We assert that it is possible for therapists to both respect client diversity and adopt a strategy for therapy that endorses moral values that facilitate human growth, functioning, and interpersonal relationships. We have called these *health and human welfare values* (see chap. 5 in this book). How can therapists implement this strategy? The most ethical and effective way is to adopt an explicit minimizing value stance. *Explicit minimizers* believe that "I can't keep my values out of therapy, nor is it desirable to totally do so." Explicit minimizers believe that it is important for therapists to be open about the values that influence their therapeutic decisions and recommendations throughout the course of therapy. They also believe that they should openly discuss and help clients examine the values that may be affecting the client's mental health and interpersonal relations. Explicit minimizers believe that by being explicit about values and actively endorsing

TABLE 6.3
Responses by Mental Health Professionals to 10 Value Themes

Theme and Sample Items	Important for a Positive, Mentally Healthy Lifestyle		Important in Guiding and Evaluating Psychotherapy in All or Many Clients
	Total % Agree[a]	% Agree[b]	% Agree
Theme 1 (5 items): Competent perception and expression of feelings	97	87	87
29. Increase sensitivity to others' feelings	98	93	92
30. Be open, genuine, and honest with others	96	86	87
Theme 2 (10 items): Freedom, autonomy, and responsibility	96	88	85
7. Assume responsibility for one's actions	99	98	98
5. Increase one's alternatives at a choice point	100	96	96
11. Increase one's capacity for self-control	99	86	89
10. Experience appropriate feelings of guilt	88	70	65
Theme 3 (9 items): Integration, coping, and work	95	81	81
50. Develop effective strategies to cope with stress	99	97	97
49. Develop appropriate methods to satisfy needs	99	95	94
53. Find fulfillment and satisfaction in work	97	86	82
54. Strive for achievement	83	52	58
Theme 4 (5 items): Self-awareness and growth	92	74	77
37. Become aware of inner potential and ability to grow	96	89	90
42. Discipline oneself for the sake of growth	82	54	59
Theme 5 (12 items): Human relatedness and interpersonal and family commitment	91	77	73
12. Develop ability to give and receive affection	97	94	95
35. Increase respect for human value and worth	98	88	79
17. Be faithful to one's marriage partner[c]	91	78	70
19. Be committed to family needs and child rearing	90	80	76
41. Become self-sacrificing and unselfish	52	26	30

TABLE 6.3 *(cont.)*

Theme and Sample Items	Important for a Positive, Mentally Healthy Lifestyle		Important in Guiding and Evaluating Psychotherapy in All or Many Clients
	Total % Agree[a]	% Agree[b]	% Agree
Theme 6 (3 items): Self-maintenance and physical fitness	91	78	71
45. Practice habits of physical health	94	77	69
46. Apply self-discipline in use of alcohol, tobacco, and drugs	95	83	75
Theme 7 (6 items): Mature values	84	66	68
56. Have a sense of purpose for living	97	87	85
14. Regulate behavior by applying principles and ideals	96	81	78
55. Adhere to universal principles governing mental health	67	47	55
Theme 8 (4 items): Forgiveness	85	64	62
60. Forgive others who have inflicted disturbance in oneself	93	77	78
62. Make restitution for one's negative influence	79	54	51
Theme 9 (9 items): Regulated sexual fulfillment	63	51	49
27. Understand that sexual impulses are a natural part of oneself	97	94	85
24. Have sexual relations exclusively within marriage	63	49	49
25. Prefer a heterosexual sexual relationship	57	43	39
17. Be faithful to one's marriage partner	91	78	70
Theme 10 (6 items): Spirituality and religiosity	49	34	29
69. Seek spiritual understanding of one's place in the universe	68	53	41
68. Seek strength through communion with a Higher Power	50	34	31
67. Actively participate in a religious affiliation	44	28	25

Note. N = 425. The Mentally Healthy Lifestyle Scale provided for seven possible ratings: hi, med, and lo agree; uncertain; and lo, med, and hi disagree. The Guiding and Evaluating Psychotherapy Scale provided for four categories: applicable to all, many, few, or no clients.
[a] Hi, med, and lo.
[b] Hi and med only.
[c] This item appears under two themes (5 and 9). The full scale included 69 items.

consensus values that promote healthy functioning, while also communicating to clients that they have the right to disagree with the therapist's values without fear of therapist condemnation, clients' freedom of choice is maximized.

As they seek to model and teach health and human welfare values, therapists need to keep in mind that they are only one of potentially many "value agents" in their clients' lives. Mainstream society, religious organizations, ethnic-cultural groups, families, and professional organizations (including the psychotherapy profession) potentially have an influence on the values of clients. Although they should not seek to undermine or supplant the other value agents in clients' lives, therapists should help promote clients' awareness of whether these different value influences are affecting them in healthy or unhealthy ways.

Therapists should help clients examine and understand the value influences in their lives and make thoughtful, reasoned choices about what values they wish to internalize and live in harmony with. In attempting to help clients make healthy value choices, it may often be appropriate for therapists to openly but nondogmatically share and discuss their own values, the psychotherapy profession's (mental health) values (see Bergin, 1985; Jensen & Bergin, 1988), and the client's religious tradition's values. However, therapists' primary goal should always be to promote clients' self-determination, not to be a "missionary" for a particular value (Bergin, 1985, 1991). In this sense, we disagree with London's (1986) notion that therapists are or should be "secular priests" but agree with him that moral and values issues must be discussed. Although the "missionary" or "religious authority" roles have appropriate places, they should be distinguished from the role of professional psychotherapists. In chapters 7 and 9, we discuss further our views about how psychotherapists should handle value issues in therapy.

The Therapist's Spiritual Preparation

Another distinctive contribution a theistic strategy makes to one's understanding of the therapist's role is that therapists may seek, and on occasion obtain, transcendent spiritual guidance and enlightenment as they assess, conceptualize, and intervene in their clients' lives. We recognize that this assertion may seem radical, unscientific, and even irrational to nonreligious and atheistic therapists.

However, many therapists, even nonreligious or atheistic ones, probably would agree that psychotherapy is both a rational-empirical and a creative-intuitive process. Many also would acknowledge that as they work with clients, they at times experience "gut-level" hunches or intuitive insights about what assessment questions to ask or interventions to make. We recognize that such experiences need not be interpreted in spiritual terms. In fact, we do not believe all intuitive hunches are examples of transcendent spiritual insights or enlightenment. Sometimes hunches may occur when the complete gestalt of one's clinical experience and impressions come together in a nonrational, holistic manner. Such experiences are difficult to explain in cognitive or intellectual terms, but spiritual explanations need not necessarily be invoked to account for them.

Nevertheless, the belief that God can guide and enlighten human beings spiritually is embraced by orthodox and devout believers in all the theistic world religious traditions. We and other psychotherapists believe that transcendent spiritual guidance and enlightenment, or what we call *meta-empathy*, is possible (Chamberlain, Richards, & Scharman, 1996; C. R. Rogers, personal communication, 1986). Meta-empathy is the ability to synthesize ordinary clinical observations in the creative way that all good clinicians do, but it goes beyond that empirical process to include an openness to inspirational impressions that convey spiritual insights or convictions about the individual that differ from ordinary diagnostic categories or treatment "hunches."

This requires that the therapist enter into meditative, reflective, or prayerful moments before, during, or after sessions. Steady practice with this, based on a degree of faith that "something more" can happen, will result in the ability to separate inspired insights from ordinary clinical hypothesizing or speculating. We think that psychotherapists who believe this should seek to prepare themselves spiritually so that, if God is willing, they occasionally can receive spiritual guidance and enlightenment about how they can assess and treat their clients more effectively. We believe that some of the most powerful healing moments in therapy happen when this occurs. An illustration of such an experience is provided in the following case related by one of us:

A young man who had recently returned from military service sought help from me with a problem of compulsive masturbation. He had a Beck Depression Inventory score of 11 and was diagnosed as dysthymic with identity confusion. As I first analyzed the problem, I decided to use a cognitive–behavioral approach, including rational–emotive therapy and self-regulation techniques. However, during the fourth session, while reflecting meditatively on the client's lack of progress, the meta-empathic intuition came to me that "masturbation is not the problem."

I discussed the meaning of this thought with the client for some time, and we concluded that the real issues concerned his sense of self, his purpose in life, his relationships, and his plans for the future. This was a deeply spiritual and moving experience for both of us. This resulted in a remarkable change in his demeanor and motivation to take responsibility for the next steps, which he did. It also took the focus away from masturbation as a target symptom. Two outside reviewers of the videotape of this session concluded that a tremendous transformation occurred in him during this hour, from a dysthymic state to an integrated sense of focus about self and life that was very hopeful. His case was presented at our weekly Clinical Psychology Case Conference at Brigham Young University's comprehensive clinic. One comment from the audience was, "His therapy is finished. His problem has been resolved!" He did not return for any further counseling for several months.

One of the steps we had felt impressed to focus on in the last session was the client's relationship with three fathers: his Heavenly Father, his biological father, and the father (bishop) of his congregation. He took initiatives on his own in these three areas and then returned months later for a fifth session to discuss how he was progressing and to receive some feedback. The session was oddly different from ordinary therapy because, essentially, he had now taken charge of his own change process. This was a time for using the therapist as a reliability check on his sense of progress. Several months later, we had our sixth encounter, during which he explained that his sense of self and his life focus had become better integrated and that he had chosen to do humanitarian service as a missionary in another country. His posttreatment depression score was a 1!

Consider another meta-empathy experience related by a psychiatrist interviewed in Chamberlain et al.'s (1996) qualitative study of experienced Mormon therapists:

> I have a certain intake format that I use for clients. But I was impressed to ask this woman something about somebody, a grandfather. I said, "Was there anything with your grandpa?" Well, that's not in my history, I don't ask that kind of thing. I ask generally if there was any abuse of any kind, but this was a 65 or 68 year old [woman], who just broke down and cried about how her grandfather had sexually abused her and she'd never told anyone her entire life. . . . I mean, ordinarily, I would never have pursued that. Instead, I would have taken just the general history. (p. 63)

These cases illustrate our view that there are spiritual resources for change that exist beyond the ordinary natural ones that are used clinically, and that some intuitive insights and hunches that occur in therapy come from the divine source. We believe that most often such experiences are not dramatic but that they come as quiet, gentle impressions to the mind and heart of the therapist. These impressions, if genuinely spiritual in nature, will give the therapist important insight into the client and his or her problems and interventions that may be effective. If heeded, such impressions should facilitate clients' therapeutic growth, and clients will often confirm their validity by their reactions.

When therapists receive such impressions, they should not, of course, announce to clients that they have received a revelation from God on the client's behalf. Rather, such impressions should be received quietly, humbly, and privately. Therapists should act on their intuitive impressions cautiously and nondogmatically, remaining open to the possibility that they could be wrong. We hope that therapists who believe in the reality and possibility of spiritual guidance and enlightenment will more often seek it as they assess and treat their clients. Such a practice should increase therapists' capacity to understand accurately the nature of their clients' issues and intervene more effectively.

THE CLIENT'S ROLE

The major psychotherapy traditions, and the theistic, spiritual strategy, have certain common expectations about what clients are supposed to do during therapy. First, they need to show up for therapy and disclose to their therapists their concerns, problems, and symptoms. Clients also are expected to provide background history and assessment information to help their therapists understand them and their perceptions of self, others, and the world. Clients also are expected to try out or participate in interventions designed to assist them in coping with and resolving their presenting problems and concerns and to promote their long-term healing and growth.

The theistic strategy also makes three additional unique contributions to the understanding of the client's role in psychotherapy. First, for complete healing and growth, it is important for clients to examine and understand how their religious and spiritual background and beliefs affect their emotional and interpersonal functioning. Clients are not forced to do this, of course, but are invited to explore how their beliefs may affect their lives. Second, it is important for clients to attend to their spiritual needs and growth, along with their emotional or interpersonal issues and to understand how these may be intertwined. This may involve an examination of doubts and concerns or an exploration and facilitation of the client's spirituality and spiritual goals and aspirations. Third, it is important for clients to draw on the spiritual resources in their lives to assist them in their efforts to change. Clients who believe in God are encouraged to seek God's guidance, enlightenment, and healing power to help them cope, heal, and grow better. They also may need to seek and obtain social, emotional, or spiritual support and guidance from members of their spiritual community.

NATURE OF THE THERAPY RELATIONSHIP

We agree with Rogers (1951, 1961) that unconditional positive regard, warmth, genuineness, and empathy are essential conditions of a professional therapeutic relationship. In addition to these foundational conditions, as discussed earlier, we think it is essential that the therapeutic relationship is spiritually open and safe. Clients need to know that it is okay to talk about their religious and spiritual beliefs and concerns and that when they do, their therapist seeks to understand and empathize with them. Clients must also know that they have the right to have different religious and spiritual beliefs than those of their therapist and that their therapist will not attempt to proselyte or convert them.

According to our theistic spiritual strategy, the therapeutic relationship must also be characterized by honesty and a respect for clients' autonomy and freedom of choice. Therapists should encourage clients honestly and openly to explore their values and lifestyle choices, particularly if therapists perceive that clients' values and lifestyle choices are contributing to their presenting problems and symptoms. However, therapists must do this respectfully and with utmost regard for their clients' autonomy and freedom of choice. Therapists may find it necessary on occasion to tell clients that they regard their values or lifestyle choices as physically or psychologically unhealthy, but this should be done in a noncondemning, nonshaming manner. Therapists should also make it clear that their clients have the right to disagree with them regarding values, beliefs, and lifestyle choices without fear of punishment or arbitrary withdrawal of services.

According to our spiritual strategy, to be optimally healing, the therapeutic relationship must also include the quality of charity or brotherly and sisterly love (Fromm, 1956). According to Fromm,

> the most fundamental kind of love, which underlies all types of love, is *brotherly love*. By this I mean the sense of responsibility, care, respect, knowledge of any other human being, the wish to further his life. This is the kind of love the Bible speaks of when it says: love thy neighbor as thyself. Brotherly love is love for all human beings. (p. 39)

According to our theistic spiritual strategy, there is a spiritual quality to the therapeutic relationship at its best that is characterized by brotherly and sisterly love and a deep spiritual connection. Therapists should seek to care about and love their clients in an ethically appropriate manner. By caring deeply about their clients' emotional and spiritual welfare, growth, and autonomy, therapists can create a climate and therapeutic relationship that is emotionally and spiritually healing.

We believe that another important characteristic of the therapeutic relationship is that it should be spiritually affirming. Therapists should seek to affirm in culturally sensitive and appropriate ways that their clients are creations or children of God who have eternal, divine potential and worth. According to our spiritual strategy, and as illustrated in our case reports in chapter 5, when clients experience a deep affirmation of their eternal, spiritual identity and worth, this is often a life transforming event for them. Feeling God's love and the love of others (including their therapist) is often what helps connect clients with their sense of spiritual identity and worth. We think, therefore, that love has great power for healing clients' wounds.

Of course, many clients are not easy to care about. In addition, many clients, and some therapists, have problems with maintaining appropriate

TABLE 6.4
Unique Contributions of the Theistic, Spiritual Strategy to the Understanding of Psychotherapy

Goals of Therapy	Therapist's Role in Therapy	Role of Spiritual Techniques	Client's Role in Therapy	Nature of the Therapy Relationship
Spiritual view is part of an eclectic, multisystemic view of humans and so therapy goals depend on the client's issues. Goals directly relevant to the spiritual dimension include the following: (a) Help clients affirm their eternal spiritual identity and live in harmony with the Spirit of Truth; (b) assess what impact religious and spiritual beliefs have in	Adopt an ecumenical therapeutic stance and, when appropriate, a denominational stance. Establish a warm, supportive environment in which the client knows it is safe and acceptable to explore his or her religious and spiritual beliefs, doubts, and concerns. Assess whether clients' religious and spiritual beliefs and activities are affecting their	Interventions are viewed as very important for helping clients understand and work through religious and spiritual issues and concerns, and for helping clients draw on religious and spiritual resources in their lives to assist them in better coping, growing and changing. Examples of major interventions include cognitive	Examine how their religious and spiritual beliefs and activities affect their behavior, emotions, and relationships. Make choices about what role religion and spirituality will play in their lives. Set goals and carry out spiritual interventions designed to facilitate their spiritual and emotional growth. Seek to use the religious and spiritual resources in their	Unconditional positive regard, warmth, genuineness, and empathy are regarded as an essential foundation for therapy. Therapists also seek to have charity or brotherly and sisterly love for clients and to affirm their eternal spiritual identity and worth. Clients are expected to form a working alliance and share in the work of change. Clients must

clients' lives and whether they have unmet spiritual needs; (c) help clients use religious and spiritual resources to help them in their efforts to cope, change, and grow; (d) help clients resolve spiritual concerns and doubts and make choices about role of spirituality in their lives; and (e) help clients examine their spirituality and continue their quest for spiritual growth.

mental health and interpersonal relationships. Implement religious and spiritual interventions to help clients more effectively use their religious and spiritual resources in their coping and growth process. Model and endorse healthy values. Seek spiritual guidance and enlightenment on how best to help clients.

restructuring of irrational religious beliefs, transitional figure technique, forgiveness, meditation and prayer, Scripture study, blessings, participating in religious services, spiritual imagery, journaling about spiritual feelings, repentance, and using the client's religious support system.

lives to assist them in their efforts to heal and change. Seek God's guidance and enlightenment about how to better cope, heal, and change.

trust the therapist and believe that it is safe to share their religious and spiritual beliefs and heritage with the therapist. Clients must know that the therapist highly values and respects their autonomy and freedom of choice and that it is safe for them to differ from the therapist in their beliefs and values, even though the therapist may at times disagree with their values and confront them about unhealthy values and lifestyle choices.

interpersonal boundaries. Thus, in saying that therapists should seek to have brotherly or sisterly love for their clients, we wish to add some caveats. First, with some clients, perhaps the best that therapists can do is to tolerate them. In some cases, even this cannot be achieved, and making an appropriate referral is the best option. Second, by loving clients, we of course do not mean that therapists may get sexually involved with them. Sexual intimacies between therapists and clients are clearly unethical (American Psychological Association, 1992) and harmful. When therapists become sexually involved with clients, their caring and love becomes destructive and pathologizing instead of healing. Therapists must keep their boundaries clear and maintain appropriate professional relationships with all their clients.

CONCLUSION

The unique and important contributions that a theistic, spiritual strategy makes to the understanding of psychotherapy (Bergin, 1988; Bergin & Payne, 1991) are summarized in Table 6.4. We believe that psychotherapists who incorporate this strategy into an integrative form of therapy will be more likely to (a) fully understand and empathize with their religious clients; (b) recognize cultural blind spots that cause them to unknowingly show disrespect or a lack of sensitivity to their clients' religious and spiritual values; (c) successfully contextualize their interventions so that they are in harmony with their clients' religious and spiritual beliefs; and (d) competently use religious and spiritual resources in their clients' lives that can powerfully assist their clients' efforts to cope, heal, and grow (P. S. Richards & Potts, 1995a).

7

ETHICAL ISSUES AND GUIDELINES

Psychotherapist have . . . two functions, one scientific and one moralistic . . . the scientific function . . . is that of manipulators of behavior . . .
their moralistic function is that of a secular priesthood.

—*Perry London*

Psychotherapists who use a theistic, spiritual strategy are faced with
a number of potentially difficult ethical questions and challenges. Dual
relationships (religious and professional), displacing or usurping religious
authority, imposing religious values on clients, violating work-setting
(church–state) boundaries, and practicing outside the boundaries of professional competence have been cited as potential ethical pitfalls for such
therapists (Bergin, Payne, & Richards, 1996; P. S. Richards & Potts, 1995a;
Tan, 1994; Tjelveit, 1986; Younggren, 1993).

We agree that such dangers do exist, although therapists can take steps
to minimize and avoid them. In this chapter, we discuss each of these
ethical dilemmas mentioned earlier. We also provide a checklist of ethical
recommendations regarding each one to help therapists implement a spiritual strategy ethically. Throughout this chapter, we also present a number
of ethical dilemma case vignettes to illustrate the principles we discuss and
to stimulate reflection and critical analysis. Note that the guidelines and
suggestions offered here are for psychologists and other mental health profes-

sionals, not for pastoral counselors or clergy. Although clergy members may find some of these perspectives useful, we acknowledge their right to define their own ethical guidelines.

DUAL (RELIGIOUS AND PROFESSIONAL) RELATIONSHIPS

The ethical guidelines and codes of all of the major mental health professions contain cautions and prohibitions against engaging in dual or multiple relationships with clients (e.g., American Association for Marriage and Family Therapy [AAMFT], 1985; American Counseling Association [ACA], 1995; American Psychiatric Association, 1986; American Psychological Association [APA], 1992; National Federation of Societies for Clinical Social Work [NFSCSW], 1985). Such relationships are discouraged, and sometimes prohibited, because it is widely recognized that they place clients at risk of being exploited or otherwise harmed by therapists (Corey, Corey, & Callanan, 1993; Herlihy & Golden, 1990; Pope, 1985). There are a variety of dual relationships that psychotherapists should avoid; for example, they should not be a client's (a) therapist and lover, (b) therapist and personal friend, (c) therapist and business partner, (d) therapist and professor, or (e) therapist and supervisor (Corey et al., 1993; Keith-Spiegel & Koocher, 1985).

Religious psychotherapists also should seek to avoid therapist–religious leader and therapist–religious associate dual relationships, except when well-defined pastoral counseling with clear boundary conditions has been set up as a congregational service. Therapist–religious leader dual relationships occur when therapists who hold ecclesiastical positions in their religious denomination (e.g., priest, minister, rabbi, or bishop) provide therapy in a mental health setting, or charge a fee for therapy, to members of their faith over whom they have ecclesiastical responsibility or authority. Although such relationships are not common because only a minority of psychotherapists hold ecclesiastical positions, when they occur they are problematic for several reasons.

First, in such situations, there is a great danger that boundaries between the roles of mental health professionals and ecclesiastical leaders will be violated. For example, therapists might perform ecclesiastical functions in the professional setting that they should perform only in the religious setting and in their ecclesiastical role (e.g., absolving or pardoning their clients' sins on behalf of a church). Second, clients may feel unsafe freely disclosing and exploring all of their concerns when the therapist has religious authority over them. For example, clients may feel less willing to discuss sexual problems, violent episodes, or financial misdeeds if the therapist has authority to take ecclesiastical action against them (e.g., excommunicate them). Third, the potential for a conflict of interest is greater in such situations. For example, to profit financially, therapists could misuse their ecclesiastical authority by referring large numbers of members over whom they have ecclesiastical authority to their private practice psychotherapy office. Fourth, normal friendships or working relationships requiring close cooperation within the congregation and the counseling itself could be compromised by the ecclesiastical leader being privy to too much private information about too many people with whom he or she associates and works. Fifth, in the case of confessed child abuse, clergy may not be legally required to report it, but therapists are. If religious leaders provide professional therapy to members of their congregation, they would have to violate the "clergy-penitant" privilege and report the abuse, thereby undermining the confidence and trust they enjoy as a religious leader.

Because of such potential problems, therapist–religious leader dual relationships should be avoided. This does not mean that ecclesiastical leaders, even those who are licensed therapists, cannot ever provide counseling to members of their own congregations. Ecclesiastical leaders may have this right by virtue of their religious calling, but we believe they should only provide such services (a) free of charge; (b) in an appropriate religious setting; (c) after making it clear that they are providing the counseling or therapy in their role as the member's ecclesiastical leader; and (d) with the understanding that the content addressed will be specific to pastoral issues and not range indiscriminately into the wide variety of emotional problems members may be subject to, which generally would be best referred to a mental health professional.

Therapist–religious associate dual relationships occur when psychotherapists who are active in their religious community but who do not hold positions of ecclesiastical authority provide therapy to members who belong to the same religious congregation (see Exhibit 7.1 for a case example). Such relationships are more common than therapist and religious leader dual relationships and are problematic for several reasons. First, if therapists provide psychotherapy to members of their own congregation, the likelihood that they will be unable to avoid outside social contacts with such clients is greater because they will, in all likelihood, see these clients in the religious setting. When frequent social contacts outside the therapy hour occur, the risk increases that the therapist will get caught in a therapist–personal friend, therapist–lover, or therapist–business partner dual relationship. Second, clients who are working with a therapist from their own congregation may feel awkward and uncomfortable when they see the therapist at religious meetings and social gatherings because they know the therapist has heard their whole life story with all of its embarrassing details. Some clients may actually avoid attending religious meetings and activities out of embarrassment or fear that they will see the therapist. Third, there is a greater risk that therapists will inadvertently violate their clients' privacy and confidentiality when they also have contact with their clients in a religious setting. For

EXHIBIT 7.1
Ethical Dilemma Case Vignette 1: Therapist–Religious Associate Dual Relationships

Case Description

While living in a small rural community in the midwestern United States during the last year of his doctoral program, Bill was contacted by the religious leader of his congregation and asked whether he would provide marital counseling to a couple who also attended this congregation and with whom Bill and his wife had socialized on occasion. Bill explained to the religious leader that it would be inappropriate for him to provide counseling to the couple because of dual relationship concerns. The religious leader told Bill that the couple had specifically requested to meet with him because he was a member of their faith (Seventh-Day Adventist) and that they would not go to a non-Adventist therapist. The religious leader pointed out that there were no other Seventh-Day Adventist therapists available within 150 miles of their community and again petitioned Bill to see the couple.

Questions

1. Do you believe Bill should consider seeing the couple? If so, why? If not, why?
2. Bill tells the religious leader that he must consult with his supervisor to determine whether he can see the couple. If you were Bill's supervisor or colleague, what would you advise him?
3. If Bill decides to talk to the couple, what are some conditions or boundaries he should establish in this situation to minimize the risks?
4. What are the ethical principles that should guide Bill's decision making in this case?

Discussion

In our view, there are two ethical principles that must be considered in this case: (a) avoiding dual relationships and (b) promoting the couple's welfare. We believe that Bill should not engage in a dual relationship with the couple. Although it might seem that Bill is failing to promote the clients' welfare by not providing therapy to them, he might actually harm them more by doing so. We would advise Bill to talk to the couple and express his wish that he could help them, but also help the couple understand the problems associated with dual relationships and that, ultimately, his efforts to help them could do them more harm than good. Bill could discuss with the couple their concerns about seeing a non-Adventist therapist and recommend one that he felt confident would understand and respect their religious beliefs and values. He could invite them to call him if they had any questions or concerns about their non-Adventist therapist, although again making it clear that he could not become their therapist. If the couple refused to see the therapist Bill recommended, Bill could recommend some marital self-help literature for the couple. He could also recommend that they counsel with their religious leader further about their problems. Bill could also offer to provide some information and training about marriage counseling to the religious leader. Bill could also consider offering an educationally oriented (nontherapeutic) marriage enrichment seminar for couples in the community and invite the couple to attend.

example, therapists may have difficulty remembering in which setting they learned something about the client and may inadvertently disclose something that the client told them during therapy that should have been kept confidential. Even telling a client that one needs to reschedule an appointment could represent a major breach of confidentiality if it is done in the religious setting and is overheard by someone. Fourth, clients may broach therapy concerns in the religious setting (e.g., about their issues or concerns about treatment) that can be awkward and even destructive of the religious associate relationship.

Because of these and other potential concerns, therapist–religious associate dual relationships should be avoided. We recognize that it is not always easy to avoid requests to provide professional services to members of one's own religious congregation. Many religious people do prefer to seek psychological help from professionals who share their religious faith (Worthington, 1986), and so they will often request assistance from a professional in their own congregation whom they already know and trust. This is particularly true in rural communities where there are few mental health professionals and even fewer who share the client's religious beliefs. Nevertheless, great care needs to be exercised before entering into such relationships, even in situations such as the one just mentioned. Protection can be provided for both client and therapist by having such therapeutic arrangements approved and monitored by an agreed-on third party or board of review.

Checklist of Ethical Recommendations: Avoiding Dual Relationships

The following represents our attempt to outline some central "dos and don'ts" for therapists in avoiding dual relationships:

1. Therapists should avoid therapist–religious leader and therapist–religious associate dual relationships.
2. After carefully considering the circumstances, if a therapist believes that a dual relationship may be in a person's best interest, the therapist should, before entering into such a relationship, consult with his or her supervisor and professional colleagues to see whether they agree.
3. If the therapist and professional colleagues agree that the risk of a professional–religious dual relationship is warranted, the therapist should carefully define and limit the extent of the dual relationship and explain the risks and boundaries to the client.
4. The therapist should consult frequently with his or her professional colleagues about the case as the dual relationship proceeds. If, at any time, the client, the therapist, or the thera-

pist's professional colleagues believe the client is being harmed by the dual relationship, the therapist should terminate the relationship and refer the client to another therapist.

5. The therapist should continue to consult with and inform professional colleagues about the case until the dual relationship has ended and until the case has been carefully documented.

DISPLACING OR USURPING RELIGIOUS AUTHORITY

Another ethical danger that all psychotherapists need to be aware of and avoid is that of displacing, usurping, or undermining the authority and credibility of their clients' religious leaders. We recognize, as discussed in chapter 2, that some early leaders in psychiatry and psychology (along with other scientists) deliberately sought to challenge and undermine religious tradition and authority. As the authority of religious leaders declined, some psychotherapists tended to play the role of "secular priests," thus assuming some important functions traditionally fulfilled by religious leaders (London, 1964, 1986; Lowe, 1976). In discussing this phenomenon, Lowe (1976) observed that "many therapists would happily preempt the theologian's traditional role completely" (p. 233). Lowe's observation is probably still correct. We believe that it is time for this to change.

There are several ways in which psychotherapists may undermine the authority and credibility of their clients' religious leaders. Perhaps the most benign way this occurs is by therapists' failure to consult, cooperate with, or refer to the religious leader or pastoral counselor. Ethical guidelines of the mental health professions state that their members should treat helpers from other professional specialties with respect and collaborate with or refer to these professionals if this would appear to be in the best interest of their clients (ACA, 1995; American Psychiatric Association, 1986; APA, 1981, 1992). Most psychotherapists routinely consult and collaborate with allied mental health professionals (e.g., marriage and family therapists, psychiatrists, psychologists, school counselors, social workers), and they also occasionally do so with other professionals (e.g., physicians, educators, lawyers). However, most mainstream psychotherapists rarely consult, collaborate with, or refer to their clients' ecclesiastical or religious leaders.

Not consulting with clients' religious leaders is unfortunate because clients' religious leaders and community can sometimes be a great resource. For example, when clients are suicidal, isolated, grieving, or lonely, the social support of members of the religious community can be of great assistance in helping clients cope. Some religious communities can provide financial or employment assistance when clients need such help. When clients feel a lack of meaning and life purpose, religious communities can provide opportunities for fulfilling altruistic service. Psychotherapists have an ethical obligation to make efforts to tap into these resources, when appropriate, on behalf of their clients (see Exhibit 7.2).

Another way therapists may displace the authority of their clients' religious leaders is to confuse the boundaries between their role and the role of their clients' authorized ecclesiastical leaders. This occurs when the therapist takes on tasks and functions that are only appropriately performed by the client's ecclesiastical or spiritual leaders or when the client perceives that the therapist is performing such tasks and functions. Therapists who use spiritual interventions may be vulnerable to such boundary violations and need to give careful thought about how they can keep their role clear from that of their clients' religious leaders (see Exhibit 7.3).

Unfortunately, it is not easy to keep these role boundaries clear because there is considerable overlap between the roles and functions that each profession fulfills (Ganje-Fling & McCarthy, 1991). For instance, both psychotherapists and spiritual leaders provide counseling and direction to their

EXHIBIT 7.2
Ethical Dilemma Case Vignette 2: Consulting With Religious Leaders

Case Description
Debbie was a licensed psychologist in Texas who worked in a private practice outpatient setting. George, a devout Christian (Baptist), presented for treatment because of severe depression that began after his wife divorced him approximately 6 months after they moved to Texas. During the first session, Debbie's assessment revealed that George was very suicidal. Debbie also ascertained that George had no family members or close friends in the area because of his recent arrival in Texas and because George had depended almost exclusively on his ex-wife to fulfill his emotional and social needs.

Question
1. In addition to typical psychological interventions (e.g., getting a contract, removing weapons and toxic drugs from George's home, instilling hope), how might consulting with George's religious leader help him?

Discussion
As part of the treatment of suicidality, therapists should help clients build support systems to avoid isolation. Because George is a devout Baptist, it is possible that he has established some contact with a Baptist congregation in the community. Even if he has not yet, Debbie should encourage him to reach out to members in his religious community during his time of isolation and need. She should also ask George for permission to contact George's religious leader. Once permission is granted, Debbie should contact George's leader and help him or her understand George's circumstances and needs and ask the leader if there is any support and resources available in the religious community to assist George. Hopefully, George's religious leader will mobilize some fellowshipping and social support from within the religious community to assist George and perhaps some meaningful activities and service that George can become involved in to help him overcome his isolation and hopelessness.

EXHIBIT 7.3
Ethical Dilemma Case Vignette 3: Displacing Religious Authority

Case Description
Steve was a licensed psychologist who provided therapy for an outpatient mental
    health clinic in Utah. Steve was an active member of the Mormon church. The
    Mormon church has a lay priesthood, and, in addition to his professional work,
    Steve was an "elder" in the church and served in a leadership position in his
    congregation. As part of his work at the mental health clinic, Steve led a
    therapy group for Mormon men and women who struggled with depression.
    One evening, near the end of an emotional group session in which a client
    named Janet (who was not a member of Steve's congregation) had shared
    spiritual concerns and doubts she was struggling with, another group member
    suggested that Steve give Janet a priesthood blessing (a religious and spiritual
    ordinance normally provided by religious leaders or close family members).
    Janet immediately expressed her desire for Steve to do this, and one of the
    male group members offered to assist Steve in giving the blessing.

Questions
1. Should Steve give Janet a priesthood blessing? Why or why not?
2. What ethical principles should guide Steve's decision?
3. What would be the best way for Steve to handle this dilemma?

Discussion
In our view, Steve should not give Janet a blessing. If Steve were to do so, he
    would be performing a function that, in the Mormon tradition, should be ful-
    filled by Janet's religious leaders or authorized family members. If Steve gave
    the blessing, he would be displacing or taking over a role that was not rightfully
    his. He would also be engaging in a dual relationship (therapist–religious
    leader or therapist–friend). Steve should remind Janet and the other group
    members that priesthood blessings should be given through appropriate
    priesthood channels and that he is not in such a position; he is her profes-
    sional psychotherapist, and it is inappropriate for him to step out of that role
    into some other role. Steve should validate Janet's desire to receive a blessing
    and encourage her to seek it from her religious leaders or authorized family
    members.

clientele. They may also explore similar issues with clients (e.g., personal-
emotional, relationships, religious and spiritual; Ganje-Fling & McCarthy,
1991). Nevertheless, in most religions there are some official functions that
ecclesiastical leaders perform that lay members, or nonmembers, are not
allowed to perform (e.g., absolving or pardoning sins, making authoritative
pronouncements about doctrine, performing religious ordinances or rituals,
giving blessings or ordinations). Psychotherapists should not perform such
functions unless they have ecclesiastical authority themselves and are clearly
and appropriately functioning in an ecclesiastical role.

The most blatant way therapists undermine the credibility of religious
leaders is to say or do things that denigrate or otherwise communicate a
lack of respect for them (e.g., ridicule advice clients receive from their
religious leaders; suggest that clients' religious leaders are superstitious, in-
competent, or deluded; make derogatory comments about religion or religious leaders in general). Such behavior is not only unethical, but it is also

often unhelpful to the client and may even backfire and undermine the credibility of the therapist. Many devoutly religious clients hold their religious leaders in high regard, even if the leaders have done something to hurt or offend them. Clients could feel offended, and lose trust in their therapists, if therapists ridicule or criticize the leaders whom they respect and admire.

This does not mean that if clients wish to express feelings of anger, distrust, or ridicule toward religious leaders themselves that it should not be permitted. Listening and seeking to understand and empathize with clients who express such feelings can be appropriate and helpful, but therapists should not use such situations as an opportunity to air their own issues and biases toward religious authorities. It would benefit many clients if therapists moved beyond historical and personal biases and rifts and made greater efforts to cooperate and collaborate with their clients' religious or spiritual leaders.

Checklist of Ethical Recommendations: Collaborating With Religious Authorities

The following represents our attempt to outline some central "dos and don'ts" for therapists in collaborating with their clients' religious leaders:

1. In initial assessment interviews with clients, therapists should find out whether their clients (a) are affiliated with any particular religious tradition or denomination and (b) view their religious leaders as a possible source of support and assistance.
2. If clients view their religious leaders and community as a source of support, therapists should ask such clients whether they are willing to allow the therapist to consult and cooperate with their religious leaders if it seems appropriate.
3. Therapists should obtain a written release from their clients before consulting or talking with clients' religious leaders. When obtaining the written release, therapists should clearly explain to clients the purpose of the consultation and what general information they plan to share with religious leaders. Therapists should also ask clients to give their religious leaders a release of information.
4. When consulting with a religious leader, therapists should (a) briefly introduce themselves; (b) mention they are seeing_____ (the client's name) in therapy and that the client gave them permission to talk to the religious leader; (c) clearly explain that the purpose of the phone call is to provide information, or seek information, about the client

for the purpose of helping the person better cope with and resolve his or her problems; and (d) confirm that the client has also given the leader permission to talk about his or her case.

5. If the religious leader communicates a willingness to talk, the therapist and leader should share only information that they believe is needed for both of them to be of optimal assistance.

6. Therapists should respectfully thank religious leaders for their assistance, ask for permission to contact the leader again if needed, and invite him or her to contact them for assistance with the client, if needed.

7. Before using spiritual interventions, therapists should explicitly explain to their clients that "they have no religious or ecclesiastical authority over the client and that they cannot speak for or act on behalf of the church or its leaders" (P. S. Richards & Potts, 1995a, p. 169). Therapists may wish to put this in writing in their informed consent document, or they can explain this verbally.

8. Therapists should make efforts to find out what functions their clients' religious leaders might perform on behalf of their members that require official ecclesiastical authority (e.g., hearing confessions, absolving or pardoning sins, giving blessings). Therapists should not perform such functions themselves.

9. Therapists should clarify where their therapeutic role overlaps with the role of their clients' religious leaders. For example, therapists and religious leaders often both provide individual, marital, and family counseling, and both may explore career, emotional, sexual, relationship, and spiritual issues. Therapists should be sensitive to these areas of overlap and make sure clients understand that they have a choice about from whom they seek assistance. It may often be appropriate for clients to seek assistance from both a professional therapist and their religious leader, and therapists should encourage clients to do this when appropriate.

10. When using a particular spiritual intervention (e.g., prayer, religious imagery), therapists should make sure their clients believe that it is appropriate for them to participate in that intervention during therapy. Clients may believe that some spiritual interventions or activities should be done only in private or in cooperation with their religious leader. Therapists should ascertain whether this is the case before proceeding with a spiritual intervention.

11. Therapists should not demean, criticize, or ridicule their clients' religious leaders.

12. When clients criticize or express anger toward God or their religious leaders, it is appropriate for therapists to listen empathically and to seek to understand and sensitively explore their clients' feelings and experiences. However, therapists should not add their own criticisms or tell their own "horror stories" about religion in such situations.

13. Therapists should let their clients know that, in general, they view religious leaders and communities as a potential resource and support.

14. In their relationships with clients and religious leaders, therapists should attempt to communicate and demonstrate courtesy and respect.

IMPOSING RELIGIOUS VALUES

The ethical guidelines of the mental health professions encourage their members to respect individual differences in values (AAMFT, 1985; ACA, 1995; American Psychiatric Association, 1986; APA, 1992; NFSCSW, 1985). For example, the APA's (1992) ethical guidelines state that "in their work related activities, psychologists respect the rights of others to hold values, attitudes, and opinions that differ from their own" (p. 1599).

It is now widely recognized that psychotherapy is a value-laden process and that all psychotherapists, to one degree or another, communicate their values (e.g., health, political, social, philosophical, religious) to their clients (Bergin, 1980a; Tjeltveit, 1986). Thus, Christian, Jewish, Muslim, atheist, agnostic, feminist, gay activist, Democrat, Republican, or Marxist therapists could be susceptible to imposing their values on clients, and they need to make conscious efforts to avoid doing this. By the word *imposing*, we mean using coercive methods to indoctrinate or influence clients, especially concerning therapy session content that is not relevant to the disorder or problem being treated. As we discussed in chapter 6, this does not preclude sharing ideas about value issues pertinent to clients' problems in an open and nonthreatening manner.

Critics of, and some participants in, the spiritual therapy movement have expressed concern that therapists who use a spiritual strategy may be especially likely to violate ethical guidelines by imposing their religious values on clients (P. S. Richards & Potts, 1995a; Seligman, 1988). We do not believe that therapists who use a spiritual strategy are any more likely to violate their clients' value autonomy than are other therapists. In fact, the spiritual strategy's emphasis on therapists' making their values explicit at appropriate times during therapy (see chap. 6 in this book) actually makes it less likely that this will occur. Nevertheless, there is still a danger that therapists who use a spiritual strategy could try to impose their values on clients. There are several ways that this could occur.

One form of religious value imposition occurs when therapists attempt to preach, teach, or otherwise persuade clients that their own particular religious or spiritual ideology, denomination, cause, or worldview is the most correct, worthwhile, moral, or healthy. Examples of religious proselytizing include but are not limited to (a) giving clients literature about the therapist's religious denomination or spiritual tradition, (b) inviting clients to attend services at the therapist's place of worship, and (c) teaching clients about the therapist's religious beliefs when such information is irrelevant to the client's issues and goals. Such religious proselytizing is clearly unethical. Therapists should not use therapy as a vehicle for promoting their particular religious or spiritual ideology or cause. This does not mean therapists cannot tell clients about their religious and spiritual beliefs at times. However, therapists should share such information only if clients ask them to, if it is clear that the therapist's beliefs may be pertinent and useful in helping clients with their issues and problems, and if the risks to the relationship caused by self-disclosure are minimal. Therapists should not disclose such information with the intent of converting clients to the therapist's ideology or denomination, but only for the purpose of alleviating the specific personal difficulties for which the client is seeking help.

Another form of value imposition occurs when therapists explicitly or implicitly tell clients that they are spiritually bad or deficient because of their behavior or lifestyle choices (e.g., regarding abortion, sexual orientation, gender roles, marital fidelity). It may be appropriate for ecclesiastical and spiritual leaders to tell people they behaved wickedly, but it is not for psychotherapists. Although therapists need to help clients examine their lifestyle choices, and the consequences of them, therapists should not attempt to influence clients to change their values or lifestyle by condemning or shaming them. This does not, however, preclude using the therapeutic technique of moral confrontation, which has proved useful in work with abusers and addicts.

This also does not mean that therapists should not make judgments about the possible consequences of their clients' lifestyle choices and warn clients about them. Nor does it mean that therapists cannot tell clients that they disagree with their clients' values or lifestyle choices. For example, therapists should inform clients that certain behaviors may put their physical, mental, and spiritual health at risk (e.g., drug abuse and promiscuous sex could increase the risk of AIDS, marital conflict and divorce, addiction, legal charges, and excommunication from the church) and that they disagree with such behaviors (see Exhibit 7.4). However, such information should be given to clients respectfully, with an explicit message that clients have

EXHIBIT 7.4
Ethical Dilemma Case Vignette 4:
Confronting Unhealthy Client Values

Case Description

Fran was a psychotherapist and a devout Lutheran who worked in a community mental health center in a midsize city in the eastern United States. For 6 weeks, Fran had been providing therapy to Robert, a 27-year-old, nonreligious, married man. Robert's presenting concerns were marital problems and depression. During the past two sessions, Robert had disclosed to Fran that on two occasions recently while his wife was out of town on business trips, he had arranged for sexual liaisons with prostitutes. Robert had also admitted to a long history of sexual promiscuity beginning in his teenage years and continuing to the present. He said he believed his wife was not aware of his marital infidelity because of her heavy involvement in her career. Robert expressed little concern about his behavior; in fact, he discounted it by saying, "For all I know, when she's on her business trips, she's doing the same thing." Fran was concerned about Robert's dishonesty and sexual promiscuity for two reasons: (a) because of her religious belief that such behavior is morally and spiritually wrong and (b) because, as a mental health professional, she believed that such behavior is destructive to mental health and relationships.

Questions

1. Should Fran confront Robert in any way about his dishonesty to his wife and about the potential damaging effects of his risky sexual behavior. Why or why not?
2. If Fran decides to confront Robert, how can she do so without shaming or condemning him?

Discussion

In our view, Fran should confront Robert about his unhealthy, sexually promiscuous behavior. She needs to do this carefully, however, to minimize the possibility that Robert will feel condemned or shamed. One way for Fran to approach this would be to tell Robert that she is concerned about his sexually promiscuous behavior because she is afraid that it may be harming him and his marriage. She should tell Robert that she has a belief, a value, that honesty and sexual fidelity are necessary for a successful marriage and for good mental health. She could say that this belief or value comes partly from her religious beliefs and partly from her training and experience as a mental health professional. She could tell Robert that most mental health professionals do believe that honesty and marital fidelity are important for mental health (see Jensen & Bergin, 1988). She should affirm Robert's right to disagree about this and reassure Robert that she is not going to condemn him or terminate her work with him if he continues his sexually promiscuous lifestyle. She could then express that she feels an obligation nevertheless to point out some of the potential consequences for Robert of such behavior: (a) He is putting himself and his wife at risk for AIDS and other STDs; (b) his infidelity and dishonesty is damaging and impairing his relationship with his wife; and (c) his sexually promiscuous behavior is a symptom of, maintains, and contributes to his own self-hate and emotional problems. After sharing these concerns, Fran should give Robert the opportunity to express and explore his thoughts and feelings about what she has said and about his sexual promiscuity and how he feels about it.

the right to disagree with the therapist about value and lifestyle choices. An exception to this is when clients inform therapists they have made (or plan) lifestyle choices that the therapist is legally required to report or take action to prevent (e.g., abusing children, plans to physically harm others or self). In such situations, therapists need to clearly inform clients that they disagree with such behaviors and that they are required to take action to report or prevent it.

Another form of religious value imposition occurs when therapists implicitly or subtly pursue moral, religious, or spiritual goals that are contrary to clients' values and lifestyle preferences. A example of such an imposition is a therapist who agrees to help a gay client work on improving his homosexual relationship but covertly attempts to undermine the relationship and convince the client that a heterosexual lifestyle is best. Another example is a therapist who agrees to help a female business executive overcome her depression but also decides to implicitly convince her that her career is the source of her depression and that she should do "God's will" by giving up her career, getting married, and becoming a full-time mother and homemaker. These examples concern therapists with religiously conservative views attempting to coerce clients to adopt their conservative values.

Religiously and politically liberal therapists are also guilty, at times, of attempting to get clients to adopt their liberal values. This also is unethical. For example, some therapists attempt to coerce religiously conservative clients to give up their religious beliefs against homosexuality and to accept the gay lifestyle. Some therapists try to influence religiously conservative women to give up their full-time homemaker role to pursue a career. Regardless of their personal views, therapists should not attempt to coerce clients into decisions or lifestyles that are contrary to the clients' values, wishes, and cultural context (see Exhibit 7.5).

Another form of religious value imposition occurs when therapists use religious and spiritual interventions without their clients' consent. An example of this is a therapist who prays out loud with clients at the beginning of therapy sessions without asking clients if they would like to do so. Another instance is a therapist who, during a relaxation or self-hypnosis training session, introduces religious or spiritual images into the script without first obtaining the client's permission. Of course, clients should be given the opportunity to consent to all interventions, not just spiritual ones.

Whenever therapists use an intervention (psychological or spiritual), they have made a value judgment about (a) what interventions are acceptable, good, or efficacious and (b) what goals or outcomes are good for their clients. For example, when therapists use a cognitive therapy intervention, they are assuming that cognitive therapy is a valid and useful perspective and approach and that it is desirable for clients to modify their dysfunctional or irrational thinking. When therapists ask their clients to read scriptures

EXHIBIT 7.5
Ethical Dilemma Case Vignette 5: Core Value Conflicts

Case Description
Lee was an orthodox Jewish man who was in training to become a clinical psychologist. During his internship year, a couple having serious marital difficulties presented for treatment. The marriage was an interfaith marriage; the woman was Jewish and the man was Roman Catholic. As Lee worked with the couple, he realized that the couple's problems seemed to be caused primarily by a lack of communication and conflict resolution skills and sexual difficulties. The couple did not seem to have any concerns or misgivings about their interfaith marriage. However, because of his orthodox belief that interfaith marriages are not acceptable to God, Lee had serious concerns about the marriage. Lee found himself struggling with feelings of guilt both for trying to help the couple stay together and for hoping that they would get divorced.

Questions
1. Do you believe Lee should share his belief with the couple that interfaith marriages are unacceptable to God and that they might be best off getting divorced?
2. If you were Lee's supervisor and he disclosed his conflict to you, what would you advise him?
3. Does Lee have the right to refer this couple to a therapist who does not have a value conflict with interfaith marriages?

Discussion
Obviously, it would be unethical for Lee to "hold back" in his efforts to help the couple or to covertly attempt to influence them into getting a divorce. In our view, it would be best if Lee, with the support of his supervisor, referred this couple to a therapist who is comfortable with interfaith marriages. A supervisor who insisted that Lee should disregard his deeply held religious beliefs against interfaith marriages and continue to work with this couple would be guilty of cultural-religious insensitivity toward Lee. Although it is crucial for therapists to be open-minded and to seek to increase their multicultural sensitivity and unconditional acceptance for diverse clients, they should not be forced to help clients pursue goals that conflict with their core values. Lee should let the couple know that he does not feel he can be as helpful to them as another therapist he knows and that, to ensure that they get the best possible services, he would like to refer them to this therapist. If the couple asks Lee to tell them specifically why he feels this way, Lee should be honest and let them know that because of his religious beliefs against interfaith marriages, he finds himself conflicted, that is, wanting to help them but feeling guilty for doing so. He should reassure the couple that this is his issue, not theirs, and he should point out that many therapists do not share his views about interfaith marriages.

in the Bible, they are assuming that the Bible is a valuable source of spiritual englightenment and that it is desirable for their clients to seek guidance from this source. Clients may or may not agree with such beliefs, and they should have the right to make an informed decision about whether they wish to participate in such interventions. Permission to use general types of interventions (e.g., cognitive, behavioral, spiritual) can be obtained during informed consent procedures at the beginning of therapy. Before using a specific intervention, therapists should also briefly describe it and make certain that the client is willing to participate in it.

Checklist of Ethical Recommendations: Respecting Clients' Values

The following represents our attempt to outline some central "dos and don'ts" for therapists in respecting their clients' values:

1. Therapist should respect the right of clients to hold religious beliefs that differ from their own, regardless of whether the client is a member of the therapist's religious denomination or tradition.

2. Therapists should not proselytize or attempt to convert clients to their own religious ideology or denomination. Passing out religious literature, inviting clients to attend religious services, and teaching clients religious doctrines or traditions with the intent of converting clients to the therapist's faith are inappropriate.

3. Therapists should not arrogantly condemn their clients when they engage in value and lifestyle choices with which therapists disagree or believe to be destructive. However, therapists are obligated to help clients examine the legal, physical, social, and mental health consequences of their lifestyle choices. If clients wish, therapists also can help clients examine the moral and spiritual consequences and implications of their values and choices. Therapists should assist clients with such explorations in a morally and religiously open manner that is oriented toward resolving clinical problems rather than ideological indoctrination.

4. When value conflicts between therapists and clients arise during therapy, therapists should respectfully and explicitly (a) express their own values, (b) acknowledge the client's right to hold different values, (c) explore whether the value disagreement could undermine the success of therapy, and (d) decide whether referral to another therapist is indicated. Therapists should do their best in such situations to safeguard their clients' autonomy and welfare and to remain aware of their relatively more powerful position in the therapeutic relationship, a power that should not be abused.

5. Therapists should pursue religious and spiritual goals in therapy only when clients have explicitly expressed their desire to do so.

6. Before implementing a religious or spiritual intervention in therapy, therapists should briefly but clearly describe the in-

tervention to their clients and why they believe it could help them. Therapists should ascertain whether their clients feels comfortable with an intervention and obtain consent from their clients to use it.

VIOLATING WORK SETTING (CHURCH–STATE) BOUNDARIES

Another ethical pitfall for therapists who use a spiritual strategy in civically funded settings is the possible danger of violating laws or policies regarding the separation of church and state. A therapist surveyed by P. S. Richards and Potts (1995a) said, "I personally believe that the use of spiritual and religious techniques in therapy depends on the nature of the work place. I work for the state . . . and am not at liberty to use spiritual or religious techniques I would like" (p. 167).

There are no professional ethical guidelines that prohibit therapists in civic settings from discussing religious issues or using spiritual interventions with clients. However, therapists are ethically obligated to obey the law (AAMFT, 1985; ACA, 1995; American Psychiatric Association, 1986; APA, 1992; NFSCSW, 1985), and there are some legal regulations that could affect therapists' freedom to use certain spiritual interventions in these settings.

The First Amendment of the United States Constitution states that "Congress shall make no law respecting an establishment of religion, or prohibiting the free exercise thereof" (Constitution of the United States of America, 1791). Hudgins and Vacca (1995, p. 419) explained that these are referred to as the "free exercise" and "establishment of religion" clauses of the Constitution and that

> the free exercise clause means that a person may believe what he wishes. He may believe in his God or no God, and government will not interfere with that belief. Government may, however, restrict the practice of one's belief if it harms or abuses the rights of others.
>
> The establishment clause means that government is neutral in matters of religion. It does not favor one religion over another, many religions over some, or all religions over none. It does not promote one religious activity over another nor does it compel participation in a religious activity. (Hudgins & Vacca, 1995, p. 419)

Fischer and Sorenson (1985) pointed out that "although the [first] amendment seems to restrict only Congress, the same restrictions apply to all government action . . . because the fourteenth amendment has incorporated the first and thus applies it to any and all 'state action'" (pp. 219–220).

The proper interpretation and application of the religious clauses of the First Amendment have been issues of perennial controversy in the

United States (Drakeman, 1991; Flowers, 1994; Hudgins & Vacca, 1995; Weber, 1990). Despite the long history of controversy, we are not aware of any legal cases and rulings that specifically discuss how these clauses apply to psychotherapists and their work with clients. Most court cases and legal rulings regarding the separation of church and state that define appropriate behavior for government employees have involved public school teachers and administrators. Although therapists are different from officials and teachers in some important ways, they also wield considerable power to influence students and clients, and so legal rulings that have affected schoolteachers and administrators may also apply, in some ways, to them.

The establishment clause has been the guiding principle for setting limits on what is considered appropriate behavior in government settings. Public school teachers and administrators are not allowed to do anything in the work setting that would make it appear that the government or its employees seek to promote, endorse, or establish religion (Fischer & Sorenson, 1985; Flowers, 1994; Hudgins & Vacca, 1995; Staver, 1995). Requiring or permitting public prayers (e.g., in the classroom or at commencement exercises), requiring or permitting public readings of the Bible or other Scriptures for devotional purposes, sponsoring religious meetings, and proselytizing or otherwise endorsing religious doctrines are out of bounds for schoolteachers and administrators (Drakeman, 1991; Fischer & Sorenson, 1985; Flowers, 1994; Hudgins & Vacca, 1995; Staver, 1995).

Both students and teachers do "enjoy constitutional protection of free speech and free exercise or religion" (Staver, 1995, p. 37). Students and teachers have the right to pray, meditate, or read scriptures individually and privately in the school setting. Teachers should not, however, invite or allow students to participate in such activities with them. Students may participate in student-initiated and student-led Bible (religious) clubs on public school property, and a teacher sponsor may attend these meetings, but the teacher may not actively lead or direct the club (Staver, 1995). Students have the right to express belief or disbelief in God and religion verbally or in written papers as long as their speech does not substantially disrupt school activities (Staver, 1995). Teachers may also express their beliefs "with other teachers in the school lounge or between classes" (Staver, 1995, pp. 75–76), but they must be cautious about expressing their religious beliefs to students because of the danger of proselytizing. According to Staver (1995),

> while on school campus but before or after school hours, teachers may have certain restrictions imposed by the First Amendment Establishment Clause. . . . The younger the student, the more careful the teacher must be in matters of religion. The courts have reasoned that younger students are not able to easily separate the acts of the teacher from the acts of the school. . . . Unfortunately, no clear line has been decided as to when this age differential changes. No matter the age,

however, teachers may not proselytize students in a captive setting. . . .
However, "a teacher does not have to be so paranoid as to avoid a
student's religious inquiry." (p. 76)

Given all of this, what can we conclude about therapists who wish to
use a spiritual strategy in civic settings? Which spiritual interventions are
appropriate for therapists to use and which are not? First, therapists do have
the right to explore clients' spiritual issues and concerns when their clients
initiate such discussions or when therapists believe that such issues are
pertinent to their clients' presenting problems and the clients agree. Therapists also have the right to disclose their religious beliefs to their clients if
their clients ask about the therapist's views. However, it is illegal (and
unethical) for therapists in civic settings to promote, proselytize, or attempt
to persuade clients, covertly or overtly, to their religious viewpoint or tradition. Of course, as we discussed earlier in this chapter, ethical therapists
should not do this regardless of the setting in which they practice.

Second, some spiritual interventions are risky to use in civic settings
even with adult clients. We would advise therapists in civic settings working
with adults to be cautious about praying with clients, reading or quoting
Scriptures during therapy sessions, or giving clients religious bibliotherapy
literature. Before doing so, it would be wise for therapists to give clients
and supervisors a document that clearly explains the purpose of such interventions and to obtain written permission to use them. Other spiritual
interventions that are initiated by the therapist and carried out during therapy sessions, such as discussing religious or theological concepts, religious
relaxation or imagery, and religious confrontation, also may be somewhat
risky. Such interventions may increase the risk that the therapist will be
perceived as someone who is seeking, with governmental authority, to endorse, promote, or establish religion. Again, obtaining written permission
from clients and supervisors to use these interventions would probably reduce the therapist's legal risk.

Less explicit interventions, and those that clients or therapists do on
their own outside of therapy sessions, such as praying silently for clients,
modeling mature values and healthy spirituality, suggesting that religious
clients pray on their own outside of therapy sessions, encouraging clients
to forgive others, and consulting with clients' religious leaders, are less risky.
In general, therapists who work with adult clients in civic settings should not
be at significant risk of being accused of violating church–state regulations as
long as they work within their clients' value systems and obtain explicit
written client consent before using spiritual interventions. Generally, it will
prove safest to be open with colleagues and supervisors about the spiritual
aspects of one's approach and to have their support in advance. This has
worked successfully in many public agencies, especially when applying 12-
step programs for dealing with addictive behaviors. Many government agen-

cies also allow and even encourage spiritual counsel and the presence of chaplains (e.g., state hospitals, prisons, the military, legislative bodies).

Another consideration for therapists who work in publicly, tax-supported settings when deciding whether it would be safe and appropriate to use a given spiritual intervention is the age of the client (Staver, 1995). When working with children and adolescents, therapists should be particularly cautious about using spiritual interventions because actual or perceived abuses of governmental influence is more likely to occur (see Exhibit 7.6). In light of legal rulings about school prayer, devotional Scripture reading, and proselytizing (Staver, 1995), we would advise school counselors, school psychologists, and other therapists who work with minors in civic settings not to pray with clients, read Scriptures to them, or pass out religious literature. Other religiously explicit interventions such as discussing religious or theological concepts, religious relaxation or imagery, referral to religious leaders, and confrontation about discrepancies between religious values and behavior also may be risky and should not be used without written client, parental, and supervisor consent. Ecumenical interventions that are not religiously or spiritually explicit, or that therapists do privately, such as modeling healthy values, encouraging clients to forgive others, and praying privately for clients, are less risky and should not require parental permission.

Checklist of Ethical Recommendations: Respecting Church–State Boundaries

The following represents our attempt to outline some central "dos and don'ts" for therapists in respecting church–state boundaries:

1. Therapists in civic settings should make sure they understand and adhere to laws and work-setting policies regarding the separation of church and state. Therapists should also work to protect both their clients' and their own free exercise of religion rights within such settings. Open discussion, negotiation, and mutual agreement among staff in the work setting are preferable to hidden agendas or power struggles over policies in this realm.
2. Therapists in civic (and other) settings should always work within a client's value framework; they should not use spiritual interventions to promote or impose a particular religious viewpoint. In their informed consent document, therapists should inform clients that this is their policy.
3. Therapists in civic settings should obtain written client and supervisor consent before using spiritual interventions. When working with children and adolescents, therapists should also

EXHIBIT 7.6
Ethical Dilemma Case Vignette 6: Church–State Boundaries

Case Description

Mary was a school counselor and a devout Roman Catholic who worked in a public school in a large city in the western United States. Recently, with the knowledge and permission of the client's father, Mary began providing counseling to Sandra, a 15-year-old Presbyterian girl who was struggling with grief over the recent death of her mother. During the second session, Sandra shared her religious beliefs about death and the afterlife, and, during this discussion, Mary disclosed to Sandra that she also believes in an afterlife. During the next session, Sandra talked about her mother's funeral and shared her feelings about how helpful and kind the members of the church have been since her mother's death. Sandra also opened a Bible and read a passage from the New Testament that had special meaning and comfort to her. At the beginning of the next counseling session, Sandra told Mary that she greatly appreciated how Mary had listened to her and understood her as she talked about her mother's death and her religious beliefs about the afterlife. Sandra then said, "I feel close to you and would like to pray with you at the start of our sessions."

Questions

1. Do you think Mary should pray with Sandra? Why or why not?
2. Would it make a difference, in your opinion, who offered the prayer?
3. Do you think it was appropriate for Mary to discuss Sandra's religious beliefs with her?
4. Do you think Mary should have disclosed that she also believes in an afterlife?
5. If you were Mary's colleague and she consulted with you about how to handle this case, what would you advise her?

Discussion

In our view, Mary herself should not pray because of the danger that by doing so she could be violating church–state boundaries. There also is a danger that Mary may be perceived as attempting to convert Sandra into her faith. Perhaps it could be appropriate for Mary to permit Sandra to offer a prayer, but even this may be risky. We believe that Mary has acted appropriately in her decisions to discuss Sandra's religious beliefs and spiritual concerns with her and to listen as Sandra read the biblical Scripture to her. Therapists have a right, even in civic settings with minors, to discuss whatever issues their clients wish to discuss. We think it can also be appropriate for therapists to disclose their own spiritual beliefs in some situations if it seems it will be helpful to clients. In this case, Mary's disclosure regarding her beliefs about an afterlife was done to affirm and support Sandra's beliefs, and so we believe it was an appropriate disclosure. We do think that Mary should not initiate scriptural readings with Sandra, nor should she give her other religious literature to read. If Mary wishes to use explicitly spiritual interventions, such as religious imagery or encouraging Sandra to pray and meditate outside of sessions, she should not do so without written consent from Sandra and her father.

---

obtain written parental consent before using spiritual interventions.

4. Therapists in school or other civic settings who work with children and adolescents are advised not to pray with clients, quote or read Scriptures, or pass out religious bibliotherapy literature.

PRACTICING OUTSIDE THE BOUNDARIES OF COMPETENCE

The ethical guidelines of most mental health professions prohibit their members from practicing outside the boundaries of their professional competence (e.g., AAMFT, 1985; ACA, 1995; American Psychiatric Association, 1986; for example, the APA (1992) ethical guidelines state that

(a) psychologists provide services, teach, and conduct research only within the boundaries of their competence, based on their education, training, supervised experience, or appropriate professional expertise.

(b) Psychologists provide services, teach, or conduct research in new areas or involving new techniques only after first undertaking appropriate study, training supervision, and/or consultation from persons who are competent in those areas or techniques.

(c) In those emerging areas in which generally recognized standards for preparatory training do not yet exist, psychologists nevertheless take reasonable steps to protect patients, clients, students, research participants, and others from harm. (p. 1600)

In light of such ethical guidelines, it is clear that therapists need to make sure that they receive adequate training before incorporating a spiritual strategy into their therapeutic approach (see Exhibit 7.7). Unfortunately, most professional mental health training programs are inadequate at preparing therapists to intervene in the spiritual dimensions of their clients' lives (Bergin, 1980a, 1983). Despite the fact that they give considerable attention to other types of diversity, few mainstream mental health programs provide course work or supervision on religious and spiritual issues in mental health and psychotherapy (Kelly, 1993; Shafranske & Malony, 1990; Tan, 1993). Most psychotherapists therefore will need to acquire additional education and training beyond that provided by their graduate programs before they will be adequately prepared to use a spiritual strategy. Because "generally recognized standards for preparatory training do not yet exist" (APA, 1992, p. 1600) in this domain of psychotherapy, it is not necessarily easy for therapists to decide what training or education they need or how they can obtain such training.

Fortunately, many resources are now available to help therapists acquire training and competency in the religious and spiritual domains. For example, there is large body of professional literature that provides insight into the relations among religion, spirituality, mental health, and psychotherapy (e.g., Bergin, 1980a, 1983, 1991; Bergin & Payne, 1991; Collins, 1977; Gartner, Larson, & Allen, 1991; Hood, Spilka, Hunsberger, & Gor-

EXHIBIT 7.7

EXHIBIT 7.7
Ethical Dilemma Case Vignette 7: Respecting Boundaries of Competence

Case Description

Richard was a licensed psychologist who had been trained in a respected APA-accredited program in counseling psychology. Richard had received no training during his program about working with religious and spiritual clients and issues in therapy, nor had he received any since his graduation 4 years before. Richard's own worldview could be characterized as agnostic; he believed that the Christian beliefs "shoved down his throat" by his orthodox parents were "foolishness." He had not set foot in a church since he left home at the age of 18. Recently, Nagib, a devout Muslim client who is originally from Egypt, and his American wife, Julie, a recently converted Muslim, presented for treatment at Richard's private practice office. Nagib and Julie were experiencing severe marital conflict that seemed largely due to differences in their cultural and religious beliefs, particularly about gender roles and sexuality.

Questions
1. Should Richard attempt to work with this couple? Why or why not?
2. What type of therapist would be qualified to work with this couple?

Discussion

In our view, Richard should immediately refer this couple to a therapist who has a strong background and expertise in working with religious clients and issues, and preferably with an in-depth knowledge of the Islamic faith and culture. Richard is not prepared to work with this couple for two reasons. First, he is antireligious himself and has clearly not examined or worked through his own issues (that originated in his childhood) about religion. Second, he has made no effort to study or seek training about working sensitively with religious and spiritual issues and clients in therapy. It would be unethical for him to attempt to help this couple, or other clients, whose religious and spiritual background and beliefs are clearly intertwined with their presenting problems. Richard has an ethical obligation to seek training and supervision so that he will be better prepared to assist religious clients in the future (American Psychological Association, 1992).

such, 1996; Jones, 1994; Kelly, 1995; Krippner & Welch, 1992; Larson, Lu, & Swyers, 1996; Lovinger, 1984, 1990; Miller & Martin, 1988; Payne, Bergin, & Loftus, 1992; Payne, Bergin, Bielema, & Jenkins, 1991; Propst, 1988; Propst, Ostrom, Watkins, Dean, & Mashburn, 1992; P. S. Richards & Potts, 1995a; Shafranske, 1996; Spero, 1985; Stern, 1985; Tan, 1996; Worthington, 1986, 1989a, 1990, 1993; Worthington, Kurusu, McCullough, & Sanders, 1996; Wulff, 1997). Some universities now offer specialized courses on the psychology and sociology of religion and on religious and spiritual issues in counseling and psychotherapy. For several years, APA's Division 36 offered a continuing education workshop on these topics (Jones, 1994). In addition, many universities offer courses on different world religions and cultures. Because such resources are now available and are continuing to increase in availability, we believe that specific standards of education and clinical training in this domain are now warranted.

Checklist of Ethical Recommendations: Education and Training Standards

The following represents our attempt to outline some essential educational and training standards for professional psychotherapists:

1. The foundation of effective religious and spiritual counseling is multicultural attitudes and skills (see chap. 6 in this book). Therapists should therefore study and be trained in multicultural counseling.

2. Therapists should read several good books on the psychology and sociology of religion (e.g., Crapps, 1986; Hood et al., 1996; Roberts, 1990; Wulff, 1997) and on religious and spiritual issues in counseling and psychotherapy (e.g., Lovinger, 1984; Kelly, 1995; Stern, 1985; Shafranske, 1996; this book).

3. Therapists should read current scholarly literature about religion and spirituality in mainstream mental health journals and in specialty journals devoted to these topics (e.g., *Counseling and Values, Journal for the Scientific Study of Religion, Journal of Psychology and Theology*).

4. Therapists should take at least one workshop or class on religion and mental health and spiritual issues in psychotherapy.

5. Therapists should read one or two good books on world religions (e.g., Nigosian, 1994; Smart, 1994) or, if possible, take a class on world religions.

6. Therapists should acquire specialized knowledge about religious traditions that they frequently encounter in therapy (e.g., by inviting clients to share information about their faith; reading literature published by and about the religious tradition; and immersing themselves in the religious culture when appropriate, such as attending worship services).

7. Therapists should seek supervision or consultation (or both) from colleagues when they first work with clients from a particular religious or spiritual tradition or when clients present challenging religious or spiritual issues the therapist has not encountered before.

8. Therapists should seek supervision or consultation (or both) from colleagues when they first begin using religious and spiritual interventions in their work or whenever they use new, untested spiritual interventions.

OTHER CONCERNS ABOUT SPIRITUAL INTERVENTIONS

We are aware of two other major concerns that have been raised about the use of spiritual interventions in psychotherapy: becoming enmeshed in superstition and trivializing the numinous or sacred. We do not view these issues as ethical dilemmas; they really are just fears that scientists and religionists each have that their respective profession or domain will be contaminated by the other one. Nevertheless, we discuss these concerns here because they are often mentioned along with the ethical dilemmas discussed earlier by those who object to the idea of a spiritual strategy for psychotherapy.

Some therapists and researchers have objected to the use of spiritual perspectives and interventions on the grounds that they are unscientific and could return clinicians to the religious superstitions and irrational dogmas of past centuries (e.g., Ellis, 1971, 1980; Sagan, 1995). Although such a danger could exist, as we discussed in chapters 3 and 5, the gap that once existed between science and religion is no longer as wide as was once believed (Appleyard, 1992; Barbour, 1990; Jones, 1994). Explicitly theistic perspectives are no longer viewed as necessarily being antithetical to the progress of science (Appleyard, 1992; Barbour, 1990; Jones, 1994). In addition, the movement toward methodological pluralism has opened the door to the study of phenomena such as spiritual beliefs and practices that were once excluded from scientific investigation. Religious and spiritual perspectives and interventions can and should be studied empirically. Thus, a theistic, spiritual strategy need not be less rational, scientific, or empirical than any other therapeutic approach.

Some therapists have objected to the use of spiritual "techniques" on the grounds that the use of such interventions trivializes sacred things. As stated by a therapist surveyed by P. S. Richards and Potts (1995a),

> my understanding of the divine and my experience both persuade me to avoid consciously-planned use of explicit religious or spiritual matters in my work in therapy. I even cringe of thinking of these as "techniques," just as I am troubled by having such matters as "love" and "faith" spoken of as "techniques." . . . My primary concern is not our corrupting our therapy. . . . My concern is our trivializing the numinous, our losing our awe of the divine, our forgetting the fear of the LORD. (p. 167)

In light of such concerns, it is appropriate for therapists to remember that the majority of spiritual interventions that therapists have used are practices that have been engaged in for centuries, in one form or another, by spiritual believers. For example, prayer, meditation, Scripture study, blessings (laying on of hands), attending church or synagogue, worshipping, repentance, and confession are religious and spiritual practices that are taught and advocated by one or more of the major world religions (Carmody & Carmody, 1989; Farah, 1994; Nigosian, 1994; Palmer & Keller, 1989; Smart, 1994). Perhaps there is a danger that therapists could trivialize these sacred practices when using them as interventions in therapy. However, whether this occurs depends on the therapist's attitude and approach.

If therapists routinely and irreverently use spiritual interventions not because they believe in their healing power but solely because they view them as helpful for manipulating their clients, this would trivialize or degrade sacred religious practices. We do not think therapists should do this. On the other hand, if therapists respectfully and reverently encourage clients to participate in selected religious practices that they believe will help their clients cope, heal, and grow spiritually and emotionally, this would actually be a way of honoring and validating these practices and traditions. It would be a way of expressing respect for and faith in their healing power. Therapists who are unwilling to help clients access the healing powers available to them through their religious beliefs, practices, and community may be most guilty of trivializing or degrading sacred religious practices and traditions. Simply ignoring or failing to use the potential healing power of these practices is itself a form of trivialization and disrespect.

CONCLUSION

Readers may have noticed that some of the ethical dangers we have discussed are more likely to be of concern when therapists are working with clients from religious traditions other than their own (e.g., failing to consult or collaborate with a client's religious leaders, religious proselytizing, practicing outside the boundaries of one's competence). Generally speaking, we believe it is safer for therapists to use a spiritual strategy with clients from their own religious tradition because misunderstandings and doctrinal disagreements are less likely (P. S. Richards & Potts, 1995a). However, some ethical violations may actually be more likely to occur when therapists are working with clients of their own religious faith (e.g., dual relationships, usurping religious authority by confusing role boundaries, imposing values by assuming that the client believes as the therapist does). Thus, regardless of their client's religious beliefs, therapists need to be alert to the ethical dangers we have discussed and seek to follow the recommendations we have offered.

We believe that the recommendations we have made will help therapists function more ethically and effectively in both ecumenical and denominational therapeutic situations. However, more denominationally specific ethical guidelines may be needed to supplement the general guidelines we have offered. For example, because the role distinctions between religious leaders and therapists may differ somewhat from one religious tradition to another, guidelines about which spiritual interventions therapists should not use to avoid usurping religious authority may need to be denominationally tailored. We therefore hope that psychotherapists within each religious tradition, perhaps in consultation with their religious leaders, will articulate additional ethical recommendations that may be needed for their particular religious tradition. Finally, we do not intend for this chapter to be the final word on ethical issues and guidelines in this domain. We believe more discussion, debate, and research is needed as this approach evolves to ensure that therapists continue to progress in their capacity to use a spiritual strategy ethically and effectively.

8

RELIGIOUS AND SPIRITUAL
ASSESSMENT

We must distinguish between two kinds of religious orientation, the
extrinsic value and the intrinsic value . . . the extrinsic uses his religion
. . . [intrinsics] serve it . . . then live by it.

—*Gordon W. Allport*

Because of the eclectic movement, and the growing recognition that
human beings are multisystemic organisms (Bergin, 1988; Beutler &
Clarkin, 1990; Garfield & Bergin, 1986; Norcross & Goldfried, 1992),
comprehensive assessment approaches have frequently been advocated in
the psychotherapy profession during the past 20 years (e.g., Beutler &
Clarkin, 1990; Lazarus, 1973, 1976). Many therapists now routinely seek
information about multiple aspects of their clients' background and functioning when doing their assessments (e.g., physical, psychological, behavioral, cognitive, educational, racial-ethnic, and familial). Unfortunately,
most therapists rarely systematically seek information about their clients'
religiosity and spirituality.

In this chapter, we discuss a number of reasons why it is important
for all psychotherapists to assess clients' religious and spiritual backgrounds
and status along with the other aspects of their lives. We identify and
describe dimensions of religiosity and spirituality that are clinically relevant.
We then describe a multilevel, multisystemic assessment strategy and discuss

how a religious-spiritual assessment fits into such a strategy. We also discuss how intake questionnaires, clinical interviews, and standardized tests can be used to facilitate a religious-spiritual assessment.

REASONS FOR CONDUCTING A RELIGIOUS-SPIRITUAL ASSESSMENT

There are at least five major reasons why therapists should assess their clients' religious and spiritual backgrounds, beliefs, and lifestyle.

1. *Conducting a religious-spiritual assessment can help therapists better understand their clients' worldviews and thus increase their capacity to empathically understand and work with them sensitively.* During the past 50 years, many helping professionals have asserted that it is important for therapists to gain an empathic understanding of their clients' subjective world or internal frame of reference (e.g., May, 1961; Rogers, 1951, 1957, 1961; Yalom, 1980). Psychotherapy outcome research has supported this assertion by documenting that therapist empathic understanding is consistently associated with positive therapy outcomes (Lambert & Bergin, 1994; Orlinsky, Grawe, & Parks, 1994). In recent years, multicultural writers have helped clinicians realize that it is difficult for White therapists to fully understand and empathize with racial minority clients because of differences in worldviews and life experiences (Ibrahim, 1985; Ponterotto et al., 1996; D. W. Sue & Sue, 1990). These writers have argued that therapists must seek an understanding of racial minority clients' worldviews if they are to avoid cultural insensitivity and bias (Ibrahim, 1985; D. W. Sue & Sue, 1990). Therapists also should follow this advice with their religious and spiritual clients. The worldviews and values of mainstream psychotherapists often conflict with those of their religious clients (Bergin, 1980a; Bergin & Jensen, 1990; Jones, 1994). It is essential for therapists to do an assessment of the spiritual worldview and values of their religious clients if they are to empathically understand them and avoid religious insensitivity and bias.

2. *Conducting a religious-spiritual assessment can help therapists determine whether clients' religious-spiritual orientation is healthy or unhealthy and what impact it is having on their presenting problems and disturbance.* Current theory and research suggest that religion is a complex, multidimensional phenomenon that has diverse effects on mental health (Bergin, 1983). For example, religious intrinsicness or devoutness has usually been found to be associated with better physical health, social adjustment, and emotional well-being (Batson, Schoenrade, & Ventis, 1993; Bergin, Masters, & Richards, 1987; Gartner, Larson, & Allen, 1991; Payne, Bergin, Bielema, & Jenkins, 1991; P. S. Richards, 1991; see also chap. 5 in this book). On the other hand, extrinsic religiousness has usually been associated with poorer emotional well-being and social adjustment (Batson et al., 1993; Bergin, 1983; Bergin

et al., 1987; P. S. Richards, 1991). Therefore, the empirical associations between religiousness and mental health vary depending on the definitions and measures of religiousness and mental health that are used (Batson et al., 1993; Gartner et al., 1991; Payne et al., 1991; see also chap. 5 in this book).

In the clinical situation, therapists are likely to encounter all of this complexity. For some clients, their religious background and beliefs may be causing their emotional disturbance (Ellis, 1980). For others, their religious beliefs may be intertwined or interacting with existing emotional problems (Bergin, Stinchfield, Gaskin, Masters, & Sullivan, 1988; Moench, 1985; P. S. Richards, Smith, & Davis, 1989). For still other clients, their religious beliefs and lifestyle may be acting as a therapeutic influence that is helping to prevent or alleviate emotional problems (Bergin et al., 1987; Bergin et al., 1988; P. S. Richards et al., 1989). For any given client, their religious background, beliefs, and lifestyle could be operating in all of these ways simultaneously (P. S. Richards et al., 1989). To best assist clients, it is the job of therapists to gain an understanding of what impact clients' religiousness is having on their lives. An assessment of clients' religious and spiritual background, beliefs, and lifestyle is essential if therapists are to succeed at this challenging task.

3. *Conducting a religious-spiritual assessment can help therapists determine whether clients' religious and spiritual beliefs and community could be used as a resource to help them better cope, heal, and grow.* An important part of any psychological assessment is to ascertain what strengths and resources clients have that could assist them in their efforts to cope, heal, and change. For example, when assessing a severely depressed, suicidal client, it is important for therapists to determine (a) what beliefs or values the client has that could reinforce the client's desire to live and (b) whether there are family members or friends available to provide support and companionship to the client in times of crisis. Client strengths and resources may include clients' personal characteristics, such as their beliefs, values, abilities, and financial and employment status, as well as clients' significant others, such as their family members, friends, and social community.

Religious and spiritual theologies and communities are a potential rich source of support for clients and therapists (Duncan, Eddy, & Haney, 1981; Koltko, 1990; Pargament et al., 1987; Pargament, Silverman, Johnson, Echemendia, & Snyder, 1983). For example, religious beliefs such as "there is a God who loves me," "there is a divine purpose to my life," "I have an eternal spiritual identity," "God wants me to love and forgive others," "suffering and trials are a necessary part of God's plan for me," and "God will give me strength and guidance to help me with my problems" can assist clients in times of crisis or at other times in therapy (Duncan et al., 1981; Koltko, 1990). In addition, religious communities can provide people with a sense of belonging and support, feelings of stability, a sense of order and purpose, opportunities to provide and receive charitable service, and even financial and employment support (Pargament et al., 1987, 1983). A religious-spiritual assessment can help therapists determine whether such resources are available in their clients' lives.

4. *Conducting a religious-spiritual assessment can help therapists determine which spiritual interventions could be used in therapy to help their clients.* There is now widespread agreement within the psychotherapy profession that therapists should tailor their treatment interventions for each client individually on the basis of a careful assessment of the client's unique symptoms, problems, goals, and resources (Bergin & Garfield, 1994; Beutler & Clarkin, 1990; Lazarus, 1989). A treatment tailoring approach should also be used with spiritual interventions. Because spiritual interventions are not indicated for all clients or for all problems, they should not be applied routinely or uniformly. For example, spiritual interventions may be contraindicated with severely disturbed delusional, psychotic, or obsessive–compulsive clients.

Clients may fail to improve, or, worse yet, ethical violations and negative outcomes might occur if therapists use spiritual interventions indiscriminately or inappropriately (P. S. Richards & Potts, 1995a). Therapists need to decide whether spiritual interventions are indicated given the client's symptoms, presenting problems, and goals. They also need to determine whether their clients are willing and ready to participate in such interventions. Information about clients' religious and spiritual background, beliefs, and current status is clearly essential if therapists are to integrate spiritual interventions into their treatment plans ethically and effectively. In chapter 10 (see Table 10.7 in particular), we discuss in more depth the types of client, therapist, and process variables that could influence the appropriateness and effectiveness of spiritual interventions and that should be considered when conducting a religious-spiritual assessment.

5. *Conducting a religious-spiritual assessment can help therapists determine whether clients have unresolved spiritual doubts, concerns, or needs that should be addressed in therapy.* According to the theistic, spiritual view of human nature, all human beings have certain spiritual needs and issues (e.g., the need to experience and affirm their eternal spiritual identity and divine worth, to feel connected and in harmony with God and the Spirit of Truth, to feel a transcendent sense of life purpose and meaning, to love and serve God and others altruistically, to spiritually understand suffering and death, to live in harmony with spiritual moral values, and to develop and actualize their spiritual potential). When people have religious and spiritual needs and concerns, the majority of them seek assistance and counsel from their spiritual leaders; however, some do seek help from psychotherapists (Ganje-Fling & McCarthy, 1991).

Although it may often be appropriate for therapists to refer clients who have spiritual issues to their religious leaders, this may not always be in the client's best interest. For example, clients may not feel safe enough to discuss their spiritual doubts with their religious leader and may prefer to do so with a more neutral, nonjudgmental therapist. In addition, clients' spiritual concerns and needs may be intertwined in complex ways with their emotional and interpersonal problems (Bergin et al., 1988; P. S. Richards et al., 1989). Thus, when clients present with religious and spiritual concerns, there may be psychological and interpersonal roots to these problems that need to be addressed. For example, it has been our clinical experience that some clients who express feelings of alienation from and lack of trust in God were abandoned or abused by their parents as children. With such clients, their spiritual issues are rooted in the abandonment or abuse and the associated psychological trauma (Ganje-Fling & McCarthy, 1994). Therapists may be more qualified than religious leaders to assist such clients in the process of healing and change.

Therapists also need to be alert to the possibility that when clients present with psychological and interpersonal problems, there may be religious or spiritual roots to these problems. According to the multisystemic view of human nature discussed in chapter 5, problems in the spiritual system of people's lives may affect their psychological and social functioning. For example, we have observed that clients who struggle emotionally and interpersonally with low self-esteem, shame, lack of self-confidence, and social isolation often lack a felt sense and assurance of their eternal spiritual nature and divine worth. We believe that the root of their problems is alienation from their core spiritual identity. The most powerful psychological and interpersonal healing and change occurs when these clients receive a spiritual assurance of their divine identity and worth.

Therefore, it is not desirable for therapists to compartmentalize the different systems of human functioning and work only on psychological and interpersonal issues with clients. To help clients resolve their emotional and interpersonal problems, therapists may frequently need to help clients address their spiritual issues. A religious-spiritual assessment is clearly essential if therapists are to adequately understand and assist clients with their religious and spiritual issues.

CLINICALLY IMPORTANT DIMENSIONS OF RELIGIOSITY

What dimensions of religiosity and spirituality should therapists assess when conducting a religious-spiritual assessment? This is a challenging question that defies a simple answer. Although early researchers often used unidimensional and single-item measures when studying religiosity (e.g., religious affiliation, frequency of church attendance), it is now widely recognized that religion is a complex phenomenon (Bergin, 1983; Smart, 1983, 1994; Spilka, Hood, & Gorsuch, 1985). During the past 30 years, theorists and researchers have described and operationalized numerous dimensions of religiousness and spirituality. For example, Glock and Stark (1965) described 5 dimensions of religiousness, King and Hunt (1969) 11, Malony (1985, 1988) 8, and Smart (1983) 6. Numerous one- and two-dimensional models of religiousness and spirituality also have been described (e.g., Allen & Spilka, 1967; Allport & Ross, 1967; Ellison, 1983; Fullerton & Hunsberger, 1982; Hood, 1975).

Given this complexity, and the fact that research and clinical experience with religious-spiritual assessment is still in an early stage, therapists must rely heavily on clinical wisdom and hunches when deciding what religious and spiritual information to seek about their clients. Nevertheless, on the basis of preliminary research and our clinical experience, we briefly discuss what we think are some of the most clinically relevant religious and spiritual dimensions that have been described. We hope that this information will help therapists in their efforts to assess and conceptualize their clients' religiosity and spirituality.

Metaphysical Worldview

A metaphysical worldview is composed of the beliefs a person holds about the universe and the nature of reality. As we discussed in chapter 4, according to Wilhelm Dilthey there are three major types of metaphysical worldviews: naturalism (e.g., scientific, naturalistic), idealism of freedom (e.g., Western, monotheistic world religions), and objective idealism (e.g., Eastern world religions; Kluback & Weinbaum, 1957; Rickman, 1976). To fully understand their clients' inner subjective world and empathize with them, we believe that it is crucial for therapists to gain insight into their clients' metaphysical worldviews. Therapists should seek to understand their clients' beliefs about questions such as the following: How did human beings come to exist? Is there a Supreme Being or Creator? What is the purpose of life? How should people live their lives to find happiness and peace? What is moral and ethical? Why is there suffering, grief, and pain? Is there life after death? Insight into their clients' beliefs about such questions will help therapists better understand how their clients view themselves, their relationships, and their problems.

Religious Affiliation

The majority of people in the world are affiliated or associated, to one degree or another, with a religious denomination or tradition (Barrett, 1996). Religious affiliation is an important demographic characteristic of clients. Although religious affiliation alone does not tell therapists much about the relative importance of religion in clients' lives, it does provide therapists with some basic orienting information as they begin to understand their clients. For example, if a client states that his or her religious affiliation is Roman Catholic, although the therapist knows nothing without further inquiry about what type of Roman Catholic the client is, the therapist does know that the client is not Jewish, Muslim, or Protestant. The therapist has narrowed the assessment field considerably just by finding out the client's religious affiliation. Assuming that the therapist is familiar with the client's religious tradition and culture, knowledge of the client's religious affiliation also provides the therapist with a rich source of potential insight into the client's religious and cultural background and experiences. Such information should be viewed as a source of tentative hypotheses about the client that can be checked out and explored in more depth if it seems clinically relevant.

Religious Orthodoxy

Religious orthodoxy is the degree to which a person believes in and adheres to the traditional doctrines and moral teachings of his or her religion (e.g., Fullerton & Hunsberger, 1982; Stark & Glock, 1968). More specifically, *belief orthodoxy* is the acceptance of the doctrinal beliefs of one's religion, and *behavior orthodoxy* is adherence to the moral teachings and practices of one's religion.

It is important for therapists to assess their clients' level of religious orthodoxy because orthodoxy may be related to several important treatment considerations. For example, religiously orthodox clients are more likely to prefer therapists who share their religious beliefs (Worthington, 1988; Worthington, Kurusu, McCollough, & Sanders, 1996). Building trust and credibility may be more difficult with highly orthodox clients (Worthington, 1988). Referral to religious leaders or consultation with religiously orthodox therapists may be more necessary with such clients. Religiously orthodox clients also are more likely to view their religious beliefs and lifestyle as being relevant to their presenting problems and concerns than are less orthodox clients. Thus, the exploration of religious and spiritual issues, and the use of religious-spiritual interventions, may be more necessary and appropriate for religiously orthodox clients. Clients who are nonreligious or religiously affiliated but unorthodox may be more likely to view religion negatively and to resent it if therapists attempt to discuss religious issues or use spiritual interventions.

Religious Problem-Solving Style

A person's religious beliefs can influence the manner in which she or he seeks to cope with and solve life's problems and difficulties (e.g., Pargament, 1996; Spilka, Shaver, & Kirkpatrick, 1985). Pargament et al. (1988) described three styles of religious problem solving or coping: self-directing, deferring, and collaborative). In the self-directing style, people believe that it is their own responsibility to resolve their problems; "God is not involved directly in this process. . . . Rather, God is viewed as giving people the freedom and resources to direct their own lives" (Pargament et al., 1988, p. 91). In the deferring style, people "defer the responsibility of problem-solving to God. Rather than actively solve problems themselves, they wait for solutions to emerge through the active efforts of God" (Pargament et al., 1988, p. 92). In the collaborative style, people believe that "responsibility for the problem-solving process is held jointly by the individual and God. . . . Both . . . are viewed as active contributors working together to solve problems" (Pargament et al., 1988, p. 92).

Therapists should assess their clients' religious problem-solving style because this information may help therapists determine what therapeutic style (e.g., directive, nondirective, collaborative) and types of interventions may be most appropriate for a given client. For example, deferring clients may not only defer to God, but they may also defer to the therapist for resolution of their problems. Therapists may, initially at least, need to be highly directive with deferring clients. When using spiritual (and other) interventions with deferring clients, therapists may also need to strongly emphasize the client's role and responsibility for making these interventions succeed. Self-directing clients may be highly motivated and responsible clients, but, because of their belief that resolving their problems is really all up to them, they may not wish to participate in spiritual interventions that assume that God may actively intervene to assist or guide them (e.g., praying for guidance, seeking a blessing of comfort and healing from their religious leader). Spiritual interventions that require more responsibility and active involvement from the client may work best with self-directing clients. Such clients may also find it difficult to accept active support and assistance from their therapist, and so therapists may, initially at least, need to use a more nondirective therapeutic approach. Collaborative clients may be most open to a wide range of spiritual and secular interventions and may be most able to enter into a collaborative helping relationship with the therapist.

Spiritual Identity

Spiritual identity refers to a person's sense of identity and worth in relation to God and his or her place in the universe. According to our theistic spiritual perspective, people who have a positive sense of their spiritual identity and worth believe that they are eternal spiritual beings who are creations, or children, of God. As such, they believe that they have divine worth and potential and they feel spiritually connected to God's love. They believe that their eternal potentialities are unlimited and that one purpose of life is to seek to actualize and fulfill their great potential.

Such people also believe that their inner spirit, or core identity, is eternal and that their identity and consciousness persists beyond the death of the physical body.

People who lack a positive identity do not feel that they have divine worth or potential. They may or may not believe intellectually that they are creations of God, but in either case, they feel unworthy and worthless. They do not feel God's love in their life, and they doubt whether they have any special potential, worth, or purpose. They may also doubt whether they have an inner spirit that persists beyond the grave.

According to our theistic view of personality, having a positive sense of one's spiritual identity and worth is crucial for healthy development and lifestyle functioning (see chap. 5). People who have a strong spiritual identity tend to function better emotionally, interpersonally, and spiritually. Some preliminary evidence suggests that religious people who receive an affirmation of their spiritual identity and worth seem to heal more quickly and completely and to make healthy and enduring lifestyle changes (Bergin et al., 1994; P. S. Richards & Potts, 1995b).

Assessing clients' spiritual identity is important for several reasons. First, positive spiritual identity probably bodes well for healing and growth. In our experience, such clients are better able to cope with severe challenges and stresses because of their faith in God's love, their own capacities, and in the ultimate purpose in life's tests. With such clients, therapists may find that clients' feelings of spiritual worth can serve as a powerful resource to help them cope and endure painful challenges.

Second, if clients lack a positive spiritual identity, therapists may wish to be alert to the possibility that these deficiencies in identity and worth are at the core of other problems and symptoms that have been presented. Much has been written over the years about the centrality of identity and self-esteem in relation to psychological and interpersonal functioning (e.g., Erikson, 1968; Rogers, 1961). For religious and spiritual clients, we believe that a deficit in their spiritual identity is significant diagnostically and has important implications for treatment. With such clients, therapists may wish to consider using interventions that would help clients get more in touch with their spiritual identity and worth (e.g., prayer, meditation, spiritual imagery, spiritual direction).

God Image

God image is a person's perceptions or representations of God (Wulff, 1997). God is perceived by some people as loving, kind, and forgiving, whereas others perceive God as wrathful, vindictive, and impersonal (P. L. Benson & Spilka, 1973). A number of factors appear to influence people's perceptions of God, including parental relationships, relationships with significant others and groups, self-esteem, religious instruction, and religious practices, although it appears that parental relationships and self-esteem exert the strongest influences. People who experienced loving, nurturing parental relationships and who have positive self-esteem tend to view God as loving, accepting, and forgiving (P. L. Benson & Spilka, 1973; Dickie, Merasco, Geurink, & Johnson, 1993; Wulff, 1991).

There are at least two reasons why therapists should seek to understand how their clients perceive or visualize God when conducting a religious-spiritual assessment. First, with regard to treatment tailoring, if clients have low self-esteem and perceive God to be harsh, vengeful, and impersonal, spiritual interventions that enable them to personally feel God's love and support could have powerful healing effects on their sense of self-esteem and worth. Interestingly, in a recent survey of Mormon therapists (P. S. Richards & Potts, 1995b), an increase in clients' self-esteem and feelings of worth was the most frequently reported outcome of spiritual interventions. In the case reports provided by the therapists, several therapists attributed the change in their clients' feelings of self-esteem and self-worth to the clients receiving a witness and assurance of God's love and concern (P. S. Richards, 1995). Nevertheless, despite the positive possibilities, much caution should be exercised when using spiritual interventions with clients who perceive God negatively. Such clients may doubt the efficacy of spiritual interventions and may prefer not to participate in them. Negative outcomes may occur if spiritual interventions are attempted and fail (P. S. Richards & Potts, 1995a).

A second reason why therapists should assess how clients perceive God is that this information could help therapists better understand their clients' psychological and interpersonal problems. According to some object-relations theorists and some research (e.g., Dickie et al., 1993; Grom, cited in Wulff, 1991; Spero, 1992), clients' perceptions of God are intimately connected to their perceptions of parents, significant others, and self. Insight into a client's God image, and how it is related to the client's image of self, parents, and significant others, will give the therapist a more complete understanding of the client's internalized object relations and potentially more leverage for promoting therapeutic change.

Value–Lifestyle Congruence

Value–lifestyle congruence is the degree to which a person's lifestyle choices and behaviors are congruent with their professed moral, religious, and spiritual values. According to our spiritual view of personality discussed in chapter 5, as people affirm their spiritual identity and grow in sensitivity to the Spirit of Truth, they internalize and seek to live in harmony with healthy values. Congruence between one's values and lifestyle choices, therefore, is a hallmark of healthy personality and spiritual development and functioning. A lack of congruence between one's values and lifestyle choices creates guilt and anxiety and may contribute to emotional disturbance and problems in interpersonal relationships.

With such a view, it is perhaps obvious why we believe it is important to assess clients' degree of value–lifestyle congruence. In the clinical situation it is often important for therapists to know whether their clients' religious and spiritual beliefs and values are a source of guilt and anxiety or of comfort and strength. Where there is value–lifestyle incongruence, usually there is emotional and interpersonal distress. It may be helpful for therapists to help such clients identify and own their incongruencies and explore and clarify their values. Sometimes this process results in an affirmation of new values and lifestyles. Other times it can produce a stronger internalization of clients' values and a turning away from destructive lifestyle choices. Table 8.5 provides an interview and assessment guide for helping therapists consider whether their clients' values and lifestyles are healthy and adaptive or unhealthy and maladaptive.

Doctrinal Knowledge

Doctrinal knowledge involves people's understanding and knowledge of the religious doctrines and theology of their religious tradition. Doctrinal or religious knowledge has been viewed by several theorists and researchers as an important, basic dimension of religiosity (e.g., Glock & Stark, 1965; King, 1967). We believe that it is important for therapists to assess clients' doctrinal knowledge because we have found that many clients get into emotional trouble because they misunderstand the doctrines of their religion. As expressed by P. S. Richards, Smith, and Davis (1989),

> some clients have a tendency to misunderstand or oversimplify church leaders' statements and church doctrines. Some of the clients' misunderstandings seem to be due to a lack of knowledge of the church doctrine. It also appears that problems arise because simplistic religious concepts and beliefs which the clients acquired as children, or early in their church membership, have not been critically examined. (p. 518)

The doctrines that clients misunderstand and get into emotional trouble over will undoubtedly vary from one religious tradition to another (Lovinger, 1984). Therapists who gain an in-depth understanding of the doctrines of their clients' religious traditions will be in the best position to recognize when their clients' have misunderstood specific doctrines (e.g., Koltko, 1990). When working from a denominational therapeutic stance in which they enjoy high credibility and trust with their clients, therapists may greatly help clients by helping them examine, challenge, and modify dysfunctional interpretations of religious doctrines. In ecumenical situations, when therapists are not viewed as trusted experts on the client's religious tradition, therapists may still help clients examine religious beliefs that appear dysfunctional. They can do this by referring clients to religious leaders for clarification about specific religious doctrines or by encouraging clients to do some research to determine whether their understanding of a doctrine is accurate.

Religious and Spiritual Health and Maturity

During the past century, a number of theorists and researchers have undertaken the challenging task of attempting to distinguish healthy, mature forms of religiosity and spirituality from unhealthy, immature ones (e.g., Allport, 1950, 1959, 1966; Allport & Ross, 1967; Chandler, Holden, & Kolander, 1992; Ellison, 1983; Fowler, 1981; James, 1902/1936; Malony, 1985; Meadow, 1978; Moberg, 1979, 1984). Perhaps the most influential conceptualization of religious and spiritual maturity has been Allport's (1950, 1959, 1966; Allport & Ross, 1967; Donahue, 1985) theory of intrinsic and extrinsic religious orientation. According to Allport and Ross (1967), people with an immature, extrinsic religious orientation

> use religion for their own ends. . . . Persons with this orientation may find religion useful in a variety of ways—to provide security and solace, sociability and distraction, status and self-justification. The embraced creed is lightly held or else selectively shaped to fit more primary needs. . . . The extrinsic type turns to God, but without turning away from self. (p. 434)

People with a mature, intrinsic orientation

> find their master motive in religion. Other needs, strong as they may be, are regarded as of less ultimate significance, and they are, so far as possible, brought into harmony with the religious beliefs and prescriptions. Having embraced a creed the individual endeavors to internalize it and follow it fully. It is in this sense that he lives his religion. (Allport & Ross, 1967, p. 464)

Despite complexities and some controversy about Allport's theory (e.g., Hunt & King, 1971; Kirkpatrick, 1989; Kirkpatrick & Hood, 1990), the conclusion that intrinsicness is a mature religious orientation that tends to be positively associated with a variety of indicators of personality, emotional and social adjustment has been remarkably consistent and robust (Donahue, 1985; Gartner et al., 1991; Payne et al., 1991). In addition, extrinsicness has usually been uncorrelated or negatively correlated with adjustment (Donahue, 1985; Gartner et al., 1991; Payne et al., 1991).

Allport's theory provides a useful starting point for helping therapists consider whether their clients' religious and spiritual orientation is healthy and mature versus unhealthy and immature. Therapists should assess whether their clients are intrinsically or extrinsically religiously motivated because such information will help give therapists a global understanding of how integrated and mature their clients' religious orientation is. Clients who are involved in their religion only because of the social or personal benefits such activity brings them may be experiencing a lack of congruence between their beliefs and actions. Such clients may profit from an examination of their extrinsic religious motivations and involvement and any emotional conflict that may be associated with it.

Clients who are intrinsically religious are more likely to view their religious beliefs and lifestyle as a source of meaning, support, and strength. Such clients are more likely to benefit from spiritual interventions and from an exploration of how their religious and spiritual beliefs and community can help them cope, heal, and grow. This is not to suggest that intrinsic clients' religious beliefs and lifestyles are necessarily uniformly benevolent. There is evidence that people with an overall healthy, intrinsic orientation may nevertheless harbor some unhealthy religious beliefs and tendencies (e.g., perfectionistic ones; Batson et al., 1993; Bergin et al., 1988; P.S. Richards et al., 1989, 1993). Thus, intrinsic clients also may benefit from an examination of how their religious beliefs and lifestyle may be affecting their presenting problems and emotional disturbance.

Since Allport's groundbreaking contributions, several other theorists and researchers have formally proposed and empirically tested theories of religious and spiritual well-being, development, and maturity, such as Fowler's (1981) six-stage model of faith development, Paloutzian and Ellison's (1979; Ellison, 1983; Paloutzian & Ellison, 1991) two-dimensional model of spiritual well-being, and Malony's (1985) eight-dimensional model of Christian maturity. Several other informal, empirically untested models of healthy and unhealthy religiosity and spirituality also have been proposed, such as Bergin's (1993) description of adaptive-healthy versus maladaptive-unhealthy religious values and lifestyles and Clinebell's (1965) tests for mentally healthy religion. We believe that any or all of these models could prove useful to therapists as they attempt to assess and conceptualize the healthiness and maturity of their clients' religious and spiritual orientations. Summary descriptions of each of these theories and models of religiosity and spirituality are provided in Tables 8.1–8.5.

In addition to the models of religious and spiritual maturity presented in Tables 8.1 through 8.5, it is also important for us to mention that several abnormal or pathological forms of religious experiences and behavior have been described in the literature and are sometimes observed in clinical situations; for example, demonic possession, scrupulosity ("obsessive overconcern for one's sinfulness"), ecstasy or frenzy, repetitive denominational shifting, acedia ("spiritual languor or depression"), glossolalia (speaking in tongues "when the personal milieu does not esteem this activity"), sudden

TABLE 8.1
Fowler's (1996) Stages of Faith and Selfhood

Stage and Description

I. Primal faith (infancy): A prelanguage disposition of trust forms in the mutuality of one's relationships with parents and other caregivers to offset the anxiety that results from separations that occur during infant development. The incorporative self.

II. Intuitive-projective faith (early childhood): Imagination, stimulated by stories, gestures, and symbols and not yet controlled by logical thinking, combines with perception and feelings to create long-lasting images that represent both the protective and the threatening powers surrounding one's life. The impulsive self.

III. Mythic-literal faith (childhood and beyond): The developing ability to think logically helps one order the world with categories of causality, space, and time; to enter into perspectives of others; and to capture life meaning in stories. The imperial self.

IV. Synthetic-conventional faith (adolescence and beyond): New cognitive abilities make mutual perspective taking possible and enable one to integrate diverse self-images into a coherent identity. A personal and largely unreflective synthesis of beliefs and values evolves to support identity and to unite one emotional solidarity with others. The interpersonal self.

V. Individuative-reflexive faith (young adulthood and beyond): Critical reflection on one's beliefs and values using third-person perspective taking; understanding of the self and others as part of a social system; the internalization of authority; and the assumption of responsibility for making explicit choice of ideology and lifestyle open the way for critically self-aware commitments in relationships and vocation. The institutional self.

VI. Conjunctive faith (early midlife and beyond): The embracement of polarities in one's life, an alertness to paradox, and the need for multiple interpretations of reality mark this stage. Symbol and story, metaphor, and myth (from one's own traditions and that of others) are newly appreciated (second, or willed naiveté) as vehicles for expressing truth. The interindividual self.

VII. Universalizing faith (midlife and beyond): Beyond paradox and polarities, individuals in this stage are grounded in a oneness with the power of being. Their visions and commitments free them for a passionate yet detached spending of self in love devoted to overcoming division, oppression, and violence and in effective anticipatory response to an in-breaking commonwealth of love and justice.

Evaluation: This is a useful model for helping therapists think about how developed and mature their clients' religious and spiritual faith is. Critics of this model have argued that it is (a) contaminated by liberal attitudes, (b) based on assumptions of relativism and universalism, and (c) heavily cognitive in emphasis and neglects faith's affective component (Wulff, 1991). Therapists should keep in mind these potential biases and limitations when using this model.

TABLE 8.2
Paloutzian and Ellison's (1979; Ellison, 1983) Two-Dimensional Model of Spiritual Well-Being

Dimension and description

Religious Well-Being
Religious well-being is defined as the vertical dimension of spiritual well-being. People with religious well-being feel close to God and believe that their relationship with God contributes to their sense of well-being. They perceive that God loves and cares about them, gives them strength and support, and is concerned about their problems.

Existential Well-Being
Existential well-being is defined as the horizontal dimension of spiritual well-being. People with existential well-being feel a sense of well-being about the way their lives are going. They feel a sense of purpose, meaning, and life direction and look forward to their future with optimism and confidence. They also feel happy and satisfied with how their lives are going.

Evaluation: We believe that it is an oversimplification to view spiritual well-being as a two-dimensional phenomenon; a number of theorists agree that it is multidimensional. Nevertheless, religious well-being, as defined by Paloutzian and Ellison, is an important dimension of spiritual well-being for many theistic clients. Assessing how such clients feel about their relationship with God is often useful in clinical situations. It is often also useful to assess clients' sense of existential well-being. When doing so, we believe that therapists should determine whether clients' religious and spiritual beliefs are contributing to their clients' existential well-being.

conversion, and crisis (panic or catastrophe with religious implications) (Lovinger, 1984, p. 179, 1996; Pruyser, 1971). Meadow and Kahoe (1984) also described a number of abnormal religious experiences including religious delusions, compulsions, and masochism. In recent years, media attention has been drawn to destructive religious behaviors such as mass suicides of religious cult members, ritualistic child abuse, and satanic worship.

Depending on the settings in which they work, therapists may at times be called on to assess whether their clients' religious behaviors and experiences fall into the abnormal and pathological extremes. As a general guide, when assessing whether religious behaviors and expressions are abnormal or pathological, it is important for therapists to have a sound understanding of both psychopathology and religious beliefs and behaviors that are considered normative and healthy (as well as abnormal) within the client's religious and cultural tradition. Of course, relying solely on group norms to determine whether a religious belief or behavior is unhealthy or pathological is not sufficient; for some groups at times engage in religious practices that are unhealthy and pathological (e.g., mass suicides, ritualistic child abuse). It is beyond the scope of our book to discuss these extremes in detail and so we refer readers to Lovinger (1984, 1996), Meadow and Kahoe (1984), Pruyser (1971), Meissner (1996), and Galanter (1996) for additional helpful information about these issues.

TABLE 8.3
Malony's (1985) Eight-Dimensional Model of Christian Maturity

Dimension and Description

Awareness of God

Mature persons

Stand in awe before God as creatures and are aware of their Creator

Express awareness of their dependence on the Creator but also recognize their capabilities

Show humility in the face of life's problems but do not deny their own capacity for productive action

Worship God as an expression of reverence and love

Pray as a means of spiritual sustenance and communion with God and as a way of honestly expressing concerns

Acceptance of God's grace and love

Mature persons

View God as loving them unconditionally

Use God's love and forgiveness as an impetus for new life and responsible action

Appreciate God's love and manifest this through a sense of joy and gratitude

Have the ability to find meaning, based on trust in God and his goodness, in the suffering and difficulties of life

Being repentant and responsible

Mature persons

Accurately accept personal responsibility without denying other factors, such as the environment, in personal difficulties and sin

Attitudes toward repentance are based on constructive sorrow that leads to a concern to correct the situation

Are aware of their inner impulses and accept them as a legitimate part of their humanness

Are able to request and accept forgiveness from others without feeling threatened or self-depreciating

Are forgiving of others

Knowing God's leadership and direction

Mature persons

Express trust in God's leadership for life yet also recognize their role in that process

Express an optimistic, yet realistic, hope based on trust in God

Are confident, without denying present problems, that God is in control of life

Have a positive sense of role identity that provides meaning in relation to faith

Involvement in organized religion

Mature persons

Experience regular weekly involvement with others in religious worship, prayer, study, and service

Evidence active involvement and commitment to religious activities

Are involved in church or in a religious group as an index of their desire to grow in their faith

Experiencing fellowship

Mature persons

Experience relationships at various levels of intimacy including interdependent, growth-oriented relationships with other believers

Identify positively with the family of God and have a sense of community with other believing persons as well as with people everywhere

Have a sense of commonality with all of God's creatures and with God's creation

TABLE 8.3 *(cont.)*

Dimension and Description

Being ethical
  Mature persons
    Follow their ethical principles in a flexible but committed manner
    Have a religious faith that strongly underlies and guides their ethical be-
      havior
    Show a concern for personal and social ethics
    Are concerned about individual responsibility and social justice
    Have a sense that they are serving others through their work or vocation

Affirming openness in faith
  Mature persons
    Have a faith that provides a directive for life as a whole
    Spend a significant time reading about their faith and discussing it with
      others as an expression of a desire to grow in faith
    Show a tolerance for other viewpoints and evidence a willingness to exam-
      ine others' beliefs in an honest manner while expressing confidence in
      their own view
    Have a faith that is differentiated and composed of a relatively large number
      of categories and elements

Evaluation: Malony's model provides therapists with a comprehensive description of characteristics and attitudes of mature religious people from a Christian perspective. The major shortcoming of the model is that it is uncertain
  how well it applies outside of the Protestant Christian tradition. Research is
  needed to investigate this. Models of religious maturity from Catholic, Jewish,
  Muslim, Buddhist, Hindu, and other religious perspectives may be needed. In
  the meantime, therapists need to be cautious about applying this model to
  non-Christian clients.

Note. Adapted from Malony (1985) by permission.

THE PROCESS OF RELIGIOUS-SPIRITUAL ASSESSMENT

We believe that a religious-spiritual assessment should be embedded
in a multilevel, multisystemic assessment strategy. Figure 8.1 helps illustrate
what we mean by this. The circle in Figure 8.1 represents a person, and
the pie-slice-shaped divisions within the circle represent the different
systems within the person that therapists should assess: the physical,
social, behavioral, intellectual, educational-occupational, psychological-
emotional, and religious-spiritual systems. When therapists first begin working with clients, they need to do a brief global assessment of all the major
systems mentioned earlier. We refer to this as a *Level 1 multisystemic assessment* (represented in Figure 8.1 by the outer ring of the circle). During a
Level 1 assessment, therapists rely primarily on clients' perceptions and self-
descriptions of how they are functioning in each system of their life.

Depending on the client's presenting problems and goals, and the
information obtained during the Level 1 multisystemic assessment, thera-

TABLE 8.4
Clinebell's (1965) Tests for Mentally Healthy Religion

Question

Does a particular form of religious thought and practice . . .

1. Build bridges or barriers between people?

2. Strengthen or weaken a basic sense of trust and relatedness to the universe?

3. Stimulate or hamper the growth of inner freedom and personal responsibility?

4. Provide effective or faulty means of helping people move from a sense of guilt to forgiveness? Does it provide well-defined significant ethical guidelines, or does it emphasize ethical trivia? Is its primary concern for surface behavior or for the underlying health of the personality?

5. Increase or lessen the enjoyment of life? Does it encourage a person to appreciate or depreciate the feeling dimension of life?

6. Handle the vital energies of sex and aggressiveness in constructive or repressive ways?

7. Encourage the acceptance or denial of reality? Does it foster magical or mature religious beliefs? Does it encourage intellectual honesty with respect to doubts? Does it oversimplify the human situation or face its tangled complexity?

8. Emphasize love (and growth) or fear?

9. Give its adherents a frame of orientation and object of devotion that is adequate in handling existential anxiety constructively?

10. Encourage the individual to relate to his or her unconscious through living symbols?

11. Accommodate itself to the neurotic patterns of the society or endeavor to change them?

12. Strengthen or weaken self-esteem?

Note. Adapted from Clinebell (1965).

pists then proceed with more in-depth assessments of the systems that seem clinically warranted. For example, if after completing the Level 1 assessment the client reports that he or she is not experiencing any significant physical problems or symptoms, the therapist would probably not do any further assessment of the client's physical status. If during the Level 1 assessment the client did report that he or she was experiencing significant depression and anxiety and that he or she had some religious concerns (e.g., guilt over violating one's religious values) that seemed to be contributing to these symptoms, the therapist would proceed with more in-depth assessments of both the affective symptoms and the religious issues. More focused, probing questions would be asked during clinical interviews, and the therapist might

TABLE 8.5
Religious–Spiritual Values, Lifestyles, and Mental Health:
An Interview and Assessment Guide

Adaptive–Healthy Values and Lifestyles and Eternal Identity	Maladaptive–Unhealthy Values and Lifestyles and Mortal Overlay
1A. Intrinsic* Sincere Congruent Lives religion Personal faith	1B. Extrinsic* Role-playing Incongruent Uses religion Normative faith
2A. Actualizing Growth-oriented* Self-regulated agency* Experiential–creative Self-renewing–repentant Integrates ambiguity and paradox	2B. Perfectionistic Righteous performances Over-controlled inefficacy* Ritualistic–stagnant* Self-punitive–depressed Anxious about the unanticipated
3A. Reforming–renewing Change-oriented Benevolent–reforming power* Tolerant Egalitarian	3B. Authoritarian* Rigid Dogmatic–absolutistic Intolerant–prejudiced Controlling–dominating
4A. Interpersonal–social orientation Networking–familial–kinship* Cooperative Open–authentic–integrity* Self-sacrificing	4B. Narcissistic Self-aggrandizing Competitive Manipulation–deception* Self-gratifying
5A. Nurturing Tender–protective Warm–faithful*–intimate* Caring Facilitating growth* Empathic*	5B. Aggressive Angry–abusive–violent* Antisocial–unfaithful* Sadistic Power-seeking* Insensitive
6A. Reconciling Forgiving* Humble Appropriately direct Problem-solving	6B. Dependent Pleasing–submissive Compliant–masochistic Passive–aggressive Conflict–avoidant
7A. Inspiring Attunement to spirit of truth* Prophetic Mystical-good reality testing	7B. Hyperspiritual God-controlled–externalizing Occult*–evil inspired* Mystical-poor reality testing

Note. This schema shows how personality and lifestyle dimensions can be intertwined with values, religion, and spiritual themes. It also illustrates applications of the personality and psychospiritual themes in Table 5.4 and chapter 5 to lifestyles. This table may be used by clinicians as an interview and assessment guide for evaluating how healthy and adaptive clients' religious and spiritual values and lifestyles are at the beginning and throughout therapy. It also is a helpful outline for setting therapeutic goals that are in harmony with the values and conceptual framework presented in chapter 5. Terms in Table 8.5 that were discussed in chapter 5 are starred (*). Adapted from Bergin (1993).

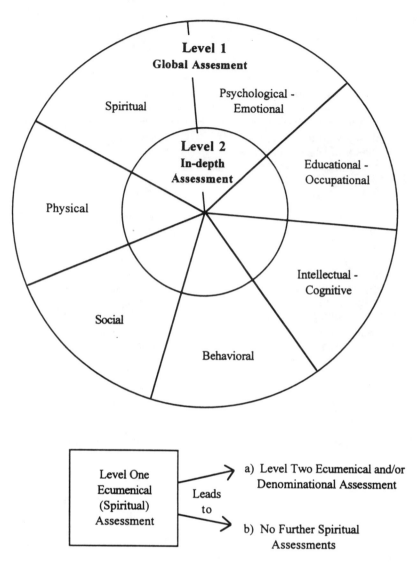

Figure 8.1. A multilevel, multidimensional assessment strategy.

also wish to have the client complete some standardized assessment measures.

We refer to these more focused, in-depth assessments as *Level 2 assessments* (represented by the inner ring of the circle in Figure 8.1). Therapists can pursue Level 2 assessments in as much depth and detail as they feel is warranted. During Level 2 assessments, therapists do not rely primarily on clients' perceptions and self-descriptions of their problems and functioning, but draw more heavily on clinical theory, experience, and objective measures in assessing and conceptualizing clients' issues. We now discuss Level 1 and Level 2 religious-spiritual assessment approaches in greater detail.

A Level 1 Ecumenical Approach

An ecumenical assessment approach is one that is appropriate for clients of diverse religious and spiritual beliefs and affiliations. During an ecumenical assessment, spiritually oriented questions on intake questionnaires and standardized measures, and those asked by therapists in clinical interviews, should not be expressed in narrow, denominationally specific language or concepts but in more general, ecumenical terms. For example, a good ecumenical question might be "Do you believe in a Supreme Being or Higher Power?" A denominational question might be "Do you believe that Jesus Christ is the Son of God?"

When clients present for treatment, as part of a multisystemic assessment therapists should conduct a Level 1 ecumenical assessment to gain a global understanding of their clients' spiritual worldview and current status. Even when a client belongs to the same religious denomination as the therapist, therapists should still conduct such an assessment. Out of respect for individual differences, therapists should not just assume that they understand a client's religious beliefs and values on the basis of religious affiliation alone. Depending on the client's presenting problems and the information obtained in the Level 1 ecumenical assessment, therapists should then either proceed with a more in-depth Level 2 assessment or discontinue any further religious-spiritual assessments.

During a Level 1 multisystemic assessment, it is not feasible to devote a lot of time to making in-depth inquiries about clients' religious and spiritual status. There is too much other information about other systems (e.g., psychological, social, physical) that also must be gathered to obtain a comprehensive, global understanding of clients. Therapists must quickly collect only that information that will help them understand their clients' spiritual worldview and whether their clients' religious and spiritual background and status may be relevant to their presenting problems and treatment planning. Seeking insight into the following seven global assessment questions will help therapists make such a determination:

1. What is the client's metaphysical worldview (e.g., Western [theistic], Eastern, naturalistic-atheistic, naturalistic-agnostic)?
2. What was the client's childhood religious affiliation and experiences?
3. What is the client's current religious affiliation and level of devoutness?
4. Does the client believe his or her spiritual beliefs and lifestyle are contributing to his or her presenting problems and concerns in any way?
5. Does the client have any religious and spiritual concerns and needs?

6. Is the client willing to explore his or her religious and spiritual issues and to participate in spiritual interventions?
7. Does the client perceive that his or her religious and spiritual beliefs and community are a potential source of strength and assistance?

Gaining insight into these Level 1 assessment questions need not be difficult or time-consuming for therapists. Currently, the most viable methods for seeking this information are written intake history questionnaires and clinical interviews. As we discussed earlier, a Level 1 multilevel assessment should begin on clients' first visit to the psychotherapy office. After clients complete whatever paperwork is necessary to begin treatment (e.g., insurance forms, release of medical information form, therapist informed consent document), we recommend that therapists ask clients to complete a client intake history questionnaire. Such questionnaires are used routinely by many therapists and generally solicit information from clients about a variety of topics, including client identifying information (e.g., age, gender, marital status); history and description of presenting problems; psychiatric and counseling history; educational and career history; health and medical history; social and developmental history; and family, marital, and sexual history (e.g., W. H. Cormier & Cormier, 1991; Trzepacz & Baker, 1993). To be useful for a Level 1 ecumenical assessment, such questionnaires also must solicit relevant information about clients' religious and spiritual history and status.

Some therapists do not use written questionnaires, but prefer to gather such information during a semistructured clinical interview with clients. We believe that during a Level 1 ecumenical assessment, therapists should use both methods if possible. Therapists can ask clients to complete a written intake history questionnaire and then supplement this information by probing further during the initial clinical interviews. Table 8.6 provides a list of specific religious–spiritual questions that can be included on client history questionnaires or asked by therapists during clinical interviews. An approach to deepening such queries is provided by Nancy Kehoe's (1997) Religious/Spiritual History Questionnaire that was developed at Cambridge Hospital in Massachusetts.

Level 2 Assessment Approaches

A Level 2 religious-spiritual assessment is conducted only if a Level 1 ecumenical assessment suggests that it is indicated. Generally speaking, further assessment and exploration of religious and spiritual issues, and the use of spiritual interventions, are indicated for clients who have a religious and spiritual worldview and lifestyle, perceive that their spiritual beliefs are

TABLE 8.6
Religious-Spiritual Client Intake Assessment Questions

1. Are religious or spiritual issues important in your life? ____ Yes ____ No ____ Somewhat

2. Do you wish to discuss them in counseling, when relevant? ____ Yes ____ No

    If not, you do not need to answer the remaining questions about religion and spirituality.

3. Do you believe in God or a Supreme Being? ____ Yes ____ No

    Please elaborate if you wish _____

4. Do you believe you can experience spiritual guidance? ____ Yes ____ No

    If so, how often have you had such experiences: often ____ occasionally ____ rarely ____ never ____

5. What is your current religious affiliation (if any)? _____

6. Are you committed to it and actively involved? ____ Yes ____ Somewhat ____ No

7. What was your childhood religious affiliation (if any)?

8. How important was religion or spiritual beliefs to you as a child and adolescent?

    ____ Important ____ Somewhat important ____ Unimportant
    Please elaborate if you wish _____

9. Are you aware of any religious or spiritual resources in your life that could be used to help you overcome your problems? ____ Yes ____ No

    If yes, what are they? _____

10. Do you believe that religious or spiritual influences have hurt you or contributed to some of your problems? ____ Yes ____ No

    If yes, can you briefly explain how? _____

11. Would you like your counselor to consult with your religious leader if it appears this could be helpful to you? ____ Yes ____ No ____ Maybe

    If yes, a permission and confidentiality form will be provided for you to sign.

12. Are you willing to consider trying religious or spiritual suggestions from your counselor if it appears that they could be helpful to you? ____ Yes ____ No

relevant to their presenting problems, and are willing and ready to explore spiritual issues with the therapist.

A Level 2 religious-spiritual assessment can be conducted in an ecumenical or denominationally specific manner. The major difference between these two approaches is that a Level 2 ecumenical assessment approach is used with clients whose religious affiliation and beliefs differ significantly from those of the therapist. A Level 2 denominational assessment approach is appropriate to use only with clients who perceive that the therapist is someone who deeply understands, accepts, and respects their spiritual beliefs (e.g., they belong to the therapist's religious denomination or to some other religious tradition of which the therapist has an in-depth understanding).

When using a Level 2 ecumenical assessment approach, therapists must continue to be careful to use language and assessment measures that are ecumenical in nature to avoid confusing or offending their clients. When using a Level 2 denominational assessment approach, therapists can use language and measures that are tailored more specifically to the subtle nuances of the client's religious beliefs and tradition. Aside from these differences, these two assessment approaches are similar. In both approaches, therapists follow up leads obtained during their Level 1 assessment with more probing, detailed questions and measures. Many of the same dimensions of clients' religiousness and spirituality may be of interest in both approaches. The same basic assessment methods may be used in both (e.g., written questionnaires, clinical interviews, objective self-report tests).

There are a variety of assessment questions that may be important to explore during a Level 2 religious-spiritual assessment depending on the client's presenting problems and what has been revealed during the Level 1 assessment. The general objective of a Level 2 spiritual assessment is to determine whether the client's religious-spiritual orientation is healthy or unhealthy and what impact it is having on the client's presenting problems and disturbance. We list some specific Level 2 assessment questions that we have found clinically useful to pursue:

1. How orthodox is the client in his or her religious beliefs and behavior?
2. What is the client's religious problem-solving style (i.e., deferring, collaborative, self-directing)?
3. How does the client perceive God (e.g., loving and forgiving vs. impersonal and wrathful)?
4. Does the client have a sound understanding of the important doctrines and teachings of his or her religious tradition?
5. Is the client's lifestyle and behavior congruent with his or her religious and spiritual beliefs and values?
6. What stage of faith development is the client in?

7. Does the client have a spiritual assurance of his or her eternal spiritual identity and divine worth?
8. Does the client feel a sense of spiritual well-being (e.g., Is his or her relationship with God a source of comfort and strength)?
9. Is the client's religious orientation predominantly intrinsic, healthy, and mature or extrinsic, unhealthy, and immature (and in what ways)?
10. In what ways, if any, are the client's religious and spiritual background, beliefs, and lifestyle affecting his or her presenting problems and disturbance?

Currently, the most viable method for seeking insight into the Level 2 assessment questions is the clinical interview. By using the models of religiosity and spirituality presented in Tables 8.1 through 8.5 to guide them in their thinking, therapists can ask questions during clinical interviews that can give them in-depth insight into their clients' religiosity and spirituality. When interviewed by Chamberlain et al. (1996), 13 therapists who were experienced in using a spiritual strategy stated that they believed clinical interviewing was the preferred method for conducting religious-spiritual assessments. In fact, all the therapists reported that they relied exclusively on clinical interviews when conducting such assessments.

One reason for an exclusive reliance on clinical interviews is that there currently is little available to assist therapists in the way of standardized, commercially distributed, objective, or projective religious and spiritual tests or measures. There are a relatively large number of objective religious and spiritual research measures that have been developed from within a Christian theological framework (Robinson & Shaver, 1973; Spilka et al., 1985), but few of them have been standardized for use in clinical situations. When working with Christian clients in Level 2 ecumenical or denominational assessment situations, therapists may find some of these measures useful. T. W. Hall, Tisdale, and Brokaw (1994) provided a helpful, more in-depth review of a number of potentially useful religious–spiritual measures. In our own work, we sometimes supplement our clinical interview assessments by administering measures of intrinsic and extrinsic religious orientation (Gorsuch & McPherson, 1989) and spiritual well-being (Ellison, 1983). These give us a quick standardized indication of clients' general levels of religious and spiritual maturity and well-being. Copies of the Intrinsic–Extrinsic and Spiritual Well-Being scales are reprinted in Tables 8.7 and 8.8.

Because most religious and spiritual measures have not been validated in clinical situations, therapists should use them only after they have carefully examined them and verified in their own minds that they are suitable for their clients. Even then, therapists should interpret them tentatively. Normative data are so limited for most of these measures that sharing norma-

TABLE 8.7
Gorsuch and McPherson's (1989) Revised Age Universal
Intrinsic–Extrinsic Scale

Directions: The following items deal with various types of religious ideas and social opinions. Please indicate the response you prefer, or most closely agree with, by circling the number corresponding to your choice in the right margin (e.g., 1 = *strongly disagree*, 5 = *strongly agree*). If none of the choices expresses exactly how you feel, indicate the one that is closest to your own views. If no choice is possible, you may omit the item. There are no right or wrong answers.

Scale	Item
Intrinsic	1. I enjoy reading about my religion.
Extrinsic (Social)	2. I go to church because it helps me to make friends.
Intrinsic[a]	3. It doesn't much matter what I believe so long as I am good.
Intrinsic	4. It is important to me to spend time in private thought and prayer.
Intrinsic	5. I have often had a strong sense of God's presence.
Extrinsic (Personal)	6. I pray mainly to gain relief and protection.
Intrinsic	7. I try hard to live all my life according to my religious beliefs.
Extrinsic (Personal)	8. What religion offers me most is comfort in times of trouble and sorrow.
Extrinsic (Personal)	9. Prayer is for peace and happiness.
Intrinsic[a]	10. Although I am religious, I don't let it affect my daily life.
Extrinsic (Social)	11. I go to church mostly to spend time with my friends.
Intrinsic	12. My whole approach to life is based on my religion.
Extrinsic (Social)	13. I go to church mainly because I enjoy seeing people I know there.
Intrinsic[a]	14. Although I believe in my religion, many other things are more important in life.

Note. A 5-point response format ranging from *strongly disagree* to *strongly agree* is used. Strongly disagree = 1; disagree = 2; somewhat agree, somewhat disagree = 3; agree = 4; and strongly agree = 5 (except on reversed-scored items, in which strongly disagree = 5, disagree = 4, etc.).
[a] Reverse-scored item
This table was reprinted from Gorsuch R. L., and McPherson, S. E. (1989). Intrinsic/extrinsic measurement: I/E revised and single-item scales. *Journal for the Scientific Study of Religion, 28,* 248–254. Reprinted here by permission from the Society for the Scientific Study of Religion.

tive comparisons with clients should be avoided. At most, these measures should be used only to give therapists some tentative insights into their clients and perhaps as a tool to help clients engage in exploration and self-discovery.

We do not know of any objective religious or spiritual self-report measure that is appropriate for non-Christian clients. Although there are some measures that do not contain items whose content is obviously and exclusively Christian, such as the Spiritual Well-Being Scale (Ellison, 1983), the "age universal" intrinsic–extrinsic scale (Gorsuch & McPherson, 1989; Gorsuch & Venable, 1983), and the Adjective Ratings of God (Gorsuch, 1968), they currently lack research evidence that would justify their clinical

TABLE 8.8
Paloutzian and Ellison's (1991) Spiritual Well-Being Scale

Instructions: In the following items, a variety of experiences are described. Please indicate how closely these experiences define your own personal religious experiences and attitudes by circling the appropriate number in the right margin (e.g., 1 = *strongly disagree*, 6 = *strongly agree*).

Scale	Item
Religious Well-Being[a]	1. I don't find much satisfaction in private prayer with God.
Existential Well-Being	2. I feel that life is a positive experience.
Religious Well-Being	3. I believe that God loves me and cares about me.
Existential Well-Being[a]	4. I don't know who I am, where I came from, or where I'm going.
Religious Well-Being[a]	5. I believe that God is impersonal and not interested in my daily situation.
Existential Well-Being[a]	6. I don't enjoy much about life.
Religious Well-Being	7. I have a personally meaningful relationship with God.
Existential Well-Being[a]	8. I feel unsettled about my future.
Religious Well-Being[a]	9. I don't get much personal strength and support from God.
Existential Well-Being[a]	10. I feel that life is full of conflict and unhappiness.
Religious Well-Being	11. I believe that God is concerned about my problems.
Existential Well-Being	12. I feel very fulfilled and satisfied with my life.
Religious Well-Being[a]	13. I don't have a personally satisfying relationship with God.
Existential Well-Being[a]	14. Life doesn't have much meaning.
Religious Well-Being	15. My relationship with God helps me to not feel lonely.
Existential Well-Being	16. I feel a sense of well-being about the direction my life is headed in.
Religious Well-Being	17. I feel most fulfilled when I am in close communion with God.
Existential Well-Being	18. I believe there is some real purpose in life.
Existential Well-Being	19. I feel good about my future.
Religious Well-Being	20. My relationship with God contributes to my sense of well-being.

Note. A 6-point response format ranging from *strongly disagree* to *strongly agree* is used. Strongly disagree = 1, disagree = 2, somewhat disagree = 3, somewhat agree = 4, agree = 5, and strongly agree = 6 (except on reversed-scored items, in which strongly disagree = 6, disagree = 5, etc.). See Paloutzian and Ellison (1991) and Bufford, Paloutzian, and Ellison (1991) for a manual and norms for the spiritual well-being scale.
[a] Reverse-scored item.
From Paloutzian, R. F. and Ellison, C. W. (1991). *Manual for the Spiritual Well-Being Scale*. Nyack, NY: Life Advances. Copyright 1991 by R. F. Paloutzian and C. W. Ellison. All rights reserved. Not to be duplicated unless express written premission is granted by the authors or by Life Advances, Inc., 81 Front Street, Nyack, NY.

use with non-Christian clients. Therefore, there is a great need for denominationally specific measures for the major non-Christian religious traditions and denominations (e.g., Judaism, Islam, Buddhism, Hinduism). Measures that are truly ecumenical in nature, that is, those that can be used validly with clients from diverse religious traditions (both Western and Eastern), are also greatly needed. Promising work in this direction has been conducted by Carole A. Rayburn and Lee J. Richmond (1996; Rayburn, 1997) in Silver Spring, Maryland; they have constructed separate inventories on religiousness and spirituality. Also valuable, and perhaps less difficult to develop, would be some limited-scope ecumenical measures, that is, measures for clients who have a Western theistic, spiritual worldview and other measures for clients who have an Eastern (pantheistic or polytheistic) spiritual worldview. We and our colleagues have begun work on a limited-scope, multidimensional, ecumenical measure for theistic clients. We hope that another research team will begin work on one for clients with an Eastern worldview.

Developing valid, clinically relevant religious and spiritual measures will be a challenging task. To be useful in clinical situations, it is essential for both ecumenical and denominational measures of religiosity and spirituality to meet accepted professional test standards. For example, such measures must provide (a) evidence of reliability and validity, (b) adequate normative data, (c) evidence and information concerning the test's clinical use and relevance, (d) clear administration and scoring instructions, and (e) a detailed test manual (American Psychological Association, 1985). We look forward to the day when measures of religiosity and spirituality that meet such standards are available.

Meta-Empathy and Assessment

For psychotherapists who believe that God can inspire and enlighten human beings, a religious and spiritual assessment will always be more than just gathering and conceptualizing information that has been gathered in intake questionnaires, clinical interviews, and objective or projective assessment measures. As we discussed in chapters 5 and 6, for such therapists, a spiritual assessment includes an effort to seek and remain open to spiritual impressions and insights about clients and their problems that may come from the divine source. Meta-empathy, the capacity to receive felt impressions and insights about clients that go beyond ordinary clinical hypothesizing or hunches (Chamberlain et al., 1996; C. Rogers, personal communication, June 9, 1986), is not well understood or often reported. Nevertheless, we have become convinced that it is a reality. As therapists engage in the process of client assessment and conceptualization, we hope that they will take the time, on occasion, to pray and contemplate about their clients. As they do, they may experience spiritual impressions and insights that deepen their understanding of their clients and increase their ability to help them.

CONCLUSION

Compared with the domains of intellectual, personality, and psychopathology assessment, in which volumes on theory and research have been published and numerous standardized, commercially published tests are available, religious-spiritual assessment is in its infancy. There is obviously much more theoretical and research work that is needed on religious-spiritual assessment approaches and methods. We hope that this work will soon be done and that there will be many more resources available to assist therapists in this domain.

9

RELIGIOUS AND SPIRITUAL PRACTICES AS THERAPEUTIC INTERVENTIONS

The everlasting God . . . the Creator of the ends of the earth . . . giveth power to the faint; and to them that have no might he increaseth strength.

Even the youths shall faint and be weary, and the young men shall utterly fall: But they that wait upon the LORD shall renew their strength; they shall mount up with wings as eagles; they shall run, and not be weary; and they shall walk, and not faint.

—Isaiah 40: 28-31
Holy Bible, King James Version

As we mentioned earlier in this book, what religiously oriented psychotherapists have referred to as spiritual interventions are actually practices or traditions that have been engaged in for centuries in some form by religious believers (e.g., prayer, meditation, Scripture reading, forgiveness). In this chapter, we describe a number of practices that we think have therapeutic potential in ecumenical therapy and across a variety of denominational situations. We also offer some tentative clinical suggestions regarding how these practices can be implemented in therapy appropriately.

Each of the religious and spiritual practices described in this chapter are, in one form or another, advocated by most of the world religious traditions. These practices have endured for centuries because, in different ways, they express and respond to people's deepest needs, concerns, and problems. Research indicates that there is significant healing power in many of them (e.g., H. Benson, 1996; Borysenko & Borysenko, 1994; Krippner & Welch, 1992; W. R. Miller & Martin, 1988). We briefly discuss this evidence in the sections that follow. We hope that spiritual practices can be more frequently used as interventions in therapy to assist clients in their efforts to cope, heal, and grow. In chapter 10, we describe and provide specific examples of how therapists have applied these practices in therapy.

PRAYER

The word *prayer* was defined by James (1902/1936) as "every kind of inward communication or conversation with the power recognized as divine" (p. 454). Prayers can be offered verbally or nonverbally (Meadow & Kahoe, 1984). Prayer is advocated by all the Western (theistic) world religious traditions and by several of the Eastern traditions (e.g., Hinduism, Mahayana Buddhism, Religious Taoism, and Shintoism), although the specific forms of prayer advocated varies from religion to religion.

A variety of different forms of prayer have been described in religious and psychological literature, including, for example, prayers of

> *petition*, asking something for one's self, and *intercession* (asking something for others). There are also prayers of *confession*, the repentance of wrongdoing and the asking of forgiveness; *lamentation*, crying in distress and asking for vindication; *adoration*, giving honor and praise; *invocation*, summoning the presence of the Almighty; and *thanksgiving*, offering gratitude. (Dossey, 1993, p. 5; see also Finney & Malony, 1985a; Heiler, 1932/1958; Meadow & Kahoe, 1984; Poloma & Pendleton, 1991; D. G. Richards, 1991)

Thus, prayers can differ across a variety of dimensions, including the purpose of the prayer, how formal the prayer is, who is being prayed to, and what people are doing and thinking during the prayer.

Considerable research has been done investigating the effects of prayer on physical and psychological health. A number of researchers have attempted to determine whether intercessory prayer on the behalf of people who do not know they are being prayed for promotes their physical and psychological healing (e.g., Byrd, 1988; Collipp, 1969; Finney & Malony, 1985a; Joyce & Welldon, 1965; see also Dossey, 1993, for a critical review of these and other prayer studies). Although there is some intriguing evidence that anonymous intercessory prayer can have positive effects on those being prayed for, overall, this domain of research remains controversial and inconclusive (Dossey, 1993; McCullough, 1995). However, there is no doubt that people who pray do believe that prayer helps them physically and psychologically. Whether this is because of the placebo effect, the "relaxation response," the power of the mind–body connection, or a transcendent healing influence remains scientifically uncertain (H. Benson, 1996; Borysenko, 1993; Dossey, 1993; McCullough, 1995). There also is some evidence that different types of prayer may have different effects on people's emotional well-being and life satisfaction (e.g., Duckro & Magaletta, 1994; Finney & Malony, 1985c; McCullough, 1995; Poloma & Pendleton, 1991; D. G. Richards, 1991). For example, people who engage solely in ritual prayer are more likely to be sad, lonely, depressed, and tense, whereas meditative and colloquial prayer are more likely to be associated with well-being and happiness (Poloma & Pendleton, 1991).

Research has revealed that in their professional work, psychotherapists sometimes (a) pray silently for clients during or outside of therapy sessions, (b) pray vocally with clients during sessions, and (c) encourage clients to pray by themselves outside of therapy sessions (Ball & Goodyear, 1991; Chamberlain et al., 1996; Jones, Watson, & Wolfram, 1992; P. S. Richards & Potts, 1995a; Worthington, Dupont, Berry, & Duncan, 1988). The studies just cited have provided evidence that therapists engage in or encourage clients to engage in petitionary and intercessory prayers, but we do not know whether therapists engage in or encourage other forms of prayer. Finney and Malony (1985b) suggested that therapists may wish to encourage clients to engage in contemplative prayer. Given the preliminary evidence that different forms of prayer may be associated differentially with well-being and life satisfaction, it would seem important for therapists to give careful consideration to what forms of prayer they encourage or engage in with clients.

Therapists who believe in God and think that God can enlighten and guide people would be wise to regularly pray for God's inspiration and guidance to assist them in their work with clients. Prayer and transcendent guidance should not be viewed as a substitute for therapists' professional competency and psychological health. Nevertheless, for therapists who have good psychological health and sound professional competencies and ethics, prayer and spiritual guidance can be an added resource to help them assist their clients. From time to time in therapy, such therapists may experience intuitive insights, impressions, and promptings that help them guide clients through critical change moments in therapy (Chamberlain et al., 1996).

It also may be appropriate at times for therapists to encourage religious clients to turn to God through prayer for assistance, strength, and wisdom. Even therapists who do not believe in God or prayer themselves need to remember that clients' perceived relationships with God can be a great source of strength and comfort to them. In their darkest hours, many people are sustained by their belief that God is there and loves them (Duncan,

Eddy, & Haney, 1981). Prayer is one religious practice that helps many people feel God's love and healing power, and so encouraging clients who are struggling with serious problems to pray for strength, comfort, and wisdom could be a powerful intervention for helping clients cope and heal.

We have some serious reservations about therapists praying with clients during therapy sessions. In the studies that have distinguished between praying with clients and client or therapist solitary prayers, it has been found that praying with clients during sessions is a relatively rare practice (Jones et al., 1992; P. S. Richards & Potts, 1995a; Shafranske & Malony, 1990). In P. S. Richards and Potts's (1995a) survey of Mormon therapists, 33 therapists mentioned specifically that they believed psychotherapists should not pray with clients during sessions. In general, we tend to agree with this position.

Praying with clients during sessions increases the risk that role boundaries will become confused. Clients may find it more difficult to keep clear in their minds the differences between the roles of professional therapists and religious leaders. The danger of potentially unhealthy transference issues arising in therapy also is greater. We suspect that clients who have unresolved issues of anger toward or dependency on God and religious authorities are more likely to project these issues onto the therapist if their therapist prays with them. Of course, we recognize that when such transference issues arise during therapy they can be used to a therapeutic advantage, but we believe the risks may outweigh the potential benefits.

We are not saying that therapists should never pray with their clients during therapy sessions. Praying with clients may be more appropriate in some settings and with some types of clients than with others. For example, therapists who practice in religious settings (e.g., religious universities, church social service agencies) may find that it is expected, comfortable, and helpful to pray with clients individually or in group sessions. Therapists in private practice settings who work with generally well-functioning religiously devout clients also may find that praying with clients can be helpful. In some inpatient settings in which religious services are included as part of the treatment milieu, it also may be appropriate. However, therapists in such situations who pray with their clients should be alert to the possible dangers of such a practice.

Finally, when praying with clients or encouraging clients to pray, therapists need to make sure that they work within their clients' religious belief systems so that they do not impose their own beliefs about and practices of prayer on their clients. In denominational therapeutic situations, with clients who do not understand how to pray but who would like to learn, it may be appropriate for therapists to teach clients about prayer and how it could help them. In ecumenical therapy situations, it may be appropriate for therapists to explore clients' beliefs about prayer and to encourage them to pray for help with their problems. However, in ecumenical situations, if clients lack an understanding of prayer, we believe that, in general, it may be most appropriate for therapists to avoid teaching such clients about prayer themselves and to refer them to their religious leaders or members of their religious community for such instruction and guidance. Such a practice will reduce the possibility that therapists will impose their own beliefs about prayer on clients from other religious faiths.

CONTEMPLATION AND MEDITATION

The word *contemplate* is defined in the *American Heritage Dictionary of the English Language* (1992) as "to consider carefully and at length; meditate on or ponder" (p. 406). According to J. P. Miller (1994), "contemplation includes meditation as well as spontaneous and unstructured moments when we experience a connection with the unity of things. . . . Meditation is a form of contemplation that involves concentrated practice" (pp. 2–3). Meditation was defined by J. C. Smith (1975) as a "family of mental exercises that generally involve calmly limiting thought and attention. Such exercises vary widely and can involve sitting still and counting breaths, attending to a repeated thought, or focusing on virtually any simple external or internal stimulus" (p. 558). Specific types of meditation include, for example, vipassans (insight), mindfulness, transcendental, Zen, visualization, and devotional meditation (H. Benson, 1996; Borysenko & Borysenko, 1994; Carlson, Bacaseta, & Simanton, 1988; Hirai, 1989; J. P. Miller, 1994; Sweet & Johnson, 1990). J. P. Miller (1994) categorized meditation approaches into four general types: intellectual (i.e., a focus on awareness and discrimination), emotional (i.e., connect with the heart), physical (i.e., involves various forms of movement), and action-service (i.e., service oriented).

Many forms of contemplation and meditation have come directly from the Eastern religious traditions, most notably, Hinduism, Jainism, and Buddhism. Some writers have expressed concerns that the passive forms of meditation (i.e., those that encourage shutting down of mental activity) advocated by some Eastern traditions may not be compatible with the Western (theistic) religious traditions (e.g., Carlson et al., 1988; McLemore, 1982). However, other writers have pointed out similarities between Eastern and Western forms of contemplation, meditation, imagery, and centering prayer (e.g., Carlson et al., 1988; Finney & Malony, 1985b). Martin and Carlson (1988) suggested that there is a relationship between relaxation, meditation, and some forms of prayer; we would also add contemplation and spiritual imagery to this list. All of these spiritual practices require a trusting, passive attitude of release and surrender of control, isolation from distracting environmental noise, active focusing or repetition of thoughts, task awareness, and muscle relaxation (Martin & Carlson, 1988; Payne, Bergin, & Loftus, 1992).

Research has revealed that psychotherapists have occasionally recommended or used contemplation, meditation, and spiritual imagery with clients, although, relatively speaking, these interventions are used less frequently than most other spiritual interventions (Ball & Goodyear, 1991; Jones et al., 1992; P. S. Richards & Potts, 1995a; Sweet & Johnson, 1990; Worthington et al., 1988). Given the relatively large amount of empirical evidence that such practices can have significant healing effects on the mind and body (H. Benson, 1996; Borysenko & Borysenko, 1994), it is surprising that they are not used more frequently in psychotherapy. Perhaps most psychotherapists have been trained and are more comfortable with secularized versions of these practices, such as biofeedback, progressive muscle relaxation, and hypnosis.

On the basis of his clinical practice as a physician, H. Benson (1996) concluded that interventions designed to promote the relaxation response are more powerful when they draw on people's deepest religious and spiritual convictions. He referred to this as "the faith factor" and indicated that it appears that people's faith in an "eternal or life-transcending force" enhances "the average effects of the relaxation response" (H. Benson, 1996, pp. 151, 155). Carlson et al. (1988) also found evidence of this in an empirical study that compared the relative effectiveness of devotional meditation and progressive muscle relaxation. Individuals who engaged in devotional meditation reported less anger, anxiety, and muscle tension than did those who engaged in progressive muscle relaxation. Thus, there is reason to believe that spiritual practices such as meditation, contemplation, and religious imagery could have more powerful healing effects with religious and spiritual clients than secular interventions that have purged all religious and spiritual content or meaning. More comparative studies are needed, but, in the meantime, we believe that therapists should be more open to encouraging or using contemplation, meditation, and spiritual imagery with their religious and spiritual clients.

Contemplation, meditation, and spiritual imagery may be especially indicated in therapy with spiritually devout clients who are at risk physically and psychologically because of Type A coronary prone behavior pattern (Martin & Carlson, 1988). Clients struggling with stress-related problems, such as reactive depression, anxiety, panic attacks, adjustment disorders, and posttraumatic stress disorder, as well as those who have health problems, such as hypertension, cardiovascular problems, cancer, and weakened autoimmune systems, may also benefit psychologically, spiritually, and physically from such practices (H. Benson, 1996; Martin & Carlson, 1988). Of course, many psychotherapy clients, to one degree or another, struggle with higher-than-normal levels of emotional distress, and therefore it may be that some form of contemplation, meditation, or spiritual imagery could be beneficial for most religiously and spiritually devout clients. Clients who are active, busy, and performance focused may not find contemplative practices appealing. However, such clients may benefit most from practices that help them slow down, focus inward, and get more in touch with their emotional and spiritual feelings (H. Benson, 1996; Borysenko & Borysenko, 1994; J. P. Miller, 1994).

Therapists need to be sure that the forms of contemplation, meditation, and spiritual imagery they encourage or use with clients are consistent with clients' religious and spiritual beliefs. Some Eastern forms of meditation, for example, may be viewed negatively by some Christian clients (McLemore, 1982). Selecting forms of meditation that are more active and Bible centered may be essential with such clients. When therapists are working in a denominational therapeutic stance, and thus have an in-depth knowledge of their clients' religious beliefs, it should not be difficult for them to tailor contemplative practices to fit the beliefs of their clients. In ecumenical situations, therapists will need to rely heavily on their clients' input to help them select forms of contemplation, meditation, and spiritual imagery with which clients feel comfortable. In ecumenical situations, it may often be most appropriate to encourage clients to engage in these practices outside of therapy to reduce the possibility of therapist value imposition and client discomfort. Because of the amount of time contemplation and meditation can take, therapists should limit how much in-session time is spent engaging in these practices. Once clients understand how to engage in contemplative practices, and appreciate their purpose and possible benefits, they should normally be encouraged to engage in these practices outside therapy.

READING SACRED WRITINGS

All the major world religious traditions have some type of text or writings that devout followers view as sacred and as a source of spiritual wisdom and insight (Nigosian, 1994; see also chap. 4 in this book). According to Whiting (1983),

> holy books are usually ones which contain teaching revealed by God or gods and so they are of very special value to their religions. . . .
>
> Holy books are usually given a place of honour in the worship building and may be ceremoniously carried in during services. Readings from them are considered most important and a sermon (instructive talk) may be based on some passage from them. . . .
>
> The contents of holy books are varied. They are likely to contain some historical facts as well as biographies of leading characters, rules to be followed, songs or poems to be recited, and myths. (p. 46)

Each of the major theistic world religious traditions teach that God, the Supreme Being, has revealed himself and his words to human beings through that tradition's Scriptures or sacred writings (McCasland, Cairns, & Yu, 1969; Smart, 1994; Whiting, 1983). For example, Jews believe that God revealed himself and his law to Moses, as recorded in the Torah. Jews also revere the Talmud, which is "a huge collection of traditions to explain the Torah, as well as the oral law handed down by word of mouth from previous generations" (Whiting, 1983, p. 57). Christians believe that God revealed himself and his will through his son, Jesus Christ, as recorded in the Holy Bible (particularly the New Testament). Some Christian denominations also believe in other sacred writings; for example, Mormons accept the Book of Mormon as a record of God's revelations to prophets of the appearance of the resurrected Christ in ancient America. Muslims believe that Allah (God) revealed his eternal speech and words to human beings through the angel Gabriel to Mohammed, as recorded in the Qur'an. Zoroastrians believe that God revealed himself to human beings in the Avesta. Sikhs believe that God revealed himself through gurus whose inspired words, along with those of other holy men, are recorded in the Guru Granth Sahib.

The major Eastern world religious traditions view their sacred writings as a source of spiritual and moral wisdom, although not all of them claim that these writings are necessarily a revelation from God or the gods. For example, in Hinduism, there are two types of sacred writings: Sruti (hearings) and Smriti (memory). The Sruti include the Vedas, Brahmanas, Aranqakas, and Upanishads and are viewed as wisdom the "rishis (holy men) heard from the gods" (Whiting, 1983, pp. 46–47; Roger R. Keller, personal communication, March 12, 1997). The Smriti are long collections of stories that "were remembered from generation to generation and then written down by wise men" (Whiting, 1983, p. 47). They are considered less authoritative than the Sruti. In Buddhism, there are several sacred writings, including the Tripitaka, which are the scriptures of the Theravada Buddhists (Nigosian, 1994; Whiting, 1983). The Tripitaka contains teachings of Buddha and his followers as well as stories about Buddha. Mahayana Buddhists accept the Tripitaka, but they also accept many other sacred texts, which contain sayings, rules, and stories (Nigosian, 1994; Whiting, 1983). In Jainism, there are two canons of sacred writings: those of the Svetambaras and Digambaras (Nigosian, 1994). The Svetambara canon consists of 45 texts that deal with matters such as the origin of the universe, astronomy, geography, doctrines, and rules on ascetic life (Nigosian, 1994). The Digambara canon "consists of two major works that address the doctrines of karma and passions" (Nigosian, 1994, p. 162). The Jain canons are thought to contain Mahavira's (Jainism's founder) basic teachings and those of his followers.

This brief description of the sacred writings of some of the world's major religious traditions illustrates that there is great diversity among these traditions about what texts or writings are viewed as sacred or holy. Not only do each of the major religions differ in what writings they consider sacred, but individuals within each tradition differ in the degree of orthodoxy with which they view their tradition's sacred writings. Some people are highly orthodox and view their tradition's sacred writings as infallible and as literally and completely the word of God. At the other extreme are religious believers who might view the sacred writings of their tradition as a source of spiritual wisdom, insight, and poetic metaphors for how to live but nevertheless as the fallible writings of human beings that also contain errors, myths, and false traditions. Religious and spiritual people also differ in how frequently they read or study the sacred texts of their traditions. Some study the Scriptures daily, whereas others never read their tradition's sacred writings but rely on memories, cultural traditions, or the teachings and interpretations of their spiritual leaders.

People also differ in the purpose for which they read sacred writings. Some believers study their tradition's Scriptures for intellectual reasons, to gain a more complete doctrinal understanding of their tradition's theology or philosophy. Others find comfort, insight, and enjoyment as they read the narrative stories and myths found in these writings. Many also read and reflect on sacred writings because they feel that doing so brings them into the presence of the divine (i.e., they feel a sense of spiritual communion and enlightenment). Regardless of how infallible or fallible people view the sacred writings of their tradition, or how frequently or in what manner they read these writings, a belief most religious people share is that their tradition's sacred writings can be a source of understanding, instruction, guidance, comfort, insight, and enlightenment (Nigosian, 1994; Smart, 1993, 1994; Whiting, 1983). An indication of the social and psychological importance of sacred writings was disclosed by a survey in the United States by the Book of the Month Club. In reply to the question of what book had most influenced their lives, respondents identified the Bible more frequently than any other book. Even Albert Ellis (1993), who is an atheist, acknowledged that the Bible has been the single, most significant self-help book in human history.

Research has revealed that psychotherapists are using Scriptures and sacred writings in therapy in a number of different ways and that they are doing so frequently. Therapists have (a) quoted Scriptures[1] to clients, (b) interpreted Scriptures to clients, (c) made indirect reference to Scriptures while discussing or teaching religious concepts, (d) related stories from the Scriptures, (e) encouraged clients to memorize Scriptures, (f) encouraged clients to read and study Scriptures outside therapy sessions, and (g) used Scriptures to challenge clients' dysfunctional or irrational beliefs (Ball &

---

[1] We use the term *Scriptures* as a convenience to include both canonized texts such as the Bible as well as other sacred or inspirational writings that do not have such a formal status.

Goodyear, 1991; Jones et al., 1992; Propst, 1980; Propst, Ostrom, Watkins, Dean, & Mashburn, 1992; P. S. Richards & Potts, 1995a; Tan, 1987; Worthington et al., 1988). Overall, it appears that some variation of scriptural discussion, interpretation, and study is engaged in more frequently during psychotherapy than any other spiritual intervention (Ball & Goodyear, 1991; Jones et al., 1992; Moon, Willis, Bailey, & Kwasny, 1993; P. S. Richards & Potts, 1995a; Worthington et al., 1988). This is interesting, especially considering that little research has been done to evaluate the effects of reading or studying Scriptures or sacred writings.

It is true that cognitive therapy treatment approaches that have included Scriptures to help challenge dysfunctional beliefs have been successful at reducing clients' depression (e.g., Pecheur & Edwards, 1984; Propst, 1980; Propst et al., 1992). In addition, scriptural readings and reflections, combined with prayer and quiet time, have been shown to help reduce anger, anxiety, and muscle tension (e.g., Carlson et al., 1988). However, in all these studies, Scriptures were just one part of a multifaceted treatment program, and so it is impossible to isolate the effects of the scriptural interventions. Making reference to Scriptures was the most frequently reported "effective" spiritual intervention in the case reports of 215 Mormon therapists (P. S. Richards & Potts, 1995a). Despite these suggestive findings, we are aware of little conclusive evidence that reading, studying, interpreting, discussing, or reflecting on Scriptures and other sacred writings have beneficial psychological or physical effects. We believe that such practices and interventions are often therapeutic, but there is clearly a need for research to explore how this may be so.

It appears that sacred writings can be used for a variety of purposes in therapy, such as helping clients (a) challenge and modify their dysfunctional beliefs; (b) reframe and understand their problems and lives from an eternal, spiritual perspective; (c) clarify and enrich their understanding of the doctrines of their religious tradition; and (d) seek God's enlightenment, comfort, and guidance. Before implementing a spiritual intervention that uses sacred writings in some way, therapists, of course, should assess their clients' beliefs and feelings about scriptures and sacred writings carefully. Therapists should use only scriptural interventions that are compatible with their clients' spiritual beliefs.

Therapists should avoid getting into scriptural or theological debates with their clients. Some clients would probably enjoy such power struggles, but others may be deeply offended by it. Scriptural debates could lead to unethical therapist value imposition. Thus, in our opinion, such debates are rarely appropriate or helpful. When questioning clients' scriptural understandings or offering their own scriptural interpretations, we believe that therapists should do so nondogmatically, making it clear that they do not speak with any official authority (cf. Lovinger, 1984).

When therapists believe that their clients' scriptural understandings are dysfunctional, it may be best for them to refer such clients to their religious leaders for doctrinal discussions and clarification. This is most effective when the therapist has permission to converse with or sit in with the leader. If client and therapist are both of the same belief system, it may be appropriate for therapists to invite clients to explore specific writings that would help clarify their misunderstandings, but even here therapists should be cautious not to set themselves up as authorities.

It appears that most religiously oriented therapists have used Scriptures as a cognitive intervention to influence and modify clients' religious understandings and cognitions (see also Table 10.3 in chap. 10 in this book for an example of a biblical Scripture used by Propst for this purpose). We believe that Scriptures also have much potential as affective and transcendent interventions. The stories and narratives in sacred writings can serve as powerful metaphors for connecting with clients affectively and spiritually. Much has been written in recent years about the power of metaphors and stories (e.g., Barker, 1996; Kopp, 1995; Mills & Crowley, 1986; Siegelman, 1990; Vitz, 1990, 1992a, 1992b), and scriptual stories are some of the most powerful and meaningful in all of literature.

Many religious people believe that sacred writings are a means for helping them communicate with God and know of his will for them. With clients who believe this, it may be appropriate for therapists to encourage them to read, ponder, and reflect on the Scriptures with the purpose of seeking transcendent insight into their problems and concerns. Of course, such an intervention could be misused. Clients have sometimes reported that they had received the advice from family or religious leaders that "If you'll just read the Scriptures and pray about it, everything will be fine." Reading Scriptures and praying about problems may help many clients, but such practices should not be recommended as if they were a magical cure for all of life's problems. If clients do read the Scriptures seeking enlightenment about how to cope with and overcome their problems and feel that they do not gain such insight, therapists need to be prepared to process such "failures" with their clients.

FORGIVENESS AND REPENTANCE

The word *forgive* is defined in the *American Heritage Dictionary of the English Language* (1992) as "to excuse for a fault or an offense; pardon" and "to renounce anger or resentment against" (p. 713). The word *repent* is defined as "to feel remorse, contrition, or self-reproach for what one has done or failed to do" and "to make a change for the better as a result of remorse or contrition for one's sins" (*American Heritage Dictionary of the English Language*, 1992, p. 1530). Repentance can be viewed as a prelude to forgiveness; that is, in repentance, people seek forgiveness from God or from those they have hurt or offended, and it includes reform in thought, feeling, and action (McCullough, Sandage, & Worthington, 1997; McCullough & Worthington, 1994a, 1994b; Payne et al., 1992). All the theistic world religions teach that people should forgive those who have harmed or offended them and seek forgiveness for wrong doings (R. R. Keller, personal communication, May 8, 1996). There are, of course, differences in the specific beliefs about to whom, when, and how forgiveness should be granted and sought. For example, within the Christian tradition, believers are told to forgive "all enemies and offenders in an unqualified way" (Payne et al., 1992, p. 183). In the Jewish tradition, it may not be viewed as desirable to "forgive people who do not acknowledge the injury, or even worse, rationalize their injurious behavior as having been deserved" (Lovinger, 1990, p. 177). In some religious traditions (e.g., Catholic, Mormon), confession to church authorities is viewed as a necessary step in seeking forgiveness, whereas in other traditions, confession to religious authorities is not viewed as necessary.

From a religious perspective, forgiveness is viewed as an act that has important spiritual consequences. For example, within the Christian tradition, forgiveness is thought to restore people's relationship with God, help them qualify for salvation, and demonstrate their faith in God and Jesus Christ and their desire to do God's will (McCullough & Worthington, 1994b). From a psychological perspective, writers have suggested that forgiveness can (a) promote positive changes in affective well-being, (b) physical and mental health, (c) restoration in a sense of personal power, and (d) reconciliation between the offended and offender (Bergin, 1988; McCullough & Worthington, 1994a, 1994b). Hope (1987) suggested that by choosing to forgive, people increase their options and freedom to grow. When seeking forgiveness, people take responsibility for their wrongdoings and thus make it easier for those they have hurt to heal.

Research reveals that encouraging forgiveness is one of the most frequently used spiritual interventions by psychotherapists (Ball & Goodyear, 1991; DiBlasio, 1992; DiBlasio & Benda, 1991; DiBlasio & Proctor, 1993; Freedman & Enright, 1996; Jones et al., 1992; Moon et al., 1993; P. S. Richards & Potts, 1995a; Worthington et al., 1988). Therapists have encouraged clients to forgive (a) parents and others who have hurt, abused, or offended them; (b) themselves for their own mistakes and transgressions; and (c) God. They also have encouraged clients to repent and seek forgiveness from others and from God. Preliminary evidence does provide support for the belief that forgiveness is an important component of interpersonal and psychological healing (Freedman & Enright, 1996; Hebl & Enright, 1993; Worthington, Kurusu, McCollough, & Sanders, 1996), but more research is needed to substantiate this further. Despite the relative lack of empirical evidence, we do believe that forgiveness is a powerful healing practice, and we endorse its careful use in psychotherapy.

Encouraging forgiveness is an intervention that can be used without any reference to religious or spiritual concepts; indeed, DiBlasio (1993; DiBlasio & Benda, 1991) found that therapists' religious beliefs were weakly or completely unrelated to their attitudes about the importance and usefulness of forgiveness in therapy. However, consistent with H. Benson's (1996) assertion that connecting people's religious and spiritual beliefs to relaxation techniques can enhance the potency of the relaxation response, the effectiveness of forgiveness may be enhanced by relating it to clients' deeply held beliefs. Bergin's (1988) transitional figure technique illustrates what we mean by this. Bergin suggested that clients should be encouraged to become a transitional person in the history of their family, absorbing the pain of past victimization, stopping its transmission into future generations, forgiving perpetrators, and adopting a redemptive role between previous ancestors and future progeny. With devout Christian clients, the parallels between a client's redemptive role in the family and the redemptive role of Jesus Christ can be discussed explicitly to strengthen clients' sense of purpose, meaning, and resolve.

Before encouraging clients to forgive others, or seek forgiveness from others, we believe that it is crucial for therapists to assess clients' readiness for such an intervention. Forgiveness is a spiritual and emotional process that takes time, sometimes a lot of time. When clients have been abused and severely hurt by others, they often must go through a stagelike healing process: (a) shock and denial; (b) awareness and recognition that they have been abused, hurt, and offended; (c) feelings of hurt, grief, anger, and rage and the opportunity to appropriately express these feelings to others; (d) the need for validation that they have been wronged and, if possible, to see justice done and restitution occur; (e) boundary repair (i.e., the opportunity to affirm and ensure that the abuse or offenses will not happen again); and (f) letting go, forgiving, and moving on with life. If therapists encourage clients to forgive others before they have had the opportunity to appropriately work through the confrontation–forgiveness–healing process, considerable emotional and spiritual harm could be done. When people attempt to forgive prematurely, the healing process is prevented from occurring, and invalidated and unresolved feelings of pain, grief, guilt, shame, anger, and rage continue to create problems for them in their lives.

We have found that some clients, because of feelings of religious obligation, have attempted to forgive those who have offended them prematurely. Some devoutly religious clients we have worked with have said that they felt unworthy and unrighteous because they were not able to forgive others more quickly. We have found it helpful to teach such clients that forgiveness involves a process of reconciliation that often takes considerable time and may require real or imagined encounters with the perpetrators of their pain. With such clients, we have found that reframing the client's dilemma in the following manner sometimes has been helpful: "It isn't that you haven't forgiven your [parents], it's just that you are still involved in the process of forgiving. You are part way through the process, and hopefully our work together will help you eventually complete that process. In the meantime, it appears that you still have a lot of hurt, grief, and anger that you need to talk about and work through." Reconciliation between the offender and offended is the ideal, but is not always possible. In such cases, the needed inward reconciliation can be facilitated by faith in God's ultimate justice and mercy.

Therapists also should be careful not to encourage clients to seek forgiveness before they have truly taken responsibility for their behavior and done all they can to make restitution for their wrongdoings. If clients who have wronged others have not yet fully owned and taken responsibility for their wrongdoings, and do not yet have a sincere desire to make restitution to whatever extent possible, then any attempts to confess and ask for forgiveness may be wasted. Even worse, the victim of the wrongdoer may be further harmed by premature or insincere solicitations of forgiveness. Thus, therapists need to be cautious not to prematurely encourage clients to forgive others or seek forgiveness. Often, most of the work therapists must do is to help clients work through the painful and difficult initial stages of healing, such as the shock and denial, awareness and recognition, hurt, grief, anger, rage, and shame. By the time it is appropriate for therapists to encourage clients to forgive others or to seek forgiveness, most of the difficult therapeutic work should have been done. See Carter, McCullough, Sandage, and Worthington (1994), Ganje-Fling and McCarthy (1994), Hope (1987), McCullough et al. (1997), and McCullough and Worthington (1994a, 1994b) for additional clinically useful information about the process and role of forgiveness in healing.

WORSHIP AND RITUAL

The word *worship* is defined as "the reverent love and devotion accorded a deity" (*American Heritage Dictionary of the English Language*, 1992, p. 2059). The word *ritual* is defined as "the body of ceremonies or rites used in a place of worship" or a "ceremonial act or a series of such acts" (*American Heritage Dictionary of the English Language*, 1992, p. 1557). Not all rituals are oriented toward a deity (Roger R. Keller, personal communication, March 12, 1997). All the major world religious traditions encourage their followers to engage in various acts of private and public worship or ritual (Parrinder, 1961; Smart, 1983; Whiting, 1983). Believers can worship in many ways:

I can worship God in my heart and you cannot in any obvious way see that is going on. But it is also typical and somehow more basic for worship to take a partly outward form. Worshippers bow down, or kneel, or stand up and sing. More elaborately they may pay their reverence to God or a god by making a sacrifice or going on a pilgrimage. Ritual is often assisted by various external visible means, such as the use of candles, flags, chapels, temples, statues, icons, and so on. Look at a cathedral and you are, so to speak, looking at an act of worship frozen into stone. Look at a crucifix and you are looking at a feeling of faith congealed into wood and metal. And music, that wonderful and word-less way of expressing feelings, can be audible adoration, a flow of sound dedicated to sacred things. (Smart, 1983, pp. 130–131)

The theistic world religious traditions promote and support their fol-lowers' need to worship and engage in rituals in a number of ways: (a) providing places of worship (e.g., temples, shrines, mosques, churches, syn-agogues); (b) conducting and promoting religious rituals (e.g., special pray-ers; reciting vows; singing hymns; ritualistic acts such as bowing and kneel-ing; bathing and washing; fasting or abstaining from food, water, or sexual relations; lighting candles; partaking of sacramental emblems such as bread and wine; baptism); (c) sponsoring and supporting religious festivals (e.g., Divali or Festival of Lights [in Hinduism, a new year festival in which Vishnu and his bride are welcomed into every house and light or good overcomes darkness or evil]; Wesak [in Theravada and Mahayana Bud-dhism, a festival that commemorates Buddha's birth, enlightenment, and entry into nirvana]; Pesach, or Passover [in Judaism, the 8-day "Feast of the Unleavened Bread," which marks God's passing over the Jews in Egypt sparing their firstborns during the plagues and their freedom from enslave-ment in about 1300 B.C.]; Easter [in Christianity, to commemorate the resurrection of Jesus Christ]; Ramadan Fast and Id al Fitr [in Islam, the Ramadan Fast is held during the 9th month of the Islamic year and marks the time when Mohammed received Allah's first revelation of the Koran and Id al Fitr is a celebration marking the end of Ramadan]); and (d) requiring, encouraging, or permitting religious pilgrimages, that is, journeys to holy places (e.g., Hindus make pilgrimages to the city of Benares and bathe in the River Ganges, Muslims make a pilgrimage to the city of Mecca, many Jews and Christians make pilgrimages to Israel and Jerusalem).

From a spiritual perspective, acts of worship and ritual can serve a number of purposes for believers: (a) expressing one's devotion, love, and respect toward God or the gods; (b) committing or recommitting oneself to a spiritual and moral life; (c) demonstrating devotion and piety to other members of one's religious community; (d) offering penitence and sacrifice for sins or wrongdoings; (e) demonstrating one's solidarity with other mem-bers of the religious community; and (f) seeking spiritual enlightenment, guidance, and healing (Smart, 1983, 1993, 1994). Acts of worship and ritual may also be psychologically and physically healing. H. Benson (1996) suggested that worship services "are full of potentially therapeutic elements—music, aesthetic surroundings, familiar rituals, prayer and contemplation, distraction from everyday tensions, the opportunity for socializing and fellowship, and education" (p. 176). H. Benson (1996) also described why he believed religious rituals can be therapeutic:

> There is something very influential about invoking a ritual that you may first have practiced in childhood, about regenerating the neural pathways that were formed in your youthful experience of faith. In my medical practice, this has proven true. . . . Even if you experience the ritual from an entirely different perspective of maturity and life history, the words you read, the songs you sing, and the prayers you invoke will soothe you in the same way they did in what was perhaps a simpler time in your life. Even if you don't consciously appreciate that there is any real drama or emotion attached to the ritual, the brain retains a memory of the constellation of activities associated with the ritual, both the emotional content that allows the brain to weigh its importance and the nerve cell firings, interactions, and chemical releases that were first activated. (p. 177)

Research reveals that psychotherapists do not often encourage clients to engage in acts of worship and ritual (Ball & Goodyear, 1991; Jones et al., 1992; P. S. Richards & Potts, 1995a; Tan, 1987; Worthington et al., 1988). Religious rituals such as anointing with oil, laying on of hands, blessings, encouraging clients to attend worship services, and fasting tend to be rarely or infrequently used or mentioned interventions. Of course, there are many other acts of religious worship and ritual besides those that have been included to date in surveys of therapists. Perhaps these surveys have not given therapists an adequate opportunity to indicate what acts of worship and ritual they encourage clients to perform. A more careful examination of this question is needed, but for now the best evidence we have suggests that acts of worship and religious ritual are not frequently recommended by therapists. This seems unfortunate because some forms of religious worship and ritual may promote better physical and psychological health (e.g., H. Benson, 1996; Gartner, Larson, & Allen, 1991; Matthews, Larson, & Barry, 1993–1995). On the other hand, many clients engage in such rituals regularly, but their significance is rarely discussed in the clinical situation. Discussing them may enhance the healing significance of both the rituals themselves and the therapy sessions.

Forms of worship and ritual that help clients affirm their spiritual heritage, identity, worth, life purpose, and involvement with their religious community may be especially helpful for clients who struggle with a lack of life purpose and meaning or who struggle with guilt, shame, alienation, anxiety, depression, and grief. Such forms of worship and ritual also could help people integrate and cope with major life transitions such as marriage, poor health, death, and divorce and the birth, growth, and departure of children. Of course, we recognize that acts of worship and ritual also could be promoted and used in extreme, rigid, perfectionistic, and shaming ways that could harm people physically and psychologically. Thus, we do not indiscriminately endorse all acts of worship and ritual for use in psychotherapy, but we believe that therapists should consider carefully those that could have healing properties. When such forms of worship and ritual are identified, therapists and researchers should test and evaluate them in clinical situations.

In both ecumenical and denominational therapeutic situations, therapists should be cautious about engaging in acts of religious worship or ritual with clients during therapy sessions because this could confuse role boundaries (see chap. 7 in this book). For example, we think that therapists should normally not give clients blessings (laying on of hands) or pray with them. There may be some exceptions to this, such as in therapy settings clearly affiliated with a religious institution. Also, in some inpatient settings in which clients do not have normal access to their religious community, it may be appropriate to provide opportunities for worship and ritual on the unit. In such situations, therapists may wish or need to lead or participate in such experiences or services (see Case Report 4 in chap. 11 in this book for an example of a therapist who did this). If they do, therapists should make efforts to carefully define their roles in relation to their clients' spiritual leaders.

Therapists also should be cautious about participating with their clients in acts of religious worship or ritual outside of therapy sessions (e.g., attending church or synagogue with clients). There is a great danger that religious leader–therapist role boundaries will be confused and crossed if therapists do this. Therapists should normally encourage clients to engage in religious worship and rituals outside of therapy sessions, either in private, with family members, or with religious leaders and other members of their religious community. If therapists believe that it may be appropriate to engage in religious worship or ritual with a particular client, we recommend that they consult with professional colleagues before doing so to ensure that they fully examine and minimize the potential risks.

In both denominational and ecumenical therapy situations, it might be helpful for therapists to explore with clients whether there are acts of religious worship or ritual that clients might find meaningful and therapeutic. It may be appropriate in denominational therapeutic situations for therapists to teach clients how to engage in different religious practices and rituals if clients lack an understanding of these practices and why they might be of benefit to them. In ecumenical situations, to avoid teaching religious practices that are not consistent with clients' religious beliefs, it often may be preferable for therapists to refer clients to their religious leaders for instruction in how to worship or engage in various religious rituals. Therapists should, of course, always be careful to teach clients religious practices only that are clearly consistent with clients' religious beliefs.

FELLOWSHIP AND SERVICE

The word *fellowship* is defined in the *American Heritage Dictionary of the English Language* (1992) as the "condition of sharing similar interests, ideals, or experiences, as by reason of profession, religion, or nationality" (p. 670). The word *service* is defined as an "act of assistance or benefit to another or others; a favor" (*American Heritage Dictionary of the English Language*, 1992, p. 1649). All the major world religious traditions encourage their followers to engage in fellowship with members of their religious community and to perform (and be the recipients of) various acts of altruistic service (Nigosian, 1994; Smart, 1993, 1994; Whiting, 1983). According to H. Benson (1996), fellowship activities may take many forms:

> Be it weekly church or synagogue services, daily masses or temples devoted to prayer several times each day, be it Bible study or bingo night, confirmation classes, preparation for bar mitzvah or bat mitzvah, potluck suppers or youth groups, marriage encounter weekends or church camps, Sunday school or soup kitchens, religious institutions ensure that their members get ample doses, not just of faith but of healthy social interactions. (p. 181)

Altruistic service also can take many forms, including, for example, giving food to the hungry, clothing and money to the poor, visiting the sick, providing emotional support to those who are discouraged or grieving, and serving in volunteer positions in one's religious community. The specific types of fellowship and service, and the frequency with which they are engaged in or received by followers varies somewhat in different religious traditions. The basic need for fellowship, mutual support, and service, however, is universal among human beings, and all the great world religious traditions encourage and provide opportunities for the expression and fulfillment of these needs.

From a spiritual perspective, fellowship, support, and altruistic service have a number of potential benefits in believers' lives: (a) strengthening them spiritually when their faith is weak and in times of trial; (b) fortifying them against worldly (evil) influences and pressures; (c) helping them avoid self-preoccupation and to forget or place their own problems in a broader social and spiritual perspective; (d) teaching them to be unselfish and loving; (e) helping them feel a sense of belonging and social acceptance; (f) endowing them with a sense of purpose and meaning; (g) filling their hearts with joy and love for their fellow human beings; (h) helping them feel a sense of harmony with God; and (i) providing extra help in coping with stress, death, disease, and trauma (Pargament, 1996).

There also is considerable evidence that fellowship and altruistic service have beneficial physical and psychological effects. For example, Levin (1994) concluded that epidemiological studies suggest that the social support and fellowship provided by religion "serve to buffer the adverse effects of stress and anger, perhaps via psychoneuroimmunologic pathways" (p. 9). In *The Healing Power of Doing Good*, Luks (1993) reported the results of a survey of thousands of volunteers across the United States. He found that people who helped other people consistently reported better health than other people and that many believed that their health improved when they began doing volunteer work. The vast majority of those surveyed said that helping others gave them a physical sensation or rush, including a sudden warmth, increased energy, a sense of euphoria, and greater calm and relaxation. Results of numerous other studies suggest that the social support and fellowship opportunities provided by religious communities contribute to better physical and psychological health and decreased mortality rates (e.g., H. Benson, 1996; Berkman & Syme, 1979; Martin & Carlson, 1988; Pargament, 1996; Payne, Bergin, Bielema, & Jenkins, 1991; Spiegel, Bloom, Kraemer, & Gottheil, 1989).

Research is unclear about how often psychotherapists encourage clients to engage in mutual fellowship or altruistic service. P. S. Richards and Potts (1995a) found that using the client's religious community was a frequently used intervention by the Mormon therapists they surveyed. Using the religious community also was occasionally reported in two studies of Protestant therapists reported in Ball and Goodyear (1991). However, it is unclear in all three of these studies in what way clients' religious communities were used. We do not know to what extent clients were encouraged to engage in fellowship with members of their religious community or to perform and receive altruistic service. Little and Robinson (1988) reported that one component of their moral reconation group treatment approach for offenders was requiring participants to engage in community service. Tan (1996) encouraged therapists to consider referring their clients to groups within their religious community for fellowship and support. To our knowledge, however, there are no other empirical studies that have investigated how frequently therapists encourage the use of fellowship and altruistic service as an intervention. The best evidence we have seems to indicate that psychotherapists do not often encourage clients to engage in fellowship with members of their religious community or to perform and accept acts of altruistic service. We are not sure why this is the case, but we believe it is unfortunate considering the potential healing power of such activities.

Therapists could more routinely consider ways that they can involve clients in fellowship and service activities within their religious communities. Such interventions may be particularly helpful with clients who are socially isolated, lonely, depressed, or experiencing major life changes (e.g., death of loved one, divorce, loss of job). With suicidal clients, the social support and concern that may be available within the religious community could help save their lives. Not all clients, of course, will necessarily need or benefit from involvement in fellowship or service. Some clients we have worked with are already overinvolved in their religious communities, even to the point of being burned out from fellowship and service. Such clients may need help reducing their amount of involvement in their religious communities so that they have more time to attend to their own needs and growth. Some clients have been abused or otherwise hurt by members of their religious community. Such clients may need to, at least temporarily, distance themselves from their community while they work through feelings of hurt, grief, anger, and rage. Thus, interventions that provide clients with opportunities to engage in fellowship and to receive and give altruistic service are not indicated for all clients, but such interventions may greatly assist many other clients in coping with, reframing, and resolving their problems.

We recognize that it is not necessarily easy to enlist the appropriate support of clients' religious communities or to find appropriate ways to involve clients in fellowship and service. Many clients do feel isolated from their community and will resist therapists' efforts to get them more involved in it. In addition, therapists need to be cautious about how and whom they involve their clients with in the religious community. Although there are many people with good intentions in such communities who would be willing to engage in fellowship and provide service to needy clients, not all of these people are capable of providing quality help. Some of them are needy or disturbed themselves and could exploit or otherwise relate in harmful ways to clients, as has been noted in cases of clergy abuse of children or exploitation of adults for financial or sexual gain.

The discussion so far illustrates that therapists need to do their homework before attempting to involve their clients in religious fellowship or service. Therapists should seek to gain an understanding of the intricacies of their clients' religious communities. Therapists should seek to develop contacts within these communities with religious leaders and helping professionals whom they can trust and consult. Therapists should always be sure that they fully understand clients' perceptions and feelings about their religious communities before deciding whether it would be appropriate to attempt to involve them in fellowship or service or both. Of course, therapists should also obtain written consent from clients before they make contacts in the religious community on behalf of their clients.

SEEKING SPIRITUAL DIRECTION

Spiritual direction was described by Ganje-Fling and McCarthy (1991) as "a relationship which has as its major objective the on-going development of the spiritual self" (p. 104). Worthington et al. (1996) defined it as "guided reflection about the spiritual aspect's of one's life" (p. 465). Believers in all the world religious traditions at times seek guidance and direction from their religious and spiritual leaders, such as their priest, minister, pastor, rabbi, bishop, guru, spiritual director, elder, or prophet (R. R. Keller, personal communication, May 8, 1996). The focus of the direction varies somewhat from religion to religion in that in some traditions it focuses exclusively on spiritual matters, whereas in others it also may include temporal concerns of an emotional, physical, familial, financial, or career nature. The duration of the spiritual direction may also vary, ranging from one or two brief meetings to extended periods of training and instruction. The degree of formality also may vary, ranging from informal, optional, unstructured, and spontaneous to formal, required, structured, and planned.

Although seeking spiritual direction and guidance from religious leaders is a time-honored practice in the world religious traditions, research investigating the spiritual and psychological effects of spiritual direction and counseling by religious leaders is relatively rare. Some surveys indicate that people generally believe that they are helped with emotional problems by clergy and by mutual help or support groups, many of which are sponsored by religious organizations (Bergin & Lambert, 1978; Lambert & Bergin, 1994). Also, a well-designed, controlled outcome study on the treatment of depression showed that the efficacy of clergy was equivalent to that of professional therapists (Propst et al., 1992). It would seem that believers might benefit in a variety of ways spiritually and psychologically from seeking spiritual guidance and direction from their spiritual leaders, including, for example, receiving (a) increased spiritual enlightenment and growth; (b) absolution from sin and relief from guilt and shame; (c) advice and information about how to cope with and overcome emotional, marital, and family challenges and problems; (d) social support and acceptance; and (e) financial and temporal assistance. We hope that research on the effects of spiritual direction will be conducted so that psychotherapists might better understand the potential benefits of this practice for their clients.

Research also is unclear about how often psychotherapists refer clients to religious or spiritual leaders for direction and guidance. P. S. Richards and Potts (1995a) found that Mormon therapists occasionally referred clients to religious leaders for blessings (laying on of hands). In addition, Ball and Goodyear (1991) found that some Protestant therapists indicated that they sometimes referred clients to their pastor for guidance about specific spiritual questions. We are not aware of any other studies that provide insight on how frequently therapists refer clients to their religious leaders for spiritual direction. Thus, the evidence to date suggests that therapists do this only occasionally. This is unfortunate considering the potential benefits to clients of working cooperatively with religious leaders.

Although therapists generally should more often work collaboratively with clients' religious leaders by consulting with and referring to them, we recognize that doing so may not always be in the clients' best interests. We have worked with some clients who seemed to be experiencing emotional problems, at least partly, because of poor advice and counsel given to them by their religious leaders. Not all leaders are helpful to their followers. Some leaders use shame and even abuse their followers or provide simplistic, unhelpful advice. In addition, not all clients are ready to seek spiritual direction. Some clients have unresolved anger and resentment toward such leaders or institutions and would react negatively to suggestions to seek direction from them. Thus, therapists need to use caution before recommending to clients that they seek spiritual direction. Before doing so, a careful assessment of clients' feelings toward their religious leaders is needed. In addition, whenever possible, therapists should attempt to get personally acquainted with clients' spiritual advisors to determine how helpful they might be. Of course, therapists should always obtain a written release from clients before such a consultation. In chapter 7 in the section on displacing or usurping religious authority, we offer specific suggestions about how therapists can go about consulting with clients' religious leaders (see particularly Ethical Recommendations 3–6).

If these cautions are followed, religious personnel often can be a great help to clients and the therapy process. They can provide meaningful spiritual and emotional guidance and comfort. They also can be a powerful ally in encouraging people to get the psychological help they need. Without such encouragement, many clients would not be willing to enter psychotherapy in the first place. Because of their spiritual authority, religious leaders often have more credibility and leverage with clients than do therapists, and they can get clients to comply with therapeutic recommendations when therapists might not. They also can often quickly mobilize social and financial resources in their religious community on clients' behalf. They also can be a valuable source of diagnostic and assessment information by providing therapists with helpful history and insight into clients' functioning outside therapy. Finally, when it is time for therapists to terminate with clients, religious leaders can be of valuable assistance in setting up social support to help clients maintain the progress they have made in therapy. Thus, in this day of managed care and briefer therapy, consulting with and referring clients to spiritual advisors may be interventions therapists should use more often.

MORAL INSTRUCTION

One of the major functions of all the world religious traditions is to transmit religious, moral, and ethical values from one generation to another

(Smart, 1983, 1993, 1994). Leaders of religions teach and instruct their followers in the values of that tradition, and adults instruct children and adolescents. This is done in a variety of ways, including the telling of religious and moral stories and myths, the study and discussion of religious and moral guidelines found in sacred texts, and through example or modeling (Smart, 1993, 1994).

There also is considerable agreement among the world religions about the general religious and moral values that need to be transmitted from generation to generation. According to Smart (1983), "the major faiths have much in common as far as moral conduct goes. Not to steal, not to lie, not to kill, not to have certain kinds of sexual relations—such prescriptions are found across the world" (p. 117). Dong Sull Choi, a world religion scholar, also affirmed that there are general moral principles that all of the theistic world religions endorse, including do not kill, do not lie, do not steal, do not covet, honor one's parents, love all people, do not worship idols, and do not take oaths (D. S. Choi, personal communication, October 9, 1996). There is, however, much variety in the specific interpretations of these religious and moral values (D. S. Choi, personal communication, October 9, 1996; Smart, 1983, 1993, 1994). There also is some variation in the manner in which the religious and moral rules and values are viewed:

> There are different models of virtue. For the Jew and Muslim, for instance, the rules are part of the fabric of divinely instituted law. . . . Obedience to the rules is obedience to God. . . . In Buddhism the rules of morality are part of the "eightfold path" which leads to ultimate liberation. It is not that God has to be obeyed, but rather that, as part of the general effort at self-purification, it is wise to be good. The model for the monotheist is the obedient person of faith, such as Abraham. The model Buddhist is the person of superior insight. (Smart, 1983, pp. 117–118)

The transmission of religious and moral rules and values is essential for the survival of societies and human life. Such values and rules

> are found across the world because such rules are necessary if there is to be a society at all. The widespread breaking of these rules would lead to chaos. Society can exist only where such wrong acts are in the minority. (Smart, 1983, p. 117)

Not only does the transmission of moral values and rules help preserve societies, but, as we discussed in chapter 5, moral values are essential for the healthy psychosocial and spiritual functioning of human beings. One of the hallmarks of healthy functioning is the capacity to self-regulate in a healthy manner (Bergin, 1985, 1991; Jensen & Bergin, 1988). Without a set of guiding moral and ethical values, people have no basis from which to regulate their behavior in a consistent and healthy manner (Bergin, 1985, 1991).

Many people recognize that the religious and moral rules and values taught by the great world religious traditions are "recipes for living that have been evolved, tested, and winnowed through hundreds of generations of human social history" (Campbell, 1975, p. 1103). In addition, many people view these religious and moral rules and values as God-given or as laws that are a "part of the nature of the world" and "fabric of the cosmos" (Smart, 1983, p. 118). Such a view of religious and moral values tends to increase people's commitment to their values and may increase their ability to self-regulate. As expressed by Bergin (1985),

> self-regulation can never be optimally successful unless a commitment is made to values, and that commitment can be stronger and more lasting if the client feels that he or she is committing to something that is lawful and moral; not just because somebody said so but because it is built into the universe and is part of our nature. (p. 26)

Thus, it may be that people's religious and spiritual beliefs can enhance their commitment and capacity to regulate their behavior in healthy ways. The finding that religious people have been found to have lower rates of alcoholism, drug abuse, divorce, suicide, delinquency, and sexual promiscuity (e.g., Gartner et al., 1991; Payne et al., 1991) is consistent with this idea.

Research reveals that some psychotherapists do occasionally engage in religious and moral values instruction, clarification, or correction with their clients (Ball & Goodyear, 1991; Jones et al., 1992; Moon et al., 1993; P. S. Richards & Potts, 1995a). For example, the second most frequently used intervention reported by Christian therapists in Ball and Goodyear's (1991) study was the teaching of religious concepts, which included engaging in values clarification with clients. Christian psychologists surveyed by Jones et al. (1992) said that they confronted approximately 27% of their clients about sinful life patterns. P. S. Richards and Potts (1995a) found that Mormon therapists occasionally confronted clients about discrepancies between their religious values and behaviors. Christian therapists surveyed by Moon et al. (1993) said they encouraged approximately 25% of their clients to be obedient to God's will. Despite these studies and research that reveals that the majority of therapists do believe that values are important for mentally healthy lifestyles and for guiding and evaluating psychotherapy (Jensen & Bergin, 1988), researchers know little about how therapists go about engaging in religious and moral value instruction, clarification, or correction with clients, nor do they know the frequency of usage or effectiveness of such interventions.

Therapists should be sensitive to value issues throughout the course of therapy, although explicit value discussions with clients should not be overemphasized (Bergin, 1991). Nevertheless, we believe that there are certain occasions during therapy when therapists should actively endorse values that they believe are healthy and explicitly own their values and the consensus religious and psychotherapy values mentioned in chapter 6. These occasions are described briefly in Table 9.1 and are discussed in more detail by Richards, Rector, and Tjeltveit (in press).

As therapists seek to handle values in therapy appropriately, it can be useful to distinguish among values clarification, correction, and instruction (Tjeltveit, 1986). We define *values clarification interventions* as those that help clients clarify what their religious and moral values are. Values clarification interventions can be appropriate in both ecumenical and denominational therapeutic situations. Such interventions may be appropriate when therapists observe incongruencies between clients' lifestyle behaviors and their professed moral values (e.g., an adolescent who professes to believe

TABLE 9.1
Occasions During Therapy When Therapists Should Explicitly Own and Endorse Values That They Believe Are Healthy

1. During informed consent, therapists should disclose the values they believe in that influence the goals they pursue and the approach they use.

2. When asking clients to complete assessment measures, therapists should explain why they believe these particular measures are valuable (i.e., what assessment information they value).

3. When helping clients set goals for therapy, therapists should explain why they believe the goals they endorse are valuable to pursue.

4. Before implementing therapeutic interventions, therapists should explain why they believe the intervention will be helpful (i.e., what valued outcome it might promote).

5. When deciding whether to terminate therapy, therapists should explain what criteria (valued outcomes) they use to judge whether therapy has been successful.

6. When major value conflicts between the therapist and client become apparent that could threaten the therapeutic relationship or jeopardize mutual collaboration on therapeutic goals, therapists should explicitly disclose and own their values while reaffirming clients' rights to differ from therapists.

7. When therapists perceive that clients' value choices are contributing to their emotional or relationship problems, therapists should help clients explicitly examine the value choices and suggest more healthy alternatives.

8. When clients admit confusion about what their values really are or manifest discrepancies between their professed values and behavior, therapists should explicitly help clients examine and explore their confusion and incongruencies.

9. When clients lack an understanding of mental health values, therapists should explicitly teach clients what psychotherapists tend to regard as mentally healthy values.

10. When clients lack an understanding of their religious (or cultural) tradition's values, therapists should explicitly teach clients what the values are (if they know), or they should encourage clients to seek this information from religious leaders or other members of their religious community.

in honesty but frequently lies to his or her parents). In such circumstances, it may be appropriate for therapists to point out or confront their clients about these incongruencies. Value incongruencies should not be pointed out in a harsh or condemning manner, but with caring and as an invitation for clients to engage in self-exploration and self-examination.

Therapists also may engage in values clarification interventions when clients verbally acknowledge confusion or uncertainty about what their moral values are. When engaging in values clarification interventions, therapists should attempt to remain as value neutral as possible to give clients as much freedom as possible to explore how they feel about their values and lifestyle behaviors. By giving clients the opportunity to explore fully their values and behaviors in a nonjudgmental relationship, we hope that clients will be able to clarify and affirm what they value and how they wish to behave. Therapists need not remain silent if they believe clients are choosing unhealthy, destructive values, but they should inform clients of their views of the value alternatives openly and honestly (Bergin, 1991). After doing this, however, therapists must be willing to "step aside and allow the person to exercise autonomy and face consequences" (Bergin, 1991, p. 397).

Values correction interventions are those in which therapists attempt to correct deficiencies or distortions in clients' religious and moral values. It may be appropriate for therapists to engage in such interventions when it is clear that clients' religious and moral values (or lack of them) are affecting them in unhealthy or dysfunctional ways (e.g., a female client says she should obey and submit to her husband even though he emotionally and physically abuses her; a male client puts himself and his spouse at risk with his sexual promiscuity). Therapists need to be cautious about how they go about correcting and modifying clients' religious and moral values because if therapists do this inappropriately, clients may feel the therapist is attacking them personally or being disrespectful of their views.

Shaming and condemning clients, or questioning the truthfulness of their religious faith and tradition, are unethical. However, therapists can ask clients to examine how a particular belief or value seems to be affecting them without condemning them or challenging the truthfulness of their religious faith or tradition. Therapists also can question clients' understanding or application of a religious or moral value without questioning the truth of their religion.

In ecumenical therapy situations, therapists may be wise to consult with their clients' religious leaders to get authoritative interpretations of potentially problematic religious or moral values. In ecumenical situations therapists may be wise to refer clients to their religious leaders, if possible, for values correction to minimize the possibility of therapist religious or moral value imposition. In denominational situations, therapists may feel that they have sufficient credibility and trust with their clients to themselves correct and modify distortions or deficiencies in clients' religious and moral values. Even in denominational situations, of course, therapists should do this nondogmatically and with respect for clients' autonomy.

Values instruction interventions are those in which therapists teach and inform clients about the religious and moral doctrines of the client's religious tradition. Such interventions may be appropriate when clients lack an understanding of the religious and moral values and rules of their religious tradition (e.g., they do not know what their religious tradition's view is on birth control), particularly when the therapist is employed by a religious social services organization. In ecumenical therapy situations, we believe that it would be preferable for therapists to refer clients to their religious leaders or community for such instruction. It would seem presumptuous, and the risk of value imposition would be high, if therapists engaged in religious and moral value instruction with clients from religious traditions different from their own. In denominational situations, referring clients to their religious leaders for values instruction may also be the best option, although in some cases it may be appropriate for therapists themselves to provide some religious and moral value teaching and instruction (e.g., with clients who have specific questions about values).

We recognize that there are dangers in suggesting that therapists engage in religious and moral value clarification, correction, and instruction. The greatest danger is that therapists could purposely or unknowingly impose private beliefs that are irrelevant to mental health on vulnerable clients. As we discussed in chapter 6, such a practice is inappropriate and unethical. Bergin (1991) acknowledged that it is a delicate and challenging task for therapists to manage values issues in therapy and suggested that

> the therapy process can best be compared with that of good parenting: Trust is established; guided growth is stimulated; values are conveyed in a respectful way; the person being influenced becomes stronger, more assertive, and independent; the person learns ways of clarifying and testing value choices; the influencer decreases dependency, nurturance and external advice; and the person experiments with new behaviors and ideas until he or she becomes more mature and autonomous. (Bergin, 1991, p. 397)

Bergin (1991) also cautioned that

> a strong interest in value discussions . . . can be problematic if it is overemphasized. It would be unethical to trample on the values of clients, and it would be unwise to focus on value issues when other issues may be at the nucleus of the disorder, which is frequently the case in the early stages of treatment. It is vital to be open about values but not coercive, to be a competent professional and not a missionary for a particular belief, and at the same time to be honest enough to recognize how one's value commitments may or may not promote health. (p. 399)

In theory, therapists historically have eschewed the role of moral guide or teacher, although the impossibility of them fully avoiding this role is now widely acknowledged (e.g., Bergin et al., 1996; London, 1986; Lowe, 1976). As we suggested in chapter 6, therapists need to more fully accept that they function as moral guides or teachers and think carefully about how they can function ethically and effectively in this role without becoming missionaries or usurping clerical functions. Ultimately, we believe that therapists will find that they can better help clients overcome unhealthy lifestyle behaviors if they use clients' religious and spiritual beliefs and values to help motivate and reinforce clients' efforts to change and self-regulate. To this end, we hope that a wider variety of interventions that help therapists in their efforts to provide religious and moral value clarification, correction, and instruction to clients will be designed.

CONCLUSION

We do not claim that we have described all religious and spiritual practices that could be useful in psychotherapy, but we have described several promising ones that could have wide application in ecumenical and numerous denominational therapy situations. There may be some therapeutic religious practices that are unique to individual religious traditions. We hope that therapists who have an expertise in specific traditions will identify and apply in therapy those religious and spiritual practices that have the greatest therapeutic value for clients from those traditions.

We hope that for each religious or spiritual practice we have described in this chapter, therapists will adapt or use that practice in a variety of ways in psychotherapy. To some extent, this has already occurred. For example, therapists have already developed and used a variety of prayer interventions as well as numerous contemplative, meditative, and scriptural interventions (Ball & Goodyear, 1991; Jones et al., 1992; Moon et al., 1993; P. S. Richards & Potts, 1995a; Worthington et al., 1988). Given the creativity of psychotherapists, we are confident that an even wider variety of religious and spiritual interventions will eventually be available to assist therapists in their efforts to help clients cope, heal, and grow.

10

SPIRITUAL INTERVENTIONS USED BY CONTEMPORARY PSYCHOTHERAPISTS

Cognitive restructuring could be defined as a type of spiritual transformation of the mind—a spiritual exercise.

—*L. Rebecca Propst*

In this chapter we describe and give specific examples of how therapists have adapted or applied the religious and spiritual practices described in chapter 9 to the psychotherapy situation. Some spiritual practices are used in therapy in a manner that is identical to how such practices might be used or recommended by religious leaders in religious settings (e.g., encouraging clients to pray for guidance in overcoming their problems). Other spiritual practices have been adapted or integrated by therapists to some degree with secular concepts or interventions so that the practice is used in therapy somewhat differently than it typically would be practiced within the religious community (e.g., asking clients to read specific spiritual literature to challenge and modify their irrational cognitions). Ultimately, however, most spiritual interventions that have been used in therapy can be traced to some religious or spiritual practice that is advocated by one or more of the world religions.

We first describe some of the specific purposes of religious and spiritual interventions. We then review the empirical literature to determine what spiritual interventions therapists have used and how frequently they have used them. We discuss several schemes for classifying them and briefly describe a number of specific interventions. We also describe treatment packages that integrate spiritual with secular modalities and briefly discuss the use of spiritual interventions in child, adolescent, group, marital, and family therapy. Finally, we discuss when spiritual interventions are contraindicated and offer some general process suggestions.

PURPOSE OF SPIRITUAL INTERVENTIONS

In Table 10.1 we briefly summarize the views of some of the major psychotherapy traditions regarding the general purpose of interventions in therapy and compare their views about interventions with those of the theistic, spiritual strategy. The general purpose of religious and spiritual interventions is to facilitate and promote clients' religious and spiritual coping, growth, and well-being. We believe that clients who are growing in spiritually healthy ways are more likely to function effectively in the other areas of their lives.

In addition to the general purpose stated earlier, there are more specific reasons why therapists may want to use religious and spiritual interventions. For example, such interventions can be used to help clients more effectively or fully (a) experience and affirm their eternal spiritual identity and divine worth; (b) seek guidance and strength from God to assist them in their efforts to cope, heal, and grow; (c) obtain social, emotional, and material support from their religious community and leaders; (d) examine and modify dysfunctional religious and spiritual beliefs and practices; (e) reframe or understand their problems from an eternal, spiritual perspective; (f) explore and work through religious and spiritual doubts and concerns; (g) emotionally and spiritually forgive and heal from past abuse and pain; (h) accept responsibility and make restitution for their own harmful and selfish behaviors that have hurt others; and (i) grow in faith and commitment to their religious and spiritual beliefs and values.

Undoubtedly, there are other purposes or reasons therapists may want to use religious and spiritual interventions, but it is beyond the scope of this chapter to attempt to enumerate all of them. The most important point we emphasize here is that such interventions enable therapists to intervene directly in and use the religious-spiritual system of their clients therapeutically. None of the mainstream psychotherapy traditions have developed interventions for this purpose, and so the spiritual strategy contributes uniquely to the profession in this regard (Bergin, 1988; Bergin & Payne, 1991).

VARIETY AND PREVALENCE OF SPIRITUAL INTERVENTIONS

Although the empirical literature on spiritual interventions is still limited, several studies have recently been done that reveal that a wide variety

TABLE 10.1
The Role of Therapeutic Techniques in the Major Psychotherapy Traditions Compared With the Spiritual Strategy

Psychodynamic	Behavioral	Cognitive	Humanistic	Family systems	Spiritual
The major interventions are the analysis and interpretation of free-association material, dreams, resistance, and transference. The purpose of these interventions is to promote client insight into unconscious dynamics and to help the client work through core conflicts and defenses so they can resolve their symptoms and function better in their life.	These are a wide variety of techniques that were developed out of the scientific base of behaviorism and social learning theory. Examples of major interventions include relaxation training, systematic desensitization and other exposure methods, token economies and other reinforcement techniques, modeling, assertiveness training, and self-monitoring. The purpose of these techniques is to help people change their symptomatic behavior without necessarily analyzing the past or the dynamics thereof.	Examples of major techniques include examining and challenging irrational or dysfunctional cognitions, teaching the A–B–C model, rational–emotive imagery, and shame attacking exercises. These are viewed as highly important for helping clients modify their irrational or dysfunctional cognitions, which in turn can modify affects and behaviors.	Techniques are viewed as being secondary to the therapeutic relationship. Major interventions are the relationship skills of reflective listening and responding, nonjudgmentalness, and communicating warmth, empathy, and authenticity. The purpose of these relationship skills is to provide a therapeutic climate that allows the client to deeply explore their beliefs, values, feelings, and interpersonal conflicts.	Examples of major interventions include family sculpting, genograms, teaching communication skills, paradoxical intention, reframing, and detriangulating. Techniques are viewed as highly important for perturbing, or creating change in the family system. Diagnosis and treatment assume that disorders are systemic and reflect dysfunctions in systems of interaction.	Examples of major interventions include cognitive restructuring of irrational religious beliefs, transitional figure technique, forgiveness, meditation and prayer, Scripture study, blessings, participating in religious services, spiritual imagery, keeping a journal about spiritual feelings, repentance, and using the client's religious support system. Interventions are viewed as highly important for facilitating and promoting clients' religious and spiritual coping, healing, and growth and for helping clients draw on the spiritual resources in their lives.

of them have been used by professional therapists. Worthington, Dupont, Berry, and Duncan (1988) investigated how frequently seven Christian psychotherapists who had a degree in social work or rehabilitation counseling used spiritual guidance techniques. After each therapy session, both therapists and clients were asked to complete a session inventory, in which they indicated which of 19 Christian spiritual guidance techniques were used during the session. The most frequently used interventions by the seven Christian therapists were religious homework assignment, quoting from Scripture, interpretation of Scripture, and discussion of faith. Religious imagery, rededication, meditation, confession, laying on of hands, and anointing with oil were rarely or never used.

Shafranske and Malony (1990) surveyed members of the American Psychological Association's Division 12 (Clinical Psychology) and asked them to indicate which of six religious interventions they had used in therapy. The most frequently used religious interventions used by the 409 clinical psychologists who responded were assessing their clients' religious backgrounds (91%) and using religious language or concepts (57%). Less frequently used were recommending participation in religion (36%), using or recommending religious or spiritual books (32%), praying privately for a client (24%), and praying with a client (7%).

Ball and Goodyear (1991) surveyed doctoral-level clinical members of the Christian Association for Psychological Studies (CAPS) and asked them to list interventions that they had used with Christian clients that they regarded as "distinct to Christian counseling" (p. 146). The 174 CAPS members who responded listed and described 436 interventions that were then grouped by raters into 15 clusters or categories. The most frequently mentioned spiritual interventions were prayer, teaching of religious concepts, and making reference to Scripture. Integration techniques, Scripture memorization, anointing with oil, confrontation and challenge, and screening and intake were rarely used.

Jones, Watson, and Wolfram (1992) surveyed graduates of explicitly Christian doctoral and master's programs in clinical psychology and asked them to estimate what percentage of clients they had used various spiritual interventions with and how appropriate they believed each technique is for Christian clients and for general practice. The most frequently used interventions reported by the 640 alumni were implicitly teaching biblical concepts, praying for clients outside the session, discussing forgiveness, explicitly teaching biblical concepts, and confronting clients over sinful life patterns. Praying for direct divine healing and deliverance or exorcism from the demonic were rarely used.

P. S. Richards and Potts (1995a) conducted a national survey of members of the Association of Mormon Counselors and Psychotherapists, and asked them to indicate how frequently they had used various religious and spiritual interventions during the past year in their professional practices.

The most frequently used interventions by the 215 Mormon therapists who responded were therapist silent prayer, encouraging forgiveness, using the religious community as a resource, and teaching spiritual concepts. Therapist and client in-session prayer, blessings by the therapist, and Scripture memorization were rarely used.

The studies just described document and provide insight into the variety of religious and spiritual interventions that have and are being used by more than 1,400 religiously oriented licensed therapists in clinical and counseling psychology, clinical social work, psychiatry, and marriage and family therapy. Worthington et al. (1988) identified 21 different spiritual interventions, Shafranske and Malony (1990), 6 interventions; Ball and Goodyear (1991), 14; Jones et al. (1992), 11; and P. S. Richards and Potts (1995a), 18. Definitions or descriptions of the interventions were not provided in all the studies, so it is difficult to determine how much they overlapped. Nevertheless, it appears that at least 25 distinct interventions were reported in the five studies. In Table 10.2 we provide definitions and examples of those reported by Ball and Goodyear (1991) and P. S. Richards and Potts (1995a).

Those studies also have given us insight into which religious and spiritual interventions have been used most frequently and which ones have been rarely used. Currently, it appears that the most frequently used interventions tend to be praying privately (or silently) for clients, teaching religious and spiritual concepts, encouraging forgiveness, and making reference to Scriptures. Less frequently used interventions include spiritual meditation, religious relaxation and imagery, religious-spiritual assessment, and vocal therapist and client in-session prayer. Rarely used interventions include blessings (e.g., laying on of hands, anointing with oil), Scripture memorization, praying for direct divine healing, and exorcism from the demonic (Ball & Goodyear, 1991; Jones et al., 1992; P. S. Richards & Potts, 1995a; Worthington et al., 1988). There were some exceptions to these trends in Shafranske and Malony's (1990) study. For example, a high percentage of therapists in that study reported that they assessed clients' religious backgrounds and that relatively few of them prayed for their clients. However, Shafranske and Malony included greater diversity in the religious backgrounds of the therapists (i.e., they included large numbers of Roman Catholic, Jewish, Unitarian, and nonaffiliated therapists) than did the other researchers, so this may account for the differences. To date, most research studies on therapists' use of religious and spiritual interventions have been limited to Protestant and Mormon therapists.

The studies discussed earlier and others (e.g., Chamberlain et al., 1996; Payne, Bergin, & Loftus, 1992) also have revealed that most psychotherapists do not use religious and spiritual interventions exclusively but as part of an eclectic, integrative approach that includes mainstream secular therapeutic perspectives and interventions. The relative frequency with

TABLE 10.2
Definitions and Examples of Various Religious and Spiritual Interventions

Intervention	Definition	Examples of intervention
Therapist prayer	Therapist silent prayer	Prayer to help clients develop a bigger picture of their suffering and look beyond their current circumstances.
Teaching spiritual concepts	Teaching or instructing clients about theological issues and spiritual concepts	Teaching an awareness of biblical promises of peace, love, and faith. Help clients view self-worth based on what God says about them.
Reference to Scripture	Direct quotation or citation of Scripture to establish a point	Instruction by scripture to counter inappropriate feelings such as perfectionistic striving. Therapist cites references to Christ's emotions to help clients feel at ease about their problems.
Spiritual self-disclosure	Therapist self-discloses or models spiritual experiences or behaviors in an attempt to influence the client	Therapist shares aspects of his or her own spiritual experience. Therapist attempts to model grace and affirmation.
Spiritual confrontation	Interventions that confront a client concerning religious or spiritual beliefs and values	Therapist asks clients in bad relationships what they think the Bible says about the relationship. Therapist gently confronts clients about the incongruencies between their professed religious values and their current behavior.
Spiritual assessment	Using the initial counseling session as a way to assess the client's religious and spiritual status	Therapist takes a history of the client's spiritual development when he or she first sees him or her." Therapist gives clients the Spiritual Well-Being Scale to assess how they feel about their relationship with God.
Religious relaxation or imagery	The use of guided imagery, meditation, or relaxation with direct reference to spiritual concepts	During guided imagery, therapist asks clients to visualize being embraced by and speaking to Jesus. Therapist uses imagery and metaphor in biblical stories for relaxation.
Therapist and client prayer	Vocal in-session prayer with client	Therapist prays on behalf of clients that they will have the strength to deal with strong, painful feelings. Therapist invites the client to pray at the beginning of a session to petition God's guidance and help during the session.
Blessing by therapist	Use of priesthood blessings (laying on of hands) in session to help client cope or work through impasses	Therapist lays hands on a client's head, blessing him or her that he or she might receive comfort, strength, and insight.
Encouraging forgiveness	Discussing the concept of forgiveness with client; encouraging client to forgive parents or others	Therapist discusses how to have forgiveness when a client reports guilt about a behavior or feeling. Therapist uses forgiveness in restoring broken relationships.
Use religious community	Using the client's religious community as an extratherapy resource	Therapist refers to a pastor for specific spiritual or theological questions. Therapist sends a person to a Christian attorney for information.

TABLE 10.2 *(cont.)*

Intervention	Definition	Examples of intervention
Client prayer	Encouraging client private prayers	Therapist encourages a client to pray for help to know how to better relate to his or her spouse. Therapist suggests that a client pray for strength to resist whenever he feels tempted to view pornography.
Encouraging client confession	Encouraging the client to confess violations of moral code to appropriate persons and to seek repentance	Therapist suggests that a client admit that he was overly harsh and emotionally abusive to his children and ask them to forgive him. Therapist supports a client in her decision to confess a sexual transgression to her religious leader.
Referral for blessing	Encouraging client to request priesthood blessing from home teacher or religious leader to help client cope and work through impasses	Therapist suggests that a client seek a blessing from her spiritual leader for assistance in gaining the emotional and spiritual strength to cope with the death of her child.
Religious journal writing	Asking client to keep journal concerning spiritual struggles, insights, and experiences	Therapist assigns journal keeping of answered prayer. Therapist suggests to some clients that they record spiritual insights or impressions they have.
Spiritual meditation	Encouraging meditation about spiritual matters to promote client spiritual growth	Therapist suggests meditation or meditative imagery focusing on Christ and his love. Therapist suggests quiet times when the client can ponder and contemplate about his or her life and God's will for her.
Religious bibliotherapy	Giving clients religious and spiritual literature to read	Therapist encourages clients to read the Book of Job in the Bible. Therapist gives some clients tapes or articles of talks by leaders in the church.
Scripture memorization	Interventions specifically using client memorization of Scriptures to affect change	Therapist suggests Scripture memorization for thought stopping of obsessive clients and as a means of coping during panic attacks.

Note. Definitions and examples were adapted from two sources. Ball, R. A., and Goodyear, R. K. (1991). Self-reported practices of Christian psychologists. *Journal of Psychology and Christianity, 10*, 144–153. Reprinted here by permission from the Christian Association for Psychological Studies. Richards, P. S., and Potts, R. W. (1995a). Using spiritual interventions in psychotherapy: Practices, successes, failures, and ethical concerns of Mormon psychotherapists. *Professional Psychology: Research and Practice, 26*, 163–170. Copyright 1995 by the American Psychological Association.

which different therapists use religious-spiritual versus secular interventions is not clear. There is probably a great deal of variation between therapists and perhaps within therapists in this regard. Some therapists probably use religious and spiritual interventions almost exclusively, whereas others probably rely almost exclusively on secular techniques. Some therapists may rely heavily on religious and spiritual interventions with some of their clients but use secular interventions exclusively with other clients. Research is needed to investigate these possibilities.

A 1985 national survey of psychotherapists in psychiatry, clinical psychology, marriage and family therapy, and clinical social work by Jensen, Bergin, and Greaves (1990) revealed that 17% of eclectic therapists included a religious-transpersonal component in their overall integrative approach. Although this study did not provide specific information about what types of spiritual interventions were used or how frequently the therapists used them, it does suggest that even a decade ago a sizeable number of mainstream psychotherapists were attempting to integrate spiritual perspectives and interventions into their therapeutic approach. Shafranske and Malony's (1990) study also provided some evidence that significant numbers of mainstream clinical psychologists use at least a few religious and spiritual interventions in psychotherapy. The generalizability of the findings in their study is somewhat limited, however, because psychologists who were more interested in and sensitive to spiritual issues were overrepresented in the sample. In addition, only six religious interventions were included on the survey, so this study did not provide information on the wide variety of other religious and spiritual interventions that have been developed. Thus, it is still unclear how widespread the use of various religious and spiritual interventions is within the psychotherapy profession as a whole, but it appears to be a growing phenomenon. Additional studies are needed to investigate this possibility.

CATEGORIES OF SPIRITUAL INTERVENTIONS

We now discuss several ways that the wide variety of religious and spiritual interventions described earlier can be conceptualized or categorized so that therapists will better understand the types of spiritual interventions that are available to them. We limit our descriptions to several categorization schemes that may have some clinical relevance and utility. Specific examples of applications of spiritual interventions are provided in Table 10.2, in the section on treatment package approaches, and in the case studies provided in chapter 11.

Religious Versus Spiritual Interventions

One way of categorizing religious and spiritual interventions is according to whether the intervention is "religious" or "spiritual." As one might have guessed from our previous use of these terms, it is difficult to define the difference between them precisely because the terms *religious* and *spiritual* are interrelated and can be distinguished from each other along several dimensions (e.g., denominational vs. ecumenical, external vs. internal, cognitive and behavioral vs. affective, ritualistic vs. spontaneous, public vs. private). We define *religious interventions* as those that are more structured, behavioral, denominational, external, cognitive, ritualistic, and public. Examples of religious interventions include quoting or paraphrasing Scriptures; encouraging clients to attend church, engage in religious rituals and traditions, and use resources available within the institution; and suggesting that clients read (and possibly reinterpret) Scriptures or the writings of their religious leaders. We define *spiritual interventions* as those that are more experiential, transcendent, ecumenical, cross-cultural, internal, affective, spontaneous, and personal. Examples of spiritual interventions include private prayer, spiritual meditation, spiritual imagery with images that are personally meaningful to the client, encouraging forgiveness, and keeping a spiritual journal. Although distinguishing between religious and spiritual interventions is helpful, because of the somewhat imprecise and overlapping nature of these categories, other schemes for categorizing and conceptualizing such interventions also are needed.

In-Session Versus Out-of-Session Interventions

Another way of categorizing interventions is according to whether they are used in or out of the session (e.g., P. S. Richards & Potts, 1995a). *In-session interventions* are those that therapists or clients actually carry out during the therapy session. Examples of in-session interventions include therapist vocal or silent in-session prayers, teaching clients spiritual concepts, quoting or paraphrasing Scriptures, spiritually confronting clients about discrepancies between their religious beliefs and behaviors, and using guided religious or spiritual imagery activities during the session. *Out-of-session interventions* are those that are prescribed or suggested as homework activities for clients. Out-of-session interventions, of course, must be recommended and discussed during the therapy session, but the actual activity or experience occurs outside the session without the therapist. Examples of out-of-session interventions include suggesting that clients attend religious worship services, encouraging them to privately pray and meditate during the week, encouraging them to confess violations of their moral code to their religious leader, suggesting that they request help and support from their religious leaders or congregants, and asking them to keep a journal about their spiritual struggles, experiences, and insights.

P. S. Richards and Potts (1995a) found that Mormon therapists reported that, on the average, they used out-of-session religious and spiritual interventions more frequently than in-session interventions. It was unclear why this was the case, but they speculated that the therapists believed that there was less risk of confusing role boundaries or offending clients when out-of-session interventions were used. Out-of-session interventions generally are less risky because there is less chance when using them that therapists will cross role boundaries by engaging in religious activities that would be more appropriately performed by the client's religious leader or that would cause the client to perceive the therapist as a religious authority. In addition, when recommending out-of-session interventions, therapists can convey support of clients' spiritual beliefs and growth with less risk of influencing or coercing clients into spiritual activities that are alien to them. The risk of coercion is lower with out-of-session interventions because clients can choose more easily not to participate in them. Clients can simply choose not to do their homework when out-of-session interventions are recommended, but when therapists suggest in-session interventions, clients must directly tell therapists they do not wish to participate.

This is not to say that we believe out-of-session interventions should always be preferred over in-session interventions. The little research evidence available suggests that in-session interventions can be highly effective (e.g., P. S. Richards & Potts, 1995a). Therapists should simply keep in mind that in-session interventions may be somewhat more risky than out-of-session ones with some clients and proceed accordingly.

Denominational Versus Ecumenical Interventions

Another useful way of categorizing interventions is according to whether they are denominational or ecumenical. We define *denominational interventions* as those that contain theological content or meaning that makes them suitable only for clients who belong to a particular religious tradition. Within the category of denominational interventions, numerous subcategories could be created, such as several subcategories for Jewish clients (e.g., Orthodox, Conservative, and Reformed), numerous subcategories for Christians (e.g., Roman Catholic, Greek Orthodox, Lutheran, Baptist, Mormon, Seventh-Day Adventist), several for Muslims (e.g., Sunni, Shi'ah), and so on. Examples of denominational interventions include encouraging Jewish clients to attend their synagogue, using spiritual imagery activities with Christian clients that contain images of Jesus, and discussing verses from the Koran with Muslim clients.

Many interventions can be adapted and used in a denominationally specific manner across a variety of different denominations (Lovinger, 1984). For example, therapists working with Jewish clients may discuss with them Scriptures from the Torah and therapists working with Christian clients may discuss with them New Testament Scriptures. Therapists who have an in-depth knowledge of several religious traditions may find that they can apply the same intervention (e.g., discussing scriptural teachings) with clients from each of these traditions by adapting the content of the intervention to suit each client. Generally speaking, however, therapists should use interventions in a denominational manner only when they have adopted a denominational therapeutic stance as discussed in chapter 6.

We define *ecumenical interventions* as those that do not contain any theological content or meaning that would identify the intervention with a specific religious tradition. The content and meaning of ecumenical interventions is general, flexible, and as universal as possible so that they can be accepted and used with clients from a variety of religious and spiritual traditions. Examples of ecumenical interventions include encouraging theistic clients to pray or commune with their God or Higher Power, suggesting that clients keep a journal in which they record their spiritual experiences and insights, and using spiritual imagery when clients are invited to supply their own spiritual images at certain moments during the experience (H. Benson, 1996). We recognize that it may be almost impossible to use interventions that are completely ecumenical in nature because almost all interventions contain some content or meaning that could exclude some clients. Nevertheless, some interventions are clearly more ecumenical than others. If therapists are careful to use language that is general and nondenominational, many interventions that are typically used in denominational therapeutic situations also may be suitable when therapists are working from an ecumenical therapeutic stance.

Transcendent Versus Nontranscendent Interventions

Another useful way of categorizing religious and spiritual interventions is according to whether the intervention is a transcendent or a nontranscendent one. We define *transcendent interventions* as those that assume and petition transcendent spiritual influences on behalf of clients or the therapy process. Transcendent interventions require that the client or the therapist or both believe in God and in the reality of transcendent spiritual influences. Examples of transcendent interventions include client or therapist prayer, blessings from religious leaders, and spiritual meditation when such practices are engaged in with the intent of seeking spiritual guidance, enlightenment, and strength.

We define *nontranscendent interventions* as those that do not require that the therapist or the client believe in God or in spiritual influences, or assume or petition transcendent spiritual influences on behalf of clients or the therapy process. Examples of nontranscendent interventions include discussing clients' understanding of Scriptures, confronting discrepancies between clients' professed religious values and their behaviors, assessing clients' religious and spiritual background and status, encouraging clients to forgive others, referral to the religious community, and keeping a spiritual journal. Of course, some nontranscendent interventions could be used with the hope that the client will be blessed with transcendent spiritual assistance (e.g., a therapist may encourage a client to read Scriptures with the hope that the client will have a transcendent spiritual experience while doing so). Thus, some interventions could be viewed as either transcendent or nontranscendent depending on the purpose or intent for which they are used.

Affective, Behavioral, Cognitive, and Interpersonal Interventions

Another useful way of categorizing religious and spiritual interventions is according to the primary modality (e.g., affective, behavioral, cognitive, or interpersonal) through which the intervention attempts to affect the client. Such a classification scheme also has been useful for categorizing the interventions of the mainstream psychotherapy traditions (e.g., L. S. Cormier, Cormier, & Weisser, 1984; L. S. Cormier & Hackney, 1987).

We define *affective spiritual interventions* as those that are designed to help clients by changing their religious and spiritual feelings and emotions. Clients who are emotionally sensitive and expressive, and who use their emotions in problem solving and decision making, may be the most receptive to affective interventions (L. S. Cormier & Hackney, 1987). Examples of affective spiritual interventions include client prayer, spiritual imagery, blessings, keeping a spiritual journal, and spiritual contemplation and meditation.

We define *behavioral spiritual interventions* as those that are designed to help clients by changing their religious and spiritual practices and lifestyle. Clients who have a strong goal orientation and who like to be actively doing something may be the most receptive to behavioral interventions (L. S. Cormier & Hackney, 1987). Examples of behavioral spiritual interventions include encouraging clients to participate in religious practices and rituals (e.g., attending worship services, visiting a temple or shrine, participating in a religious festival), reading and memorizing Scriptures, pointing out discrepancies between clients' professed religious values and their behaviors, modeling spiritual values, and encouraging clients to confess and forsake unhealthy and sinful behaviors.

We define *cognitive spiritual interventions* as those that are designed to help clients by changing their religious and spiritual religious beliefs and understandings. Clients who are logical and rational in their problem-solving approach, and who find ideas, theories, and concepts appealing, may be most receptive to cognitive interventions (L. S. Cormier & Hackney, 1987). Examples of cognitive spiritual interventions include teaching and discussing spiritual concepts, paraphrasing and interpreting Scriptures, and scriptural study homework assignments.

We define *interpersonal spiritual interventions* as those that are designed to help clients by changing the amount and nature of their involvement with members of their religious community. Clients who have good social skills and who are open to relationships with other people may be the most receptive to interpersonal interventions (L. S. Cormier & Hackney, 1987). Examples of interpersonal spiritual interventions include encouraging clients to engage in fellowship with members of their religious community, providing service to people in need, and serving in ecclesiastical or volunteer positions in their religious congregation.

Because of the complex interplay among affect, behavior, cognitions, and interpersonal relationships, it is often difficult to know what type of intervention will be most helpful for a given client. Just because a client may be receptive to interventions that use a certain modality does not mean such interventions will be effective. Interventions that clients are initially the least receptive to may help them the most. For example, clients who are socially unskilled and interpersonally isolated may find interpersonal spiritual interventions threatening and difficult to participate in but extremely beneficial.

Summary

None of the categorization schemes we have described are meant to be *the* correct one. Each of these schemes has some advantages and limitations. We hope that these schemes will be studied empirically to evaluate their clinical usefulness. Perhaps other clinically relevant categorization schemes will be proposed and tested. Ultimately, perhaps the ideal classification scheme for interventions would be one that categorizes them according to the type of client problems or issues with which the intervention is effective. For example, it would be useful to have a categorization scheme that indicates which interventions are most likely to (a) help clients develop a healthier sense of self-esteem and identity, (b) overcome depression and suicidal ideation, and (c) improve their marital relationship. Whether such a classification scheme will ever be possible remains to be seen.

TREATMENT PACKAGE APPROACHES

All the practices and interventions we have described up to this point can be, and usually are, used in an eclectic, treatment tailoring manner (Payne et al., 1992; P. S. Richards & Potts, 1995a). That is, therapists implement these interventions flexibly along with whatever secular interventions they may be using whenever it seems indicated for individual clients. However, spiritual interventions also have been integrated into structured, multicomponent treatment plans. In such *treatment package approaches*, therapists implement selected spiritual interventions along with secular ones with all clients who are receiving the treatment package at specific times or phases of the treatment process.

There are a number of treatment package approaches that have been described in the literature. We briefly describe three prominent examples: Propst's (1980, 1996) religious cognitive therapy approach, the 12-step program of Alcoholics Anonymous (AA; Hopson, 1996), and Ornish's (1990) Opening Your Heart program for modifying Type A behavior and reversing heart disease. We also briefly discuss some of the advantages and disadvantages of treatment package approaches and offer suggestions about how such approaches can be used ethically and effectively.

Religious Cognitive Therapy

Propst (1980, 1988, 1996) has pioneered efforts to integrate religious and spiritual interventions with cognitive therapy. Propst (1988) developed a cognitive therapy treatment protocol for depression that includes religious rationales for the treatment approach, religious arguments to counter dysfunctional thoughts, religious imagery procedures, and religious motivations for behavior change. As explained by Propst (1996),

> because cognitive therapy emphasizes that patients must understand and believe that their thoughts and assumptions strongly influence their emotions and psychological well-being, religious patients may be given a religious rationale for this framework as well as a religious rationale for assessing their thoughts and assumptions. . . .
>
> After patients accept the value of thought monitoring and can apply this skill, the next process in cognitive therapy is the actual challenging and subsequent changing of thoughts and assumptions. Themes from most religious belief systems can play an important role in this process. Indeed, the religious ideas can actually become cognitive restructuring techniques. . . .
>
> An additional cognitive restructuring technique that is helpful within a religious context is the use of religious imagery. . . . Images . . . may allow patients to focus more fully on emotionally laden ideas, so that patients may more effectively restructure the thoughts and images surrounding a traumatic event. . . .
>
> Behavior modification is often also a part of cognitive-behavioral therapy. Here also, religious patients could profit from a religious motivation for behavior changes. (pp. 399–401)

Examples of religious cognitive restructuring and religious imagery techniques from Propst's (1988) book, *Psychotherapy in a Religious Framework: Spirituality in the Emotional Healing Process*, are provided in Table 10.3. Propst and colleagues have conducted two well-designed outcome studies that have provided evidence that religious cognitive therapy with religious clients is as effective, and sometimes more effective, than standard cognitive therapy (Propst, 1980; Propst, Ostrom, Watkins, Dean, & Mashburn, 1992).

Propst's writings have stimulated other theoretical and research efforts. For example, Tan and colleagues have critiqued and provided guidelines for a biblical (Christian) cognitive therapy approach (e.g., Craigie & Tan, 1989; Tan, 1987). Pecheur and Edwards (1984) empirically compared a religious (Christian) cognitive–behavioral treatment approach with a secular one. They found that the religious cognitive–behavioral treatment was

TABLE 10.3
Examples of Religious Cognitive Therapy Techniques
From Propst (1988)

Religious Rationales for Challenging Dysfunctional Thinking

I. *"Defeatism versus perfectionism*: The perfectionist believes in the dictum, 'I must be thoroughly competent, adequate, and achieving in all possible respects if I am to consider myself worthwhile' (Ellis & Harper, 1975, p. 102). According to David Burns (1980), these same individuals are also guilty of all-or-nothing thinking. If their performance falls short of perfect, they see themselves as total failures" (Propst, 1988, p. 111).

Theological Rationale

"Scripture does not speak of our spirituality as necessarily based on perfection. St. Paul, in his Epistle to the Romans, for example, declares that all have sinned. We all fail in some ways. He then proceeds to use the entire book of Romans to say, in effect, that even though we are not okay, we are okay. In other words, we are accepted by God anyway, through his forgiveness" (Rom. 3:23–34). . . .

"Ultimately, it will be our acknowledgement and acceptance of our imperfections that free us to live a fuller life. . . . We will never be perfect. We will always be striving. We can never arrive, because the Holy Spirit is continually inspiring new aspirations. This sense of imperfection should be taken as a merciful voice from God leading us in new directions" (Propst, 1988, p. 112).

Religious Imagery

"Because the images of Jesus play such a central role in correcting our own self-definitions, visual images of Jesus and ourselves can also be used profitably within the psychotherapy process. At least four different types of relationships between ourselves and the image of Jesus are possible. (1) There is the image of surrender. Various images of giving oneself to Christ can be therapeutic. (2) There is the image of Christ's reaction to us. (3) There is the image of Christ with us as we engage in specific tasks, and finally, (4) there is the image of Christ within us" (Propst, 1988, p. 128).

Christ with us in a difficult situation: The image of Christ with us can be helpful in at least two different ways:

"A mental rehearsal of an anticipated event has been found to be a great aid in enabling an individual eventually to carry out that behavior. This rehearsal can be enhanced by imagining Christ with you in the situation, as you rehearse an anticipated conversation or action that you have found difficult in the past.

Imagery can be a useful method whereby we may experience more fully the truth of scripture that Christ has promised to be with us in all things.

A second method of imagining Christ with us is to visualize a difficult or painful past situation in which Christ is with us in that situation. When Christ is added to the painful traumatic event, the tone and flavor of such an image may be changed. Such a process is actually a cognitive restructuring of the image as we remember it. Often, such images are so intense and so painful, that only other equally intense images will be able to have impact on them.

For some patients, Christ will change the actual content of the image. For others, Christ's presence will give the original painful content new meaning" (Propst, 1988, p. 136).

Note. This material was adapted from Propst, R. L. (1988). *Psychotherapy in a religious framework: Spirituality in the emotional healing process* (pp. 111–112, 128, 136). New York: Human Sciences Press. Adapted here by permission from Human Sciences Press.

significantly more effective than the waiting-list control group, although it was equivalent to the secular approach. Johnson and colleagues developed a treatment protocol for Christian rational–emotive therapy and compared it with secular rational–emotive therapy (Johnson, 1993; Johnson, Devries, Ridley, Pettorini, & Peterson, 1994; Johnson & Ridley, 1992). They found that both religious and secular forms of rational–emotive therapy were equally effective with depressed Christian clients. P. S. Richards, Owen, and Stein (1993) pilot tested a religiously oriented group therapy cognitive intervention for perfectionistic Mormon students. They found that by the end of treatment, the students had experienced significant reductions in depression and perfectionism and increases in self-esteem and existential and religious well-being. Thus, research provides support for the efficacy of religious cognitive therapy treatment package approaches and incentive for further efforts to refine and evaluate them.

12-Step Programs

The 12-step program of AA is the largest and most influential self-help group in contemporary society (McCrady & Delaney, 1995). AA estimates that they have approximately 87,000 groups in 150 countries and more than 1.7 million members worldwide (Alcoholics Anonymous World Services, 1990). Numerous other fellowships that subscribe to the AA 12-step model of recovery have been created, such as Narcotics Anonymous, Gamblers Anonymous, and Sex and Love Addictions Anonymous. Although empirical evidence supporting the effectiveness of 12-step programs is relatively sparse (Hopson, 1996; McCrady & Delaney, 1995), 12-step programs do enjoy considerable acceptance among helping professionals. Many therapists look to 12-step groups as a source of assistance and support for their clients and as an important supplement to professional treatment (Castaneda & Galanter, 1987; Hopson, 1996; McCrady & Delaney, 1995).

It is well-known that the 12-step program of AA, and many other 12-step programs, is based on a spiritual worldview (Hopson, 1996). The 12-step program of AA starts with the assumption that, to recover from alcoholism, people must humble themselves before God or their Higher Power and acknowledge that they need God's assistance. As can be seen in Table 10.4, the entire 12-step process is a spiritual model of healing and recovery. As explained by Hopson (1996),

> The 12-step programs view spirituality in recovery from addiction as the basis of a lifestyle change. Rather than denying the reality of his or her condition, the addict must begin to see the addiction as destructive to the self. Spirituality involves an assertion of the will to bring one's behavior in line with the reality of one's condition. Acknowledgment of one's helplessness leads to the recognition that one must turn

TABLE 10.4
The Twelve Steps of Alcoholics Anonymous

Step
1. We admitted we were powerless over alcohol—that our lives had become unmanageable.
2. Came to believe that a Power greater than ourselves could restore us to sanity.
3. Made a decision to turn our will and our lives over to the care of God *as we understood Him.*
4. Made a searching and fearless moral inventory of ourselves.
5. Admitted to God, to ourselves, and to another human being the exact nature of our wrongs.
6. Were entirely ready to have God remove all these defects of character.
7. Humbly asked Him to remove our shortcomings.
8. Made a list of all persons we had harmed, and became willing to make amends to them all.
9. Made direct amends to such people wherever possible, except when to do so would injure them or others.
10. Continued to take personal inventory and when we were wrong promptly admitted it.
11. Sought through prayer and meditation to improve our conscious contact with God *as we understood Him,* praying only for knowledge of His will for us and the power to carry that out.
12. Having had a spiritual awakening as the result of these steps, we tried to carry this message to alcoholics, and to practice these principles in all our affairs.

Note. From AA World Services. (1980). Alcoholics Anonymous. New York: Author. The Twelve Steps are reprinted with permission of Alcoholics Anonymous World Services, Inc. Permission to reprint the Twelve Steps does not mean that AA has reviewed or approved the contents of this publication, nor that AA agrees with the views expressed herein. AA is a program of recovery from alcoholism *only*—use of the Twelve Steps in connection with programs and activities which are patterned after AA, but which address other problems, or in any other non-AA context, does not imply otherwise.

to something outside the self to begin the process of recovery (Buxton et al., 1987, p. 280). That something outside the self that will support recovery is the higher power. Recovery is made possible at the junction between the surrendered self and the higher power. The quest that has compelled someone to use a substance is redirected toward the beneficent higher power. (pp. 536–537)

Religious and spiritual interventions that are potentially used to facilitate the recovery process in 12-step programs include confession, making restitution, seeking forgiveness from God and others, prayers of petition and invocation, meditation, and service to others. Some 12-step groups also use scriptural interventions; that is, they make explicit connections between the Bible and the 12 steps (Friends in Recovery, 1994; McCrady & Delaney, 1995). Secular 12-step programs also have been developed for clients and therapists who have less interest in a theistic, spiritual approach (Dupont & McGovern, 1994).

Ornish's (1990) Reversing Heart Disease Program

There have been numerous treatment programs developed to help people modify Type A coronary prone behavior pattern and heart disease. Some of these treatment programs have integrated religious and spiritual interventions into the treatment package (e.g., Friedman et al., 1984; Ornish, 1990; Powell & Thoresen, 1987). Perhaps the most well-known of these is Ornish's (1990) Opening Your Heart program (Friend, 1995). Ornish's program has received national attention because well-designed research studies have proved that it can stop and even reverse coronary heart disease (Friend, 1995; Ornish, 1990).

Ornish's (1990) treatment program is more than just a medical intervention; it seeks to help people physically, psychologically, and spiritually. As explained by Ornish (1990),

> physically, this program can help you begin to open your heart's arteries and to feel stronger and more energetic, freer of pain. Emotionally, it can help you open your heart to others and to experience greater happiness, intimacy, and love in your relationships. Spiritually, it can help you open your heart to a higher force (however you experience it) and to rediscover your inner sources of peace and joy. (p. 3)

Ornish's (1990) program encourages patients to engage in comprehensive lifestyle changes and includes a number of treatment components: low-fat diet, smoking cessation program, exercise program, techniques for reducing stress, interventions for improving communication and intimacy with others, and methods for seeking spiritual communion with God or a Higher Power. Spiritual practices and interventions that are used in Ornish's program include yoga; "inner teacher" visualization; encouraging altruism, compassion, and forgiveness; meditation; and prayer or devotion (Ornish, 1990).

Ornish (1990) believed that the spiritual component of treatment is essential for treatment success:

> Your mind, body, and spirit are all intimately interconnected. Because of this, coronary heart disease occurs on emotional and spiritual levels as well as physical ones. The Opening Your Heart program is designed to address *all* of these levels, not just the physical ones.
>
> If we limit our treatments only to the physical heart, then the disease tends to come back again and again—or the treatments may be worse than the illness. If we also address the emotional and spiritual dimensions, then the physical heart often begins to heal as well. (p. 250)

In recent years, numerous physicians have discussed the potential health benefits of spiritual beliefs and practices such as meditation, imagery, and prayer (e.g., H. Benson, 1996; Borysenko & Borysenko, 1994). Table

10.5 provides examples of two meditation techniques from Borysenko and Borysenko's (1994) book, *The Power of the Mind to Heal: Renewing Body, Mind, and Spirit.*

There are at least two advantages of integrating spiritual interventions into structured, multicomponent treatment packages. First, well-designed, integrated treatment packages may be more therapeutically potent than individual interventions. Systematically combining promising spiritual interventions with empirically proved secular interventions could maximize therapists' ability to help clients with specific problems and disorders. Second, because treatment package approaches tend to follow structured treatment plans, it is more feasible to write detailed treatment manuals for them than it is for eclectic, flexible treatment approaches. Treatment manuals are valuable because they make it easier to train therapists in an approach, and they make controlled psychotherapy outcome research more feasible (Kazdin, 1994; Lambert & Bergin, 1994). Thus, therapists could find spiritual–secular treatment package approaches easier to learn and empirically evaluate than less structured spiritual treatment approaches.

One major concern we have about treatment package approaches is that they could lead to the rigid application of religious and spiritual interventions without regard for clients' values and needs (cf. Kazdin, 1994). When using such approaches, all clients are supposed to receive the same interventions; thus, there is perhaps a greater risk that therapists could impose their values on clients and coerce them into participating in spiritual interventions that are alien to their religious beliefs. However, therapists can apply interventions flexibly even when using treatment package approaches. Spiritual interventions could potentially be dropped from the treatment package for individual clients if they conflict with the client's religious and spiritual beliefs. Perhaps the best way therapists can avoid value imposition when using treatment package approaches is to carefully select for treatment only those clients whose beliefs are compatible with the spiritual interventions included in the treatment package. To accomplish this, advertising materials and informed consent documents should describe all spiritual interventions that may be included in the treatment program, and therapists should explicitly ascertain whether clients are willing to participate in these interventions.

Another concern we have about treatment package approaches is that they could lead to the misapplication and trivialization of sacred religious and spiritual practices (P. S. Richards & Potts, 1995a). There may be some religious and spiritual practices that people should only engage in spontaneously or when prompted by transcendent, spiritual influences. For example, should therapists prescribe precisely when during treatment that clients should pray, meditate, ask for blessings from religious leaders, or seek transcendent spiritual guidance? Perhaps some spiritual practices and experiences should not, or cannot, be rigidly orchestrated to fit into thera-

TABLE 10.5
Meditation Scripts From Borysenko and Borysenko (1994)

Meditation Script

Holy moment meditation

"Take a few letting-go breaths, and remember a time when you felt present in the moment—absorbed in a sunset, marveling at fresh-fallen snow, enchanted by the smile of a baby. . . . If several memories come, choose just one. . . .

Enter the memory with all of your senses. Remember the sights and colors . . . the fragrances . . . the position and movement of your body . . . the emotional or felt sense. . . .

Let the memory go and meditate on the feelings that remain—the stillness and joy of your own Higher Self."

TONGLEN: The meditation of forgiveness and compassion

"Close your eyes and take a stretch and a few letting-go breaths. . . . Begin to notice the flow of your breathing, allowing your body to relax and your mind to come to rest. . . .

Imagine a Great Star of Light above your head, and feel it washing over you like a waterfall and running through you like a river runs through the sand at its bottom. . . . Allow it to carry away any fatigue, pain, illness, or ignorance. . . . See these wash through the bottom of your feet into the earth for transformation. As you are washed clean, notice that the light within your heart begins to shine very brightly. . . .

Now imagine yourself as a child, choosing whatever age seems most relevant to you at this time. . . . You, better than anyone, know the pain in your heart at that time. Breathe it in as a black smoke (or dark clouds), and breathe out the light in your heart to yourself. . . .

Imagine yourself as you are right now, as if you could see yourself in a mirror. See whatever pain or illness you have as a black smoke around your heart. Inhale the smoke and exhale the light of your Higher Self. . . . Fill your heart with light. . . .

Bring to mind a person that you love. . . . Think about the pain or illness that might be in their heart. . . . Inhale that pain as a black smoke, and exhale the light of your own true nature back into their heart.

Bring to mind someone whom you are ready to forgive. Imagine them in as much detail as you can. Imagine their pain, illness, or illusion as a black smoke around their heart. . . . Breathe in the smoke, and breathe back the light of your own true nature into their heart.

Think of someplace in the world where there is suffering. If possible, bring a specific example of that suffering to mind—a starving child, a grieving parent. . . . Breathe in the pain of that suffering as a black smoke, and let it part the clouds of darkness around your own heart. Breathe out the light of your Higher Self.

End with a prayer or a short period of mindful meditation. You may also want to dedicate the fruits of this meditation to alleviate the suffering of all beings:

> May all beings be happy.
> May all be free from suffering.
> May all know the beauty of
>   their own true nature.
> May all beings be healed."

Note. Reprinted from Borysenko, J., and Borysenko, M. (1994). *The power of the mind to heal* (pp. 127, 172–174). Carlsbad, CA: Hay House, Inc. Reprinted here by permission from Hay House, Inc.

pists' structured treatment plans (P. S. Richards & Potts, 1995a). The most therapists should do in the case of many religious and spiritual interventions is to encourage clients to engage in these practices if and when they feel ready.

APPLICATIONS TO DIFFERENT THERAPEUTIC MODALITIES

It appears that spiritual interventions have been used the most frequently in individual psychotherapy with adult clients (Ball & Goodyear, 1991; Chamberlain et al., 1996; Jones et al., 1992; Payne et al., 1992; P. S. Richards & Potts, 1995a; Worthington et al., 1988). Spiritual interventions also have been used in group therapy (e.g., Little & Robinson, 1988; Propst, 1980; P. S. Richards et al., 1993), marital and family therapy (e.g., L. Sperry & Giblin, 1996; Worthington, 1989b, 1990), and less frequently with children and adolescents (e.g., Wells, in press). Examples of the use of spiritual interventions in group therapy were provided earlier in this chapter in our discussions of cognitive therapy (Propst, 1980; Propst et al., 1992; P. S. Richards et al., 1993), 12-step groups (Hopson, 1996), and Type A behavior pattern groups (Ornish, 1990).

Descriptions of the use of spiritual interventions in marital and family therapy recently have been provided by L. Sperry and Giblin (1996); Wright, Watson, & Bell, (1996), and Worthington (1989b, 1990). Table 10.6 provides a summary outline of Worthington's (1989b, 1990) Christian marriage counseling approach. Worthington's approach is suitable for committed Christian couples and integrates Christian perspectives and spiritual interventions (e.g., prayer, quoting and explaining biblical Scriptures, and encouraging forgiveness) with secular marital therapy concepts and techniques (e.g., systemic and structural). L. Sperry and Giblin (1996) provided a helpful description of an eclectic, ecumenical marriage and family therapy approach that includes an overview of relevant theory and concepts from the secular literature, a discussion of religious beliefs and practices that may influence therapy, techniques for assessing religion and spirituality, and descriptions of religious and spiritual interventions that they believe are suitable for couples and families. Spiritual interventions they recommend include prayer; exploration of spiritual content in dreams; discussion of Scriptures; encouraging forgiveness and acceptance; spiritual bibliotherapy; and the infusion of spiritual content into gestalt, empty chair, and letter-writing techniques.

In one of the few publications we are aware of that discusses the use of spiritual interventions with children and adolescents, Wells (in press) provided a helpful review of theory and research on religious development in children, including discussions of Elkind's (1978, 1982) work on children's understanding of prayer and institutional identification, Fowler's (1981, 1991) faith development theory, Oser's (1991) descriptions of children's

TABLE 10.6
Summary of Worthington's (1989b, 1990) Christian Marriage
Counseling Approach for Christian Couples

Christian Marriage Counseling Approach

Basic Assumptions and Goals

"I believe that people are created in the image of God, which endows them with a variety of laudable personal qualities. They were created as individuals, but they were created to be in relationship with God and with humans, most importantly with a spouse, with whom they are 'one flesh,' but also with their offspring, members of their family of origin, and others both Christian and non-Christian. Despite their positive qualities, people are corrupted by the Fall, which acts as a distal cause of psychological and relationship problems. I believe that people can be redeemed by admitting their sinfulness and trusting in Jesus as their savior. Their redemption will often help heal their personal and relationship problems but rarely will it completely cure them or prevent all future problems.

A Christian marital therapist has a two-pronged goal: (a) to help people grow spiritually and psychologically through (b) helping them solve their marital problems" (Worthington, 1990, p. 5). During the course of therapy, whenever he feels that it is appropriate, Worthington prays with couples and encourages their prayers, discusses Scriptures, and encourages Scripture reading and other Christian literature.

Therapy Process and Interventions

A. Relationship establishment and gaining a commitment to working
  1. Graph "closeness to the Lord" and "closeness to each other."
  2. Discuss and read literature about of the meaning of covenant (and marriage covenant) from a Christian perspective.
  3. Get initial agreement with couple to meet for three assessment sessions.
B. Assessment questions and measures
  1. What are the main difficulties in the marriage?
  2. What is the couple's relationship history?
  3. Administer the Personal Assessment of Intimacy in Relationships.
  4. How do they use time each week, and how does this effect the balance of intimacy, distance, or coaction?
  5. Assess the couple's communication skills through their self-reports and by observing them discussing issues during sessions.
  6. Assess the couple's conflict management skills by having them discuss for 7 min an issue about which they habitually disagree. This discussion is recorded and analyzed later.
  7. To what degree is there unresolved and unforgiven hurt, blame, and sin, and what is each partner's capacity for additional forgiveness?
C. Therapeutic goals and interventions used
  1. Change patterns of intimacy
    a) Read aloud together about conflict negotiation and other marital topics written from a Christian perspective.
    b) Have the couple plan different ways to arrange their time schedule to include more time together.
    c) Assign the couple tasks and activities that will help them increase their pleasant interactions and feelings of closeness.
  2. Improving communication
    a) Ask the couple to describe their parents' communication patterns to see how parents may have influenced them.
    b) As a tool for helping the couple discuss communication of feelings, discuss Crabb's (1982) *The Marriage Builder: A Blueprint for Couples and Counselors* (provides a Christian view of successful marriage).

TABLE 10.6 *(cont.)*

Christian Marriage Counseling Approach

3. Conflict negotiation
   a) Use Stuart's (1980) powergram to help the couple state whom they perceive has decision-making responsibility in conflictual issues.
   b) Identify major areas of conflict and the couple's differences in goals.
   c) Tackle one issue in which there is moderate disagreement to discuss. Tape record the interaction. Observe the effects of communication patterns on each partner. Process it to help the couple understand their patterns and learn new ones.
4. Promoting forgiveness
   a) Use Worthington and DiBlasio's (1990) forgiveness intervention. Each spouse compiles a list of things he or she has done to hurt the other. They each describe ways they have sinned against their partners and ask their partner for forgiveness.
D. Consolidating changes
   1. Hypothetical graph is shown to the couple depicting typical progress of couple and the ups and downs in marital satisfaction culminating in an increase in satisfaction. Couples are encouraged to persevere toward their goal despite ups and downs.

religious thinking, and Tamminen's (1991) research on the religious development of Finnish children and youth. Wells (in press) also discussed implications of this theory and research for clinicians and suggested that religious and spiritual interventions may be the most useful for children and adolescents with internalizing (mood) disorders and adjustment disorders. He discussed the coping value of religious beliefs and suggested that spiritual interventions such as prayer, meditation, participation in religious rituals, and using religious metaphors and narratives may be therapeutic with children and adolescents (see also Keith-Lucas, 1992; Komp, 1993).

Spiritual interventions that make use of play, art, stories, dance or movement, games, drama or role-play, imagery, puppets, and music also may be useful for children and younger adolescents (Bradley & Gould, 1993). Given that the major psychosocial tasks of adolescence concern issues of identity, meaning, values, and sexuality (Erikson, 1968; Havighurst, 1972), spiritual interventions that help adolescents affirm their sense of identity, worth, and belonging and clarify and internalize healthy values may be useful for them. Prayer, meditation, spiritual literature and music, fellowship and service with peers in the religious community, and spiritual direction from leaders may be helpful in this regard. There is reason to believe that such interventions also may help prevent common problems of adolescence such as substance abuse, promiscuity and pregnancy, STDs, depression and suicide, violence, delinquency, and gang involvement (Pargament, 1996; Payne et al., 1992).

All of the foregoing illustrates that many spiritual interventions can be applied in therapy regardless of the modality being used. Nevertheless, there are some unique challenges when therapists use spiritual interventions with children and adolescents, groups, couples, or families. As we discussed in chapter 7, when working with children and adolescents, it is crucial for therapists to obtain explicit parental consent before using religious and spiritual interventions. Even with such consent, given the power differential that exists between adults and minors, therapists must be extra cautious not to impose their religious beliefs and values on children and adolescents. Therapists also must make sure they adapt religious and spiritual interventions to fit the language, cognitive abilities, and developmental needs of children and adolescents (Vernon, 1993; Wells, in press).

When working with groups, couples, or families, it is crucial for therapists to be sensitive to individual differences in the degree of comfort with various religious and spiritual interventions. Not all group and family members or partners will necessarily be receptive to spiritual interventions. In groups, couples, and families, religion could be an emotionally laden issue. Deep differences in religious belief and practice may exist. In addition, some partners or family members may use religion as a weapon or source of control during conflicts (P. S. Richards & Potts, 1995b). Thus, when working with groups, couples, and families, therapists must carefully assess each client's religious and spiritual background and current status. It may be that spiritual interventions will be appropriate for some group or family members or partners, but not all. Certainly, there are some spiritual interventions that can be tailored to fit the unique needs of individual clients without compromising treatment efforts with other members of the group, family, or couple. We refer readers who would like more insight into the use of religious and spiritual interventions with children and adolescents, groups, couples, and families to Little and Robinson (1988), Propst (1988), L. Sperry and Giblin (1996), Wells (in press), and Worthington (1989a, 1990).

CONTRAINDICATIONS FOR SPIRITUAL INTERVENTIONS

There are at least four situations in which religious and spiritual interventions are clearly contraindicated: (a) clients who have made it clear that they do not want to participate in such interventions; (b) clients who are delusional or psychotic; (c) spiritual issues are clearly not relevant to clients' presenting problems; and (d) clients who are minors and their parents have not given the therapist permission to discuss religious issues or use spiritual interventions. There also may be other situations in which religious and spiritual interventions are not clearly contraindicated but in which it would be too risky or otherwise inadvisable to use religious and spiritual interventions.

It is widely recognized in the psychotherapy profession that the effectiveness of a therapeutic intervention does not depend solely on the nature of the technique but also on a host of other influences (Bergin & Garfield, 1994). In Table 10.7 we summarize some of the major client, process, and therapist variables that could influence whether a religious or spiritual intervention would be appropriate and effective. Generally speaking, such interventions are probably more risky or less likely to be effective when clients are young (children and adolescents), severely psychologically disturbed, anti-religious or nonreligious, or spiritually immature; view their spirituality or religion as irrelevant to their presenting problems; perceive God as distant and condemning; and have a deferring (passive) religious problem-solving style. Therapist-initiated, denominationally specific, religiously explicit, and in-session spiritual interventions are probably more risky than client-initiated, ecumenical, religiously implicit, and out-of-session interventions. It also is probably more risky to use spiritual interventions in civic- and government-supported settings than in private and religious settings. Spiritual interventions also are probably more risky and less likely to be effective if the therapeutic alliance is weak and there is low therapist–client religious value similarity. Of course, spiritual interventions are less likely to be used effectively and ethically by therapists who lack multicultural and religious sensitivity and awareness, have limited denominational expertise, and are spiritually immature. Empirical investigation of these hypotheses are needed; however, until then, therapists should at least keep these possibilities in mind as they seek to evaluate whether it would be appropriate to use such interventions with a given client.

GENERAL PROCESS SUGGESTIONS

Assuming that spiritual interventions are not contraindicated, how should therapists go about implementing them during the therapeutic hour? We do not believe that a cookbook description of how to implement religious and spiritual interventions is warranted or helpful. As we have discussed before, we advocate a treatment tailoring approach in which therapists do their best to select and apply interventions that fit the unique needs, beliefs, and circumstances of each client. Therapists must thoughtfully, sensitively, and carefully select and implement the interventions that they believe will be helpful to clients.

We offered a number of general suggestions earlier in this book to guide therapists in this process. These process suggestions are summarized in Table 10.8. The guiding principles behind these suggestions include (a) deep respect for clients' autonomy and freedom, (b) sensitivity to and empathy for clients' religious and spiritual beliefs, and (c) flexibility and responsiveness to clients' values and needs. It is essential for therapists to be committed to these principles and values if they are to integrate religious

TABLE 10.7
Client, Therapist, and Process Variables
That May Influence the Appropriateness and Effectiveness
of Religious and Spiritual Interventions

Variable	Hypothesized influence
Client	
Amount of psychological disturbance	More disturbed clients may be less likely to bene-fit from spiritual interventions, particularly de-lusional, psychotic, and obsessive–compul-sive clients.
Degree of religious orthodoxy	Clients who are more religiously orthodox may be more open to discussing religious issues and participating in spiritual interventions, but perhaps only with therapists of their own faith and in a denominationally specific manner.
Degree of religious and spiritual health and maturity (intrinsic, devout)	More religiously and spiritually healthy and ma-ture clients may be more open to discussing spiritual issues and effectively using spiritual interventions regardless of the therapist's reli-gious affiliation.
Type of problems or symptoms	The more clearly clients' religious and spiritual backgrounds and beliefs are connected or rel-evant to their presenting problems and symp-toms, the more likely it is that spiritual inter-ventions may be appropriate and effective.
Religious affiliation	Clients' religious affiliation may influence their willingness to discuss spiritual issues and the kinds of spiritual interventions they are willing to participate in (i.e., they may wish to discuss issues and participate in interventions that are compatible with their religion).
Age	Younger clients (children and adolescents) may be more willing to discuss religious and spirit-ual issues and participate in spiritual interven-tions, but the risk of ethical and legal viola-tions may be greater depending on the setting and situation.
God image	Clients who have had positive religious experi-ences and that perceive God as being forgiv-ing, active, and supportive are more likely to believe that God will help them and participate in spiritual interventions.
Religious problem-solving style	Clients who have a collaborative religious prob-lem-solving style are more likely to participate in and benefit from spiritual interventions. Clients who have an extreme deferring (pas-sive) or self-directing style are less likely to par-ticipate in and benefit from such interventions.
Therapist	
Multicultural and ecumenical sensitivity and awareness	Therapists who are sensitive and aware of their own religious values and biases and who have developed multicultural and ecumenical atti-tudes and skills should be more capable of using spiritual interventions appropriately and effectively.

(Table continues)

TABLE 10.7   *(cont.)*

Variable	Hypothesized influence
Denominational expertise	Therapists who have in-depth knowledge and experience with one or more specific religious denominations should be more capable of using spiritual interventions with clients from those denominations.
Religious and spiritual maturity	Therapists who are more religiously and spiritually healthy and mature themselves should be more capable of modeling and facilitating their clients' spiritual exploration, healing, and growth.
Therapist–client religious value similarity	Greater client–therapist religious belief and value similarity should increase clients' willingness to discuss specific issues and participate in spiritual interventions.

Process

Variable	Hypothesized influence
Client-initiated discussions	When clients initiate the discussion of religious and spiritual issues, it generally should be safer and more appropriate to explore spiritual issues and use spiritual interventions because this suggests that clients are willing and ready to participate in this manner.
Ecumenical versus denominational approach	Generally, implementing spiritual interventions in an ecumenical manner should reduce the risk of offending clients, particularly early in therapy with clients whose religious affiliation or beliefs differ from those of the therapist. When high client–therapist religious value similarity exists, implementing spiritual interventions in a denominational manner may enhance their effectiveness.
In- versus out-of-session interventions	Out-of-session spiritual interventions generally should reduce the risk of dual relationships and coercing or offending clients, although there is no reason to believe that out-of-session interventions are more effective than in-session ones.
Setting	Generally, it is probably safer for therapists to use spiritual interventions in religious and private settings than in public and state settings. Clients are more likely to expect and welcome spiritual interventions in religious and private settings and legal complications are less likely to arise.
Spiritually open and safe therapeutic alliance	When a spiritually open and safe therapeutic alliance has been established, spiritual interventions will be more appropriate, safer to use, and more effective in their outcomes.

TABLE 10.8
**General Process Suggestions for Using Religious
and Spiritual Interventions**

Suggestion
1. Therapists should inform clients during their informed consent procedures that they approach therapy with a spiritual perspective and sometimes (when appropriate) use religious and spiritual interventions.
2. Therapists should assess clients' religious and spiritual background and current status before using religious and spiritual interventions.
3. Therapists should establish a relationship of trust and rapport with clients before using religious and spiritual interventions.
4. Therapists should consider carefully whether religious and spiritual interventions are indicated (or contraindicated) before using them.
5. Therapists should clearly describe religious and spiritual interventions they wish to use and obtain clients' permission to do so before implementing them.
6. Therapists should use religious and spiritual interventions in a respectful manner, remembering that many of the interventions are regarded as sacred religious practices by religious believers.
7. Therapists should work within their clients' value framework and be careful not to push their own spiritual beliefs and values on clients, although they should challenge and help clients examine beliefs that are clearly irrational or self-defeating and linked to the presenting problem.
8. Therapists should not apply religious and spiritual interventions rigidly or uniformly with all clients but use them in a flexible, treatment tailoring manner.
9. Therapists who believe in God and in the reality of transcendent spiritual guidance should seek spiritual enlightenment and inspiration to guide them in what interventions to use and when to use them.

and spiritual interventions into their therapeutic approach ethically and effectively.

CONCLUSION

Although significant efforts have been made to develop and implement religious and spiritual interventions into psychotherapy practice, the profession is still in its infancy in this domain. There is so much that is not known or understood about religious and spiritual interventions, questions about prevalence, appropriateness, process, and outcome. For example, what types of religious and spiritual interventions do mainstream therapists believe are appropriate for use in therapy? What types of interventions are different types of clients most comfortable with? When and how can specific interventions be implemented ethically and effectively? Are spiritual interventions more effective than secular interventions and, if so, when? What types of spiritual interventions are most effective with what types of clients and problems? These and other questions beg to be answered. In chapter 12, we discuss a theistic, spiritual view of psychotherapy research and offer suggestions for research in this domain that we believe will help the profession begin to investigate them. First, however, we provide a number of case examples to further illustrate the use of spiritual perspectives and interventions.

11

CASE REPORTS OF SPIRITUAL ISSUES AND INTERVENTIONS IN PSYCHOTHERAPY

> Any appearance of God and religion in treatment [is] a normal manifestation of significant developmental and dynamic issues . . . the potential to be used as a defense . . . [and] their equally strong potential to aid in . . . psychic integration. . . .
>
> —Ana-Maria Rizzuto

In this chapter we present eight case reports of psychotherapy with religious clients from several different religious traditions. The therapists who wrote these reports, except for P. Scott Richards, did so without having read our book. Thus, the inclusion of their cases does not mean that the therapists necessarily agree with all our views. Nevertheless, these reports help illustrate the variety of ways that a spiritual strategy can be applied to assist clients. In each of these cases, the clients' spiritual beliefs and issues were intertwined with their presenting problems and, in our view, treatment could not have been completely successful if the issues had not been addressed sensitively. These cases also illustrate the successful integration of a variety of different spiritual interventions with secular therapeutic approaches.

OVERVIEW OF THE CASE REPORTS

The first three cases are examples of therapists working with clients whose religious affiliation differed from their own. Case 1 describes Edward

P. Shafranske's work with Sheila,[1] a 38-year-old Hispanic born-again Christian. This case illustrates how spiritual interventions such as prayer, scriptural readings, and referral to the client's spiritual leader can be effectively integrated in an ecumenical manner with a long-term psychodynamic therapeutic approach. Case 2 describes P. Scott Richards's work with Jack, a 22-year-old mixed-race Roman Catholic. This case illustrates how spiritual interventions such as encouraging involvement in the client's religious community and discussions about the client's spiritual beliefs and goals can be integrated in an ecumenical manner with crisis intervention and cognitive–behavioral techniques. Case 3 describes Clifford H. Swensen's work with Janet and Bill, a young (late 20s to early 30s) White couple who were members of an evangelical Christian church. This case illustrates how a client's religious beliefs contributed to the woman's decision to work to improve an unfulfilling marriage. It also illustrates how a spiritual intervention (asking a couple to pray for each other each day) can enhance long-term marital satisfaction and stability.

Cases 4–8 are examples of therapists working with clients from their own religious tradition. Case 4 describes Lisa Miller's work with Rebecca, Jerry, Sol, and Bill, four Jewish patients on a psychiatric inpatient unit in New York City. This case illustrates how prayer and religious ritual can supplement psychopharmacological treatment and short-term inpatient psychotherapy. Case 5 describes Carolyn A. Rayburn's work with Odessa, a 50-year-old Black Seventh-Day Adventist. This case illustrates the denominationally specific integration of spiritual interventions such as prayer, forgiveness, and theological discussions and reinterpretations with rational–emotive, transactional analysis, and feminist therapy approaches.

Case 6 describes Alan C. Tjeltveit's work with Kristen, a 32-year-old White Lutheran. This case illustrates how biblical Scriptures and theological discussions can be integrated in a denominational manner to enhance the potency of a cognitive therapy approach. It also is a good example of how a client can benefit when mental health professionals work cooperatively with the client's religious leader (pastor). Case 7 describes Wendy L. Ulrich's work with Helen, a middle-aged (early 40s) White Mormon. This case illustrates how spiritual interventions such as scriptural and doctrinal discussions and reinterpretations, spiritual metaphors, affirming the client's spiritual worth and sensitivity, and forgiveness can be integrated effectively in a denominationally specific manner with cognitive–behavioral, systemic, and psychodynamic interventions. Case 8 describes Robert J. Lovinger's work with Derek, April, and Dov, a Jewish family. This case illustrates how religious issues can be intertwined with family and marital problems. It also

---

[1] All clients' names are ficticious and identifying characteristics have been changed to protect their anonymity.

illustrates how a therapist's countertransference issues can make it more difficult to respond effectively to a client's religiosity.

Case 1: Sheila

Description of the Therapist. Edward P. Shafranske is a professor of psychology at the Graduate School of Education and Psychology at Pepperdine University and is a member of the faculty of the Southern California Psychoanalytic Institute. Shafranske, who is a Roman Catholic, has a long-standing interest in religion as a cultural, psychological, and spiritual resource. At the time of this patient's treatment, he held an academic position and provided psychological services in a community-based outpatient clinic. Although Shafranske's primary orientation is psychoanalytic, his clinical practice has been influenced by and includes theoretical and technical contributions from cognitive–behavioral therapy and existential psychotherapy. Shafranske is a fellow of the American Psychological Association (APA) and is the editor of *Religion and the Clinical Practice of Psychology* (Shafranske, 1996).

Setting. The patient was seen in a community-based clinic in a suburb of a major city in the southwestern United States. This clinic had two clinical psychologists, a neuropsychologist, a licensed clinical social worker, psychologist interns, and a consulting psychiatrist.

Client Demographic Characteristics. Sheila was a 38-year-old married Hispanic woman. She was the mother of two children, an 18-year-old son from a previous marriage and a 10-year-old daughter. She was a high school graduate and had completed the equivalent of 1 year of college. At the beginning of treatment, Sheila was employed as an administrative assistant in a manufacturing firm; previously she had held a number of jobs, often of short duration, ranging from clerical to service-related employment. Twice married, Sheila reported that her marriage was generally satisfactory with difficulties associated primarily in their sexual life.

Religion played a central role in Sheila's life. She described herself as a born-again Christian and actively participated in a freestanding, evangelical church. Although raised in a devout Roman Catholic family, Sheila reported that religion had become relevant only when she "accepted Jesus Christ as her personal savior" in her early 20s after the divorce from her first husband. In this case, the demographic feature of religious affiliation served not only to identify a salient aspect of a client's background that is brought into treatment but also to identify a potential resource to the therapeutic work.

Client History. Sheila was the third-born child and first daughter of 10 children in an intact family. Her father was a moderately successful entrepreneur who owned a number of small businesses. Her mother was a homemaker who was involved in the community and church activities.

She described her childhood as mostly uneventful, with the exception of mounting conflicts during late childhood with her mother, periods of depression and anxiety, and pronounced fear reactions associated with her mother's brother, who had lived with the family when she was 8–9 years of age. She reported having close girlfriends and recalled that she was hardworking and successful in elementary school.

The onset of adolescence brought turbulence and a pronounced period of acting out, truancy, drug abuse, and sexual promiscuity that contributed to poor academic performance, an early marriage, and an unplanned pregnancy. She reported that she had sought counseling during this period but that the result was unsatisfactory; she could not "get at what was eating at [her]." Other features of the family system suggested an environment of emotional constriction and unavailability. This was particularly the case concerning her father, whom she described as distant and mostly uninvolved in the family. Sheila was particularly resentful of serving as the "second mom" to her younger siblings and felt chronically misunderstood by her mother. Her self-reports indicated a notable lack of insight into her experiences during adolescence. Although summing up her behavior as rebellious, she noted that she never really understood why she became involved in drugs and in seemingly masochistic sexual relationships with older men. Her depiction of this period reflected a curious dissociation of her values and self-identity from her behavior.

This troubled period reached its apex in her early 20s, when she discovered that her husband, with whom she had a mostly unsatisfying emotional and sexual relationship, was involved in an extramarital affair. This event was the final straw: Sheila filed for divorce. A single mother with limited job skills, Sheila struggled to make a life on her own. It was within the context of this challenge that Sheila experienced a religious conversion that was to significantly shape her future life, including her course of psychological treatment. She married in her late 20s, had a daughter by her present husband, became active in her church, and later sought treatment to address bouts of depression and anxiety related to marital and career conflicts.

Her religious development reflected the family's particular approach to Catholicism: Involvement was duty-bound and primarily stressed rules and sacramental obligations. Her depiction suggested an essentially extrinsic religious orientation. The change in her faith in her 20s marked a significant developmental transition and, as I understood it, reflected an attempt to establish a more cohesive sense of self, to resolve intrapsychic and interpersonal conflicts, to better meet the challenges of adulthood, and to repair areas of psychic trauma. She first became involved in a storefront evangelical church that focused its mission on youth and young adults, many of whom were dealing with alcohol and substance abuse. Within this congregation, Sheila began studying the Bible and attending prayer services. She reported that during a prayer service, she felt "the presence of the Holy Spirit" and experienced a dramatic sense of peace and love. She considered this experience to be her "conversion to Christ" and marked the beginning of a new life. Indeed, after this experience, Sheila reported a new religious fervor, commitment to her young son, and a developing confidence in her abilities. She sought out and established personal relationships, became gainfully employed, and, in short, began to address the developmental challenges and responsibilities of adulthood. Her affiliation and active involvement in religion appeared to serve as a significant resource from that day forward and reflected the quality of an intrinsic religious orientation.

Presenting Problem. The presenting problem concerned sexual conflicts in the marriage and associated features of depression and anxiety related to physical intimacy. Sheila stated that she was motivated to be sexually intimate with her husband; however, during sexual engagement she became flooded with anxiety and recoiled from further contact. In other instances, she reported dissociative experiences during which she had sexual relations. These experiences were uniformly unsatisfying and triggered episodes of free-floating anxiety and depressed mood with disturbances of sleep and concentration. These more acute symptoms appeared within the context of Sheila's long-standing lack of secure identity, self-doubt, and transient feelings of anxiety and depression. In addition to these complaints, Sheila felt stymied in her attempts to attain a number of goals; she wanted to complete her education and to enter a career path with greater personal accomplishment and satisfaction.

Assessment and Diagnosis. An assessment was conducted through a series of clinical interviews and the administration of the Minnesota Multiphasic Personality Inventory (MMPI). This procedure indicated that Sheila was a depressed, anxious, and insecure person whose psychological resources were taxed. There was no evidence of a psychotic disorder or a major affective disorder and no sufficient evidence of a personality disorder. The episodes of anxiety appeared to be central to sexual situations and in circumstances in which she perceived herself to be vulnerable to sexual attack. The depression was assessed to be related both to the immediate conflicts related to sexuality and to more long-standing difficulties characterized as dysthymia. In the nomenclature of the fourth edition of the *Diagnostic and Statistical Manual of Mental Disorders* (*DSM–IV*), the diagnosis would include the following Axis I disorders: dysthymia, depersonalization disorder, sexual aversion disorder, and female sexual arousal disorder.

The assessment took into consideration the variables of religious belief, affiliation, and practice in the genesis and maintenance of the psychological disturbance. For Sheila, sexuality was a taboo subject and was never discussed in her family, and, from her perspective, it was characterized and reinforced within Catholicism as sinful. Sexual relations had always been rife with conflict, guilt, and shame. Sexual fantasy was in and of itself as sinful as the deed and would have been a potential point of resistance and noncompliance in the treatment should visualization be encouraged as part of a program of desensitization. Furthermore, her strongly held religious beliefs placed submission to her husband's authority and needs as a value and operationally functioned as a behavioral prescription that extended into bedroom. This understanding, derived from a particular interpretation of Scripture, unwittingly set up a situation of vulnerability and reinforced experiences of loss of control and autonomy that were central to her sexual and interpersonal difficulties.

Religion also played a role in her entry into psychological treatment. In addition to the fact that previous attempts at psychological treatment had been unsuccessful, the minister and culture of her church were not supportive of secular psychological practice. In fact, Sheila demonstrated unusual autonomy in seeking treatment that, from her perspective, involved putting trust not only in God but also in a secular, humanistic science. In the early phase of consultation and throughout the treatment, careful attention was placed on a respectful appreciation and analysis of her religious and spiritual beliefs. Critical to the treatment was establishing a framework in which contributions from psychology could be accepted with those of her religious orientation without compromise and without creating what would have been an unfortunate acrimony.

Treatment Process and Outcome. The treatment consisted of individual psychotherapy with occasional conjoint consultations over the course of 3½ years. The treatment evolved from the early phase of supportive treatment, in which a therapeutic relationship and secure base was established to clarify her conflicts, to an explorative, psychodynamic form of treatment emphasizing the uncovering of psychic conflict, the interpretation of defenses, and modification of compromise formations. Throughout the course of treatment, an emphasis was placed on both the dynamic interaction between the patient and clinician and the reinforcing patterns of behavior within her relationships.

The treatment was established using free association as the central procedure. Her current anxieties were examined within genetic and transferential contexts. Clarification of points of anxiety within free association allowed Sheila to begin to observe the ubiquity of her anxiety, the specific nature of her fears, and the operations she used to avoid situations of intrapsychic and interpersonal threat. Early in the treatment process, Sheila was able to make direct connections between her behavior in a session and that with her husband. For example, she recognized that she would often initiate exploration of a particular line of thinking only to abruptly shift focus and become confused and anxious. She noted that this was a recurrent pattern with her husband; she would initiate a sexual interaction and anxiously withdraw, feeling confused and agitated. Her husband's frustration in such moments led to strained interpersonal relations and reinforced her negative attributions concerning sexuality and her marriage. The enactment of this dynamic within the treatment relationship allowed for examination of the source of her anxiety and a reconstruction through the use of her associations, memories, and dreams. Furthermore, she was able to examine her fears in vivo in respect to issues of trust with her therapist.

She located the epigenesis of this dynamic in childhood masturbatory experiences that included heightened excitement aborted by intense anxiety, guilt, and shame. Through a series of traumatic dreams, memories, and associations, clinical data accumulated concerning the possibility of sexual abuse during the period in which her uncle lived with the family. The therapist's clinical stance was to provide a "holding environment" in which fear-evoking material, including memories and fantasies, could be processed. Through treatment, a gradual desensitization occurred and an increased understanding of the genetic roots of her difficulties took place. These experiences led to an increased sense of mastery and control that allowed for further emotional expression and opened the door to new experience. The patient was better able to contain and express her affective experience in appropriate ways. The working through in this phase produced behavioral changes, including increased comfort in social situations, increased willingness to engage in and derive pleasure from sexual relations, direct confrontation of interpersonal difficulties, active career decision making, and development of friendships.

These changes produced numerous challenges and opportunities for the marriage. Through the support of timely conjoint consultations, the patient and her husband worked to make accommodations in their relationship on the basis of Sheila's developing confidence and willingness to engage in new ways of relating to her husband. These few consultations were sufficient to encourage communication and establish a mode of relating in which Sheila and her husband were able to discuss their experiences and solve problems collaboratively. At the time of termination, Sheila had graduated from college, embarked on a new career, and reported increased marital and sexual satisfaction. This case was not without significant challenges to maintaining the treatment relationship and encouraging the therapeutic process. As the work intensified during the middle phase, Sheila experienced periods of increased dysphoria, anxiety, and distrust. Sheila's religious faith played a particular role in sustaining her commitment to treatment and ultimately to facing and resolving her difficulties. She had a strong belief that her faith would not let her down. I now describe two particular areas in which religion played an important role.

Sheila's "faith in Jesus and his saving power" provided emotional as well as spiritual support throughout the treatment. In the middle phase of treatment, when she was beset with disturbing dreams and troubling memories and associations, she found prayer and the community support of her church to be essential. She began several sessions in prayer. In these moments I would quietly participate in her prayer and sometimes offer a supportive, interpretive remark about the anxiety that she was facing willingly with the support of God. My empathic support of her religious beliefs and practices, although differing to a great extent with my own faith orientation, brought into the treatment an important and vital resource. Sheila sought additional support by joining a prayer group and enrolling in a Bible study course. Within these settings she found the support and encouragement of others and was sustained through the support of her faith community. Although her husband did not share her faith, he supported her involvement.

A second area concerned Sheila's beliefs about the expression of anger and her role in a marital relationship. Sheila thought that anger, expressed in any form, was sinful. She also believed that to feel hate would mean to be estranged from God. Furthermore, she believed, and was affiliated within a congregation that also believed, in the husband's authority to make all marital decisions. The holding of these beliefs from a clinical perspective led to an inability to resolve certain aspects of her psychological and relational difficulties. Although maintaining respect for her beliefs, I engaged Sheila in both a clarifying and, to an extent, a cognitive restructuring of the implications of these beliefs. I encouraged Sheila to speak with her pastor and to study various interpretations of the Scripture. She was able to better understand biblical ideas in a way that did not compromise her integrity or reinforce experiences of powerlessness. She became more accepting of the affective responses that she was experiencing and gained ego strength through her acceptance of these states of mind. Aggressive and excitatory states no longer triggered acute anxiety or affective dysregulation. My aim in these interventions was not to convert Sheila to my faith but to encourage a process of exploration that carefully examined the relationship between her beliefs and the behavioral and emotional outcomes that followed.

Therapist Commentary. In my view, the approach taken to this patient's use of prayer and religious beliefs and practices was located at the boundary of explicit and implicit integration of religious issues in psychotherapy. A therapist confident in the use of an explicit approach to integration might have created more opportunities for prayer or might have initiated a "healing of memories" consistent with her religious tradition. Furthermore, such a therapist might have directly challenged or supported this patient's religious beliefs using personal knowledge of Scripture and theology. A more implicit approach might have required simply listening to the influences of religious faith and belief on the clinical situation. In this case, a careful walking the line between both approaches was needed. Because of the important and direct influence of religious belief on her views of sexuality and aggression and in the potential for reinforcing a pattern of loss of control, it was necessary to examine her beliefs in this clinical context. In addition, religion appeared to be the one reliable source of support in her adulthood; as such, it was viewed as a resource rather than an impediment to the treatment process.

In this case, religious beliefs contributed to the epigenesis and maintenance of psychological conflict and yet also offered a long-standing and singular source of support that ultimately sustained the course of treatment. Several clinical decision points were addressed in this course of treatment that point to areas for further ethical and practice consideration. These include how a clinician responds to prayer, religious beliefs, proscriptions and prescriptions of behavior and role within a marriage, authority and autonomy of client beliefs and attributions, and the handling of client and therapist divergence and convergence of faith perspectives. Decisions concerning each issue reflect and illustrate the value-laden nature of psychological treatment and the therapeutic encounter.

Case 2: Jack

Description of the Therapist. P. Scott Richards is an associate professor of counseling psychology at Brigham Young University and is a licensed psychologist. Richards is a devout member of The Church of Jesus Christ of Latter-day Saints. At the time he saw Jack, Richards was an assistant professor of psychology at a university in the Pacific Northwest. Richards's therapeutic orientation is eclectic. He primarily uses client-centered, cognitive–behavioral, psychodynamic, and spiritual perspectives and approaches. He is past editor of the *Journal for the Association of Mormon Counselors and Psychotherapists* and has published several articles on religious and spiritual issues in mental health and psychotherapy.

Setting. Richards saw Jack in his private practice office in a moderately sized community in the northwestern United States. This office included one other therapist, a licensed psychologist.

Client Demographics and Characteristics. Jack was a 26-year-old man of mixed race (half Black and half White). He was a member of the Roman Catholic church, although at the time he started therapy he attended church infrequently and rarely socialized with peers in his religious community. Jack was a junior in accounting with a grade point average of about 3.5. He had steadily dated Melisa, another student, for the past $2\frac{1}{2}$ years.

Client History. Jack was the youngest son in a family of four boys. His mother died when he was 18. Jack said that his childhood was "okay." His parents were not abusive, but even though he knew intellectually that they loved him, he did not *feel* loved. Although Jack's parents had been moderately religious and Jack indicated that he believed in God, religion had never been extremely important to him, although he attended church occasionally and was friends with peers in his church. Jack was an excellent football player during high school, but he did not do well academically.

His first year in college was difficult for him. He did poorly academically and felt very socially isolated and lonely. Early in his second year, he met Melisa and became emotionally involved with her. The relationship with Melisa rescued Jack from his social isolation and loneliness and also helped him turn things around academically. Melisa was a good student and helped Jack develop effective study habits and skills. During his second year of college, Jack's grades improved dramatically. Jack spent almost all of his time with Melisa and, as a result, neglected other friendships, including the peers in his religious community and his family.

Presenting Problems and Concerns. Jack presented for treatment during the second week in January. He told me that he "almost canceled his appointment" because he was "doing much better now," but he decided to go ahead with the appointment so that he could ask me a few questions about his ex-girlfriend. Jack told me that late in November, Melisa, his girlfriend of 2½ years, had told him, without warning, that she was terminating their relationship. She told him that she "needed some space to find herself" and that perhaps in time they could get back together again. For now, though, Melisa did not want to see Jack anymore. Jack then asked me a couple of questions about why I thought Melisa might do something like this. I briefly speculated with Jack and then brought the focus back to him.

"When Melisa told you she was ending the relationship, how did this affect you, Jack?" I asked. Jack immediately began to tear up and admitted that it had been difficult for him. He then said in a desperate-sounding voice, "I've just got to get on with my life though!" I then asked Jack to tell me more about how the breakup had affected him. As he did so, it quickly became clear that the breakup had triggered a major depressive episode for Jack. Jack acknowledged that he was experiencing frequent insomnia, had lost 25 lb, felt sad and depressed most of the time, did not experience pleasure anymore, felt hopeless, and was having recurrent thoughts of suicide.

When I asked him to tell me more about the suicidal thoughts, he acknowledged that he had a plan and a lethal method readily available to him (i.e., he told me he had considered walking to a high bridge in the community and jumping off). After Jack acknowledged this, he teared up again and with much intensity said, "It would be so stupid to kill myself." I responded to Jack by saying, "You don't want or plan to commit suicide, do you? You're just in so much pain, you're afraid you might." Jack quickly agreed with me, and I then proceeded to get a contract from him that he would not commit suicide and that he would call me or a crisis line if he became suicidal again. Jack assured me that he would and then tried to reassure me that he was doing better now and that he did not think he would need any more sessions with me.

I told Jack that the breakup of his relationship with Melisa was a major loss, somewhat akin to the death of a loved one. I told him that it was not surprising that this had been so difficult for him and that he might yet still have some difficult days ahead. I told him firmly that I would like to see him again the following week and that he should call me before then if he felt the need. Jack seemed relieved and quickly agreed to reschedule for another appointment.

Assessment and Diagnosis. My assessment, based on Jack's history, symptoms, and MMPI profile, led me to conclude that Jack was experiencing a major depressive episode that was triggered by the breakup with his girlfriend. I concluded that he was at moderate risk for suicide, as evidenced by his highly lethal plan but low intent to act on it. Jack's history and MMPI also revealed some dependent personality characteristics and low self-esteem. He was of above-average intelligence and had adequate social skills. His support system had become severely restricted because of his overdependent, almost exclusive relationship with Melisa. Immediately after the breakup, Jack said he had reached out to his father and brothers, but he said they were tired of hearing him talk about it and were telling him "just get on with your life." He felt he could no longer go to them for support. I concluded that Jack's social isolation increased his risk of suicide.

Treatment Process and Outcomes. The day after our first session, Jack called just before the end of the day. He said he was having a difficult time and began to cry. I asked him if he was feeling suicidal and he admitted he was. I asked him where he was, and he told me he was alone at his apartment; neither of his two roommates were there. I told Jack that I would like him to immediately go to the emergency room of the hospital so that he could get some support during the night and get started on some antidepressant medication. I asked Jack if he would be willing to do this. He immediately began crying again, but in a relieved voice said he would. I asked him if he would like me to go with him, but he said he would go on his own. I asked him to call me when he reached the hospital and told him I would wait in my office. He called 30 min later to inform me that he had been unable to get permission from his insurance company to admit himself and so had changed his mind. Jack told me he no longer felt at risk for suicide and promised me he would see his physician first thing in the morning to get some antidepressants. I accepted his decision and scheduled Jack for an appointment with me the following afternoon.

During the first few weeks of my work with Jack, I used several interventions, including two spiritual ones. In consultation with Jack's physician, we started him on some antidepressants. I also discussed the need for Jack to begin reestablishing some friendships with his peers and family. It was here that we discussed Jack's feelings about his religious community, and he expressed his plan to renew his friendships there. Early in therapy, we also discussed reasons why Jack wanted to keep living. This led to a discussion of his belief in God, that God did not want him to commit suicide, that God would help him get through this difficult time, and that God wished him to do worthwhile things with his life. Jack reaffirmed his desire to succeed in his career and to be married and have a family. This reaffirmation of

Jack's life's goals and purpose bolstered his desire to not act on his suicidal impulses.

We also explored why the breakup with Melisa had left Jack feeling so hopeless and depressed. Jack was able to identify a deeply held belief he had formed that without Melisa, his life would "go down the tubes again." Jack had felt lonely and unsuccessful before he met her, and he was terrified that without her he would again become (and remain) lonely and unsuccessful. He rightly attributed his increase in academic success to her influence, but wrongly assumed that she was totally responsible for it. I challenged this belief and pointed out that a large measure of his success was the result of his own ability and intelligence. I emphasized that Melisa had not taken this with her when she left. She also had not taken away the study skills and habits that he had learned from her. When Jack realized that he had not "lost everything" with Melisa's departure and that he still had his abilities, skills, life ambitions, and friends he could turn to for support and companionship, he quickly began to improve. Within about 3 weeks, the severity of Jack's depression lessened noticeably and his mood stabilized. His suicidal ideation ceased and he no longer felt hopeless.

During the next 5 months, I met with Jack regularly; twice a week for the first month, weekly for the next 2 months, and then tapering off to once or twice a month. During this time we worked to help Jack understand the reasons why the breakup with Melisa had affected him so severely (e.g., his overdependence on her to meet his emotional needs, his social isolation, his lack of confidence in his own abilities and skills, and his grief at losing someone he cared deeply about). During this time, Jack reestablished friendships with peers in his religious community, strengthened his relationships with his brothers and father, grew in self-esteem and emotional self-reliance, and continued to succeed academically. Three months into treatment, Jack began to date again. He also was faced with the decision of whether to reestablish his dating relationship with Melisa because she contacted him and expressed an interest in doing so. Jack told her he was not interested in dating her at that time, and, when I terminated treatment with him, he had still not done so.

Therapist Commentary. Although Jack and I were not of the same religious faith, my awareness of his religious background and orientation enabled me to draw on the spiritual resources in his life to help him through his crisis. The fact that Jack had a religious community and peers with whom he could quickly reestablish connections greatly benefited him. Without such social support, his social isolation would have been more difficult to overcome and his suicide risk, in all likelihood, would have been greater. Jack's beliefs about God and his life goals and purpose were also spiritual resources that helped inoculate him against acting on his suicidal impulses. Once Jack got through the worst of his depression and suicidal ideation, religious and spiritual issues were rarely discussed. However, even though spiritual issues and interventions were not at the foreground during most of my work with Jack, I think they contributed significantly to Jack's emotional recovery and growth, especially during the early weeks of therapy.

Case 3: Janet and Bill

Description of Therapist. Clifford H. Swensen has a doctorate in clinical psychology. Swensen is a professor of psychology at Purdue University and a diplomate in clinical psychology of the American Board of Professional Psychology. He is a member of the Church of Christ and has served as an elder and Sunday school teacher in his local congregation. Swensen has been providing therapy part time to adult clients for approximately 40 years.

Setting. Janet was seen privately in an outpatient setting. The services provided within this setting were adult psychological services, including individual, group, and family and marital therapy. The kinds of problems treated within this setting included neuroses, situational reactions, personality disorders, and marital and family problems.

Client Demographic Characteristics. The client, Janet, was a 28-year-old White woman, married with no children. She was a college graduate with a degree in interior decorating. She was working as a salesperson in a store that provided both supplies and advice for people redecorating their homes. Her husband, Bill, was a 31-year-old pharmacist who owned and operated his own neighborhood drug store. Both she and her husband were members of an evangelical, nondenominational Christian church and regularly attended services. Their religious views would probably be described as moderate (i.e., not strictly orthodox, but not strongly liberal either).

Client History. Janet was the younger of two children. Her father was an engineer and her mother a homemaker. She grew up in the suburb of a large midwestern city. She was relatively close to both of her parents. Their approval was important to her. She was an attractive and popular girl in high school, had many dates, was active in extracurricular affairs, and earned good grades. Her parents were active church members who also expected their children to attend church regularly.

After graduating from high school, Janet attended the state university, which was located within a 90-min drive from her home. She quickly developed an active social life and dated many different young men. She became particularly interested in two of them, in sequence, and took them home, in sequence, to meet her parents. Her parents did not appear to approve of either of the young men.

She then met the man who was to become her husband. He was an active member of the college students' group at the church she attended. He was 3 years older than she and was in his last year of pharmacy school. He was a serious, hardworking student who got excellent grades. She was attracted to him because he was responsible and successful academically. She also felt he was the sort of man of whom her parents would approve.

They were married when her husband completed school, at the end of her sophomore year in college. She continued going to school while her husband worked in a retail store. It had always been her husband's ambition to own his own store, so he saved as much money as he could from his work. When Janet completed her undergraduate work, she got a job working for a construction business that built and remodeled homes. Her income, combined with that of her husband, made it possible for them to accumulate enough money for her husband to buy his own store. However, the responsibility for the store began to consume her husband. The income from the store was not great enough to allow him to hire much additional help. Thus, he had to be in the store all the time it was open. These long hours meant that Janet and her husband had little time together. Furthermore, her husband's worries about the financial success of the store made him irritable and preoccupied. Her relationship with her husband was deteriorating.

Janet had formed a warm relationship with the older man who owned the company for which she worked. She told him of her distress over her husband's apparent lack of concern for her and her general dissatisfaction with the way her life was developing. Her employer had his own marital dissatisfactions, so their relationship became more intimate and resulted in them having an affair.

Both she and her employer felt guilty about the affair, so they ended up confessing to their spouses and terminating their relationship. Her husband was extremely distressed about the affair but felt that his neglect of her had contributed to her behavior. He became more attentive and considerate and restrained his irritability. Janet quit working for her employer and got another job with a firm that sold interior decorating supplies and services.

Her relationship with her husband improved for a period of time, but he again became absorbed in his business, which was declining slowly. The competition of chain stores, which could sell products more cheaply, was slowly killing the business, and he was preoccupied with trying to develop plans to survive economically.

Janet then began to become emotionally involved with a man with whom she worked. He was in the process of getting a divorce. He was proposing that she have an affair with him, and she was tempted. However, she feared that if she had an affair with this man and her husband discovered it, it would mean the end of her marriage. That thought terrified her.

Presenting Concerns and Diagnosis. It was at this point that Janet sought psychological help. She was extremely anxious because she feared that she would not be able to resist the temptation of an affair with her coworker and that this would destroy her marriage. Her goals, when she sought psychological help, were to avoid doing anything that would destroy her marriage and to do what she could to improve her relationship with her husband.

The psychologist's conceptualization of the case was that she needed close, supportive relationships with other people. She was vulnerable to the demands of those who provided such support. She was initially attracted to her husband partially because she felt that her parents would approve of him, but also because she felt that he would provide a safe, supportive life structure for her. When she no longer felt her husband's support, she became vulnerable to the attraction of other men.

Treatment Process and Outcomes. The goals of therapy were to help Janet become more self-sufficient, to have less need for the emotional support of a man, and to help her develop a more satisfying relationship with her husband. To accomplish these goals, my plans were to first provide her with support to alleviate her immediate anxiety and then to help her develop a greater confidence in her ability to manage her own life. When she had stabilized, I felt that it would be necessary to bring her husband in to work on improving their relationship with each other. The approach used was essentially a cognitive one. Religious and spiritual issues emerged as an integral part of the cognitive content of the therapy.

The initial issue within therapy was Janet's relationship with the man with whom she was tempted to have an affair. There were two sides to this issue. She felt neglected and unappreciated by her husband. Their sexual relationship was almost nonexistent. She felt appreciated, understood, and supported by the other man. Furthermore, he was sexually attractive to her. He offered emotional and sexual satisfaction. On the other hand, having an affair with him might result in the destruction of her marriage. However, her marriage was almost dead anyway, so that in itself might not be such a great loss. However, she would feel guilty for having violated her religious beliefs, and, if her marriage were destroyed it would greatly upset her parents, who would certainly disapprove of the cause of the divorce.

She was not able to resist the temptation to have the affair. However, as her relationship with the other man developed, it became apparent that he had a much different view of life from her own. He did not share her religious beliefs or values. He could not understand the guilt she felt over their relationship. With the decline in the support she felt from the relationship, she could see no purpose in continuing the affair, so she terminated it. In therapy she was able to work through her thinking about herself and her relationships and to gain some insight about why she had originally been tempted to have a relationship with another man. She also gained support from therapy, so she had no need to seek support elsewhere.

Therapy then began to focus on Janet's relationship to her husband. She began to see that she was attracted to her husband because he was a serious, capable person whom she felt would be able to provide her with a secure life. She also felt that he was a man of whom her parents would approve, and her parent's approval was important to her.

She felt that she herself was a sociable and personally attractive person, but she did not have confidence in her ability to manage her own affairs. She had spent her life being cared for by either her parents or her husband. Thus, she had never had an independent life of her own. Part of her motivation for her affair was to declare some independence from her husband behaviorally and to assert her ability to have a life of her own, apart from her parents or her husband. However, she perceived that her behavior had not been constructive. She wanted to have a mature, satisfying relationship with her husband and to develop a constructive, satisfying life for herself. She had behaved in ways that had violated her own religious and moral values and that had threatened to destroy what she wanted to achieve in life. One consequence had been severe guilt and anxiety for herself and the threat of destroying her marriage.

Her husband was a significant part of her life. She felt that he was relatively cold emotionally. He did not provide the emotional support she needed, nor did he give her the affection she wanted. Beyond that, he said and did things that indicated that he considered her immature and impulsive. He did not trust her to make wise decisions. He did not feel that she was financially responsible. Consequently, he treated her, she felt, as an irresponsible adolescent.

At this point in therapy, Janet's anxiety had dissipated and she felt more in control of her life. Her affair had ended, and she had begun a new and promising job with an interior design and decorating firm. We agreed that her husband should be brought into the therapy.

The couple was seen together. Bill expressed his feelings that Janet was immature, impulsive, and irresponsible, particularly in financial matters. Janet expressed her unhappiness with Bill's nit-picking over details, his total concern about his business, and his lack of insight into and apparent concern for her emotional needs. In the course of therapy, it became apparent that part of Bill's problem was his concern over his business. His emotional preoccupation and distress, as well as the inordinate demands on his time, were solved by him selling the store and obtaining a job in a hospital. He worked on developing more awareness of Janet's emotional needs. Janet, in turn, became more sensitive to his financial concerns and became more concerned with avoiding spending in ways and amounts that distressed her husband. They seemed to be getting along well, so therapy was terminated.

A couple of years later they returned to therapy with the same marital problems. The essence of the problem seemed to be that they were not sensitive to and responsive to the needs and feelings of the other. Again, the problems were worked out, and therapy was terminated.

A year later they returned again, with the same problems. At this point, I felt that their religious beliefs might provide a greater power to help resolve their problems. I knew that they attended church regularly and that they believed in prayer. I asked each of them to pray for the other each day. I asked them to pray each day that they would do or say that which would promote the growth and well-being of the other. They began following this prayer regime. They reported that their relationship improved steadily. Therapy was terminated. Follow-up several years later indicated that they reported that their relationship was excellent and that when problems emerged, they found that prayer helped them produce the solution.

Therapist Commentary. The religious beliefs of this patient and her husband were not a part of my original conceptualization of the case, nor were they a factor in the initial therapy planning. However, it became apparent in the course of therapy that both implicitly and explicitly, religion was a factor in the couple's conceptualization of themselves, their behavior, and their relationship.

Religion was not initially a focus in my attempt to help them solve their problems. A focus on their behavior with each other and their conceptualizations of each other and their relationship helped solve the immediate problems that came up in their relationship. However, this did not seem to supply a permanent solution to the conflicts in their relationship. The old problems were alleviated temporarily, but they kept reemerging.

Thus, it eventually occurred to me that the couple's religious beliefs could be used to help develop a more permanent solution to their problems. I knew they believed in prayer, so I asked them if they prayed for each other. They admitted that they did not. I then suggested that they pray for each other each day, praying that their spouse would be able to cope successfully with the problems met that day and that they would be able to provide the support and help their spouse needed. Prayer seemed to provide the added power needed to help them maintain a constructive relationship.

The lesson this experience taught me was that religion may form the basis of a person's most fundamental beliefs about self, other people, the world, and the nature of human existence. To fail to integrate a person's most fundamental beliefs into the therapy process is to fail to use the most powerful tools available for therapy.

Case 4: Rebecca, Jerry, Sol, and Bill

Description of the Therapist. Lisa Miller is a clinical psychologist and research fellow in the College of Physicians & Surgeons of Columbia University in New York City. She received her bachelor's degree in psychology from Yale University and her doctorate in clinical psychology at the University of Pennsylvania, where her dissertation was chaired by Martin E. P. Seligman. Miller is a devout but non-Orthodox Jew. Her therapeutic orientation is in a state of evolution toward the integration of religious experience with humanistic and existential understandings.[2]

---

[2] Portions of this case were presented at the 104th Annual Convention of the American Psychological Association held in Toronto, Ontario, Canada, in August 1996.

Setting. My first job as a clinical psychologist was on a psychiatric inpatient unit serving Manhattan from the middle-class area of 59th Street to Harlem at 135th Street. Patients came to the unit in crisis to receive psychopharmacological treatment and short-term psychotherapy. Our patients represented the diversity of the catchment area: African American, Latin American, and a sizable representation of White Jewish patients.

The Patients. Rebecca Rabinowitz, obese and 38 years old, had been admitted to the inpatient unit for an attempted suicide by overdose. She had suffered for more than 15 years from severe depressive episodes, had never married or worked a steady job, and lived with her mother. She repeatedly elicited and absorbed the hostility of other patients, which culminated in her being assaulted by a fellow patient on the unit. Ms. Rabinowitz spoke in an apologetic tone and expressed ongoing feelings of guilt and inadequacy. At times her guilt took on the tone of a moral or existential guilt, guilt for asserting her being, guilt for existing. Although she spoke little of her religious background, she seemed to be a Reform Jew. Her *DSM–IV* Axis I diagnosis was recurrent major depressive disorder.

Jerry Petrofsky, my patient in individual psychotherapy, was a large 61-year-old man. He, too, had been admitted to the unit for attempted suicide. However, unlike Ms. Rabinowitz, he had not suffered life-long depression. Mr. Petrofsky suffered an acute depression in reaction to his recent diagnosis of leukemia. Before being diagnosed with cancer, he had enjoyed a robust life. A city engineer who had married a recent emigre, Jerry was often sighted bicycling around the West Side. On the unit, however, he rarely rose from bed, appeared sullen, and spoke with derision to much of the staff. A crisis of faith, or at least a crisis of meaning, plagued Mr. Petrofsky to the point where he saw the world as cruel and abandoning. On the unit so little was spoken about religion that not until Jerry appeared at the Yom Kippur service did I know he was a Jew. His *DSM–IV* Axis I diagnosis was major depression.

Sol Stein was Jewish, 38 years of age, and had been admitted to the unit for barricading himself in a Midtown hotel room and then struggling with the police officers who attempted to extricate him. Mr. Stein's greatest fear and nemesis were other people, so much so that social interactions could trigger his psychosis. Since he graduated from college, Mr. Stein had battled several episodes of social phobia, which he managed through seclusion. On the unit he rarely left his room. I did not know much about Sol's religious background. However, it was clear that Mr. Stein had thought deeply about religious issues. His *DSM–IV* Axis I diagnosis was social phobia and major depression with psychotic features.

Bill Manning was Jewish, 42 years of age, and had struggled with a nearly incapacitating form of bipolar disorder since college. As an early adolescent, he had displayed enormous potential at Yeshiva only to find his scholarly ambitions frustrated with the onset of the disease. Contrary to his adolescent expectations, Bill had never held a job, nor had he ever dated a woman. On the unit Mr. Manning was highly volatile and displayed little impulse control. When his loneliness grew too unbearable, Bill would erupt with pressured speech, pound the walls, and speak crudely to staff with a playboy tone of seduction. He attempted to bridge his alienation through mischievous—sometimes bullying—acts of disruption. His hospital treatment included care for widespread skin rashes and the amputation of his toe, both of which were associated with his ongoing condition of diabetes. His *DSM–IV* Axis I diagnosis was bipolar I disorder.

Treatment Process and Outcomes. As Yom Kippur (the Jewish Day of Atonement) approached, I noticed that much of the staff was away in observance of the holiday and that no service was available for the Jewish patients. Although some patients were free to sign out of the locked unit in observance of the holiday, most patients either had no family to accompany them to synagogue or were too disturbed to leave the unit. How strange, I thought, that no religious service was available for interested patients who wanted to observe the most sacred of Jewish holidays.

As a devout but non-Orthodox Jew, I had attended Yom Kippur services my entire life, but I myself had never led a service. I am not a rabbi, but I assumed that as long as I was clear about my role as lay participant I could volunteer to lead a service. I cleared my intentions with the unit chief, who seemed to be a spiritual Catholic man. He responded, "Good, we need one. You know what I tell my patients who are concerned about the religious significance of medication? I tell them that the fact that we have medicines is an act of grace."

Encouraged by the remarks of the unit chief, I announced at the weekly community meeting of staff and patients that there would be a Yom Kippur service for all interested parties. Some of my colleagues were pleased, and others thought it was inappropriate. Almost all were shocked. Mild outrage came from some psychoanalytic psychotherapists, who considered my conduct of a service to be in violation of psychotherapeutic boundaries. Yet, ironically, the more senior psychoanalysts were greater supporters of the service than the more junior psychotherapists. The controversy surrounding the proper role of a psychotherapist, however, failed to address what I saw as a pressing concern: On Yom Kippur our patients' needs would not be met by psychotherapy alone.

The Service

On Yom Kippur I walked into the designated prayer room, the kitchen, to find the four Jewish patients waiting in anticipation. The patients had arrived early, had carefully arranged the furniture, and were seated waiting for the service. A strong sense of specialness, warmth, and solemnity filled the air. I immediately realized that our service was not destined to proceed like a normal group encounter on the unit.

The service began by our singing the traditional Jewish prayers of Yom Kippur. To my surprise, all four of the patients, who normally withdrew socially, immediately commenced chanting. With each refrain, our prayers quickly mounted into a robust chorus. Patients who had not said a word to me about being Jewish, un-self-consciously recited from memory the Hebrew words and traditional melodies. The tone of the service at this point was identical to any other Yom Kippur service that I had attended in synagogue.

Between songs of prayer, the patients and I took turns leading the group in responsive readings in English. In their substance, the prayer readings covered four areas of worship: (a) acknowledgment of our sins and request for forgiveness ("Forgive us, our Father, for we have sinned. Pardon us, our King, for we have transgressed. You, Oh Lord, are generous and forgiving. Great is your love for all who call to you"); (b) appreciation of G-d and his greatness ("Praised are You, Lord our G-d, King of the universe whose word brings the evening dusk. You open the gates of dawn with wisdom, change the day's divide with understanding, set the secession of seasons. . . . Your rule shall embrace us forever"); (c) historical identification as Jews ("Remember your covenant with our fathers, as promised in the Torah: 'I will remember my covenant with Jacob, Isaac, and Abraham, and the Land will I remember . . .' "); and (d) Hebrew prayers sung to familiar melodies (Sh'ma or Avinu Malkeinu).

As we continued to read responsively, I looked up to notice that the patients' eyes seemed bright. Our religious ceremony had enlivened the patients dramatically. Otherwise sullen and withdrawn, Jerry read robustly. Sol started to officiate and correct other patients on the mechanics of the service. Bill, despite being filled with energy, did not erupt in a manic display. Instead, he rocked assuredly with his eyes closed in song. Rebecca sang without the muted tone of self-effacement.

Near the end of the service, we paused to each offer a word about our individual experience of Yom Kippur. Jerry spontaneously offered, "How can you not believe in an all-powerful G-d of goodness when you look around and see the beauty of the universe!" I was completely stunned to hear such a confident statement of faith from my patient who customarily laid in bed trapped in a state of futility.

Rebecca then quickly commented, "Thank you for the service, I have nothing to say." I took my turn, "Yom Kippur for me is very important because I make mistakes, I mess up. This is a time when I ask the people in my life forgiveness and then ultimately ask G-d for forgiveness." In an immediate response, Sol turned his gaze into my eyes. "G-d will forgive you. G-d always forgives everyone." Sol was offering me counsel. Sol, who feared people to the point of barricading himself in the hotel room, was extending himself to care for me. Bill waited his turn and then bashfully confessed, "I'd like to apologize to G-d for cheating on my diabetic diet . . . but G-d knew all along."

We concluded our service and then parted ways, with much the same communal spirit I recalled feeling at the end of the Yom Kippur services I had attended in synagogue. These patients, who suffered greatly because of a lack of connection with other people, had joined together as a worship community. Communion, in the sense described by Hillman (1994), perhaps best characterized our union. Together—yet also individually—each patient accessed transcendence. We had each moved closer to the divine together.

I returned to the residents' room to find an atypically elevated tone among my colleagues. One resident pulled me aside to reveal, "You know, sometime I'll tell you—I agree with you. There is definitely something going on with the patients." I was struck by his desire to communicate about the spiritual as well as his secrecy, which suggested discomfort.

Then there was a knock at the door. It was Sol. Sol stood squarely on the threshold and reached out his hand. "I want to thank you again for the service. G-d will forgive you. He always forgives everyone." How bold for Sol. I wondered if this relatedness could be sustained for Sol in his daily exchanges.

I packed up my belongings and headed down the hall to leave the unit. From behind, Rebecca rushed up to me: "I had a realization during the service. I always knew that Yom Kippur meant you could do penance for your sins. I knew you could admit to being wrong. But the service showed me that I could be forgiven. I had never realized this before." Rebecca's realization was directly antithetical to her core issue, which relegated her entire existence to an apology.

Through insight (for Rebecca and Jerry) or in action (for Sol and Bill), each patient had been liberated from his or her core issue. Something had happened that was not happening in psychotherapy. I wondered how long these changes would last.

Follow-Up: As Days Passed.

If depression is an eclipse of the transcendent soul by the ego, then each of the patients had glimpsed at the silhouette of personal limitation. Could each of the patients weave such an epiphany into an ongoing way of living? It seemed that their challenge was the challenge that all people face in integrating religious experience into their daily encounters. The day after Yom Kippur, I looked for signs of either reversal or ongoing change in the patients.

In the staff morning report, Rebecca was described as speaking with the night nurse about forgiveness. Rebecca's psychotherapist later told me that Rebecca had continued to develop her existential insights from Yom Kippur in her ongoing psychotherapy sessions.

Jerry, by contrast, erupted with confusion and doubt the following day on receiving laboratory results suggesting a worsening of his cancer. "You, Dr. Miller, you want me to believe in a G-d. How can I believe in your all powerful G-d of goodness when this is happening to me?" Jerry did not mention another word about the service from this point forward, so I do not know whether there were any ongoing effects of the service on him. Despite his subsequent refusal to discuss the service, in retrospect I wondered whether Jerry's response to the ceremony might have been reawakened had I initiated a shared reading and discussion of Kushner's (1981) book, *When Bad Things Happen to Good People*.

In subsequent following days Sol was notably more outgoing with fellow patients. Remarkably, he played cards with fellow patients in the solarium and started to attend group psychotherapy. Over the next few weeks, however, he gradually retreated from the public space. I wondered whether ongoing participation in religious ceremony (e.g., the observation of weekly Sabbath) might have helped Sol to sustain companionship.

Bill calmed down for the duration of his stay on the unit. I heard of no more explosive displays or disrespectful comments directed at the staff. A self-respect first manifest in his contrition about cheating on his diet seemed to endure and extend to his treatment of his fellows. Weeks after the service, both Sol and Rebecca thanked me on their respective discharges from the unit.

Therapist Commentary. Through religious ceremony something happened for these patients that was not happening in psychotherapy. Although the effects of our service somewhat degraded over time, I strongly suspect that sustained involvement in religious ceremony may yield more enduring change in patients. At the least, psychotherapy might benefit from the integration of patients' insights derived from religious ceremony.

I cower at the awesome task of understanding the method of transcendence in communal prayer. I can with some confidence, however, report that in each patient transcendence seemed to spark a categorical leap of insight or change in conduct associated with a core issue. As a relatively new psychotherapist, I now look at the prevailing models of treatment, and they seem incomplete. I sense that there is something in patients, in all people, that can lift them beyond the minutia of the ego. I am unsure how to address this mighty force that lives in the center of everyone. Yet, through it seems to be people's only chance of substantial evolution.

Case 5: Odessa

Description of the Therapist. Carole A. Rayburn is a fellow of the APA's Division of the Psychology of Religion, Division of the Psychology of Women, Division of Clinical Psychology, Division of Psychotherapy, and Division of Consulting Psychology. Rayburn is a past president of the APA's

Division of the Psychology of Religion, the APA's Division of Clinical Psychology's Section on the Clinical Psychology of Women, and of the Maryland Psychological Association. She has researched, presented, or published on topics such as women and stress, women and therapy, ethics in conducting psychotherapy and counseling with religious women, pastoral counseling, spirituality, state–trait morality, and clergy stress.

Rayburn is a Euro-American, Seventh-Day Adventist of more than moderate orthodoxy and devoutness. She has three degrees in psychology (including a doctorate) and a master of divinity from her religious denomination's seminary. Rayburn had been in private practice of psychology for 18 years when she saw Odessa. Her therapeutic orientation is psychodynamic, and she also uses rational–emotive therapy and transactional analysis with occasional gestalt techniques. Currently, Rayburn is in private practice and also does consulting and conducts research in psychology.

Setting. Odessa was seen in an office setting in a cosmopolitan eastern city. Primary services offered in the office setting were individual, group, marital, and family therapies and counseling. An overall feminist therapy approach was used, and, when appropriate, a religious or spiritual perspective and intervention was used.

Client Demographic Characteristics. The client, age 50, was a Black woman originally from a southern state. She was a Seventh-Day Adventist of more than moderate orthodoxy and devoutness. A convert to the Seventh-Day Adventist faith, she was raised as a Roman Catholic. At least of high normal intelligence, she had begun the first year of junior college but had been unable to continue because of family finances. Odessa was born into a lower middle-class family; her father was a plumber's helper and her mother was a homemaker. She was the next-to-the-youngest child in a family of two sisters and two brothers. Odessa was married and had five daughters.

Client History. Odessa had two brothers who were older than she was. One of her brothers was mentally retarded. Her father and both brothers had forced her older and younger sisters to have sexual intercourse with them. When they attempted to force themselves on Odessa, she fought back in such a fierce way that she dissuaded them from any attempts to sexually assault her. However, they occasionally physically abused her from age 13 to age 18. At 18, she left home to get a job and to share an apartment with another young woman. While living with her parents, she had thoughts of seriously harming the male family members, and she harbored ambivalent feelings toward her mother for being so unprotective of her and her sisters, so passive with the father and brothers and ineffectual in general.

Her father beat her mother too, and the mother turned her head away when he and her sons attacked Odessa and her sisters because she was trying to escape his cruelty herself. Odessa, feeling vulnerable to and angry at both the persecutors and the victims in her family and at her mother for not rescuing her from that horrible predicament, nonetheless wanted both to protect and physically attack her mother. She also was furious that she had no adequate female role model and a terrible male figure in her childhood experiences. Furthermore, she resented that her parents never encouraged her to further her education. She differentiated between her parents actually having money for this (which she realized they did not) and at least motivating her to achieve.

Presenting Problems and Concerns. When she came to therapy, Odessa was feeling deep shame, guilt, and depression. Her guilt and shame concerned her familial captive position in physically being abused and witnessing her mother and sisters being abused; her inability to protect the other female family members from their abusers; and her hatred toward her parents, siblings, and herself. Her religious and spiritual background espoused love and respect for her parents and siblings, to "not let the sun go down on her anger," but she did not think that she could obey such commands without becoming seriously emotionally disturbed.

She regretted that she had married and had children. She was concerned that she would physically abuse her children when they failed to unconditionally respect and obey her. She also was angry at her husband for being passive in family matters and not taking the major part or at least sharing equally the disciplining of the children. Her self-hate and self-blame were apparent too. Her intense anger, guilt, shame, and ambivalence toward all her family members also contributed to several physical problems, such as hypertension, high blood pressure, and diabetes. She was under regular medical treatment for these problems.

When Odessa began her individual psychotherapy treatment, she had a low-level (GS-2) government job, primarily because of her hesitation in asserting herself and in learning new material on her job. She also was not willing to assert herself as head deaconess at her church: She felt plagued with too much responsibility in this role, although she felt compelled to volunteer for that level of involvement. She resented that other women in the church were not doing their share. This was reminiscent of her mother's failure and brother's abuse but her thinking that she needed to somehow respect or not report her abusive father and brothers. Her husband, the head elder in their church and a Sabbath school teacher, had a second job to help support their family. She was angry at him for not having enough time for her and the children.

Furthermore, she blamed her husband for not discouraging his many female admirers in the Sabbath school class. She wondered how much she had to accept in "Christian humility and silence" or "suffering" and how much deference she had to give to the patriarchal concept of the male head of the household. Besides the need of both of them having at least one job to give their children a religious education, they interpreted church teachings as requiring that they be busy performing Christian works most of their time. Thus, Odessa was tired much of the time; at church and work, Odessa saw herself as a religious Cinderella whose accommodating nature and deep desire to please others to gain approval were taken advantage of by a bad parent, boss, or religious leader and bad sisters, coworkers, or congregants.

Assessment and Diagnosis. In the initial therapy sessions, to diagnose the extent of Odessa's problems, I asked her to complete several figure and other drawings and the Wechsler Adult Intelligence Scale–Revised. The latter was to determine her intellectual functioning and potential and to help her to gain a more realistic idea of her abilities and lessen her thoughts of low self-esteem and self-deprecation. Diagnosed as experiencing dysthmic disorder (*DSM–IV* code 300.40) with intense guilt, anger, shame, and passivity, she had much difficulty expressing her feelings openly and appropriately. She believed that she was not allowed to set her own priorities or to say no when it was appropriate: She thought that this would be un-Christian and selfish. Odessa's religious and spiritual background led her to put respecting parents and church authorities at the top of her list of priorities.

Feeling guilty and un-Christian whenever she felt intense anger with those most significant in her life and whenever she did not want to put others' desires and wishes above her own, she did not accept, respect, or even like herself much of the time. She felt at least partly responsible for the physical abuse that she received from the men in her nuclear family, reasoning that somehow even her mother did not love her enough to shield her from a life of misery and punishment. Odessa thought that women were not supposed to assert themselves, that men were physically if not morally superior to women and could force women to obey them. Although her religious denomination encouraged all people to attain the highest educational goals feasible, she was influenced by the traditions of her church that seemed to espouse a male leadership and an auxiliary role for women. Indeed, neither the Roman Catholicism of her childhood nor the Seventh-Day Adventism of her adulthood provided her with a role model of female leadership and responsibility at the highest church levels of clergy and elder.

At work, she was often teased by her coworkers, who told her that her lifestyle of no smoking or drinking and a vegetarian diet qualified her for sainthood. They referred to her as a "goodie-goodie," and she usually became depressed and felt demeaned in the face of such comments. She experienced a great deal of stress when she attempted to respond positively to others' requests for help, maintain an image of the "sincere and loving Christian," and do too much for too long.

Treatment Process and Outcomes. Rational–emotive therapy and transactional analysis were used to better elucidate the cognitive and emotional factors in Odessa's personality that related to her problems and their solutions. This involved working on the parental messages in her thinking, the adaptive and rebellious child within her, and the persecutor role that she learned from her parents and transferred to herself when interacting with her children. Her children, in turn, saw Odessa as persecuting them and wanted their father to rescue them. However, Odessa saw her parents, brother, husband, and children as persecuting her and making her the victim. She wanted to force a protecting and nurturing role on her husband, mainly to protect her from any disrespect or unkindness from their children.

Reality testing concerning her shame, guilt, and need to understand her parents and brothers and others and to forgive them and herself so that she could get on with the rest of her life played a part in the overall plan of her treatment. The abuse was never to be condoned, but the internalized intense anger was having a noxious effect on her and was constantly getting recycled. Feminist therapy was also used to balance the male chauvinism in her familial situation and within her religious environment and to reinforce the equality of all people, or gender equality and gender fairness, in all areas of life. Indeed, such awareness of and sensitivity to gender equality seemed to have been missing in important spheres of her life during significant periods of her development.

Overall, she responded positively to these interventions. Her setbacks included her still wanting to blame and hate her parents and brothers and, to some extent, other men, even though she knew that holding on to this hate was acting as an emotional cancer in her body and mind. She resisted giving up her shame, guilt, and obsession to be perfect with its self-flagellation for not having achieved a holier-than-thou status. She also had a setback when her daughters rebelled by getting into trouble at school and getting poor grades, and Odessa reacted by wanting to hurt them for not obeying her and their teachers. She was angry with her husband for being "too close" to his mother and doing whatever his mother asked rather than listening to Odessa.

Odessa eventually had some insights into the harmful interactions between her parents and her, her brothers and her, and the ways in which she transferred her negative feelings onto her husband and children. However, she was reinforced in the justification in expecting her husband to share equally in raising their children and in spending more time with her. Eventually she became more self-confident, more self-appreciative, saw God as more forgiving and thus could be more forgiving of herself, and she saw herself as more intelligent and capable. She applied for and got a much better position in the government with far greater responsibilities and learning opportunities as well as better pay.

Although the guilt and shame over the incest and physical violence in her family negatively affected her progress, Odessa's sincere religious convictions about a loving, parental God, a nurturing and redemptive Savior (a good sibling role model for her), and an ever-present and healing Holy Spirit or teacher and guide for her daily walk in life as well as her spiritual fervor in earnestly desiring to get better led to much progress on her part. She largely overcame her depression, anger, and sorrow as she forgave others and herself. The forgiveness was not to ever be confused with condoning or even forgiving the behavior but in looking deeply into the human frailty of the abuser. She was encouraged to never take any kind of abuse again, and she readily understood this need to protect herself.

Therapist Commentary. Odessa's religiosity and spirituality were relevant to her treatment in that her shame, guilt, and belief in the commandment to love one's parents had religious origins and contributed to her problems. On the other hand, Odessa's beliefs that parents should be worthy of their children's love and respect, that there are biblical taboos against incest, that she could depend on God's forgiveness, Christ's salvific power, and the Holy Spirit working through her, and that she could forgive others and herself were religious doctrines and beliefs that contributed to her healing and growth. Also, she would not have entered into psychotherapeutic treatment with a person not of her religious beliefs. Relevant, too, was the fact that her therapist was a woman, because she had less anger with women than with men and thus could establish better rapport with women than with men at the outset of therapy. Perhaps she would have preferred a Black female therapist of her own religious denomination, but one was not available. That the therapist was the same age, gender, and religious denomination as the client seemed to be adequate.

Working with Odessa presented me with the challenge of establishing the finely tuned balance between ecclesiastical teachings and traditions and feminist egalitarian values that are necessary for the progress of the growth of all women. Too often, women come away from a religious setting with the idea that they are second-class citizens, auxiliary to the male members of their religious group, and often they are taken for granted because the pews usually contain more women than men across any denominational affiliation. Religious women often develop burnout from working so hard on others' behalf and not sensing that they are appreciated or recognized for their contributions when compared with the men in the same environment. Odessa was feeling that she was expected to single-handedly do the work of all of the deaconesses, and she needed to know that she could set her own priorities and had no moral obligation to overwork to the point of wearing herself out and perhaps even experiencing poor health. Fortunately, Odessa started her therapy sessions before such burnout became a serious problem, and she learned to better balance her home, work, and church life and to be well satisfied in all these spheres.

Overall, a positive outcome for Odessa has held up over the years, as Odessa has communicated with me at Christmas and occasionally at other times. This communication has occurred for more than eight years. She is far more comfortable with herself now as well as less impatient with or hurt by her family and others. She has learned to realistically assess her wants and needs, her strengths and weaknesses, her energy level, and her ability to allow herself to take more problems philosophically and to turn many of them over to a power outside herself. Her prayer life has been important to her throughout her treatment and continues to be now.

Case 6: Kristen

Description of Therapist. Alan C. Tjeltveit is an associate professor of psychology at Muhlenberg College in Allentown, Pennsylvania, where he maintains a small clinical practice. He received his doctorate in clinical psychology in 1984 and is a licensed clinical psychologist. Tjeltveit has published a number of articles on psychotherapy, values, and ethics and is completing a book on the ethical dimensions of psychotherapy. His therapeutic orientation is integrative, generally emphasizing cognitive–behavioral interventions with individuals.

Tjeltveit has been a Lutheran Christian since being baptized as an infant. His faith became personally meaningful to him as a teenager and continues to be important to him. He has long been interested in theology and considers himself to be a theologically moderate Lutheran, with religious breadth added by completing a course on Japanese religions in Japan, by earning a master's degree in theology at an ecumenical seminary, and through his experiences as a psychotherapist. Tjeltveit is a member of the Evangelical Lutheran Church in America, the large "mainstream" branch of American Lutheranism.

Setting. Kristen was seen in the mid-Atlantic region in a private practice setting known for the sensitivity of its practitioners to religious issues but open to clients and therapists of different religious convictions; it was not described as a "Christian counseling center." Individual psychotherapy for mental health issues was the primary service offered.

Client Demographic Characteristics. Kristen was a married, 32-year-old White woman with three children. A Lutheran, she regularly attended worship services. Religious issues were extremely important to her, but her religiosity was in some ways decidedly idiosyncratic, drawing on a variety of religious and spiritual traditions but differing from them all. The family lived in a middle-class suburban neighborhood, from which she commuted to her 25-hr-a-week clerical job at a Fortune 500 corporation.

Client History. Kristen grew up in a large eastern city, the daughter of an emotionally distant mother and an alcoholic, physically abusive father, who abandoned the family when Kristen was 13. Although he abused Kristen's mother, not her, Kristen worried about his violence when she was a child. Indeed, she reported feeling "afraid always" when growing up, trusting neither of her parents. She denied ever being abused sexually.

Religion was not especially important to her growing up. When she was 16, however, she began to develop fears of being condemned because she had committed the "unpardonable sin." She swore at God and told God she did not want to be forgiven. As a result, she became "panicky" and anxious about hell. And about much else.

She experienced severe agoraphobic symptoms from the ages of 17 to 19. She could not identify any precipitants, but the symptoms first occurred at about the same time she swore at God and developed gastritis. She improved with extensive (up to two to three times a week) behaviorally oriented therapy. Although her anxiety improved, she reported having occasional panic attacks and she remained a fairly anxious person.

She married and began a family. Symptoms (e.g., obsessions, compulsions, agoraphobic symptoms, specific phobias, and an extremely high general level of anxiety) resumed when she was 29. Her third child had just been born, and her husband had developed a serious medical condition that resulted in the loss of his job. At one point, he went to have some medical tests done, and Kristen became extremely anxious thinking about it. A high level of anxiety then became a constant factor in her life.

She sought out a cognitive–behavioral therapist, with whom she made some progress. Kristen's therapist began to notice, however, that her complex ideational system contained extensive religious content that appeared to be blocking progress. Because she was unfamiliar with her religious tradition and did not feel competent to address Kristen's religious issues, the therapist suggested that Kristen talk with her pastor to supplement their therapy sessions. (Her health maintenance organization had assigned a psychiatrist to her, but she refused to take the medication he prescribed because "God doesn't want me to get better.")

Kristen's pastor met with her on several occasions to talk about Lutheran beliefs. He soon discovered that some of her ideas (e.g., that wearing lipstick would condemn her to hell forever and that people need to earn their way into heaven by being perfect) were in sharp contrast with Lutheran Christian beliefs. He became frustrated, however, because Kristen's intellectual assent to Lutheran doctrine (e.g., the conviction that God is gracious and forgiving) had little effect on her. In addition, he did not feel competent to deal with her anxiety symptoms. So, knowing I had both theological training and a doctorate in clinical psychology, he referred her to me. She continued to see her therapist, her pastor, and her psychiatrist.

Presenting Problems and Concerns. "I would like to get to a point where God works *with* me," Kristen stated, adding that she no longer wanted to feel that God was her "adversary." Kristen also reported the following problems: agoraphobia, phobias, obsessions, compulsions, and a consistently high level of free-floating anxiety, plus depression secondary to those problems. With regard to anxiety and obsessive–compulsive symptoms, she reported that "anything" caused panic. To protect herself from God's wrath, she tried to follow all of God's laws, borrowing rules for living from all religions and cultures, just to be sure she did not leave any out. She avoided eating certain foods, following eating laws from the Hebrew Scriptures, for example, by not eating pork. Her fears of food, however, also spread to a wide variety of foods, including all meat. On hearing that people in some cultures think one ought not have one's picture taken (unless one's soul be taken up into the camera), Kristen began to be petrified every time her picture might be taken. She also avoided putting things in a mailbox or throwing things away (out of fear that she would later remember she made a mistake but not be able to recover that paper and correct it). Extensive cleaning rituals meant she devoted 2 hr to washing the dinner dishes for her family of five. She was unable to walk alone more than half a block from her house, but she was able to do so if accompanied by a family member. Her husband generally drove her to work.

Assessment and Diagnosis. I drew on the assessments provided by her other therapist and her pastor, MMPI results, and extensive interviews with her. Assessment was slow and ongoing because of the intricate complexity of her obsessional system. In addition to being embarrassed about some of her thoughts, she was convinced that God did not want her to talk about her problems or to improve. Accordingly, assessment and treatment were intertwined to an unusually great extent, as some treatment was necessary before she would talk about some of her beliefs, beliefs that are essential to a complete understanding of her cognitions.

I gave her a *DSM–III* Axis I diagnosis of obsessive–compulsive disorder. Her MMPI results (a 4-6 profile with T-score values higher than 90, with 7, 8, and 2 having T-score values higher than 80) suggested considerable distress and a wide range of psychiatric symptoms, unusual thinking that others might have trouble following, and dependency issues.

In general, I perceived her to be a severely obsessive–compulsive woman with an unusually complex, deeply entrenched belief system that was tied, in a variety of ways, to religiousness. Some symptoms were connected to religion; others were not. For instance, she reported that she performed some compulsive behaviors because she was specifically instructed by God to do so, but other behaviors were performed in the absence of divine direction.

Some of her anxiety had to do with a fear of violating God's law and being punished. She also interpreted any anxiety as a sign that she had broken one of God's laws. Her rituals alleviated some of her anxiety ("They protect me"), so she continued them and expanded them.

There were several tensions within her religious system: Consistent with her Lutheranism, she stated she knew that God forgave her. However, that thought was rapidly followed by another: "But what if . . . ?" She stated that she had only one chance in life and that she had messed up. God would not permit further mistakes, take extenuating circumstances into account, or forgive her. "God has standards," she stated. "I blew it. Now I have to be perfect." She also felt powerless in the face of a God who "pulls the strings" (another belief inconsistent with Lutheran theology), yet she also blamed herself whenever anything went wrong in her life.

In terms of the origin of her symptoms, the fact that her abusive, impossible-to-please father bore a substantial resemblance to her abusive, impossible-to-please "God" was undoubtedly no accident. Because of that and because so many of her beliefs were at odds with those of her Lutheran tradition, I saw much of the religious content of her cognitive system to be the result of her psychopathology rather than the original cause of it. Whatever the cause of her idiosyncratic religiousness, however, it served a variety of functions in her life: creating, perpetuating, exacerbating, and expressing symptoms; blocking improvement; and (potentially) helping her improve.

Her view of God as the giver of law and an unforgiving task master added to her anxiety and gave rise to some of her compulsions. Once her anxiety reached high levels, and religiously justified rituals alleviated her anxiety, she received powerful negative reinforcement for continuing the rituals. In addition, the ample variety of religious rules provided many ways for her to extend her ritualistic and compulsive behaviors. Her idiosyncratic religiousness thus perpetuated and exacerbated her symptoms.

Her religious views also stood in the way of her therapeutic progress, especially her beliefs that God did not want her to talk about herself or get better. She also was in a bind: She interpreted anxiety as evidence that she had violated one of God's laws. However, if she felt less anxious, that meant she was improving, which she thought was against the will of God. Therefore, no matter what happened to her, she assumed that she was in trouble with God, which made her more anxious, which she interpreted to mean that she had violated one of God's laws.

Her religiousness also functioned as a potential resource for her, however, both in terms of social support and as a source of adaptive cognitions to challenge the maladaptive beliefs associated with her self-constructed religion. It was on these adaptive religious resources that I drew when working with Kristen.

Treatment Process and Outcomes. I adopted a cognitive approach, focusing on the maladaptive religious beliefs that maintained her problems, and working with her to challenge those cognitions and develop new, more adaptive cognitions. Given the complex and entrenched nature of her belief system, progress was excruciatingly slow.

We spent several sessions talking about her conviction that wearing makeup is wrong, a conviction stemming from her hearing that some religious groups think it is wrong, partly because wearing makeup, and especially wearing it to church, would "defile" the church. I brought in a Bible, and we examined the verses believed to justify a ban on makeup, discussing alternative interpretations, including those of her own religious tradition (which permits complete freedom in the matter, with most members of the church, including its clergy wives and its female clergy, wearing makeup). We also examined other Scripture passages related to the freedom that

Christ brings the Christian and the forgiveness available to human beings from a God whose central attribute is believed to be grace.

In and of themselves, these discussions did not, of course, change her beliefs or behaviors. However, they provided us with a set of alternative cognitions that we, and eventually she alone, could use to challenge the automatic thoughts that it would be wrong for her to wear makeup and to replace them with more adaptive cognitions, cognitions more attuned to our theological tradition.

Using a similar approach, we addressed her beliefs that she was a "contaminant" and "evil," that God would "zap" her for talking about herself and that God would punish her if she got well. We addressed those maladaptive cognitions by challenging them with her Lutheran convictions that God is accepting and loving, that it is okay to make mistakes, and that what is most important is to love people, not to follow rules rigidly.

In general, I worked with her so that she labeled her anxiety as anxiety rather than as evidence that God was punishing her; so that she recognized that most of what she regarded as "wrongdoing" (and therefore evil) was not sinful at all (this sometimes involved biblical interpretation); so that she could see (and feel) that she was not an intrinsically evil or bad person (drawing on the Christian doctrine of creation); and so that she could believe that God loved her despite her occasional wrongdoing, that her sins were forgiven unconditionally, and that she would remain God's child even if she sinned.

Although progress was slow, Kristen eventually began changing her thinking and her symptoms began to diminish. She reported progress in decreasing her compulsions and phobias, for instance, not washing her hands as often and wearing makeup (although she still had trouble wearing makeup to church). After addressing her belief that God did not want her to take medication, she eventually agreed to her psychiatrist's recommendation and began taking medication, with progress speeding up thereafter. When she terminated with me, she reported moderate levels of anxiety and much progress in challenging the religious distortions that had helped create and sustain the symptoms that had so dominated her life.

Therapist Commentary. Several factors made it easier for me to use spiritual interventions to full advantage with Kristen. Kristen and I were members of the same denomination. She was referred to me by her pastor, and we had an explicit therapeutic contract to address the religious issues related to her problems. I had some measure of expertise in biblical interpretation and her tradition's theology. I was familiar with the literature on the interface between clinical psychology, theology, and religion. Finally, we were in a private practice setting unconstrained by the agency or insurance company rules and church–state considerations that sometimes stand in the way of therapists pursuing the best interests of their clients. The ethical issues that sometimes arise when using spiritual interventions were thus not factors in this case. It also was helpful that I knew her other therapist, could count on her to address Kristen's other issues well, and could, with integrity, dovetail my therapeutic approach with hers.

Because they played an important role in the perpetuation of her symptoms and blocked progress, Kristen's religious issues needed to be addressed directly. Although improvement might have been possible without spiritual interventions, I think there were a number of advantages to using them. That I had been referred by her pastor, was a fellow Lutheran, and used spiritual interventions aided in building a trusting relationship. Those factors also made the spiritual interventions more effective. Because religion had such a powerful effect on her life, altering the functional impact of her religious beliefs by using her Lutheran theology was especially effective. That is, we used religion against religion; the healthier religion of her tradition against the pathology-inducing, defensive religion into which she had descended. Because Kristen believed that God trumped all other considerations, addressing her concept of God from within a theological and biblical framework was especially potent. Finally, my detailed knowledge of the tradition was important because some of her distortions of Lutheran belief played subtle, yet important, roles in keeping her trapped in her pathology. By learning to identify her distorted religious cognitions and to replace them with those of her own tradition, Kristen was able to grow within that faith while reducing her symptoms and learning to function at a much higher level of mental health.

Case 7: Helen

Description of the Therapist. Wendy L. Ulrich has a doctorate in psychology and education from the University of Michigan. She also has master's degrees in business administration and psychology from the University of California, Los Angeles, and the University of Michigan. Ulrich has worked as a consultant and trainer for a variety of organizations including Marriott Corporation International, the Federal Aviation Administration, the U.S. Army, General Electric, Johnson & Johnson, United Way, and the University of Pennsylvania Medical School.

Ulrich is a White woman and is a practicing and committed member of The Church of Jesus Christ of Latter-day Saints (Mormon). She also has worked extensively as a consultant for Joy of Jesus, a nonprofit organization working to revitalize inner-city neighborhoods and provide academic, spiritual, and emotional support to minority students. She has been in private practice for 7 years. Her therapeutic orientation is eclectic, with formal training and practice in cognitive–behavioral, family, child, and psychodynamic therapy. She currently works primarily with individual adults in long-term therapy. Ulrich is the past president of the Association of Mormon Counselors and Psychotherapists and has published a number of articles on psychotherapy and spiritual issues.

Setting. The client was seen in a private practice office in the Midwest, where Ulrich practices with four other therapists. Ulrich met with Helen for regular weekly sessions for about 2 years.

Client Demographic Characteristics. When first seen, Helen was a White woman in her early 40s and a devout member of the Church of Jesus Christ of Latter-day Saints (Mormon). She was recently widowed and had two children. Although college educated and from a middle-class background, Helen was experiencing economic hardship. She had worked for many years as a secretary but was unemployed when we began meeting.

Client History. Helen was the oldest child in a large family. She was raised in the Mormon church and had been active in it all her life. She had always been devout in her faith. She did well in school through determined effort and extremely hard work, but she felt she had to work much harder than others to succeed in school. She described herself as shy and awkward. She began college but quit to work so she could help support her younger siblings—to whom she was devoted—through college and missionary service for the church. She married late and bore two children, who were in grade school when her husband died. His death left Helen with minimal income and many debts.

Presenting Problems and Concerns. Helen had been diagnosed previously with generalized anxiety disorder and dysthymia. She had taken antianxiety and antidepressant medication for many years and had seen a variety of specialists for both psychological and physical problems. She had determined that she was addicted to her medication, and, about 2 months before seeing me, she decided without medical advice to completely stop all her medication. She had become severely depressed and delusional.

By the time Helen was referred to me, she was no longer delusional but still extremely depressed, quietly desperate, and suicidal. She was troubled by a variety of obsessive thoughts and some compulsive behavior. She was extremely anxious in any social setting, to the point of having difficulty speaking at all in a group. Her voice would become difficult to understand, and she would have difficulty formulating her thoughts. She had difficulty expressing her thoughts even with me, forming her sentences carefully and deliberately as if each one required great effort.

Cooking, writing, and sewing—in fact, anything requiring fine motor skill and hand–eye coordination—were painfully slow and tedious for her. It could take her almost a minute to write her name. She had a difficult time with spatial orientation and had difficulty conceptualizing or learning spatial tasks. She was terrified about the prospect of trying to get or hold a job again, and she had virtually no support group outside of a few caring but inundated family members. Helen attributed all of these difficulties to her extreme anxiety, over which she felt a great deal of shame and frustration.

Of greatest concern to Helen, however, was her belief that she was unspiritual and unrighteous. This conclusion rested on three sets of experiences. First, she felt she had never received an answer to prayer or felt the spiritual feelings that seemed familiar to others of her faith. She had concluded that she was spiritually defective in some critical way, which left her outside the realm of salvation. Second, she had obsessive thoughts of obscene language that she tried hard, but without success, to banish from her mind. This obsession reinforced her feelings of defectiveness and her conclusion that her very thoughts would condemn her in God's eyes. Third, she attributed her overall fearfulness to a lack of faith in God, convinced that if she had faith she would be able to overcome her fear and fix her problems.

Along with her many painful symptoms, Helen had many assets. In school, Helen had been an A student through sheer determination and effort. She was a good money manager, scrupulously honest, persistent, and hard working. Helen's two children were extremely bright, caring, and capable. Helen made her life work through her own resourcefulness, good organization, and orderliness. She was extremely patient, thoughtful, and uncomplaining with associates and friends. One-on-one, she was friendly and compassionate, and she had a keen sense of reciprocity and generosity with others.

Assessment and Diagnosis. Despite much conversation on the subject, Helen was unwilling to submit to a formal psychological evaluation for fear that she would prove to be defective in some way (which would make her feel even more hopeless and depressed) or not (which would make her feel even more responsible for her failures). My assessment, based on observations and a review of her history, led me to conclude that Helen was of above-average verbal intelligence.

Although I agreed that her social anxiety exacerbated her dyspraxia, I hypothesized that the dyspraxia was primary rather than secondary to her anxiety. She also met diagnostic criteria for social phobia, mild obsessive–compulsive disorder, dysthymia, and a severe major depressive episode. Although I believe Helen's depression and anxiety also may have had biological components, I eventually concluded that Helen's primary problem was her fairly severe deficit in processing speed, spatial orientation, and fine-motor coordination. She attempted to compensate for these deficits in the only way she could: by trying really hard. However, the exceptional effort required of her to accomplish ordinary tasks also made her tense and anxious about failure. Her high verbal skill and good school performance contributed to others' perceptions that her dyspraxia resulted from anxiety as opposed to a learning disability, and she was told again and again to relax.

Helen had concluded from this repeated injunction to relax that her deficits were something that she should be able to control, but the word *relax* had become anxiety provoking for her, and she did not have the faintest idea how to relax enough to improve her performance. By the time I saw her, talking to her about relaxing had the effect of making her anxiety skyrocket. She blamed herself for not controlling her anxiety, saw the evidence of her failure every time she tried to do a task as simple as writing her name, and spiraled into increasing depression and hopelessness. Helen became highly sensitive to all public performance and situations with potential for public appraisal, developing a severe social phobia that contributed further to her sense of failure. In her chronic dysthymic state, Helen's affect was almost continuously flat and blunted, making it difficult for her to feel much of anything, including sensitive spiritual feelings.

Treatment Process and Outcomes. The therapist's initial task, particularly with a depressed patient, is to establish a basis for hope. Without a grounded basis for hope, the client cannot be expected to mobilize the effort required to attempt change. Establishing a basis for hope felt like an especially precarious process with Helen. She had virtually no expectation of anyone being able to help her, to which she seemed completely resigned. She had come to me on the recommendation of an ecclesiastical leader to whom she had gone in a last-ditch effort after she had thought of taking her own life. She had not told either of us this until later, however. Having been to many doctors and therapists before without feeling helped, she had almost no reason to believe that I would be able to help her either.

I initially accepted her assumption that chronic and excessive anxiety was at the root of her difficulties. I concluded that cognitive–behavioral techniques, relaxation training, medication, and desensitization might help her. These suggestions only added enormously to her distress, however, because they reinforced old messages that she just needed to relax, which she knew herself incapable of doing to the degree necessary to reduce her dyspraxia. I quickly recognized that my current approach reinforced rather than reduced Helen's hopelessness.

For Helen to have hope in this therapeutic process, she needed an explanation for her difficulties that made sense given her experience and that provided viable options she had not already tried and dismissed as useless. As I began to formulate the hypothesis outlined earlier, Helen and I discussed it at length. We worked together to explore the hypothesis that her hand-motor problems were a physical disability beyond her control, something she might learn to cope with better but that we did not expect her to overcome by relaxation or willpower. This was a hopeful promise, one that made sense to her and that did not require her to change things about herself that she knew from previous experience she could not change. Helen proceeded most cautiously, but once convinced she was enormously relieved by this new way of understanding herself. I spent much time simply documenting Helen's difficulties and empathizing with the enormous emotional distress they caused her, things she had seldom discussed previously.

We eventually took the same approach with her social phobia, conceptualizing it as something she could learn to cope with but was not expected to conquer. This theory made sense of Helen's experience and was therefore believable to her, and she began to experience hope and relief. With permission to avoid social situations that made her uncomfortable and to stop trying to control her social anxiety by trying to relax, Helen felt less pressure to fix herself. Over time, not feeling responsible to figure out how to relax her anxiety away actually allowed her to relax a little and to begin experimenting with some other coping skills. Helen actually found the symptoms of her social distress more tolerable when she did not feel the additional burden of trying to fix them and blaming herself for her failure to do so.

I believed antidepressant medication might offer additional relief that would help her progress. Helen was understandably reluctant to go back on medication given the enormous difficulty she had had with withdrawal from her previous medication. After much discussion about the addictive nature of various medications, she agreed to a referral to a physician, who prescribed only an antidepressant. Helen soon acknowledged that the medication helped her feel a little better and to think more clearly.

Helen's spiritual concerns were at the forefront throughout this process, but now we began trying to deal with them more directly. I shared my observations that people who are depressed have great difficulty feeling anything, including spiritual feelings. As we met I often felt spiritual feelings relative to God's love for Helen and a sense of confirmation when the approach we were taking to a problem felt spiritually right. I believed that Helen also was feeling some of these feelings. I brought these occasions to her attention, asking her to identify where in her body, mind, and heart spirituality registered for her. She began to recognize and acknowledge her own spiritual feelings with great joy. She noticed that some ideas and feelings had a particular quality of peacefulness, sensibility, and rightness that registered in both her mind and her heart. We both felt spiritual assurance that we were on the right track in how we were approaching Helen's problems, and we prayed together for further direction. It was not enough for either of us to believe something that was convenient but untrue about Helen's condition.

As Helen began to identify her own spiritual experiences, she suddenly felt included in a world of spiritual connection from which she had felt excluded before. Helen had seemed to believe that the major way God answers prayer is by giving people direct impressions or inspiration that they would recognize as a spiritual prompting. Not having recognized such experiences previously, she felt defective when others spoke of God answering their prayers. Now she believed that God also communicated with her through peaceful feelings and new insights. We also reviewed her history and discovered many incidents in which her prayers had been answered, even though those answers had not come as personal revelation to her. She saw answers to prayers that had occurred but had not been noted. These discoveries also brought joy, relief, and gratitude. She began to accept that God was involved in her life and that she was capable of receiving his help.

As they emerged in the course of therapy, we reviewed Helen's religious beliefs and attempted to correct misunderstandings and erroneous conclusions. Helen discovered that she had enormous faith in God but little in herself. She had seen her inability to conquer her difficulties as stemming from a lack of faith in God, believing that if she just had faith she could relax and perform better. We distinguished faith in God's ability to do all things, which she trusted completely, from her ability do to all things, which was not necessary to faith. We reframed her trust in God as faith, her doubts in herself as realism, and her willingness to submit to God in either healing or disability as obedience and righteousness. Seeing her disability as a physical "thorn in the flesh" rather than as a self-inflicted emotional ailment for which she was responsible freed her to apply her considerable inner resources to coping rather than stressing.

A similar approach helped her to stop feeling responsible to control the profanity that occasionally crossed her mind. Just as Helen had learned that the harder she tried to relax the more tense she became, we explored the possibility that the harder she tried to control thoughts of profane language the more her thinking would be flooded with it. I invited her to experiment with noting the profane words that bothered her and to simply watch them go by rather than trying to control them. I reminded her that God judges people by their desires as well as by their actions and thoughts and that she could probably afford to at least experiment with approaches other than more attempts at thought control. As Helen relinquished control of these thoughts, they began to relinquish control of her.

Helen developed a high level of trust in me once she knew that I would not expect something of her she knew she could not do. We painstakingly worked through the emotional hurdles entailed in seeking employment, organizing personal affairs, and raising her children. Her depression gradually lifted, and she even began to tackle her social phobia. I made some suggestions, attempted to build on what she had discovered helped her, and encouraged small experiments. We discussed the views she held of others as being superior to her and rightful judges of her and applied logic, experience, and scriptural teachings to counter these beliefs. She began to report some small successes in social situations and began to reach out more to others.

By the second year of therapy, Helen was employed, no longer clinically depressed, and realizing some small gains in her social comfort. She continued to report on the physical tasks that were difficult for her, marveling at how much harder these tasks were for her than for others, but she was relieved that she did not have to fix this. She could laugh at her disability as well as weep about it, she could see how hard she tried as a virtue instead of a problem, and she could begin to turn to other issues.

During the second year of therapy, Helen chose to focus on forgiving her family members for the ways their criticism and lack of support had contributed to her problems. Helen was concerned about her angry feelings at and disappointment with her parents. She felt guilty about these feelings and wanted to be rid of them, believing forgiveness to be a spiritual requirement for a Christian. However, she equated forgiving with admitting that her family was right and she was wrong. She wanted to forgive them but, again, could imagine this only as something she had to do perfectly and completely and through willpower alone.

We discussed at length the importance of acknowledging the things her family had done to hurt her, the effects their behavior had had on her, and what she had needed that she did not get. This was framed as an attempt to know the truth, a principle of godliness (Deuteronomy 32:4), rather than as a vendetta. Once she knew the truth, she could decide what she wanted to do about it. She could more easily make a conscious choice to be merciful and forgiving with her family when this choice did not mean saying that they had been right all along and she had been wrong.

Knowing the truth included a careful examination of the ways in which church teachings or scriptural verses had been used by others to justify others' hurtful behavior and excuse wrongdoing. For example, injunctions to honor parents and to forgive others were taken to mean that she was wrong to believe her parents had hurt her in any way (although they clearly had). We discussed a Book of Mormon Scripture stating that in the plan of God, mercy cannot rob justice (Alma 42:25), which we took to mean in part that forgiving (being merciful) does not include ignoring or detracting from what is fair and true (justice).

We also enacted her internal dialogues of self-condemnation, with her venting the condemning voice of her parents and me giving voice to her defense. Noting Christ's condemnation of those who offended little children (Matthew 18:6), I reminded her that she was simply learning to be more like Jesus when she condemned the hurtful treatment of children, including herself as a child. I allowed her to know that I, too, would have been deeply wounded by what happened to her and that I did not consider her to be overreacting. I helped her create a logic for protecting herself against the internal parental voices of condemnation. Once I had received and empathized with her story, she then could apply that empathy to those who had hurt her.

Therapist Commentary. Even though Helen and I shared the same religious background, I always worry about imposing my spiritual conclusions and convictions on those who come to me for help. Because Helen was deeply suspicious of the unhelpful information she had received from helping professionals and authority figures in the past, she was extremely cautious about every suggestion I made to her. Although this necessitated lengthy discussion, I felt her caution was warranted and served both our interests. Individual sessions often took 2 hr or more to give Helen time to work through an issue, given her need to come to her own conclusions and not rely on trusting mine and given her slow overall processing speed. Helen remained extremely responsible about owning her thoughts, conclusions, and behavioral choices. A less cautious client might be too easily led by an authority figure to conclusions that she could not really claim and that would thus not really help in the long run.

Because Helen's deep religious commitment and conviction were so central to her understanding of herself and the world, any change effort had to make sense in, and flow out of, that religious perspective. Misunderstandings of her relationship to God and others were central tenets of the cognitive structure that supported her depression and anxiety. Misunderstanding of the meaning of scriptural passages had reinforced her self-condemnation. Misunderstanding of her body and control over it had contributed to her social anxiety and hopelessness. Misunderstanding of the forgiveness process had led her to believe that she had to choose between her reality or that of her parents.

Correcting these misunderstandings required establishing a trusting relationship, central to which was Helen's confidence in both my spiritual judgment and the soundness of my doctrinal understanding of our shared faith. It also required experience with God's love and mercy and power, acquired both directly and vicariously through my empathy. It further required a painstaking review of Helen's religious beliefs, correcting faulty logic, and placing scriptural injunctions within a broader scriptural context. Finally, this process was helped along by Helen's many personal strengths, including her willingness to take a high level of personal responsibility for her actions, her extraordinary patience and courage, and her desire and willingness to learn and change.

Helen eventually found a new basis for her faith that dramatically improved her emotional sense of well-being and her ability to function independently and interdependently as a contributing member of her community. She learned to see God as a loving father whose ways were just and generous. Although she still struggles with her disabilities, she is not depressed and self-condemning. She accepts assignments in the church, reaches out to others, and displays a sense of humor and a stoic doggedness about solving life's problems.

Perhaps I alone realized the significance of Helen's willingness to offer a spontaneously created personal prayer in front of her entire congregation, a prayer of great sensitivity, tender feeling, and deep insight. Although I am certain that she was nervous, her fear no longer prevented her from participating and sharing her spiritual insights and feelings with others. It still takes Helen almost a minute to write her name, but it takes her no time at all to recognize the spiritual feelings that comfort and direct her life. Although medical, cognitive, and other therapeutic interventions contributed enormously to Helen's treatment, I sincerely doubt that an approach insensitive to her religious beliefs and spiritual desires would have led to such a positive outcome.

Case 8: A Jewish Family

Description of the Therapist. Robert J. Lovinger is a 54-year-old Jewish White man. He is married and has two adult male children. He is a fully licensed psychologist in a semirural area of Michigan with more than 15 years of clinical experience, which consists of a full-time university appointment as a professor in a doctoral-level psychology department where he teaches in the clinical psychology program and a similar number of years of part-time clinical experience, mostly in individual therapy with adults. Lovinger's theoretical orientation is psychoanalytic, primarily object relations. In practice, he is more diverse in considering alternatives if a supportive–expressive modality is not productive.

Lovinger is a member of the local synagogue, which is affiliated with the Conservative movement; he has taught in its religious instruction program and has held positions on the synagogue's board of trustees. His family did not fully observe Jewish dietary laws, although only kosher meat was used in the home. They did observe the Sabbath (in a modified fashion) and the major holidays.

Setting. At the time of this therapy, Lovinger was commuting 1 day a week to a large city in Michigan and was working and consulting in a private office owned by a psychologist acquaintance of his. There were a number of practitioners in the office, but none were employed by the owners of the practice; rather, they were associates, although the premises were owned and furnished by the primaries in the practice.

Client History and Demographic Characteristics. The history and the background of the parents was incomplete and emerged in bits and pieces over time. I typically gather history as it emerges, although I do use a personal information form with individual patients and with couples who seem adequately engaged. The father's notable reluctance from the first phone contact indicated to me that the family's involvement was tenuous and to have focused on securing these data risked the therapy's continuation. I would not have accepted the case to just "fix" the son and not involve the parents even though the son was the identified patient. The history is presented as it developed in treatment.

Presenting Problems and Concerns The father, Mr. Derek S.,[3] called me after having been referred by one of the rabbis I knew in the city. In

---

[3] Although the names have been changed, I made an effort to retain name parallelism because the names chosen have clear emotional significance.

the phone contact, he told of the partial breakdown of their family, culminating with the departure of Dov (meaning *Bear* in Hebrew) in a dispute over Dov's relationship with Mary, a young woman. The woman was about 3 years older than Dov and had an out-of-wedlock child by another man. From this material, I recommended family treatment and Mr. S reluctantly agreed.

Treatment Process and Outcomes. I saw this family for seven sessions. Mr. and Mrs. S. returned 2 years later for marital work for another eight sessions (11½ hr) and then a year later for a single session. In the intake session, Mr. S. and his wife, April, arrived separately from Dov. Both parents were attractive people. Mr. S. appeared to be in his early 40s, was somewhat taller than average, and was trim. Mrs. S. was of average height, slightly plump but also in good condition. She had a somewhat darker complexion than Mr. S. They sat next to each other in the first session. Dov, a youngster of 17, was handsome and sounded mature. I summarized the information I had up to that point. Mrs. S. rapidly asserted her view of Mary (Dov's girlfriend) as "trash," a girl of low morals who had gone out with several boys at the same time. She made it clear that Mary was totally unacceptable and Mr. S. concurred.

When I inquired, Dov acknowledged the involvement, which he saw as continuing but not leading to marriage because he planned to enter the military in about 6 months. When I asked what he liked about Mary, Mrs. S. said "s-e-x" sotto voce, but Dov saw her as active, she liked to do things, and was her own person. Mrs. S. owned a personal appearance and exercise salon that Dov worked in, beginning as a preadolescent, at his mother's invitation. This is where he met Mary, who was employed there, although this information did not emerge until the second session.

The parents asserted that they felt Dov was using them, but the way his voice choked during these discussions made that seem unlikely to me. Most of their communications were directed to me, and I noted that they communicate indirectly, as they were doing in the session, and through rules rather than discussion, a modality unsuited to a 17-year-old. At this, Mrs. S. remarked that her father had a similar mode of relating and that Dov had been "a good kid" and Mr. and Mrs. S. had a "free ride." I suggested that they all had responsibility for their interaction patterns because Dov seemed to accept it too. I also pointed out that Dov obviously cared for them and did not seem to be using them. There appeared to be some recognition of their communication pattern, but Mr. S. was clearly reluctant to continue family sessions. I asserted that the problem was between them and they agreed to return.

By the end of the session, I thought the family communication style might conceal some marital problems, but I kept that suspicion to myself. Mrs. S. was financially successful in her business and, although Mr. S. had a supervisory position in a medical field, I wondered whether he felt overshadowed. I thought the first session was actually fairly successful in engaging the mother and son because there seemed to be some softening of the mother's attitude. The father's reluctance and overall style had a narcissistic edge. The family seemed to be strongly connected to the synagogue and to things Jewish (the younger two children were named Adom [Red] and Ya'akov [Jacob]), although neither parent had either traditional or modern Jewish names.[4]

In the second session, Mrs. S. began by saying that she wanted Dov to come home for Passover but that Mr. S. did not want him to come the first night.[5] I interpreted this as a severe rejection because Dov was the firstborn child as, it later developed, was Mr. S., and the drama of the holiday pivots around the destruction of the firstborn of the Egyptians. Before this could be explored, the discussion shifted to Mary. When I raised the issue of Dov's sexual involvement, he was not able to tell me that he did not want to discuss it without considerable prompting on my part. Mrs. S.'s objections to Mary could not be elaborated beyond her being an employee and having loose morals. Because communication seemed to be a critical problem in the family, it was the major focus for the rest of the session. Although quiet, Mr. S. smiled when I did not look directly at him. Near the end, I suggested that an issue might be control. They feared, I said, that Dov did not love them so they attempted to exercise control through financial generosity. Dov wanted to negotiate a return home and asked about getting material (e.g., a driver's license) to establish his identification, but Mr. S. said Dov could do this through the motor vehicle bureau. Mr. S. seemed bitter and in essence avoided the opportunity to achieve a rapprochement with his son. The next session was in 2 weeks because of Mrs. S.'s scheduled absence. My therapy agreement with the family was that both parents and Dov would attend and that any outside communications were not private.

In the third session, Dov called to verify the appointment time, suggesting an investment in the therapy process. Before they entered the session, his mother gave him a hug. I began to explore their grievances with each other, which were expressed on a superficial level. I reflected them more intensely, and Mrs. S. and Dov agreed but Mr. S. did not and also denied my suggestion that he felt excluded from his relationship with his son. He said he talked with Dov when he had to, but he denied the obvious

---

[4] Jewish names have a definite meaning known to the bearer, and it is customary to give children Hebrew names in addition to more common English names. In the Diaspora, Orthodox Jews typically might have traditional names (e.g., David, Moshe, Avraham, Yitzhak), whereas non-Orthodox Jews who want to give Jewish names might use other names such as Amir (commander) or Guy (valley). The mixture of names suggested that the family was not Orthodox and perhaps adopted a stronger Jewish affiliation later in life.

[5] Outside Israel, the start of Passover was celebrated on the first two nights because of medieval doubts about when the holiday started in the land of Israel, which depends on lunar observations. The first night is often considered more important.

meaning to this. I suggested that Dov was actually very attached to his family and that his relationship with Mary, knowing his family's attitude, was a way to create distance. I also noted that they did not hear the meaning of his entering the military. It was then that it was disclosed that Dov had broken off his relationship with Mary. Mr. S. was resistant to additional sessions, but Mrs. S. and Dov wanted to continue. At the end, as we were leaving, Mr. S. asked whether I had seen the *Shoah*[6] series and I said I had avoided it because it was difficult to watch. He was surprised. In retrospect, I think I made an error because I was not responsive, and I think Mr. S. was reaching out to me to find a common ground, knowing that I was Jewish. My countertransference blocked a more useful therapeutic response.

Later, Mrs. S. called to tell me that my description of Mr. S. being on the outside of the family was accurate, a long-standing problem he was not aware of. She was going to invite Dov for his birthday in spite of Mr. S.'s objections.

In the fourth session, I disclosed the call from Mrs. S., but Mr. S. showed little visible reaction other than to state his requirement that Dov apologize for the breach. Dov expressed that he could say that but that it would not be sincere. I tried to reframe the issue of a developmental thrust in Dov toward differentiation, but Dov did not confirm this interpretation. Toward the end of the session, Mrs. S. said that she was always in the middle, transmitting communications between her husband and son, and I recommended she discontinue this. As the session concluded, Dov began to cry. Mrs. S. tried to comfort him, but Mr. S. did not react.

In the fifth session, the relationships were clear, with father and son facing each other and Mrs. S. in the center. Mr. S. asked whether Dov had been home. He had, but this was not what Mr. S. preferred. Dov wanted to take his bicycle, but his father said no and he would talk with his wife. Inquiry elicited that it was a gift, and, although I noted that a gift made it the receiver's property, both father and son seemed to think that Mr. S. had the right to make this decision. Mrs. S. began to talk for both of them several times, and I remarked on her behavior. Mrs. S. felt that there was a long-standing tension between her husband and son, although neither acknowledged this. Feeling that we had actually achieved the putative goal of therapy and that we were, to some degree, stalled, I asked about their perceptions of each other, and both saw the other as firm and independent. I elicited some history of the parents and on what their mutual attraction was based. Mr. S.'s mother was described as intrusive, and Mr. S. was distant from whatever family he had. He was an only child, and both parents were now deceased. Mr. and Mrs. S. met at Mr. S.'s place of work, and it was disclosed that she was Catholic but that she converted

---

[6] This was a series of filmed interviews with Jewish survivors of the Holocaust as well as Nazis and others.

before they were married.[7] Mr. S.'s mother was vehemently opposed to the marriage, and I drew the parallel between that opposition and Dov's relationship with Mary. I suggested that perhaps this parallel arose out of Dov's love for his father in repeating an aspect of the father's history. Although I thought the evidence for this was speculative, I was attempting to see whether some bridge could be built from the father to the son. Earlier in the session, Mr. S. said that Dov could have his possessions, but at this point he gave Dov his wallet. They left together.

In the sixth session, the S. family assumed the same seating arrangement. I tried to explore the motivation for Dov's actions and departure. I again interpreted this as an effort to individuate, not as an action to hurt his parents, and there seemed to be some acceptance of this. Near the end of the session, I was asked whether the separation could be healed, and I said I thought so but not on the prior basis. Mr. S. seemed a bit warmer to his son.

In the final session, to my surprise, the parents saw the situation as unchanged. They wanted Dov to come home but to acknowledge the breach as his fault. I tried to reframe the breach as having multiple contributors. I tried a paradoxical approach, saying that by asking his son to be at fault, he gave away control. By attributing blame to another, he relinquished control over what was easiest to change: his own behavior. Exploration with Dov made the issue of his desire for separation clearer. I also role-played with Mrs. S. how she might have dealt with Dov about Mary instead of trying to dictate to him, but she had trouble grasping the negotiating process. The session ran over the allotted time, and, at the end, Mr. S. surprised me by saying that I was on target but that he did not want to continue. Although Mrs. S. and Dov wanted to, Mr. S. said that there was no progress. It emerged that Dov had started to ride with them, and I asked them for a final session to discuss their situation. It was left that someone would call, but no one did.

About 2 years later, Mrs. S. called to request marital therapy because she had discovered that Mr. S. had had an affair. In these sessions a good deal of additional information about their styles of relating was revealed. When Mrs. S. discovered the affair, she told her children, her family, and the other woman's husband. Of course, none of this would facilitate healing the marital relationship. She did not want to go to the synagogue or have the children go, but she did not feel like a Christian either. Mr. S., in an individual part of the session, described the marriage as being troubled for a long time. He described incidents that were painful to his self-esteem, such as an argument that developed when the children were young and

---

[7] Conversion before marriage is not uncommon, although, technically, such a conversion is invalid because it is done for an extrinsic reason. My impression was that this was a sincere action on the part of Mrs. S.

asked about witches, which he said did not exist and Mrs. S. interrupted and disagreed.

Another incident he recalled was when Mrs. S. told him that if she could not have children with him, she would go somewhere else. Mrs. S. was furious but also absolute in her views. She wanted explanations for Mr. S.'s behavior, but psychological ones did not satisfy her. Her critical tendencies and his withdrawal became much clearer. Mrs. S.'s family was large, vocal, and expressive, whereas Mr. S.'s mother was a caustic woman who may not have wanted children. Although Mr. S.'s affair suggested that he did not care about her, there was some evidence that he did but that it was not expressed. Her attachment to Judaism was severely strained, and she was thinking of going to a Unitarian church. Later, she stated that she needed to feel that things were rock solid and she left the Catholic Church when "the rules changed," presumably after Vatican II. The presence of children, which he apparently opposed, may have meant the loss of nurturance, and Mrs. S.'s insistence and threat were probably experienced as a major narcissistic insult.

A month's vacation intervened, and the temporary patching of their relationship was strained when she was given a ticket to see a male stripper and she went after asking Mr. S. She missed the meaning in his sarcastic agreement. Each expected the other to know what his or her needs were without making them clear. Neither had any skill in negotiation. Mr. S. tended, under stress, to withdraw or make peremptory demands, whereas Mrs. S., the more expressive one, became rigid and moralistic.

A year later they returned for one session. Mrs. S. had seen Mr. S. in a car conversing with the same woman with whom he had had the affair. He protested his innocence and even offered to take a polygraph test, but she said he would not accept his answer. I recommended individual therapy and offered them names of therapists in their area.

Therapist Commentary

I think Mr. S. grew up in an emotionally deprived but intrusive environment, an only and lonely child. Mrs. S. was much warmer, more expressive, and, growing up Catholic, probably provided a relationship that would not be as anxiety provoking by being too similar to his mother. However, Mr. S.'s largely narcissistic personality made him vulnerable to the ordinary slights and wounds that are inherent in most marriages. His revenge was to seek solace with another woman, something that would hurt Mrs. S. a great deal. Her needs were somewhat less clear, but I speculate that there were significant deficits in her relationship with her father. What might have attracted her to Mr. S. is a not uncommon idea that circulates among some European ethnic groups that "Jewish men make good fathers."

Dov's action in separating himself from his family through an affair with Mary could have appeared to Mr. S. as his son being a "chip off the old block." Instead, it seems to have been experienced as a narcissistic blow; Mr. S. wanted control because he lacked confidence that he merited his son's love.

There were significant countertransference issues because Mr. S. seemed alien to my idea of a Jewish father; his wife, with all her flaws, was closer to my expectation. An irony indeed. I never felt comfortable talking about my Judaism with Mr. S., sensing the degree to which his religion served to shore up a fragile self.

As an analytically oriented therapist, I would have not been comfortable talking about the meanings of Judaism this early in therapy, especially because I sensed that for Mr. S., Judaism had mainly extrinsic value. Had I been clearer about this in my own mind at the time, I might have been able to make myself more available because responding to him as if he were neurotic was not a suitable treatment stance. Spiritually oriented interventions such as prayer or spiritual direction would, I think, usually be inconsistent with how Jews typically function. Scholarly discussion, use of various types of commentaries, analyses of Bible texts and such might form a basis for interventions that are not overtly therapeutic.

Although it is speculative, Mr. S.'s emphasis on being Jewish may have specifically served his fragile self-esteem because it was different in significant ways from the prevailing practices in a religiously conservative, Christian community. A high ethical demand inherent in Judaism may have conferred a distinctive sense of aloof superiority as a member of one of the "chosen people."[8]

It was clear that Mr. S. needed much more in the family sessions even though he achieved his ostensible goals of having Dov return to the family and breaking off his relationship with Mary. I thought that he wanted to humiliate Dov, in addition to his ostensible goal, but that he feared self-exposure in family therapy because his self-image was so fragile. He also may have feared the exposure of his affair. My early impression of marital problems was confirmed, but the lack of clear material in this regard, in addition to his tenuous attachment to the process that did expose painful deficits, suggested that Mr. S. would not have tolerated dealing with his failure both as a husband and as a father.

GENERAL COMMENTS ON THE CASE STUDIES

These cases illustrate different ways that clients' religious and spiritual beliefs and issues may be relevant in treatment and the variety of ways that therapists may choose to respond to these issues. Amidst the diversity found

---

[8] The notion of being chosen as conferring a moral or other superiority is entirely incompatible with normative Jewish thinking.

in these cases, there were also some important similarities, that we believe illustrate some of the important principles of an effective spiritual strategy. In all cases, the therapists viewed the clients' religious and spiritual beliefs and backgrounds as being important. Most of the therapists clinically assessed in what ways the clients' spiritual beliefs were intertwined with and contributed to the presenting problems and clinical issues. Many also were alert to ways in which the clients' spiritual beliefs and communities could be used as a therapeutic resource. The therapists also sought to demonstrate respect for and sensitivity to the clients' religious backgrounds and issues, even though at times this was challenging because countertransference issues (e.g., Lovinger) were present.

In all cases, the therapists worked within the clients' value systems, although, when needed, they were not reticent about examining and challenging religious beliefs that were dysfunctional or that were inconsistent with the doctrines of clients' religious traditions. Most of the therapists used one or more spiritual interventions during treatment. The spiritual interventions were not used in isolation but were integrated into secular approaches and techniques. When used, it appears that the spiritual interventions enhanced the clients' growth and healing above and beyond what could have been accomplished with secular interventions alone. We think that these cases provide a fascinating glimpse into the therapeutic potential of spiritual interventions and the variety of applications of a spiritual strategy.

IV
RESEARCH AND FUTURE DIRECTIONS

12

A THEISTIC, SPIRITUAL VIEW OF SCIENCE AND RESEARCH METHODS

I want to know how God created this world . . . I want to know His thoughts, the rest are details.

—*Albert Einstein*

If a spiritual strategy is to take its place alongside other major theories of personality and psychotherapy, it is crucial for those with interests in it to subject their ideas and practices to the scrutiny of empirical research. As we have noted throughout this book, there is much that is not known in this domain. For example, in what ways do different religious and spiritual beliefs influence personality development? When and how do spiritual practices promote physical and psychological healing? What types of spiritual interventions are most efficacious with what types of clients and problems? If psychologists are to gain more insight into these and many other important questions, much research is needed.

We recognize that there are major challenges associated with conducting research on spiritual phenomena. The study of such phenomena was excluded from psychological science more than 100 years ago because many researchers believed that it was impossible to study "subjective" and "invisible" experiences. More recently, some theorists have raised concerns that the assumptions and methods of traditional science themselves may preclude the valid study of spiritual phenomena (e.g., Slife, Hope, & Nebeker, 1996).

We agree that there are real difficulties associated with the scientific study of spirituality. Perhaps the research methodologies are, and will always be, fundamentally limited for studying spiritual phenomena. Perhaps they will never allow researchers to fully unlock the complexities and mysteries in this domain. We think, however, that research *can* help psychologists learn a great deal in this domain, at least much more than is currently known. As long as researchers recognize the limitations that their assumptions and research methodologies impose on their knowledge (Howard, 1986; Slife et al., 1996) and avoid the mistaken view that a phenomenon that cannot be directly observed with our senses or measurement instruments is therefore not real, they can proceed with the research enterprise, gaining what understanding and knowledge they can from it.

In this chapter, we first briefly review the major "ways of knowing" available to human beings. We then discuss a theistic view of epistemology and the implications of this view for our understanding of the research process. We define and discuss methodological pluralism and why we endorse it. We conclude by briefly describing major quantitative and qualitative research designs and the contributions they can make to the study of a spiritual strategy in personality and psychotherapy.

WAYS OF KNOWING

As we discussed in chapter 2, epistemology is the branch of philosophy that concerns itself with the nature and sources of knowledge (Percesepe, 1991). Most philosophers agree that there are a limited number of "ways of knowing" or sources of knowledge (e.g., Madsen, 1995; Percesepe, 1991). The most commonly acknowledged ones include *authority, sense experience/ empiricism, reason,* and *intuition/inspiration* (Madsen, 1995; Percesepe, 1991).

Authority

One way for us to gain knowledge is to seek it from experts or "authorities" in a given field, whether they be scientific, religious, or legal ones. One advantage of relying on authority as a source of knowledge is that we can learn from the experience, knowledge, and insights of others. We do not have to "reinvent the wheel." This can save us a great deal of time and effort. A major disadvantage of relying on authorities is that they can be wrong. History is replete with examples of religious and scientific "authorities" who were mistaken in their understandings of the world.

Sense Experience/Empiricism

Another way for us to gain knowledge is to observe the world with our senses, that is, by seeing, hearing, touching, tasting, and smelling the world (Percesepe, 1991). People who believe that the best way to gain a knowledge of the world is through their sensory experiences are called *empiricists* (Percesepe, 1991). Modern science is based on a belief in empiricism. One advantage of relying on one's sensory experiences as a source of knowledge is that such knowledge is grounded in observable facts. When people have observed a phenomenon for themselves (e.g., that the Earth is round), they no longer need to rely on the opinions of others or on logic or intellectual speculation.

One major disadvantage of relying on sense experience is that it is not possible to observe all phenomena in the world and universe, even with the aid of observational and measurement instruments. Clark (1971) pointed out that

> the five senses have their limitations. The unreliability of touch is exemplified by the "burn" which cold metal can give. Taste is not only notoriously subjective—"one man's meat, another man's poison"—but is also governed, to an extent not yet fully known, by genetic inheritance. So, too, smell is an indicator whose gross incapacity in humans is thrown into relief by insects that can identify members of their species at ranges of up to a mile. Sound is hardly any better. The pattern of "reality" heard by the human is different from that heard by the dog—witness the "soundless" dog whistles of trainers; while the "real" world of the near sightless bat is one in which "real" objects are "seen"—and avoided—by ultrasonic waves which play no part in the construction of the external human world.
>
> And sight . . . is perhaps the most illusory of all senses. . . . All that unaided human physiology allows in the visual search for the world around—comes through only a narrow slit in a broad curtain . . . The landscape seen with human eyes is dramatically different, yet no more "real," than the scene captured on the infrared plate and showing a mass of detail beyond human vision. . . .
>
> Thus the human species is unconsciously and inevitably selective in describing the nature of the physical world in which it lives and moves. (pp. 91–92)

Another disadvantage of relying only on sense experience as a source of knowledge is that observations and facts alone are not meaningful (Percesepe, 1991). People's sensory experiences and observations need to be organized and interpreted, and to do this people must use their reasoning abilities and prior knowledge. It is here that people's conceptual schemas and limitations influence and bias their interpretations of their experiences and observations.

Reason

Another way for people to gain knowledge is through thought or reason. Philosophers who believe reason is the primary source of knowledge are called *rationalists* (Percesepe, 1991). Rationalism is "the view that the human mind is sufficient in itself to discover truth by apprehending relations of ideas" (Percesepe, 1991, p. 161). One advantage of using reason as a source of knowledge is that people do not have to rely on the opinions of others; they can think things through for themselves. Reasoning about an issue also gives people a way of trying to gain understanding about a phenomenon when they are unable to use their senses to observe the truth about it.

One major disadvantage of relying only on reason as a source of knowledge is that it is possible to "construct a rationalistic system of beliefs that is internally consistent, noncontradictory, *and completely unrelated to the world we live in!*" (Percesepe, 1991, p. 163). Another disadvantage is that human reasoning and judgment capacities may be fundamentally limited. Human reasoning about complex phenomena may be more likely to result in errors than sound judgment or knowledge (Faust, 1984).

Intuition and Inspiration

Another way for people to gain knowledge is through intuition and inspiration. According to Percesepe (1991), intuition

> may be defined as the ability to have direct, immediate knowledge of something without relying on the conscious use of reason or sense perception. In its most general sense, it may simply mean a direct, unmediated, privileged knowledge of one's own personhood. In its strongest sense intuition can mean a type of mystical experience that gives a person direct access to a higher way of knowledge. (p. 164)

Percesepe (1991) provided examples of intuition, including the "experience of the lived body," the "rapid insight that specialists often display in their field," "artistic and religious experiences," and "our knowledge of good and evil" (pp. 164–165). One advantage of intuition as a source of knowledge is that it seems to allow people access to knowledge that is not available to use through rational or empirical means. Another is that intuitive insights or hunches often are experienced as holistic and integrative and affect those who experience them in powerful and meaningful ways.

A disadvantage of intuitive ways of knowing is that they can "land us in a mystical nowhere-land" (Percesepe, 1991, p. 165) totally cut off from reality. In other words, not all intuitive experiences can be trusted as valid; some may be delusions or hallucinations. In addition, intuitive ways of knowing are not well understood, controlled or used easily, or easy to verify or replicate publicly.

In the behavioral sciences, sense experience or empiricism has been viewed historically as the most valid way of knowing, although the importance of reason in the research enterprise has been acknowledged. Scientific and psychological "authorities," such as prominent leaders in the field, have also frequently been viewed as important sources of knowledge, but religious "authorities," such as Scriptures and the words of religious leaders, have been spurned. Intuition also has been almost totally disregarded as a way of knowing in the behavioral sciences.

A THEISTIC VIEW OF EPISTEMOLOGY

An important contribution that the theistic, spiritual worldview makes to the understanding of epistemology is that it affirms that religious authority and intuition and inspiration can be valid sources of knowledge. As we discussed in chapter 4, according to the theistic worldview, God has spiritually inspired and enlightened prophets and other holy men and women. Scriptures are thought to contain a record of the inspiration and revelation that God has given in the past to spiritual leaders, and many believers therefore view them as a valid source of knowledge and truth. Many believers also accept the words of modern-day spiritual leaders as inspired and authoritative. Inspiration through God's spirit to individual lay believers also is viewed by many people as a valid source of truth or way of knowing.

Although the theistic world religions may teach that religious authority and intuition and inspiration are the most trustworthy ways of knowing, they do not discount all other ways of gaining knowledge and understanding. According to the theistic worldview, people can learn and know much through their sensory experiences and reason. The belief that sense experience and reason are the only legitimate or valid ways of knowing does conflict with the theistic worldview. Strict empiricism or rationalism therefore is rejected. An epistemologically pluralistic view is most consistent with the theistic worldview. Authority, sense experience, reason, and intuition and inspiration all provide ways of gaining understanding and knowledge, although, as discussed earlier, each has its limitations. Inspiration from God is the most valued, authoritative source of knowledge.

A THEISTIC VIEW OF THE SCIENTIFIC PROCESS

An important contribution the theistic view of epistemology makes to our understanding of the scientific process is that it affirms that intuitive, inspirational ways of knowing may be a part of the scientific discovery process. The traditional view of the scientific process has been that scientists (a) use reason to formulate theories and hypotheses and (b) test their theories and hypotheses through sensory observation (collecting empirical data). Sensory observations are thought to lead to theory refinement and the generation of further hypotheses. Scientists may to some extent rely on authority in the sense that they build on the theories and research of other authorities in the field; however, sensory (empirical) observation is viewed as the primary epistemological method. Intuitive, inspirational processes are generally de-emphasized or ignored entirely.

There has been considerable interest in the academic world regarding the question of where great ideas and scientific discoveries come from (Bergin, 1979). For example, 70 years ago, in *The Art of Thought*, Graham Wallas, a professor emeritus at the University of London, examined this question. Wallas (1926) concluded that there are "three stages in the formation of a new thought" (p. 80): the preparation, incubation, and illumination stages.

Wallas described the *preparation stage* as a "hard, conscious, systematic, and fruitless analysis of the problem" (p. 81). During this stage, scientists become interested in a topic or problem, learn all they can about it, and think about it and examine it from various perspectives. During the *incubation stage*, the scientist does "not voluntarily or consciously think on a particular problem, and . . . a series of unconscious and involuntary . . . mental events may take place during that period" (p. 86). During this stage, the scientist relaxes (e.g., goes for a walk, goes sailing, takes a nap) and allows the brain to digest what he or she has learned. Wallas (1926) described the *illumination stage* as "the appearance of the 'happy idea' together with the psychological events which immediately preceded and accompanied that appearance" (p. 80). Wallas further explained that the flashes of insight that come in the illumination stage often are preceded by feelings of "intimation" that the flash of insight is coming. Wallas (1926) also described a *verification stage*, a period that follows the formation of the new thought "in which both the validity of the idea [is] tested, and the idea itself [is] reduced to exact form" (p. 81).

Neal E. Miller, a National Science Medal winner, described two phases of the scientific process: discovery and proof (Bergin & Strupp, 1972). As can be seen in the following quote, Miller's discovery phase seems to correspond well with the first three stages of Wallas's (1926) model.

> During the discovery or exploratory phase, I am interested in finding a phenomenon, gaining some understanding of the most significant conditions that affect it. . . . During this phase I am quite free-wheeling and intuitive—follow hunches, vary procedures, try out wild ideas, and take short-cuts. During it, I usually am not interested in elaborate controls. (Miller, in Bergin & Strupp, 1972, p. 348)

Miller's proof phase seems to correspond with Wallas's (1926) verification stage.

After I believe I have discovered a phenomenon and understand something about it comes the next phase of convincingly and rigorously proving this to myself and to the rest of the scientific community. . . . During this phase it is essential to use the controls that demonstrate that the phenomenon really is what one thinks it is. (Miller, quoted in Bergin & Strupp, 1972, p. 348)

Many scientists, musicians, and artists have described the intuitive, inspirational nature of the illumination or discovery phases of the scientific and artistic processes. For example, Helmholtz, the great German physicist, explained that after investigating "in all directions," his most important new thoughts came to him "unexpectedly without effort, like inspiration" (quoted in Wallas, 1926, p. 80). In discussing Albert Einstein, Bergin (1979, p. 450) said that

one cannot help but be intrigued by the question of where he got his ideas. His paper on the special theory of relativity, written in the summer of 1905 when he was twenty-six, was astonishing. This paper, which turned the scientific world upside down, ["lacked the notes and references which give weight to most serious expositions" (Clark, 1971, p. 73)]. . . . Einstein once declared that he "created it out of whole cloth." R. W. Clark said: "Today, two-thirds of a century after Einstein posted the manuscript of his paper to *Annalen der Physik*, the dust is still stirred by discussion of what inspired him" (Clark, 1971, p. 74). Einstein once reflected on the fact that even in his youth he had intimations of his later concepts. He also said

> When I examine myself and my methods of thought I come to the conclusion that the gift of fantasy has meant more to me than my talent for absorbing positive knowledge. . . . (quoted in Clark, 1971, p. 87). The mind can proceed only so far upon what it knows and can prove. There comes a point where the mind takes a higher plane of knowledge, but can never prove how it got there. All great discoveries have involved such a leap [of faith] (quoted in Clark, 1971, p. 622).

Mozart amazed his friends with flashes of insight and intuitions (Percesepe, 1991). Kekule von Stadonitz, the German chemist who was a founder of structural organic chemistry and introduced the cyclic structure of benzene, "had a visionary experience in which he perceived the ends of swirling molecules bending and touching one another to form a ring" (Bergin, 1979, p. 451). In discussing inspirational dreams, the prominent psychiatrist Kenneth Colby stated that "in the final analysis no one knows where great ideas come from—they are a gift from God" (quoted in Bergin & Strupp, 1972, pp. 280–281).

According to the theistic worldview, many great ideas, creations, and discoveries *are* gifts from God. Through intuition and inspiration, God enlightens human beings to make great discoveries and creations to benefit humanity. We do not, of course, expect all behavioral scientists to accept this notion. It certainly is possible to accept the well-documented fact that the scientific process involves creative, intuitive processes without attributing such creativity and intuitive insights to transcendent spiritual influences. For such researchers, the theistic view of the scientific process can simply serve as a reminder to them that the scientific process cannot easily be reduced to reason and empirical observations alone and that the creative, intuitive aspects of this process must be acknowledged and should perhaps be valued. For researchers who believe in the theistic view that intuition and inspiration is at the core of scientific discovery, it would seem that they should more consistently exercise faith in God and humbly seek for such enlightenment in their research and scholarly endeavors.

THEISTIC REALISM

As we discussed in chapter 2, the behavioral sciences were built on a 19th-century view of science and adopted classical realism, positivism, and empiricism as working assumptions. These assumptions have been challenged and found wanting (Kuhn, 1970; Lakatos & Musgrave, 1970; Manicas & Secord, 1983; Polanyi, 1962). It is now recognized that science is a value- and theory-laden process, that complete objectivity is impossible, and that scientific theories cannot be proved true or falsified easily (Kuhn, 1970; Lakatos & Musgrave, 1970; Polanyi, 1962). Several scholars also have pointed out that the research methodologies themselves can limit or distort one's understanding of the world (Howard, 1986; Slife et al., 1996). As expressed by Howard (1986),

> most researchers believe that by employing appropriate research methodology and proper experimental controls, one comes to a more precise and accurate understanding of the relationships among variables in the world. Many of the distortions and misperceptions associated with naïve observation and commonsense knowing can be avoided by utilizing experimental paradigms with their appropriate methodological controls. Research methodologies, however, do not always provide a clear and undistorted view of the world. It is simply not true that experimental methodology affords researchers a set of glasses through which the world may be glimpsed as it truly exists. (pp. 19–20)

Although we accept this revised view of science and its methods, we do not agree with some relativists who believe that there are no criteria of truth and that it is impossible to establish that some theories, ideas, practices, or behaviors are better than others (Slife & Williams, 1995). We agree with Manicas and Secord (1983) that "there is a world that exists independently of cognizing experience. Since our theories are constitutive of the known world but *not* of the *world*, we may always be wrong, but *not* anything goes" (p. 401). Howard (1986) suggested that commonsense knowledge and scientific knowledge are both

> stationed on a continuum anchored at one end by total skepticism or solipsism, in which we give up knowing or science, and anchored at the other end by total credulity. Ordinary knowing and science are in between these extremes and somehow combine a capacity for focused distrust and revision with a belief in the common body of knowledge claims. It follows from *this imperfect yet improvable* view of scientific knowledge that the cumulative revision of scientific knowledge becomes possible through a process of trusting (tentatively at least) the great bulk of current scientific and commonsense belief ("knowledge") and using it to discredit and revise one aspect of scientific belief. (pp. 20–21)

It also is important to note that such critiques of scientific models and of classical realism began not long after Newton established the "laws" of the physical universe. In the 19th century, many sophisticated scientists and philosophers proposed essentially the same arguments against classical realism that are heard today from some postmodernists. Indeed, it was the critical and original work of Kirchhoff, Mach, Maxwell, and others that laid the foundation of relativity theory, and then came quantum mechanics, and the mechanical picture of the universe disintegrated. Much of philosophy and science during most of the 20th century has been devoted to creating alternative views.

Who can question the greatness of the contributions of Newton and his contemporaries and followers who laid the foundation of modern science and technology? Indeed, it is ironic that some people with theistic and spiritual perspectives are so quick to criticize the modernist-Newtonian worldview when Newton, the great originator, was himself a devoted theistic Christian who believed that his work was inspired by God. He always believed that his work on nature was only a small part of God's picture of the universe, never the full picture. He maintained that God's power, influence, and presence were behind and in the phenomena of nature (Burtt, 1955).

According to *theistic realism* (Bergin, 1980a), it is possible to gain valid understanding and knowledge about the world. Researchers' understanding and knowledge will always be incomplete and somewhat limited by their culture and context, and it should always be held tentatively, but researchers need not lapse into relativism or nihilism (i.e., the belief that all values are baseless and that nothing can be known or communicated). By seeking knowledge and understanding through reason, sensory experience, authority, and intuition and inspiration, human beings can advance in their understanding and knowledge of truth. Thus, according to theistic realism, the scientific process at its best combines all four major ways of knowing rigorously and creatively.

METHODOLOGICAL PLURALISM

We believe that the professions of psychology and psychotherapy need to embrace a methodologically pluralistic approach to research. The term *methodological pluralism* refers to the practice of using a wide range of research designs, methods, and strategies, including quantitative and qualitative ones (Greenberg, Elliot, & Lietaer, 1994; Kazdin, 1994). Such an approach is more consistent with a theistic view of epistemology than is strict empiricism, and we think that it also is more consistent with current views in the philosophy of science.

To some extent, a movement toward methodological pluralism has already begun in psychology and psychotherapy. The postmodern critiques of 19th- and 20th-century science have broken down the rigid adherence to traditional experimental and quantitative research designs and methodologies. Qualitative, ethnographic, naturalistic, and phenomenological methodologies have been proposed and are being used with increasing frequency (e.g., Kirk & Miller, 1986; Lincoln & Guba, 1985; Reichardt & Cook, 1979). We think that this is fortunate because such approaches hold considerable promise for broadening and deepening the understanding of human beings and the complexities of personality, psychotherapy, and therapeutic change. We endorse these methodologies as long as they are used carefully and rigorously. We also endorse the continued use of traditional quantitative methodologies, including experimental, quasi-experimental, correlational, survey, single-subject, process, and discovery-oriented designs.

We recognize that some scholars view the quantitative (modernistic or positivistic) and qualitative (postmodern) research paradigms as being incompatible (e.g., Lincoln & Guba, 1985). Although these paradigms are based on seemingly conflicting assumptions about the nature of the world and science (Lincoln & Guba, 1985; Slife et al., 1996), we think that neither their assumptions nor methods are all necessarily mutually exclusive. Each paradigm offers a different language, "lenses," and methods through which researchers can seek to study and understand the world. The truth about the world and science may fall somewhere in between the philosophical and methodological extremes of these two paradigms. As researchers embrace a methodologically pluralistic approach to the research enterprise, however, it is certainly important for them to understand the underlying assumptions of the positivistic (quantitative) and postmodern (qualitative or naturalistic) paradigms and how these may limit or filter what they can know (Howard, 1986; Slife et al., 1996).

Lincoln and Guba's (1985) book, *Naturalistic Inquiry*, provides a helpful discussion of the assumptions of the positivistic and naturalistic (postmodern) paradigms. Table 12.1 is reprinted from their book and briefly contrasts some of the assumptions of these two paradigms. Slife et al. (1996) also have recently written an important article that makes explicit some of

TABLE 12.1
Contrasting Positivistic and Naturalistic (Postmodern) Axioms

Axioms about	Positivist paradigm	Naturalistic paradigm
The nature of reality	Reality is single, tangible, and fragmentable.	Realities are multiple, constructed, and holistic.
The relationship of knower to the known	Knower and known are independent, a dualism.	Knower and known are interactive, inseparable.
The possibility of generalization	Time- and context-free generalizations (nomothetic statements) are possible.	Only time- and context-bound working hypotheses (idiographic statements) are possible.
The possibility of causal linkages	There are real causes, temporally precedent to or simultaneous with their effects.	All entities are in a state of mutual simultaneous shaping, so that it is impossible to distinguish causes from effects.
The role of values	Inquiry is value-free.	Inquiry is value-bound.

Reprinted from Lincoln, Y.S., & Guba, E.G. (1985). *Naturalistic inquiry* (p. 37). Beverly Hills, CA: Sage. Copyright 1985 by Sage Publications. Reprinted by permission.

the underlying assumptions of modernistic scientific (quantitative) methods and contrasts them with postmodern (qualitative) ones. In Table 12.2 we summarize these assumptions and their methodological implications.

Slife et al. (1996) explained that modernistic science assumes that if a phenomenon cannot be operationalized, repeated or replicated, and reduced into smaller parts, factors, or dimensions, its reality or truth status is suspect. Slife et al. pointed out that such methodological requirements are based on the assumptions of universalism, materialism, and atomism, assumptions that are not necessarily true. Because these assumptions are open to debate, researchers should not proceed as if they were valid, as they commonly have during the past century. Slife et al. also argued that these assumptions create difficulties for researchers who study spirituality with modernistic methods because the researchers must alter their conceptions of spirituality to fit the assumptions of the modernistic methods (i.e., that spiritual phenomena must be operationalizable, repeatable or replicable, and subdividable into smaller parts, factors, or dimensions).

Slife et al. (1996) also discussed the alternative postmodern assumptions of contextuality, lived experience, and radical holism and the methodological implications of such views. The assumption of contextuality implies that researchers should not expect that findings in one research study will be repeated or replicated across time, places, or people because each study is context bound. Researchers should be less concerned about replication and generalization. Instead, they can search for "experiential patterns,"

TABLE 12.2
Assumptions and Methodological Implications of Modernistic and Postmodern Research Paradigms

Modernistic		Postmodern	
Assumptions	Methodological implications	Assumptions	Methodological implications
Universalism: This is "the notion that natural laws—because they are lawful—do not change in time or space . . . a law should work universally; otherwise, it only applies to one point in time and space and thus is not lawful (or truthful)" (Slife, Hope, & Nebeker, 1996, p. 11).	If a finding is valid or real, researchers in different places and times should be able to replicate it (observe it again). Valid findings should be generalizable to other times, participants, and settings.	Contextuality: There are not "timeless, immutable laws that occur without regard to context" (Slife et al., 1996, p. 26). There are "experiential 'patterns' or 'regularities' that are culturally and contextually bound. That is, they pertain to and must be wholly understood within the context in which they are found—potentially unique and nonrepeatable" (Slife et al., 1996, pp. 26–27).	Researchers should not randomly sample or attempt to replicate the findings of other researchers. They should deliberately study in context only the persons or group of interest without concern for generalizability or repeatability.
Materialism: This "postulates that the real is the visible and tangible things of the world that exist independently of the observer" (Slife et al., 1996, p. 12).	Researchers must be able to observe and measure the phenomena they study with one or more of the five senses. Inner or invisible phenomena must be operationalized (defined) in	Lived experience: "Our lived experience offers us far more than what comes through our senses, including our feelings, mental events, and even spiritual events" (Slife et al.,	Researchers should not worry about trying to use "objective" methods such as standardized tests, observational schemes, or statistics because such methods indicate little about

A SPIRITUAL STRATEGY FOR COUNSELING AND PSYCHOTHERAPY

an observable, measurable way.	1996, p. 25). "Instead of focusing on an observable, material reality that is considered to be 'behind' changing experience," we should "focus on experience itself. . . . No one, including the most rigorous of scientist, gets outside their experiences" (Slife et al., 1996, p. 25).		people's "lived experience," nor do they entirely remove the influence of the observer. Researchers should use themselves as a research "instrument" by using methods such as participant observation and interviews to understand people's perceptions, understandings, and experiences.
Atomism: This is "the notion that the material objects of our observation and knowledge can themselves be separated and divided into variables, constructs, and laws that are smaller and presumably more basic than their larger counterparts. These atoms contain within themselves all the essential properties of the larger units" (Slife et al., 1996, pp. 12–13).	Radical holism: "Rather than postulating that the whole is derived from more fundamental, atomic parts "out there" in material reality," radical holism posits that "the parts themselves depend upon the whole for their very existence" (Slife et al., 1996, p. 26).	Theorists and researchers should subdivide phenomena into smaller parts, factors, dimensions, or units to better explain and study them. Methods that help researchers do this, such as factor analysis and factorial research designs, are helpful.	Researchers should study phenomena holistically and phenomenologically. They should not try to break things into parts, factors, or dimensions or use methods for doing this such as factor analysis and factorial experimental designs.

Adapted from Slife, Hope, and Nebeker (1996) with permission.

that is, "regularities that are culturally and contextually bound" (Slife et al., 1996, p. 26), but they should not elevate them to the status of immutable laws. The assumption of lived experience implies that researchers should be less concerned about using objective, operationalized, standardized, and quantitative methods and more willing to use subjective, qualitative, and participatory ones. Rather than attempting to gain detached insight into laws and principles of human behavior stripped of their context, they should seek to understand people's perceptions, experiences, understandings, and meanings. The assumption of radical holism implies that researchers should be less concerned about subdividing phenomena into factors, dimensions, and dependent and independent variables using methods such as factor analysis and experimental designs. Rather, they should study phenomena more globally, holistically, and phenomenologically.

Slife et al. (1996) argued that the assumptions and qualitative methods of postmodernism may be more compatible with spiritual views of reality. They encouraged spirituality researchers to consider the assumptions they are adopting carefully and the conceptual "costs" of these assumptions before deciding what methods to use in their study of spiritual phenomena. We agree with this recommendation. We also think that "modernistic," or quantitative, research methods clearly do not need to be discarded in the study of spirituality. Although such methods may in some ways distort and limit the understanding of spiritual phenomena, they also can help researchers learn much in this domain. As long as researchers keep in mind the advantages and limitations of both quantitative and qualitative methodologies as they use them, progress can be made and they can avoid discounting or ignoring phenomena simply because they do not conform to their methodological assumptions.

MAJOR RESEARCH DESIGNS AND THEIR CONTRIBUTIONS TO A SPIRITUAL STRATEGY

We now briefly describe some of the major quantitative and qualitative research designs and discuss how they can contribute to the study of a spiritual strategy in personality and psychotherapy. We do not describe in detail here the various research designs because this has been done in numerous books and articles on research methodologies (e.g., Borg & Gall, 1989; Denzin & Lincoln, 1994; Greenberg, 1986; Heppner, Kivlighan, & Wampold, 1992; Kazdin, 1994; J. M. Morse & Field, 1995; Ray & Ravizza, 1988; Rice & Greenberg, 1984). Our purpose is to briefly describe the defining characteristics of the major designs, their main strengths and weaknesses, and the types of research questions regarding a spiritual strategy that they are most suitable for investigating. Although it is somewhat too simplistic to classify research designs into quantitative and qualitative categories because some research designs (e.g., survey, single subject, and discovery oriented) combine elements of each paradigm, we group them in this manner for convenience and to highlight which paradigm (positivistic or postmodern) each design has been predominantly associated with historically.

Quantitative Research Designs

There are several quantitative research designs. In Table 12.3 we summarize the key characteristics of six quantitative research designs that we believe have the potential for furthering the understanding of a spiritual strategy: analogue, survey, experimental (including quasi-experimental), correlational, single-subject, and discovery-oriented designs. Research on religious and spiritual issues in mental health and psychotherapy has been dominated by analogue, survey, correlational, and experimental designs. Worthington, Kurusu, McCollough, and Sanders's (1996) comprehensive *Psychological Bulletin* review describes numerous applications of these designs. These studies have yielded considerable insight into a variety of issues relevant to a spiritual strategy, including "(a) religion and mental health, (b) religion and coping with stress, (c) religious people's views of the world, (d) preferences and expectations about religion and counseling, and (e) religious clients' responses to counseling" (Worthington et al., 1996, p. 451). In Table 12.4 we summarize some of the major conclusions from the Worthington et al. review. We expect that analogue, survey, correlational, and experimental designs will continue to make valuable contributions to the advancement of a spiritual strategy.

Few therapy outcome studies of religious and spiritual therapies have been conducted (Worthington et al., 1996). Therapy outcome studies in which rigorous experimental designs have been used are time-consuming and expensive, but they are essential for investigating outcome questions such as the following: Are spiritual treatment approaches and interventions effective? What types of changes do they promote? Are spiritual treatment approaches more or less effective than secular ones? Is psychotherapy more effective when secular and spiritual approaches are integrated? With what types of clients and problems are spiritual interventions most effective? We hope that during the next decade, many more experimental therapy outcome studies will be done to investigate these and other questions.

We think that single-subject and discovery-oriented research designs (Greenberg, 1986; Kazdin, 1994; Mahrer, 1988) also have great potential for contributing to the advancement of a spiritual strategy. Although these designs are more limited in terms of their internal and external validity, they are more feasible to carry out in clinical settings because they are less intrusive, ethically problematic, costly, and time-consuming. They also are more clinically relevant in that they allow the exploration of research ques-

TABLE 12.3
Comparison of Major Quantitative Research Designs or Strategies

Design or strategy	Defining characteristic	Types of research questions	Type of data	Major advantages	Major limitations
Analog	Simulation of psychotherapy, does not study actual therapy situations.	Causal questions. How do different therapist, client, or process variables affect therapy process and outcomes (e.g., client religiosity)?	Quantitative measures and ratings from trained judges	Rigorous experimental control is possible. Good for addressing causal questions about the relationship between religiosity and therapy outcomes and processes.	Limited external (ecological) validity. Generalizing to real therapy situations is difficult.
Survey	Participants are contacted by phone or mail and asked to describe their beliefs, attitudes, and practices.	Good for describing therapists' and clients' attitudes, beliefs, and behaviors (e.g., clients' religious beliefs and practices).	Relatively brief, researcher-constructed questionnaires	Good for describing the self-reported religious and spiritual characteristics, beliefs, and behaviors of a population.	Relies only on self-report data with all of its potential distortions. Cannot establish causality.
Correlational	The relationship between two or more variables is explored through correlational statistics or causal-comparative methods.	What is the relationship between variables (e.g., what is the relationship between religious devoutness and various indicators of mental health)?	Quantitative measures	Good for exploring associations among religious and mental health variables when experimental manipulations of variables is not possible.	Cannot establish causal relationships.

	Procedure	Research questions	Measures	Strengths	Weaknesses
Therapy outcome study (experimental)	Random assignment to treatment conditions and control groups is used in actual therapy situations.	Are spiritual treatment approaches effective? Which spiritual treatments are most effective with what clients and problems?	Quantitative outcome measures and ratings from trained judges	Can demonstrate treatment effects and differences between various spiritual therapy approaches and between spiritual and secular approaches.	Difficult to conduct in real therapy situations: expensive, time-consuming, difficult to control all confounding variables, and ethical concerns with using control groups.
Single subject	Study one client at a time. Take repeated outcome and process measurements over the course of treatment.	Did a specific spiritual intervention work? What components of a spiritual approach were most effective? What in-session spiritual interventions or processes were associated with what outcomes?	Quantitative outcome and process measures and ratings from trained judges	High ecological validity. Feasible for therapists to use in clinical settings. Can demonstrate treatment effects of spiritual interventions and isolate the effects of specific spiritual components of treatment.	Limited external and internal validity unless the design is repeated many times with many clients and therapists.
Discovery-oriented or change process	Study significant "change" events in therapy and their immediate and long-term impact on process and outcome.	How did an in-session spiritual event or intervention affect the immediate (and long-term) processes and outcomes of therapy?	Quantitative and qualitative process and outcome measures or descriptions of clients and therapists	Clinically relevant. Good for understanding important spiritual "change events" in therapy.	Limited internal and external validity. Exploratory and descriptive in nature.

Sources consulted included Borg and Gall (1989), Greenberg (1986), Heppner, Kivlighan, and Wampold (1992), Kazdin (1994), Ray and Ravizza (1988), and Rice and Greenberg (1984).

TABLE 12.4
Major Conclusions From Worthington, Kurusu, McCollough, and Sanders's (1996) Review on Religion and Psychotherapeutic Processes

1. Most research has been done on potential, not actual, clients.

2. Numerous studies have investigated the relation between religion and mental health, personality, social behavior, and coping. Generally, these studies provide considerable evidence that religion is beneficial. Certain types of religiousness (e.g., intrinsic) appear to be healthier than others (e.g., extrinsic).

3. Several studies have been done on how religious beliefs and values influence expectations and preferences in counseling. Generally, religiously devout clients prefer and trust counselors with similar religious beliefs and values.

4. Several studies have examined the religious beliefs and practices of psychotherapists. Psychotherapists tend, on average, to be less religious than clients, although less so than was previously believed. Religious therapists are more likely to view religion as being relevant to treatment and to use spiritual interventions.

5. Large numbers of clergy provide mental health therapy, and in some localities clergy are more popular as a source of counseling than are mental health professionals. Little is known empirically about the effectiveness of the counseling provided by clergy, spiritual directors, and chaplains.

6. A few studies have been done on whether the religion of the therapist, client, or both influences clinical judgment. This research has been inconclusive, and more studies are needed.

7. Several studies have investigated the referral practices of mental health professionals and clergy. Generally, mental health professionals refer clients to clergy rarely. Clergy refer difficult cases to mental health professionals, particularly when they know and agree with the professional's religious values.

8. Numerous studies have been conducted on prayer, forgiveness, and meditation. In general, this research provides support for the therapeutic use of these practices.

9. Several outcome studies have examined the effectiveness of religious cognitive therapy interventions. Generally, these studies have shown that religious cognitive therapy is as effective as secular cognitive therapy and sometimes slightly more effective. Nonreligious therapists have successfully used religious cognitive therapy.

---

tions that are more meaningful to psychotherapists (Barlow, Hayes, & Nelson, 1984; Greenberg, 1986; Kazdin, 1994; Mahrer, 1988).

Single-subject designs could prove especially useful for evaluating the effectiveness of religious and spiritual interventions. Psychotherapists in clinical settings can use these designs relatively easily to evaluate their own practices. In a single-subject study, the client serves as his or her own control. By measuring changes in the client's symptoms or problems over time, the impact of the treatment can be seen (Kazdin, 1994). If therapists who use spiritual interventions in clinical settings are willing to invest the relatively small amount of effort needed to administer repeated outcome measures to their clients during the course of treatment, they could document the effectiveness of their own work and contribute to the establishment of a large database on the outcomes of spiritual interventions. Perhaps this will be most feasible if practicing clinicians collaborate with scholars in academic and research settings. Both clinicians and scholars would benefit from such collaboration and the database on a spiritual strategy would grow rapidly.

Qualitative Research Designs

There are numerous overlapping qualitative research designs or strategies and many ways of categorizing them (Denzin & Lincoln, 1994). In Table 12.5 we present five major qualitative research strategies that we think have considerable potential for contributing to the understanding of a spiritual strategy: phenomenology, ethnography, grounded theory, biographical, and case study. We limit our discussion to these strategies because of space limitations. In doing so, however, we are not ruling out the possibility that other strategies will prove useful in the study of a spiritual strategy.

A relatively small number of qualitative studies have been done on religious and spiritual issues in mental health and psychotherapy, although we are aware of a growing number of them that have been done in recent years (e.g., Bergin et al., 1994; Chamberlain et al., 1996; Mattson & Scharman, 1994; Preece, 1994; Scharman, 1994). Like the rest of the behavioral sciences, spirituality research has relied on quantitative methods almost exclusively (Slife et al., 1996; Worthington et al., 1996). This seems unfortunate because such methods may, to some extent, limit and distort the understanding of spiritual phenomena (Slife et al., 1996). Quantitative research has provided considerable insight into clients' symptoms and behaviors and therapeutic processes and outcomes, but it has not provided much insight into clients' inner, subjective worlds. We think that this is where qualitative strategies will contribute the most to a spiritual strategy and to mainstream psychology and psychotherapy. Such strategies will help researchers better understand clients' inner worlds, or "lived experience," thereby enabling them to understand and empathize with them more fully.

Phenomenological, ethnographic, grounded theory, biographical, and case study strategies hold considerable promise for helping researchers gain more in-depth and richer insight into clients' religious and spiritual perceptions, experiences, understandings, feelings, beliefs, values, desires, and practices and how their spirituality is intertwined with their emotions and behavior. These strategies also hold promise for yielding considerable insight into the spiritual nature and processes of therapeutic change and healing, as viewed from the perspectives of clients and therapists. Biographical and case study strategies have been used for a long time in psychology and psychotherapy (L. M. Smith, 1994; Stake, 1994) and have considerable

TABLE 12.5
Comparison of Major Qualitative Research Designs or Strategies

Design or strategy	Defining characteristic	Types of research questions	Type of data	Major advantages	Major limitations
Phenomenology	Studies the meaning of people's experiences	"Meaning questions—eliciting the essence of experiences" (J. M. Morse & Field, 1995, p. 224), such as the meaning of their spiritual experiences	"Audiotaped 'conversations'; written anecdotes of personal experiences" (J. M. Morse & Field, 1995, p. 224)	Can give insight into the meaning that clients give to their religious and spiritual experiences in life and to spiritually healing experiences in therapy.	Limited generalizability
Ethnography	Studies people's values, beliefs, and cultural practices	"Descriptive questions—of values, beliefs, practices of cultural group (J. M. Morse & Field, 1995, p. 224), such as clients' spiritual beliefs and practices	"Unstructured interviews; participant observation; field notes'" (J. M. Morse & Field, 1995, p. 224)	Can provide rich, detailed description and insight into the religious and spiritual values, beliefs, and practices of clients, therapists, and therapeutic groups and communities.	Limited generalizability

Grounded theory	Studies people's experiences over time	"Process questions—experience over time or change, may have stages and phases" (J. M. Morse & Field, p. 224), such as how do clients change spiritually during therapy?	"Interviews (tape recorded); . . . participant observation; memoing; diary" (J. M. Morse & Field, 1995, p. 224)	Can provide rich, detailed description and insight into the emotional, religious and spiritual changes that clients experience during the course of therapy.	Limited generalizability, amount of change is not quantifiable
Biographical	"Seeks to report on and document the history of a person's life (Denzin & Lincoln, 1994, p. 205)	What can be learned from this person's life (e.g., about the role of religion and spirituality in the person's functioning, growth, and healing)?	Letters, journals, memoirs, documents, and interviews	Can provide rich insight into how religious and spiritual beliefs and practices affect human development, emotional functioning, and social relationships.	May be difficult to establish the factual status of the materials used. Biases of the biographer can distort the truthworthiness of the account.
Case study	The "object of study is a specific, unique, bounded system [person or perhaps group]" (Stake, 1994, p. 236)	What can be learned from the treatment of this person or group (e.g., what role did spiritual interventions play in their healing)?	Clinical observations and recollections, case notes, client history, client self-reports, and reports of significant others	Can provide rich insight into clients' religious and spiritual issues, the process and course of treatment, and the perceived effects of specific spiritual interventions.	Limited generalizability. Biases of the therapist can distort the trustworthiness of the report. Outcomes are not objectively measured and documented.

Sources consulted included Borg and Gall (1989), Denzin and Lincoln (1994), J. M. Morse and Field (1995), L. M. Smith (1994), and Stake (1994).

potential for providing insight into religious and spiritual development and functioning over the life span and during therapy.

Qualitative studies are not easy to do. They are time-consuming, laborious, and challenging to report. However, many of the methods used for data collection in qualitative research are highly similar to the methods used in clinical practice, such as unstructured interviews, participant observation (in therapy groups), audiotaped conversations, field (case) notes, and diaries (Denzin & Lincoln, 1994). With some training in qualitative methods and permission from clients, much of what therapists do in psychotherapy could serve as data for qualitative studies (W. Miller & Crabtree, 1994). We hope that during the next decade many psychotherapists, perhaps in collaboration with scholars in academic and research positions, will study spiritual issues in personality and psychotherapy creatively and rigorously using qualitative methods.

ASSESSING THE OUTCOMES OF PSYCHOTHERAPY

It should be evident by now that we believe that the outcomes of psychotherapy should be evaluated multidimensionally. We are not, of course, the first to advocate such an evaluation approach. There has been a gradual movement toward a multidimensional evaluation approach in the past few decades. In the most recent edition of the *Handbook of Psychotherapy and Behavior Change*, Kazdin (1994) stated that

> there is general consensus that outcome assessment needs to be multifaceted, involving different perspectives (e.g., patients, significant others, mental health practitioners), characteristics of the individual (e.g., affect, cognitions, and behavior), domains of functioning (e.g., work, social, marital adjustment), and methods of assessment (e.g., self-report, direct observation). (p. 40)

In the same book, Lambert and Hill (1994) also advocated a multifaceted outcome assessment approach. They also noted that there has been much variation in the criteria therapists and researchers have used to evaluate the outcomes of therapy. It appears that indicators of psychological symptoms such as depression, anxiety, self-esteem, phobias, compulsions, personality disorders, and schizophrenia have been used the most frequently. Measures of interpersonal and social adjustment also have been used often (Lambert & Hill, 1994). Researchers who evaluate the effects of spiritual treatment approaches should use standard criteria such as those described earlier, but they also should include religious and spiritual outcome measures.

An important contribution that the theistic, spiritual strategy makes to psychotherapy outcome research is the view that an evaluation of clients' religious and spiritual status and functioning is crucial for an adequate assessment of outcome. Therapists and researchers should not ignore this dimension when assessing therapy outcome. It should be assessed along with other clinically important criteria regardless of the type of therapy approach (secular or spiritual) that is being evaluated.

Unfortunately, few therapists or researchers have used religious or spiritual outcome measures when they evaluated the effects of psychotherapy. This is not surprising given the historical neglect of religious and spiritual issues in psychotherapy; however, part of the reason also may be attributable to the lack of clinically useful religious and spiritual assessment measures. The problem with not assessing how therapy is affecting clients' religious and spiritual well-being and status is that it leaves one with an incomplete understanding of the effects of psychotherapy. Does therapy undermine and weaken clients' spiritual beliefs and faith as some religiously orthodox people have supposed (Koltko, 1990; Worthington, 1986)? Or does it strengthen clients' spiritual faith and maturity? Until the religious and spiritual outcomes of therapy are assessed empirically, such questions will remain unanswered.

We recognize that currently there is a lack of clinically useful religious and spiritual outcome assessment measures. However, in chapter 8 we identified several assessment measures that also could be used for outcome research (e.g., the Age Universal Intrinsic–Extrinsic Scale, Spiritual Well-Being Scale, Religious Problem Solving Scale). More research is needed on these measures before it is known whether they are sensitive and valid outcome measures. For now, as long as they are interpreted cautiously, they can at least provide researchers with some "semistandardized" ways of assessing the impact of therapy on clients' religiosity and spirituality.

In the spirit of the qualitative approaches discussed earlier, therapists and researchers also could use the conceptual schemes of religious maturity and health outlined in Tables 8.1, 8.2, 8.4, 8.5, and 8.6 in chapter 8 to guide them in assessing clients clinically. Therapists or researchers would need to devise a way to rate clients on these dimensions. By doing this at the beginning of treatment and at various points as therapy progresses, a crude clinical estimate of clients' progress on these religious and spiritual dimensions at least can be obtained.

The foregoing discussion highlights clearly the great need that there is for the development of reliable, valid, and clinically relevant religious and spiritual outcome measures. All the recommendations we made in chapter 8 about assessment measures apply here. In particular, we need some ecumenical measures that can be used validly with clients from diverse religious traditions. In constructing outcome measures, one needs to remember that not all assessment measures are sensitive to change, so they do not necessarily make *good* outcome measures (Lambert & Hill, 1994; Ogles, Lambert, & Masters, 1996). Outcome measures are needed that are sensitive to the types of religious and spiritual changes that may occur in therapy.

CONCLUSION

Empirical (quantitative) research on religious and spiritual issues in mental health and psychotherapy has mushroomed during the past decade, as documented by the review of Worthington et al. (1996). The methodological quality of this research has improved to the point of approaching "current secular standards, except in outcome research" (Worthington et al., 1996, p. 448). We hope that the number and quality of outcome studies on spiritual interventions will increase. We also hope that more single-subject, discovery-oriented, and qualitative studies in this domain will be conducted. When Worthington and his colleagues do their next 10-year review of the research literature in this domain, we hope a spiritual strategy for personality and psychotherapy will be solidly grounded in and supported by both quantitative and qualitative empirical research.

13

DIRECTIONS FOR THE FUTURE

Finally, if science and religion are so broadly similar, and not arbitrarily limited in their domain, they should at some time converge. I believe this convergence is inevitable . . .

—*Charles H. Townes*
Nobel Laureate in Physics

In this chapter we discuss what we believe are the needs and directions for the future relative to the advancement of a spiritual strategy in psychology and psychotherapy. We first discuss pressing theoretical and research questions that need investigation. We then discuss and make recommendations for education and clinical training. Finally, we briefly discuss a number of domains in which a spiritual strategy can make potentially important contributions to practice, including psychotherapy, medicine, health psychology, education and prevention, and religious institutions.

THEORY AND RESEARCH

Although theory and research relevant to a spiritual strategy have increased greatly during the past decade (Shafranske, 1996; Worthington, Kurusu, McCullough, & Sanders, 1996), there are still many pressing ques-

333

tions that need to be answered. The *Psychological Bulletin* review of Worthington et al. (1996) not only updates research that has been conducted on religious counseling during the past decade, but it also identifies a number of areas in which there are deficiencies in research. Worthington et al. also recommended a research agenda for the next decade. In Table 13.1 we summarize these recommendations.

We agree with this agenda and add our voices to those of Worthington et al. (1996) in calling for more outcome studies with actual clients on specific spiritual interventions and on spiritual–secular integrative treatment approaches. Studies that document the effectiveness of spiritual treatment approaches are essential if a spiritual strategy is to achieve credibility in mainstream psychotherapy. We hope that practitioners and researchers with interests in a spiritual strategy will join together in such efforts. We also want to emphasize the need for more theory and research on how religious and spiritual beliefs and practices influence people's personality development and functioning. Although researchers have gained considerable insight into ways that religion can be beneficial and harmful, knowledge in this regard is still limited. We also endorse the call by Worthington et al. for more research on religiously and culturally diverse groups. Most the-

TABLE 13.1
Worthington, Kurusu, McCullough, and Sanders's (1996) Proposed
Research Agenda for the Next 10 Years on Religion, Mental Health
and Psychotherapy

Research Agenda
1. Research on actual clients should be a priority.
2. More research needs to be done to determine more fully why religion sometimes has positive or negative effects. What forms of religiosity and spirituality are healthy and what forms are unhealthy? How does religion help people cope, change, and heal?
3. Studies documenting clients' reactions to spiritual interventions are needed (e.g., What type of clients feel comfortable with spiritual interventions? When do they feel comfortable with them? With what types of spiritual interventions are clients most comfortable?).
4. Therapy outcome studies of specific spiritual interventions and of spiritual–secular integrative treatment approaches are badly needed.
5. Studies of inpatient treatment programs are needed.
6. Studies of religiously and spiritually oriented group therapy and psychoeducational groups are needed.
7. More research on the effectiveness of counseling by clergy, chaplains, and lay religious counselors is needed.
8. Research is needed on brief forms of religious counseling.
9. More research on religious counseling with religiously and culturally diverse groups is needed.
10. More research on religious clients, religious counselors, and religious and spiritual interventions is needed.

ory and research in this domain has focused on the Judeo-Christian religious traditions and Western (Euro-American) cultures. We hope that theorists and researchers with interests and expertise in diverse religions and cultures will contribute to the literature in this domain.

In addition to endorsing the recommendations of Worthington et al. (1996), we also wish to add some of our own. There are several other areas in which more philosophical, theoretical, and research work is needed if a theistic, spiritual strategy is to advance and mature. We recognize that many of the ideas we have introduced in this book are not yet developed fully, defended adequately, or researched carefully. For example, work is needed to more fully justify, describe, explain, understand, develop, and test (a) a multisystemic, spiritual view of human personality; (b) an integrative spiritual strategy for psychotherapy; (c) the nature of spirit, spirituality, and spiritual well-being; (d) religious and spiritual development across the life span; (e) the major spiritual needs and issues of human beings; (f) the prevalence and role of intuition, inspiration, and divine intervention in therapeutic change and healing; (g) the prevalence and role of intuition and inspiration in scientific discovery and research; (h) the nature, prevalence, effects (e.g., physical, psychological, interpersonal, and spiritual), and meaning of spiritual and mystical experiences (e.g., near-death experiences, afterlife visions, inspirational and revelatory experiences, conversion experiences, healings); (i) the implications and usefulness of epistemological and methodological pluralism; (j) the conflicts and potential compatibility between the assumptions and methodologies of scientific modernism and postmodernism; (k) reliable, valid, and clinically useful assessment and outcome measures of religious and spiritual orientation and functioning that are applicable with clients from diverse religious and cultural backgrounds; and (l) research methodologies, procedures, and designs that allow researchers to study spiritual phenomena validly.

As can be seen from the recommendations of Worthington et al. (1996) and our list, there will be no shortage of fascinating and challenging projects for philosophers, theorists, and researchers in this domain during the next few decades. We invite those with interests in this domain to join us in this effort. We hope that individuals who have influence at the highest levels of academic, government, business, and religious institutions and societies will use it to help gain financial and political support for these efforts.

EDUCATION AND CLINICAL TRAINING

Most graduate training programs in the mental health professions do not adequately prepare therapists to intervene sensitively and effectively in the religious and spiritual dimension of their clients' lives (Bergin, 1983;

Shafranske, 1996). Because of this, in chapter 7 we offered several recommendations about how therapists who are interested in implementing a spiritual strategy in their work can obtain the specialized training and knowledge that they need to work more sensitively and effectively with religious and spiritual clients (e.g., reading books on the psychology of religion, taking classes in world religions, attending workshops on spiritual issues in healing and psychotherapy). Here we do not speak to individual therapists about education and training. Rather, we want to make recommendations for professional organizations and graduate training programs about the religious and spiritual content that is needed in educational and clinical training experiences.

Shafranske and Malony (1996) proposed "a number of measures to redress and remedy the current status of training" (p. 576) on religious issues in the concluding chapter of the recent book published by the American Psychological Association, *Religion and the Clinical Practice of Psychology* (Shafranske, 1996). They opined that the ideal curriculum would include four components: "a 'values in psychological treatment' component, a 'psychology of religion' component, a 'comparative-religion' component, and a 'working with religious issues' component" (Shafranske & Malony, 1996, p. 576). A model curriculum for psychiatry training has also been developed by Larson, Lu, and Swyers (1996).

Values in Psychological Treatment

This component of the training model would include studies in (a) the philosophy and epistemology of science and (b) the role of values in theory, research, professional acculturation, and clinical practice. As described by Shafranske and Malony (1996),

> in essence, we are calling for and envision a curriculum that addresses the underlying value commitments that establish the canon of science and influence its application within clinical practice. Such an investigation will include a philosophical inquiry into the nature of facts, scientific practices, models of validation and falsification, and the assumptions on which clinical theories and treatments are based. . . . [It] would also include an investigation of the role of personal values of the clinician as they are expressed in clinical thinking and practice. (pp. 577–578)

Shafranske and Malony (1996) expressed their belief that "this is critical for the profession of psychology and essential 'if a constructive relationship for religion with the science and profession of psychology' (Jones, 1996) is to be achieved" (pp. 577–578). We agree with them. Such studies are essential to help theorists, researchers, and clinicians become more aware of the profession's, as well as their own, underlying and often hidden assumptions and values. An awareness of these assumptions and values can help therapists be more aware of their influence and how they may limit and bias their views of the world, their clients, and their professional work.

Psychology of Religion

This component of the training model would include studies in the psychology and sociology of religion. Shafranske and Malony (1996) commented on the importance of this component:

> Many clinicians have not gone much deeper than a cursory reading of Freud and, perhaps, William James and are mostly unaware of the rich tradition of psychological interest in religion. . . . An exposure to the psychology of religion provides a fascinating history of American psychology in addition to its examination of essential issues concerning religion in individual and cultural experience. (p. 579)

Comparative Religions

This component of the training model would include studies in comparative world religions. Shafranske and Malony (1996) acknowledged the great diversity in religions and spiritual perspectives. They also said that

> there is a need for clinicians to have some appreciation of the variety. If nothing else, such a study would keep therapists from premature claims that they knew what was or was not orthodoxy for other traditions. In addition, an understanding of religious diversity would assist the clinician in making determinations regarding particular beliefs and practices in respect to normative religious practice in a given faith community. . . . Such knowledge is required for a clinical assessment to be proffered. Moreover, such a study might provoke a greater appreciation for the ways in which various religious traditions provide guidelines for well-being and fulfilling life adjustment. (p. 580)

Clinical Training

This component of the training model includes instruction and supervision in working with religious issues in therapy, including (a) assessment of clients' religiousness and spirituality as it relates to their mental health and (b) working with religious issues and using spiritual interventions in psychotherapy appropriately. Shafranske and Malony (1996) pointed out that there are several excellent resources available to assist in such training. They also pointed out that support for this component of training

> appears to be developing in a number of professional associations. . . . The Office of Accreditation [of the American Psychological Association] includes religion as one aspect of multicultural sensitivity that site visitors take into consideration in evaluating a program's education in cultural diversity. The American Psychiatric Association recommends,

as well, that religion be considered in the evaluation and treatment of patients within residency training. (p. 581)

We think that Shafranske and Malony's (1996) recommendations are excellent. We wish that every graduate training program in the mental health professions would incorporate them fully. However, we recognize, as did Shafranske and Malony, that these recommendations represent the ideal from the viewpoint of those who place a high value on competency in this domain. Directors and faculty in graduate training programs that are already overloaded with courses required for accreditation and licensing will undoubtedly not be eager to incorporate these recommendations fully.

So what are our recommendations for administrators who decide that they cannot or will not achieve the ideal? We think that the absolute minimum training standard in this domain would be that all students would be required to take a 3- to 5-credit multicultural issues class that includes a substantial component in religious issues and diversity and receive supervision from supervisors who have received continuing education training and acquired expertise in religious issues and diversity. In such programs, it should be made clear to students that the training they are receiving only "scratches the surface," and they should be reminded of their ethical obligation to seek continuing education and training in this domain as they progress in their careers.

We hope that many training program administrators will find ways to offer more than these minimal requirements. Several programs have shown that it is possible to offer an entire course that explores religious and spiritual issues in mental health and psychotherapy. There are now several books available, including this one, that would be useful in such a course (e.g., Kelly, 1995; Shafranske, 1996). As we documented in chapter 7, there also are numerous scholarly articles available.

Many programs, particularly those accredited by the American Psychological Association, already offer a class or classes that introduce students to the history and theoretical and philosophical foundations of the behavioral sciences. With relatively minimal effort, such courses could, as recommended by Shafranske and Malony (1996), include an examination of how the foundational metaphysical and epistemological ideas in the behavioral sciences compare with those of the world religious traditions. A careful examination of students' personal values and worldviews should be a required experience in multicultural and ethics classes as well as an ongoing concern during practicums and internships.

Many universities offer courses in comparative world religions and in the psychology and sociology of religion. Thus, many graduate training programs in the behavioral sciences would not need to design their own classes on these topics. They could simply require or encourage their students to take these classes as electives. When such courses are not available or feasible to design, students could be required or encouraged to complete independent readings on these topics for academic credit. Finally, we encourage both students and faculty to pursue continuing education training on religious issues and diversity throughout their careers by attending workshops and conventions, reading books and articles, and consulting with colleagues who have expertise in this domain.

PRACTICE

In this book we have focused mostly on describing a spiritual strategy for the practice of counseling and psychotherapy. It is in the practice of psychotherapy that the spiritual strategy has perhaps the most potential for enhancing professional practice, including individual, marital, family, and group therapies. However, there are reasons to believe that spiritual perspectives and interventions will make important contributions to practice in a number of other professional domains.

Behavioral Medicine and Health Psychology

As we discussed briefly in chapter 5, spiritual perspectives and interventions have already proved helpful in the field of medicine. There is evidence that spiritual beliefs and interventions can aid in the healing and prevention of a variety of physical diseases and help people cope with chronic pain, illness, and death and dying (Benson, 1996; Borysenko & Borysenko, 1994; Ornish, 1990; B. S. Siegel, 1986). More and more, physicians are recognizing this fact and are incorporating spiritual interventions into their work (Benson, 1996; Borysenko & Borysenko, 1994; Ornish, 1990; B. S. Siegel, 1986). For these reasons, we expect that spiritual perspectives and interventions will continue to make significant contributions to practice in the medical profession.

We also think that a spiritual strategy has much potential for contributing to the profession of health psychology (Martin & Carlson, 1988). Although a spiritual strategy does not yet appear to be a major influence in the health psychology profession, as evidenced by the lack of mention of religious and spiritual issues in some recent books on health psychology (e.g., Belar, Deardorff, & Kelly, 1987; Bishop, 1994), we believe that this will change as its contributions within the medical profession continue to receive recognition.

Values and Lifestyle Education

In our view, the spiritual strategy also holds promise for enhancing the health education and prevention efforts of schools and public health education agencies. According to the spiritual strategy, values play a crucial role in the development of healthy behavior and lifestyles. The often-repeated empirical finding that spiritual values and practices are positively associated with better physical and mental health and coping provides support for this hypothesis (e.g., Gartner, 1996; Pargament, 1996; Payne, Bergin, & Loftus, 1992). The spiritual strategy therefore provides both theoretical and empirical justification for healthy lifestyle values education efforts.

We recognize that there are difficulties with teaching lifestyle values in a pluralistic society and that such efforts will likely encounter strong resistance from some. We are not saying that schools and public health agencies should promote religion. Nevertheless, lifestyle values and practices that health professionals have documented are helpful for promoting physical and mental health through clinical practice, and empirical research should be endorsed and taught in schools and by public health agencies. Such lifestyle values and practices should be taught and promoted in an ecumenical, multiculturally sensitive, and noncoercive manner. Healthy lifestyle values and practices should be taught regardless of whether they had their origins in the world's religious traditions, medicine, or the mental health professions.

Congregation Development as Community Psychology

We think that a spiritual strategy also holds promise for strengthening and enhancing the psychosocial climate and well-being of religious institutions and their members. It is well-known that religious institutions potentially provide much social, emotional, and spiritual support to their members (Pargament, 1996). However, the psychosocial climate of religious institutions is not always positive (Pargament, Silverman, Johnson, Echemendia, & Snyder, 1983). Many people experience religious institutions as impersonal, frustrating, oppressive, rigid, shaming, or discriminatory (Pargament et al., 1983; W. H. Silverman, Pargament, Johnson, Echemendia, & Snyder, 1983). In addition, as expressed by Pargament et al. (1991), "churches and synagogues present the full range of problems . . . , from the mental health concerns of individual members, the conflicts of leaders and clergy, and questions about particular programs to issues of organizational survival, direction and growth" (p. 394).

Although the historical alienation that has existed between religion and the mental health professions has created barriers that have kept religious leaders from seeking assistance from mental health professionals, this has begun to change (Pargament et al., 1991). Mental health professionals who are sensitive to religious issues, who have incorporated a spiritual strategy into their practice, and who have established trust and credibility with leaders in religious communities may have opportunities for providing a variety of psychological services to such communities, including psychotherapy and organizational consultation. The Congregation Development Program developed by Pargament et al. (1991) is an excellent example of how mental health professionals with expertise in religious and spiritual issues can consult with and assist religious institutions and their members.

Pastoral Counseling

Pastoral counseling has a long and important history, including numerous successes in integrating psychological knowledge within the role and repertoire of clergy (e.g., Collins, 1988; Estadt, Blanschette, & Compton, 1983; W. R. Miller & Jackson, 1985; Wicks, Parsons, & Capps, 1985). As a theistic, spiritual strategy develops within mainstream psychology, the already-existing overlap between pastoral and clinical counseling will expand. This can become a problem if it creates a growing competition or a confusion in role boundaries (see chap. 7 in this book). On the other hand, a collaborative stance could greatly enhance the roles of both clergy and mental health professionals. The sharing of information, working together in helping specific clients, collaborating on designing therapeutic congregational structures and processes, joint efforts in outcome research, and so on are all exciting possibilities. Much thought and research within community psychology and the prevention movement have been done along these lines over the years (Pargament, Maton, & Hess, 1992; Pargament et al., 1991), but adding a spiritual dimension *within* psychological theory and practice could further enhance the synergy between the pastoral and clinical models of helping.

CONCLUSION

As we conclude this book, we are aware that there are many important issues regarding religion, spirituality, personality, and psychotherapy that we have not discussed. These topics will have to await future books by us and others. One need that has become apparent to us is for more information to help psychotherapists better understand the religious beliefs, cultures, practices, and clinical issues of members of specific religious denominations or communities. There was not space in this book to provide this information fully, but it is invaluable in ecumenical situations and essential if therapists want to adopt a denominational therapeutic stance with clients.

We therefore are pleased that our editor at the American Psychological Association has asked us to prepare a second book on a spiritual strategy to complement the first one. The second book will be an edited one that contains detailed information for therapists about the beliefs, practices, and clinical issues of clients from many of the Western and Eastern world religions, including the major denominations or traditions within Judaism, Christianity, Islam, Buddhism, and Hinduism.

We think that this book on religious diversity will nicely complement the first. Therapists who read both books should be well prepared to begin integrating a spiritual strategy into their therapeutic work. Of course, they should supplement the understandings they gain from our books with further readings, conferences and workshops, and clinical supervision and consultation from therapists who already have developed expertise in this strategy. We hope that this book, and the future one, will prove helpful to many mental health professionals. We welcome correspondence and feedback about the ideas that we have shared. Such dialogue will help us in our continuing efforts to implement a spiritual strategy effectively into our own professional work.

REFERENCES

Adorno, T. W., Frenkel-Brunswik, E., Levinson, D. J., & Sanford, R. N. (1950). *The authoritarian personality.* New York: Norton.

Alcoholics Anonymous World Services. (1980). *Alcoholics Anonymous.* New York: Author.

Alcoholics Anonymous World Services. (1990). *Alcoholics Anonymous 1989 membership survey.* New York: Author.

Allen, R. O., & Spilka, B. (1967). Committed and consensual religion: A specification of religion-prejudice relationships. *Journal for the Scientific Study of Religion, 6,* 191–206.

Allport, G. W. (1950). *The individual and his religion: A psychological interpretation.* New York: Macmillan.

Allport, G. W. (1959). Religion and prejudice. *Crane Review, 2,* 1–10.

Allport, G. W. (1966). The religious context of prejudice. *Journal for the Scientific Study of Religion, 5,* 447–457.

Allport, G. W., & Ross, J. M. (1967). Personal religious orientation and prejudice. *Journal of Personality and Social Psychology, 5,* 432–443.

Alston, W. P. (1991). *Perceiving God: The epistemology of religious experience.* Ithaca, NY: Cornell University Press.

American Association for Marriage and Family Therapy. (1985). *Code of ethical principles for marriage and family therapists.* Washington, DC: Author.

American Counseling Association. (1995). *Code of ethics and standards of practice.* Alexandria, VA: Author.

American Heritage Dictionary of the English language (3rd ed.). (1992). Boston: Houghton Mifflin.

American Psychiatric Association. (1986). *Principles of medical ethics, with annotations especially applicable to psychiatry.* Washington, DC: Author.

American Psychiatric Association. (1994). *Diagnostic and statistical manual of mental disorders* (4th ed.). Washington, DC: Author.

American Psychological Association. (1981). *Ethical principles of psychologists* (Rev. ed.). Washington, DC: Author.

American Psychological Association. (1985). *Standards for educational and psychological testing.* Washington, DC: Author.

American Psychological Association. (1992). Ethical principles of psychologists and code of conduct. *American Psychologist, 47,* 1597–1611.

Antoun, R. T., & Hegland, M. E. (Eds.). (1987). *Religious resurgence: Contemporary cases in Islam, Christianity, and Judaism.* Syracuse, NY: Syracuse University Press.

Appleyard, B. (1992). *Understanding the present: Science and the soul of modern man.* New York: Doubleday.

Baker, M., & Gorsuch, R. L. (1982). Trait anxiety and intrinsic-extrinsic religiousness. *Journal for the Scientific Study of Religion, 21,* 119–122.

Ball, R. A., & Goodyear, R. K. (1991). Self-reported professional practices of Christian psychologists. *Journal of Psychology and Christianity, 10,* 144–153.

Bandura, A. (1969). *Principles of behavior modification.* New York: Holt, Rinehart & Winston.

Bandura, A. (1986). *Social foundations of thought and action: A social cognitive theory.* Englewood Cliffs, NJ: Prentice Hall.

Barbour, I. G. (1990). *Religion in an age of science: The Gifford lectures 1989–1991* (Vol. 1). San Francisco: Harper & Row.

Barker, P. (1996). *Psychotherapeutic metaphors: A guide to theory and practice.* New York: Brunner/Mazel.

Barlow, D. H., Hayes, S. C., & Nelson, R. O. (1984). *The scientist practitioner: Research and accountability in clinical and educational settings.* Elmsford, NY: Pergamon Press.

Barrett, D. G. (1996). Religion: World religious statistics. In *Encyclopedia Britannica Book of the Year (p. 298).* Chicago: Encyclopedia Britannica.

Batson, C. D., Schoenrade, P., & Ventis, W. C. (1993). *Religion and the individual: A social-psychological perspective.* New York: Oxford University Press.

Bechtel, W. (1988). *Philosophy of science: An overview for cognitive science.* Hillsdale, NJ: Erlbaum.

Beck, A. T. (1976). *Cognitive therapy and the emotional disorders.* Madison, CT: International Universities Press.

Beckwith, B. P. (1985). *The decline of U.S. religious faith 1912–1984 and the effects of education and intelligence on such faith.* Palo Alto, CA: Author.

Beit-Hallahmi, B. (1974). Psychology of religion 1880–1930: The rise and fall of a psychological movement. *Journal of the History of the Behavioral Sciences, 10,* 84–90.

Belar, C. D., Deardorff, W. W., & Kelly, K. E. (1987). *The practice of clinical health psychology.* Elmsford, NY: Pergamon Press.

Bennett, W. J. (1993). *The book of virtues.* New York: Simon & Schuster.

Benson, H. (1993). The relaxation response. In D. Goleman & J. Gurin (Eds.), *Mind-body medicine: How to use your mind for better health* (pp. 233–257). Yonkers, NY: Consumer Reports Books.

Benson, H. (1996). *Timeless healing: The power and biology of belief.* New York: Scribner.

Benson, P. L., & Spilka, B. (1973). God image as a function of self-esteem and locus of control. *Journal for the Scientific Study of Religion, 12,* 297–310.

Bergin, A. E. (1969). A self-regulation technique for impulse-control disorders. *Psychotherapy: Theory, Research and Practice, 6,* 113–118.

Bergin, A. E. (1979). Bringing the restoration to the academic world: Clinical psychology as a test case. *Brigham Young University Studies, 19,* 449–473.

Bergin, A. E. (1980a). Psychotherapy and religious values. *Journal of Consulting and Clinical Psychology, 48,* 75–105.

Bergin, A. E. (1980b). Religious and humanistic values: A reply to Ellis and Walls. *Journal of Consulting and Clinical Psychology, 48,* 642–645.

Bergin, A. E. (1980c). Behavior therapy and ethical relativism: Time for clarity. *Journal of Consulting and Clinical Psychology, 48,* 11–13.

Bergin, A. E. (1983). Religiosity and mental health: A critical reevaluation and meta-analysis. *Professional Psychology: Research and Practice, 14,* 170–184.

Bergin, A. E. (1985). Proposed values for guiding and evaluating counseling and psychotherapy. *Counseling and Values, 29,* 99–116.

Bergin, A. E. (1988). Three contributions of a spiritual perspective to counseling, psychotherapy, and behavior change. *Counseling and Values, 32,* 21–31.

Bergin, A. E. (1991). Values and religious issues in psychotherapy and mental health. *American Psychologist, 46,* 394–403.

Bergin, A. D. (1993). *Adaptive/healthy versus maladaptive/unhealthy religious lifestyles.* Unpublished manuscript, Brigham Young University, Provo, UT.

Bergin, A. E., & Garfield, S. L. (Eds.). (1994). *Handbook of psychotherapy and behavior change* (4th ed.). New York: Wiley.

Bergin, A. E., & Jensen, J. P. (1990). Religiosity of psychotherapists: A national survey. *Psychotherapy, 27,* 3–7.

Bergin, A. E., & Lambert, M. J. (1978). The evaluation of therapeutic outcomes. In S. L. Garfield & A. E. Bergin (Eds.), *Handbook of psychotherapy and behavior change: An empirical analysis* (2nd ed., pp. 137–189). New York: Wiley.

Bergin, A. E., Masters, K. S., & Richards, P. S. (1987). Religiousness and mental health reconsidered: A study of an intrinsically religious sample. *Journal of Counseling Psychology, 34,* 197–204.

Bergin, A. E., Masters, K. S., Stinchfield, R. D., Gaskin, T. A., Sullivan, C. E., Reynolds, E. M., & Greaves, D. (1994). Religious life-styles and mental health. In L. B. Brown (Ed.), *Religion, personality, and mental health* (pp. 69–93). New York: Springer-Verlag.

Bergin, A. E., & Payne, I. R. (1991). Proposed agenda for a spiritual strategy in personality and psychotherapy. *Journal of Psychology and Christianity, 10,* 197–210.

Bergin, A. E., Payne, I. R., & Richards, P. S. (1996). Values in psychotherapy. In E. Shafranske (Ed.), *Religion and the clinical practice of psychology* (pp. 297–325). Washington, DC: American Psychological Association.

Bergin, A. E., Stinchfield, R. D., Gaskin, T. A., Masters, K. S., & Sullivan, C. E. (1988). Religious life styles and mental health: An exploratory study. *Journal of Counseling Psychology, 35,* 91–98.

Bergin, A. E., & Strupp, H. H. (1972). *Changing frontiers in the science of psychotherapy.* Chicago: Aldine-Atherton.

Berkman, L. F., & Syme, S. L. (1979). Social networks, host resistance, and mortality: A nine year follow-up study of Alameda County residents. *American Journal of Epidemiology, 109,* 186–204.

Bertens, H. (1995). *The idea of the postmodern.* New York: Routledge.

Beutler, L. E. (1972). Value and attitude change in psychotherapy: A case for dyadic assessment. *Psychotherapy, 9,* 262–267.

Beutler, L. E., & Clarkin, J. (1990). *Systematic treatment selection: Toward targeted therapeutic interventions.* New York: Brunner/Mazel.

Bishop, G. D. (1994). *Health psychology: Integrating mind and body.* Boston: Allyn & Bacon.

Borg, W. R., & Gall, M. D. (1989). *Educational research: An introduction* (5th ed.). New York: Longman.

Boring, E. G. (1950). *A history of experimental psychology* (2nd ed.). New York: Appleton-Century-Crofts.

Borysenko, J. (1988). *Minding the body: Mending the mind.* New York: Bantam Books.

Borysenko, J. (1993). *Fire in the soul: A new psychology of spiritual optimism.* New York: Warner Books.

Borysenko, J., & Borysenko, M. (1994). *The power of the mind to heal: Renewing body, mind, and spirit.* Carson, CA: Hay House.

Bowlby, J. (1969). *Attachment and loss: Vol 1. Attachment.* New York: Basic Books.

Boyce, M. (1979). *Zoroastrian's: Their religious beliefs and practices.* New York: Routledge.

Boyce, M. (1984). *Textual sources for the study of Zoroastrianism.* Dover, NH: Manchester University Press.

Bradley, L. J., & Gould, L. J. (1993). Individual counseling: Creative interventions. In A. Vernon (Ed.), *Counseling children and adolescents* (pp. 83–117). Denver, CO: Love.

Brown, L. B. (1994). *The human side of prayer: The psychology of praying.* Birmingham, AL: Religious Education Press.

Brown, V. L., Jr. (1981). *Human intimacy: Illusion and reality.* Salt Lake City, UT: Parliament.

Brush, S. G. (1988). *The history of modern science: A guide to the second scientific revolution, 1800–1950.* Ames: Iowa State University Press.

Bufford, R. K., Paloutzian, R. F., & Ellison, C. W. (1991). Norms for the spiritual well-being scale. *Journal of Psychology and Theology, 19,* 56–70.

Burns, D. (1980). *Feeling good: The new mood therapy.* New York: Morrow.

Burns, E. M., & Ralph, P. L. (1974). *World civilizations: Their history and their culture* (5th ed.). New York: Norton.

Burtt, E. A. (1955). *The metaphysical foundations of modern physical science.* Garden City, NY: Doubleday.

Buxton, M. E., Smith, D. E., & Seymour, R. B. (1987). Spirituality and other points of resistance to the 12-step recovery process. *Journal of Psychoactive Drugs, 19,* 275–286.

Byrd, R. C. (1988). Positive therapeutic effects of intercessory prayer in a coronary care unit. *Southern Medical Journal, 81,* 826–829.

Campbell, D. T. (1975). On the conflicts between biological and social evolution and between psychology and moral tradition. *American Psychologist, 30,* 1103–1126.

Capra, F. (1983). *The Tao of physics: An exploration of the parallels between modern physics and Eastern mysticism* (2nd ed.). Boulder, CO: Shambhala.

Carlson, C. R., Bacaseta, P. E., & Simanton, D. A. (1988). A controlled evaluation of devotional meditation and progressive relaxation. *Journal of Psychology and Theology, 16,* 362–368.

Carmody, D. L., & Carmody, J. T. (1989). *Christianity: An introduction* (2nd ed.). Belmont, CA: Wadsworth.

Carter, E. F., McCullough, M. E., Sandage, S. J., & Worthington, E. L., Jr. (1994, August). *What happens when people forgive? Theories, speculations, and implications for individual and marital therapy.* Paper presented at the 102nd Annual Convention of the American Psychological Association, Los Angeles.

Castaneda, R., & Galanter, M. (1987). A review of treatment modalities for alcoholism and their outcome. *American Journal of Social Psychiatry, 7,* 237–244.

Chadwick, B. (1993). Religiosity and delinquency among LDS adolescents. *Journal for the Scientific Study of Religion, 32,* 51–67.

Chalfant, H. P., Heller, P. L., Roberts, A., Briones, D., Aguirre-Hochbaum, S., & Farr, W. (1990). The clergy as a resource for those encountering psychological distress. *Review of Religious Research, 31,* 305–313.

Chamberlain, R. B., Richards, P. S., & Scharman, J. S. (1996). Using spiritual perspectives and interventions in psychotherapy: A qualitative study of experienced AMCAP therapists. *Association of Mormon Counselors and Psychotherapists Journal, 22,* 29–74.

Chandler, C. K., Holden, J. M., & Kolander, C. A. (1992). Counseling for spiritual wellness: Theory and practice. *Journal of Counseling and Development, 71,* 168–175.

Clark, R. W. (1971). *Einstein: The life and times.* New York: World Publishing.

Clinebell, J., Jr. (1965). *Mental health through Christian community.* Nashville, TN: Abingdon Press.

Collins, G. R. (1977). *The rebuilding of psychology: An integration of psychology and Christianity.* Wheaton, IL: Tyndale House.

Collins, G. R. (1988). *Christian counseling: A comprehensive guide* (Rev. ed.). Dallas, TX: Word Publishing.

Collipp, P. J. (1969). The efficacy of prayer: A triple blind study. *Medical Times, 97,* 201–204.

Corey, G., Corey, M. S., & Callanan, P. (1993). *Issues and ethics in the helping professions* (4th ed.). Pacific Grove, CA: Brooks/Cole.

Cormier, L. S., & Hackney, H. (1987). *The professional counselor: A process guide to helping.* Englewood Cliffs, NJ: Prentice Hall.

Cormier, L. S., Cormier, W. H., & Weisser, R. J. (1984). *Interviewing and helping skills for health professionals.* Belmont, CA: Wadsworth.

Cormier, W. H., & Cormier, L. S. (1991). *Interviewing strategies for helpers: Fundamental skills and cognitive behavioral interventions.* Pacific Grove, CA: Brooks/ Cole.

Coulson, W. R., & Rogers, C. R. (1968). *Man and the science of man.* Columbus, OH: Charles E. Merrill.

Covey, S. R. (1989). *The seven habits of highly effective people.* New York: Simon & Schuster.

Crabb, L. J., Jr. (1982). *The marriage builder: A blueprint for couples and counselors.* Grand Rapids, MI: Zondervan.

Craigie, F. C., Jr., & Tan, S. Y. (1989). Changing resistant assumptions in Christian cognitive-behavioral therapy. *Journal of Psychology and Theology, 17,* 93–100.

Crapps, R. W. (1986). *An introduction to psychology of religion.* Macon, GA: Mercer University Press.

Davies, P. (1988). *The cosmic blueprint.* New York: Simon & Schuster.

Davies, P. (1992). *The mind of God: The scientific basis for a rational world.* New York: Simon & Schuster.

Denzin, N. K., & Lincoln, Y. S. (Eds.). (1994). *Handbook of qualitative research.* Thousand Oaks, CA: Sage.

DiBlasio, F. A. (1992). Forgiveness in psychotherapy: Comparison of older and younger therapists. *Journal of Psychology and Christianity, 11,* 181–187.

DiBlasio, F. A. (1993). The role of social workers' religious beliefs in helping family members forgive. *Families in Society, 74,* 163–170.

DiBlasio, F. A., & Benda, B. B. (1991). Practitioners, religion and the use of forgiveness in the clinical setting. *Journal of Psychology and Christianity, 10,* 166–172.

DiBlasio, F. A., & Proctor, J. H. (1993). Therapists and the clinical use of forgiveness. *American Journal of Family Therapy, 21,* 175–184.

Dickie, J. R., Merasco, D. L., Geurink, A., & Johnson, M. (1993, August). *Mother, father, God: Children's perceptions of nurturing authority figures.* Paper presented at the 101st Annual Convention of the American Psychological Association, Toronto, Ontario, Canada.

Dickson, P. (1995). The phenomenology of evil. *Journal of Value Inquiry, 29,* 5–12.

Dilthey, W. (1978). *Dilthey's philosophy of existence: Introduction to Weltanschauungslehre* (W. Kluback & M. Weinbaum, Trans.). Westport, CT: Greenwood Press.

Dittes, J. E. (1971). Religion, prejudice, and personality. In M. Strommen (Ed.), *Research on religious development: A comprehensive handbook* (pp. 355–390). New York: Hawthorn Books.

Doherty, W. J. (1995). *Soul searching: Why psychotherapy must promote moral responsibility.* New York: Basic Books.

Donahue, M. J. (1985). Intrinsic and extrinsic religiousness: Review and meta-analysis. *Journal of Personality and Social Psychology, 48,* 400–419.

Dossey, L. (1993). *Healing words: The power of prayer and the practice of medicine.* San Francisco: HarperCollins.

Drakeman, D. L. (1991). *Church-state constitutional issues: Making sense of the establishment clause.* Westport, CT: Greenwood Press.

Duckro, P. N., & Magaletta, P. R. (1994). The effect of prayer on physical health: Experimental evidence. *Journal of Religion and Health, 33,* 211–219.

Duncan, H. D., Eddy, J. P., & Haney, C. W. (1981). Using religious resources in crisis intervention. *Counseling and Values, 25,* 178–191.

Dupont, R. L., & McGovern, J. P. (1994). *A bridge to recovery: An introduction to 12-step programs.* Washington, DC: American Psychiatric Press.

Eccles, J., & Robinson, D. N. (1984). *The wonder of being human: Our brain and our mind.* New York: Free Press.

Edwards, P. (Ed.). (1967). *The encyclopedia of philosophy, Vol. 6.* New York: Macmillan Free Press.

Elkind, D. (1978). *The child's reality: Three developmental themes.* Hillsdale, NJ: Erlbaum.

Elkind, D. (1982). Piagetian psychology and the practice of child psychiatry. *Journal of the American Academy of Child Psychiatry, 21,* 435–445.

Elkins, D. N. (1995). Psychotherapy and spirituality: Toward a theory of the soul. *Journal of Humanistic Psychology, 35,* 78–98.

Ellis, A. (1971). *The case against religion: A psychotherapist's view.* New York: Institute for Rational Living.

Ellis, A. (1973). *Humanistic psychotherapy: The rational-emotive approach.* New York: Julian Press.

Ellis, A. (1980). Psychotherapy and atheistic values: A response to A. E. Bergin's "Psychotherapy and Religious Values." *Journal of Consulting and Clinical Psychology, 48,* 635–639.

Ellis, A. (1986). Fanaticism that may lead to a nuclear holocaust: The contributions of scientific counseling and psychotherapy. *Journal of Counseling and Development, 65,* 146–151.

Ellis, A. (1993). The advantages and disadvantages of self-help therapy materials. *Professional Psychology: Research and Practice, 24,* 335–339.

Ellis, A. (1996, August). Discussant. In A. P. Jackson & S. L. Neilsen (Chairs), *Religiously oriented REBT: Reconciling the sacred and the profane.* Symposium presented at the 104th Annual Convention of the American Psychological Association, Toronto, Ontario, Canada.

Ellis, A., & Harper, R. A. (1975). *A new guide to rational living.* North Hollywood, CA: Wilshre Books.

Ellison, C. W. (1983). Spiritual well-being: Conceptualization and measurement. *Journal of Psychology and Theology, 11,* 330–340.

Ellsworth, S. G. (1995). *How I got this way and what to do about it.* Draper, UT: Author.

Erikson, E. H. (1963). *Childhood and society* (2nd ed.). New York: Norton.

Erikson, E. H. (1968). *Identity: Youth and crisis.* New York: Norton.

Ermarth, M. (1978). *Wilhelm Dilthey: The critique of historical reason.* Chicago: University of Chicago Press.

Estadt, B. K., Blanschette, M., & Compton, J. R. (1983). *Pastoral counseling.* Englewood Cliffs, NJ: Prentice Hall.

Farah, C. E. (1994). *Islam: Beliefs and observances* (5th ed.). Hauppauge, NY: Barron's Educational Series.

Faulconer, J. E., & Williams, R. N. (1985). Temporality in human action: An alternative to positivism and historicism. *American Psychologist, 40,* 1179–1188.

Faust, D. (1984). *The limits of scientific reasoning.* Minneapolis: University of Minnesota Press.

Fennema, J., & Paul, I. (Eds.). (1990). *Science and religion: One world changing perspectives on reality.* Norwell, MA: Kluwer Academic.

Finney, J. R., & Malony, H. N. (1985a). Empirical studies of Christian prayer: A review of the literature. *Journal of Psychology and Theology, 13,* 104–115.

Finney, J. R., & Malony, H. N. (1985b). Contemplative prayer and its use in psychotherapy: A theoretical model. *Journal of Psychology and Theology, 13,* 172–181.

Finney, J. R., & Malony, H. N. (1985c). An empirical study of contemplative prayer as an adjunct to psychotherapy. *Journal of Psychology and Theology, 13,* 284–290.

Fischer, L., & Sorenson, G. P. (1985). *School law for counselors, psychologists, and social workers.* New York: Longman.

Flowers, R. B. (1994). *That godless court?: Supreme court decisions on church-state relationships.* Louisville, KY: Westminster John Knox Press.

Fowler, J. W. (1981). *Stages of faith: The psychology of human development and the quest for meaning.* New York: Harper & Row.

Fowler, J. W. (1991). Stages in faith consciousness. In F. K. Oser & W. G. Scarlett (Eds.), *Religious development in childhood and adolescence* (pp. 27–45). San Francisco: Jossey-Bass.

Fowler, J. W. (1996). Pluralism and oneness in religious experience: William James, faith-development theory, and clinical practice. In E. P. Shafranske (Ed.), *Religion and the clinical practice of psychology* (pp. 165–186). Washington, DC: American Psychological Association.

Frankl, V. E. (1959). *Man's search for meaning.* New York: Washington Square Press.

Freedman, S. R., & Enright, R. D. (1996). Forgiveness as an intervention goal with incest survivors. *Journal of Consulting and Clinical Psychology, 64,* 983–992.

Freud, S. (1927). *The future of an illusion.* Garden City, NY: Doubleday.

Freud, S. (1961). *The future of an illusion* (J. Strachey, Ed. and Trans.). New York: Norton. (Original work published 1927).

Friedman, M., Thoresen, C. E., Gill, J. J., Powell, L., Ulmer, D., Thompson, L., Price, V., Rabin, D., Breall, W., Dixon, T., Levy, R., & Bourg, E. (1984). Alteration of Type A behavior and reduction in cardiac recurrences in postmyocardial infarction patients. *American Heart Journal, 108,* 237–248.

Friend, T. (1995, September 20). Patient calls Ornish program miraculous. *USA Today.* pp. 1–2.

Friends in Recovery. (1994). *The twelve steps for Christians: Based on biblical teachings* (rev. ed.). San Diego, CA: RPI.

Fromm, E. (1956). *The art of loving.* New York: Harper & Row.

Fuller, A. R. (1986). *Psychology and religion: Eight points of view* (2nd ed.). Lanham, MD: University Press of America.

Fullerton, J. T., & Hunsberger, B. (1982). A unidimensional measure of Christian orthodoxy. *Journal for the Scientific Study of Religion, 21,* 317–326.

Galanter, M. (1996). Cults and charismatic groups. In E. Shafranske (Ed.), *Religion and the clinical practice of psychology* (pp. 269–296). Washington, DC: American Psychological Association.

Gallup, G., & Castelli, J. (1989). *The people's religion: American faith in the 90's.* New York: Macmillan.

Ganje-Fling, M. A., & McCarthy, P. R. (1991). A comparative analysis of spiritual direction and psychotherapy. *Journal of Psychology and Theology, 19,* 103–117.

Ganje-Fling, M., & McCarthy, P. (1994, April). *Impact of childhood sexual abuse on client spiritual development: Counseling implications.* Paper presented at the annual convention of the American Counseling Association, Minneapolis, MN.

Gardner, H. (1985). *The mind's new science: A history of the cognitive revolution.* New York: Basic Books.

Garfield, S. L., & Bergin, A. E. (Eds.). (1986). *Handbook of psychotherapy and behavior change* (3rd ed.). New York: Wiley.

Gartner, J. (1996). Religious commitment, mental health, and prosocial behavior: A review of the empirical literature. In E. Shafranske (Ed.), *Religion and the clinical practice of psychology* (pp. 187–214). Washington, DC: American Psychological Association.

Gartner, J., Larson, D. B., & Allen, G. D. (1991). Religious commitment and mental health: A review of the empirical literature. *Journal of Psychology and Theology, 19,* 6–25.

Gergen, K. J. (1982). *Toward transformation in social knowledge.* New York: Springer-Verlag.

Gergen, K. J. (1985). The social constructionist movement in modern psychology. *American Psychologist, 40,* 266–275.

Gibbs, N., & Chua-Eaon, H. G. (1993, December 27). Angels among us. *Time*, pp. 56–65.

Gilligan, C. (1982). *In a different voice: Psychological theory and woman's development*. Cambridge, MA: Harvard University Press.

Glock, C. Y., & Stark, R. (1965). *Religion and society in tension*. Chicago: Rand McNally.

Gorsuch, R. (1968). The conceptualization of God as seen in adjective ratings. *Journal for the Scientific Study of Religion, 7*, 56–64.

Gorsuch, R. L., & McPherson, S. E. (1989). Intrinsic/extrinsic measurement: I/E-revised and single-item scales. *Journal for the Scientific Study of Religion, 28*, 348–354.

Gorsuch, R. L., & Venable, G. D. (1983). Development of an "age universal" I-E scale. *Journal for the Scientific Study of Religion, 22*, 181–187.

Greeley, A. W. (1989). *Religious change in America*. Cambridge, MA: Harvard University Press.

Greenberg, L. (1986). Change process research. *Journal of Consulting and Clinical Psychology, 54*, 4–9.

Greenberg, L., Elliott, R., & Lietaer, G. (1994). Research on experiential psychotherapies. In A. E. Bergin & S. L. Garfield (Eds.), *Handbook of psychotherapy and behavior change* (4th ed., pp. 509–539). New York: Wiley.

Griffin, D. R. (1989). *God and religion in the postmodern world: Essays in postmodern theology*. Albany: State University of New York Press.

Griffin, D. R., Cobb, J. B., Ford, M. P., Gunter, P. A., & Ochs, P. (1993). *Founders of constructive postmodern philosophy: Pierce, James, Bergson, Whitehead, and Hartshorne*. Albany: State University of New York Press.

Groth-Marnat, G. (1989). The near-death experience: A review and critique. *Journal of Humanistic Psychology, 29*, 109–133.

Gurman, A. S., & Kniskern, D. P. (1981). *Handbook of family therapy*. New York: Brunner/Mazel.

Hall, C. S., & Lindzey, G. (1957). *Theories of personality*. New York: Wiley.

Hall, T. W., Tisdale, T. C., & Brokaw, B. F. (1994). Assessment of religious dimensions in Christian clients: A review of selected instruments for research and clinical use. *Journal of Psychology and Theology, 22*, 395–421.

Havighurst, R. (1972). *Developmental tasks and education*. New York: McKay.

Hearnshaw, L. S. (1987). *The shaping of modern psychology*. New York: Routledge & Kegan Paul.

Hebl, J., & Enright, R. D. (1993). Forgiveness as a psychotherapeutic goal with elderly females. *Psychotherapy, 30*, 658–667.

Heiler, F. (1958). *Prayer* (S. McComb, Ed. and Trans.). New York: Oxford University Press. (Original work published 1932).

Helminiak, D. A. (1996). *The human core of spirituality: Mind as psyche and spirit*. Albany: State University of New York Press.

Henning, L. H., & Tirrell, F. J. (1982). Counselor resistance to spiritual exploration. *Personnel and Guidance Journal, 61,* 92–95.

Heppner, P. P., Kivlighan, D. M., Jr., & Wampold, B. E. (1992). *Research design in counseling.* Pacific Grove, CA: Brooks/Cole.

Herlighy, B., & Golden, L. (1990). *Ethical standards casebook* (4th ed.). Alexandria, VA: AACD Press.

Hesse, M. (1980). *Revolutions and reconstructions in the philosophy of science.* Bloomington: Indiana State University Press.

Hillman, J. (1994). *In search: Psychology and religion.* Woodstock, CT: Spring.

Hillner, K. P. (1984). *History and systems of modern psychology: A conceptual approach.* New York: Gardner Press.

Hirai, T. (1989). *Zen meditation and psychotherapy.* Tokyo: Japan Publications.

Hoge, D. R. (1996). Religion in America: The demographics of belief and affiliation. In E. P. Shafranske (Ed.), *Religion and the clinical practice of psychology* (pp. 21–41). Washington, DC: American Psychological Association.

Honer, S. M., & Hunt, T. C. (1987). *Invitation to philosophy: Issues and options* (5th ed.). Belmont, CA: Wadsworth.

Hood, R. W., Jr. (1975). The construction and preliminary validation of a measure of reported mystical experience. *Journal for the Scientific Study of Religion, 14,* 29–41.

Hood, R. W., Jr. (Ed.). (1995). *Handbook of religious experience.* Birmingham, AL: Religious Education Press.

Hood, R. W., Jr., Spilka, B., Hunsberger, B., & Gorsuch, R. L. (1996). *The psychology of religion: An empirical approach.* New York: Guilford Press.

Hope, D. (1987). The healing paradox of forgiveness. *Psychotherapy, 24,* 240–244.

Hopson, R. E. (1996). The 12-step program. In E. P. Shafranske (Ed.), *Religion and the clinical practice of psychology* (pp. 533–558). Washington, DC: American Psychological Association.

Horner, D., & Vandersluis, P. (1981). Cross-cultural counseling. In G. Althen (Ed.), *Learning across cultures* (pp. 25–38). Washington, DC: National Association for Foreign Student Affairs.

Howard, G. S. (1985). The role of values in the science of psychology. *American Psychologist, 40,* 255–265.

Howard, G. S. (1986). *Dare we develop a human science?* Notre Dame, IN: Academic Publications.

Hudgins, H. C., Jr., & Vacca, R. S. (1995). *Law and education: Contemporary issues and court decisions* (4th ed.). Charlottesville, VA: Michie Law Publishers.

Hunt, R. A., & King, M. B. (1971). The intrinsic-extrinsic concept: A review and evaluation. *Journal of the Scientific Study of Religion, 10,* 339–356.

Ibrahim, F. A. (1985). Effective cross-cultural counseling and psychotherapy: A framework. *The Counseling Psychologist, 13,* 625–638.

Ibrahim, F. A. (1991). Contribution of cultural worldview to generic counseling and development. *Journal of Counseling and Development, 70,* 13–19.

Jacobs, L. (1984). *The book of Jewish beliefs.* New York: Behrman House.

Jacquet, C. H., Jr., & Jones, A. M. (Eds.). (1991). *Yearbook of American and Canadian churches.* Nashville, TN: Abingdon Press.

James, W. (1936). *The varieties of religious experience.* New York: Modern Library. (Original work published 1902)

Jensen, J. P., & Bergin, A. E. (1988). Mental health values of professional therapists: A national interdisciplinary survey. *Professional Psychology: Research and Practice, 19,* 290–297.

Jensen, J. P., Bergin, A. E., & Greaves, D. W. (1990). The meaning of eclecticism: New survey and analysis of components. *Professional Psychology: Research and Practice, 21,* 124–130.

Johnson, W. B. (1993). Christian rational-emotive therapy: A treatment protocol. *Journal of Psychology and Christianity, 12,* 254–261.

Johnson, W. B., Devries, R., Ridley, C. R., Pettorini, D., & Peterson, D. R. (1994). The comparative efficacy of Christian and secular rational-emotive therapy with Christian clients. *Journal of Psychology and Theology, 22,* 130–140.

Johnson, W. B., & Ridley, C. R. (1992). Brief Christian and non-Christian rational-emotive therapy with depressed Christian clients: An exploratory study. *Counseling and Values, 36,* 220–229.

Jones, S. L. (1994). A constructive relationship for religion with the science and profession of psychology: Perhaps the boldest model yet. *American Psychologist, 49,* 184–199.

Jones, S. L. (1996). A constructive relationship for religion with the science and profession of psychology: Perhaps the boldest model yet. In E. P. Shafranske (Ed.), *Religion and the clinical practice of psychology* (pp. 113–147). Washington, DC: American Psychological Association.

Jones, S. L., Watson, E. J., & Wolfram, T. J. (1992). Results of the Rech conference survey on religious faith and professional psychology. *Journal of Psychology and Theology, 20,* 147–158.

Joyce, C. R. B., & Welldon, R. M. C. (1965). The objective efficacy of prayer: A double-blind clinical trial. *Journal of Chronic Disease, 18,* 367–377.

Judd, D. K. (1985). *Religiosity and mental health: A literature review 1928–1985.* Unpublished master's thesis, Brigham Young University, Provo, UT.

Jung, C. G. (1938). *Psychology and religion.* New Haven, CT: Yale University Press.

Kantrowitz, B., King, P., Rosenberg, D., Springen, K., Wingert, P., Namuth, T., & Gegax, T. T. (1994, November 28). In search of the sacred. *Newsweek,* pp. 52–62.

Kaplan, M. (1996, June 24). Ambushed by spirituality. *Time,* p. 62.

Karier, C. J. (1986). *Scientists of the mind: Intellectual founders of modern psychology.* Chicago: University of Illinois Press.

Kaufmann, Y. (1989). Analytical psychotherapy. In R. J. Corsini & D. Wedding (Eds.), *Current psychotherapies* (4th ed., pp. 119–152). Itasca, IL: F. E. Peacock.

Kazdin, A. E. (1994). Methodology, design, and evaluation in psychotherapy research. In A. E. Bergin & S. L. Garfield (Eds.), *Handbook of psychotherapy and behavior change* (4th ed., pp. 19–71). New York: Wiley.

Keith-Lucas, A. (1992). Encounters with children: Children and religion. *Residential Treatment for Children and Youth, 10,* 65–73.

Kehoe, N. (1997). *Religious/Spiritual History Questionnaire.* Cambridge, MA: Author.

Keith-Spiegel, P., & Koocher, G. (1985). *Ethics in psychology: Standards and cases.* New York: Random House.

Kelly, E. W. (1993, March). *The status of religious and spiritual issues in counselor education.* Paper presented at the annual convention of the American Counseling Association, Atlanta, GA.

Kelly, E. W. (1995). *Religion and spirituality in counseling and psychotherapy.* Alexandria, VA: American Counseling Association.

Kessell, P., & McBrearty, J. F. (1967). Values and psychotherapy: A review of the literature. *Perceptual and Motor Skills, 25* (Suppl. 2–U25), 669–690.

King, M. B. (1967). Measuring the religious variable: Nine proposed dimensions. *Journal for the Scientific Study of Religion, 6,* 173–190.

King, M. B., & Hunt, R. A. (1969). Measuring the religious variable: Amended findings. *Journal for the Scientific Study of Religion, 8,* 321–323.

Kirk, J., & Miller, M. L. (1986). *Reliability and validity in qualitative research.* Beverly Hills, CA: Sage.

Kirkpatrick, L. A. (1989). A psychometric analysis of the Allport-Ross and Feagin measures of intrinsic-extrinsic religious orientation. *Research in the Social Scientific Study of Religion, 1,* 1–31.

Kirkpatrick, L. A., & Hood, R. W., Jr. (1990). Intrinsic-extrinsic religious orientation: The boon or bane of contemporary psychology of religion? *Journal for the Scientific Study of Religion, 29,* 442–462.

Kitchener, R. F. (1980a). Ethical relativism and behavior therapy. *Journal of Consulting and Clinical Psychology, 48,* 1–7.

Kitchener, R. F. (1980b). Ethical relativism, ethical naturalism, and behavior therapy. *Journal of Counsulting and Clinical Psychology, 48,* 14–16.

Kluback, W, & Weinbaum, M. (1957). *Dilthey's philosophy of existence: Introduction to Weltanschauungslehre.* Westport, CT: Greenwood Press.

Kluckhohn, C. (1951). Values and value orientations in the theory of action. In T. Parsons & F. A. Shields (Eds.), *Toward a general theory of action* (pp. 388–433). Cambridge, MA: Harvard University Press.

Kluckhohn, C. (1956). Toward a comparison of value-emphasis in different cultures. In L. D. White (Ed.), *The state of social sciences* (pp. 116–132). Chicago: University of Chicago Press.

Kluckhohn, F. R., & Strodtbeck, F. L. (1961). *Variations in value orientations.* Evanston, IL: Row, Peterson.

Koch, S. (1959–1963). *Psychology: A study of a science* (Vols. 1–6). New York: McGraw-Hill.

Koch, S. (1981). The nature and limits of psychological knowledge: Lessons of a century of science. *American Psychologist, 36,* 257–269.

Koenig, H. G. (1997). *Is religion good for your health? The effects of religion on physical and mental health.* New York: Haworth Press.

Koltko, M. E. (1990). How religious beliefs affect psychotherapy: The example of Mormonism. *Psychotherapy, 27,* 132–141.

Komp, D. M. (1993). *A child shall lead them: Lessons in hope from children with cancer.* Grand Rapids, MI: Zondervan Publishing House.

Kopp, R. R. (1995). *Metaphor therapy: Using client-generated metaphors in psychotherapy.* New York: Brunner/Mazel.

Krasner, L. (1962). The therapist as a social reinforcement machine. In H. H. Strupp & L. Luborsky (Eds.), *Research in psychotherapy* (Vol. 2, pp. 61–94). Washington, DC: American Psychological Association.

Krippner, S., & Welch, P. (1992). *Spiritual dimensions of healing.* New York: Irvington.

Kuhn, T. (1970). *The structure of scientific revolutions* (2nd ed.). Chicago: University of Chicago Press.

Kushner, H. S. (1981). *When bad things happen to good people.* New York: Schocken Books.

Lakatos, I., & Musgrave, A. (Eds.). (1970). *Criticism and the growth of knowledge.* New York: Cambridge University Press.

Lambert, M. J., & Bergin, A. E. (1994). The effectiveness of psychotherapy. In A. E. Bergin & S. L. Garfield (Eds.), *Handbook of psychotherapy and behavior change* (4th ed., pp. 143–189). New York: Wiley.

Lambert, M. J., & Hill, C. E. (1994). Assessing psychotherapy outcomes and processes. In A. E. Bergin & S. L. Garfield (Eds.), *Handbook of psychotherapy and behavior change* (4th ed., pp. 72–113). New York: Wiley.

Larson, D. B., Koenig, H. G., Kaplan, B. H., Greenberg, R. F., Logue, E., & Tyroler, H. A. (1989). The impact of religion on men's blood pressure. *Journal of Religion and Health, 28,* 265–278.

Larson, D. B., & Larson, S. (1994). *The forgotten factor in physical and mental health: What does the research show?* Rockville, MD: National Institute for Healthcare Research.

Larson, D. B., Lu, F. G., & Swyers, J. P. (Eds.). (1996). *Model curriculum for psychiatry residency training programs: Religion and spirituality in clinical practice.* Rockville, MD: National Institute for Healthcare Research.

Laudan, L. (1984). *Science and values: The aims of science and their role in scientific debate.* Berkeley: University of California Press.

Lazarus, A. A. (1973). Multimodal behavior therapy: Treating the BASIC I.D. *Journal of Nervous and Mental Disease, 156,* 404–411.

Lazarus, A. A. (1976). *Multimodal behavior therapy.* New York: Springer.

Lazarus, A. A. (1989). Multimodal therapy. In R. J. Corsini & D. Wedding (Eds.), *Current psychotherapies* (4th ed., pp. 503–544). Itasca, IL: F. E. Peacock.

Lea, W. G. (1982). Religion, mental health, and clinical issues. *Journal of Religion and Health, 21,* 336–351.

Leahey, T. H. (1991). *A history of modern psychology.* Englewood Cliffs, NJ: Prentice Hall.

Levin, J. S. (1994). Investigating the epidemiologic effects of religious experience. In J. S. Levin (Ed.), *Religion in aging and health: Theoretical foundations and methodological frontiers* (pp. 3–17). Thousand Oaks, CA: Sage.

Levin, J. S. (1995, April). *Epidemiology of religion.* Paper presented at a conference of the National Institute for Healthcare Research, Leesburg, VA.

Lincoln, Y. S., & Guba, E. G. (1985). *Naturalistic inquiry.* Beverly Hills, CA: Sage.

Little, G. L., & Robinson, K. D. (1988). Moral reconation therapy: A systematic step-by-step treatment system for treatment resistant clients. *Psychological Reports, 62,* 135–151.

London, P. (1964). *Modes and morals of psychotherapy.* New York: Holt, Rinehart & Winston.

London, P. (1986). *The modes and morals of psychotherapy* (2nd ed.). New York: McGraw-Hill.

Lovinger, R. J. (1984). *Working with religious issues in therapy.* Northwale, NJ: Jason Aronson.

Lovinger, R. J. (1990). *Religion and counseling: The psychological impact of religious belief.* New York: Continuum.

Lovinger, R. J. (1996). Considering the religious dimension in assessment and treatment. In E. Shafranske (Ed.), *Religion and the clinical practice of psychology* (pp. 327–364). Washington, DC: American Psychological Association.

Lowe, C. M. (1976). *Value orientations in counseling and psychotherapy: The meanings of mental health* (2nd ed.). Cranston, RI: Carroll Press.

Lucas, C. (1985). Out at the edge: Notes on a paradigm shift. *Journal of Counseling and Development, 64,* 165–172.

Luks, A. (1993). *The healing power of doing good.* New York: Ballantine Books.

Lundin, R. W. (1985). *Theories and systems of psychology* (3rd ed.). Lexington, MA: Heath.

Madsen, T. G. (1995). On how we know. In *Brigham Young University 1994–95 devotional and fireside speeches.* Provo, UT: Brigham Young University Publications and Graphics.

Mahler, M., Pine, F., & Bergman, A. (1975). *The psychological birth of the human infant: Symbiosis and individuation.* New York: Basic Books.

Mahrer, A. (1988). Discovery-oriented research. *American Psychologist, 43,* 694–702.

Malony, H. N. (1985). Assessing religious maturity. In E. M. Stern (Ed.), *Psychotherapy and the religiously committed patient* (pp. 25–33). New York: Haworth Press.

Malony, H. N. (1988). The clinical assessment of optimal religious functioning. *Review of Religious Research, 30*, 3–17.

Malony, H. N., & Southard, S. (Eds.). (1992). *Handbook of religious conversion.* Birmingham, AL: Religious Education Press.

Manicas, P. T., & Secord, P. F. (1983). Implications for psychology of the new philosophy of science. *American Psychologist, 38*, 399–413.

Martin, J. E., & Carlson, C. R. (1988). Spiritual dimensions of health psychology. In W. R. Miller & J. E. Martin (Eds.), *Behavior therapy and religion* (pp. 57–110). Newbury Park, CA: Sage.

Maslow, A. H. (1968). *Toward a psychology of being* (2nd ed.). New York: Van Nostrand.

Maslow, A. (1970). *Motivation and personality* (Rev. ed.). New York: Harper & Row.

Maslow, A. H. (1971). *The farther reaches of human nature.* New York: Viking Press.

Mason, S. F. (1962). *A history of the sciences.* New York: Macmillan.

Matarazzo, J. D. (1985). Psychotherapy. In G. A. Kimble & K. Schlesinger (Eds.), *Topics in the history of psychology* (Vol. 2, pp. 219–250). Hillsdale, NJ: Erlbaum.

Matthews, D. A., Larson, D. B., & Barry, C. P. (1993–1995). *The faith factor: An annotated bibliography of clinical research on spiritual subjects* (Vols. 1–3). Rockville, MD: National Institute for Healthcare Research.

Matthews, D. A., McCullough, M. E., Larson, D. B., Koenig, H. G., Swyers, J. P., & Milano, M. G. (in press). Religious commitment and health: A review of the research and implications for family medicine. *Archives of Family Medicine.*

Mattson, R., & Scharman, J. S. (1994). Divorce in Mormon women: A qualitative study. *Association of Mormon, Counselors and Psychotherapists Journal, 20*, 29–60.

May, R. (Ed.). (1961). *Existential psychology.* New York: Random House.

May, R., Angel, E., & Ellenberger, H. (1958). *Existence.* New York: Basic Books.

McCasland, S. V., Cairns, E. G., & Yu, D. C. (1969). *Religions of the world.* New York: Random House.

McCrady, B. S., & Delaney, S. I. (1995). Self-help groups. In R. K. Hester & W. R. Miller (Eds.), *Handbook of alcoholism treatment approaches* (2nd ed., pp. 160–175). Boston: Allyn & Bacon.

McCrady, B. S., & Miller, W. R. (1993). *Research on Alcoholics Anonymous: Opportunities and alternatives.* New Brunswick, NJ: Rutgers Center for Alcohol Studies.

McCullough, M. E. (1995). Prayer and health: Conceptual issues, research review, and research agenda. *Journal of Psychology and Theology, 25*, 15–29.

McCullough, M. E., Sandage, S. J., & Worthington, E. L., Jr. (1997). *To forgive is human.* Donners Grove, IL: Intervarsity Press.

McCullough, M. E., & Worthington, E. L., Jr. (1994a). Encouraging clients to forgive people who have hurt them: Review, critique, and research prospectus. *Journal of Psychology and Theology, 22*, 15–29.

McCullough, M. E., & Worthington, E. L., Jr. (1994b). Models of interpersonal forgiveness and their applications to counseling: Review and critique. *Counseling and Values, 39,* 2–14.

McLemore, C. (1982). *The scandal of psychotherapy.* Wheaton, IL: Tyndale House.

Meadow, M. J. (1978). The cross and the seed: Active and receptive spiritualities. *Journal of Religion and Health, 17,* 57–69.

Meadow, M. J. (1982). True womanhood and women's victimization. *Counseling and Values, 26,* 93–101.

Meadow, M. J., & Kahoe, R. D. (1984). *Psychology of religion: Religion in individual lives.* New York: Harper & Row.

Meichenbaum, D. (1977). *Cognitive behavior modification: An integrative approach.* New York: Plenum Press.

Meissner, M. W. (1996). The pathology of beliefs and the beliefs of pathology. In E. Shafranske (Ed.), *Religion and the clinical practice of psychology* (pp. 241–267). Washington, DC: American Psychological Association.

Mental health: Does therapy help? (1995, November). *Consumer Reports, 6,* 734–739.

Messer, S. B., Sass, L. A., & Woolfolk, R. L. (1988). *Hermeneutics and psychological theory: Interpretive perspectives on personality, psychotherapy, and psychopathology.* New Brunswick, NJ: Rutgers University Press.

Miller, J. P. (1994). *The contemplative practitioner: Meditation in education and the professions.* Westport, CT: Bergin & Garvey.

Miller, W., & Crabtree, B. (1994). Clinical research. In D. Denzin & Y. S. Lincoln (Eds.), *Handbook of qualitative research* (pp. 340–352). Thousand Oaks, CA: Sage.

Miller, W. R., & C'deBaca, J. (1994). Quantum change: Toward a psychology transformation. In T. Heatherton & J. Weinberger (Eds.), *Can personality change?* (pp. 253–280). Washington, DC: American Psychological Association.

Miller, W. R., & Jackson, K. A. (1985). *Practical psychology for pastors.* Englewood Cliffs, NJ: Prentice Hall.

Miller, W. R., & Martin, J. E. (Eds.). (1988). *Behavior therapy and religion: Integrating spiritual and behavioral approaches to change.* Newbury Park, CA: Sage.

Mills, J. C., & Crowley, R. J. (1986). *Therapeutic metaphors for children and the child within.* New York: Brunner/Mazel.

Moberg, D. O. (Ed.). (1979). *Spiritual well-being: Sociological perspectives.* Lanham, MD: University Press of America.

Moberg, D. O. (1984). Subjective measures of spiritual well-being. *Review of Religious Research, 25,* 351–364.

Moench, L. A. (1985). Mormon forms of psychopathology. *Association of Mormon Counselors and Psychotherapists Journal, 11,* 61–73.

Moody, R. (1975). *Life after life.* New York: Bantam Books.

Moon, G. W., Willis, D. E., Bailey, J. W., & Kwasny, J. C. (1993). Self-reported use of Christian spiritual guidance techniques by Christian psychotherapists, pastoral counselors, and spiritual directors. *Journal of Psychology and Christianity, 12,* 24–37.

Morse, J. M., & Field, P. A. (1995). *Qualitative research methods for health professionals* (2nd ed.). Thousand Oaks, CA: Sage.

Morse, M. (1994a). *Parting visions: Uses and meanings of pre-death, psychic, and spiritual experiences.* New York: Harper.

Morse, M. L. (1994b). Near death experiences and death-related visions in children: Implications for the clinician. *Current Problems in Pediatrics, 24,* 55–83.

Mosak, H. H. (1989). Adlerian psychotherapy. In R. J. Corsini & D. Wedding (Eds.), *Current psychotherapies* (4th ed., pp. 65–116). Itasca, IL: F. E. Peacock.

Moyers, W. (1996, October 11–13). America's religious mosaic. *USA Weekend,* pp. 4–5.

Murray, D. J. (1988). *A history of Western psychology* (2nd ed.). Englewood Cliffs, NJ: Prentice Hall.

M. W. H. (1986, November). Letter of the month. *Minnesota Psychological Association Newsletter,* p. 10.

National Federation of Societies for Clinical Social Work. (1985). *Code of ethics.* Silver Spring, MD: Author.

National Institute for Health Care Research. (1996). *Faith and Medicine Connection.* (Vol. 1, no. 1). Rockville, MD: Author.

Neimeyer, R. A., & Mahoney, M. J. (Eds.). (1995). *Constructivism in psychotherapy.* Washington, DC: American Psychological Association.

Nielsen, N. C., Jr., Hein, N., Reynolds, F. E., Miller, A. L., Karff, S. E., Cowan, A. C., McLean, P., & Erdel, T. P. (1988). *Religions of the world* (2nd ed.). New York: St. Martin's Press.

Nigosian, S. A. (1994). *World faiths* (2nd ed.). New York: St. Martin's Press.

Norcross, J. C. (Ed.). (1986). *Handbook of eclectic psychotherapy.* New York: Brunner/Mazel.

Norcross, J. C., & Goldfried, M. R. (Eds.). (1992). *Handbook of psychotherapy integration.* New York: Basic Books.

Ogles, B. M., Lambert, M. J., & Masters, K. S. (1996). *Assessing outcome in clinical practice.* Des Moines, IA: Longwood.

Orlinsky, D. E., Grawe, K., & Parks, B. K. (1994). Process and outcome in psychotherapy: Noch einmal. In A. E. Bergin & S. L. Garfield (Eds.), *Handbook of psychotherapy and behavior change* (4th ed., pp. 270–376). New York: Wiley.

Ornish, D. (1990). *Dr. Dean Ornish's program for reversing heart disease: The only system scientifically proven to reverse heart disease without drugs or surgery.* New York: Ballantine Books.

Oser, F. K. (1991). The development of religious judgment. In F. K. Oser & W. G. Scarlett (Eds.), *Religious development in childhood and adolescence.* (pp. 5–25). San Francisco, CA: Jossey-Bass.

Ostling, R. N. (1992, December 28). Science, God and man. *Time*, pp. 39–44.

Packer, M. J. (1985). Hermeneutic inquiry in the study of human conduct. *American Psychologist, 40,* 1081–1093.

Palmer, S. J., & Keller, R. R. (1989). *Religions of the world: A Latter-Day Saint View.* Provo, UT: Brigham Young University.

Paloutzian, R. F., & Ellison, C. W. (1979, September). Developing a measure of spiritual well-being. In R. F. Paloutzian (Chair), *Spiritual well-being, loneliness, and perceived quality of life.* Symposium presented at the 87th Annual Convention of the American Psychological Association, New York City.

Paloutzian, R. F., & Ellison, C. W. (1991). *Manual for the spiritual well-being scale.* Nyack, NY: Life Advances.

Pargament, K. I. (1996). Religious methods of coping: Resources for the conservation and transformation of significance. In E. Shafranske (Ed.), *Religion and the clinical practice of psychology* (pp. 215–239). Washington, DC: American Psychological Association.

Pargament, K. I., Echemendia, R. J., Johnson, S., Cook, P., McGath, C., Myers, J. G., & Brannick, M. (1987). The conservative church: Psychosocial advantages and disadvantages. *American Journal of Community Psychology, 15,* 269–286.

Pargament, K. I., Falgout, K., Ensing, D. S., Reilly, B., Silverman, M., Van Haitsma, K., & Warren, R. (1991). The Congregation Development Program: Data-based consultation with churches and synagogues. *Professional Psychology: Research and Practice, 22,* 393–404.

Pargament, K. I., Kennell, J., Hathaway, W., Grenvengoed, N., Newman, J., & Jones, W. (1988). Religion and the problem-solving process: Three styles of coping. *Journal for the Scientific Study of Religion, 27,* 90–104.

Pargament, K. I., Maton, K. I., & Hess, R. E. (Eds.). (1992). *Religion and prevention in mental health: Research, vision and action.* New York: Haworth Press.

Pargament, K. I., & Park, C. L. (1995). Merely a defense? The variety of religious means and ends. *Journal of Social Issues, 51,* 13–32.

Pargament, K. I., Silverman, W., Johnson, S., Echemendia, R., & Snyder, S. (1983). The psychological climate of religious congregations. *American Journal of Community Psychology, 11,* 351–381.

Parrinder, G. (1961). *Worship in the world's religions.* London: Faber & Faber.

Patterson, C. H. (1958). The place of values in counseling and psychotherapy. *Journal of Counseling Psychology, 5,* 216–223.

Paul, E. R. (1992). *Science, religion, and Mormon cosmology.* Chicago: University of Chicago Press.

Payne, I. R., Bergin, A. E., Bielema, K. A., & Jenkins, P. H. (1991). Review of religion and mental health: Prevention and the enhancement of psychosocial functioning. *Prevention in Human Services, 9,* 11–40.

Payne, I. R., Bergin, A. E., & Loftus, P. E. (1992). A review of attempts to integrate spiritual and standard psychotherapy techniques. *Journal of Psychotherapy Integration, 2,* 171–192.

Pecheur, D. R., & Edwards, K. J. (1984). A comparison of secular and religious versions of cognitive therapy with depressed Christian college students. *Journal of Psychology and Theology, 12,* 45–54.

Peck, M. S. (1978). *The road less travelled: A new psychology of love, traditional values, and spiritual growth.* New York: Simon & Schuster.

Peck, M. S. (1983). *People of the lie.* New York: Simon & Schuster.

Peck, M. S. (1993). *Further along the road less traveled: The unending journey toward spiritual growth.* New York: Simon & Schuster.

Percesepe, G. (1991). *Philosophy: An introduction to the labor of reason.* New York: Macmillan.

Peterson, E. A., & Nelson, K. (1987). How to meet your clients' spiritual needs. *Journal of Psychosocial Nursing, 25*(5), 34–39.

Plantinga, A. (1984). Advice to Christian philosophers. *Faith and Philosophy, 1,* 253–271.

Plantinga, A., & Wolterstorff, N. (Eds.). (1983). *Faith and rationality: Reason and belief in God.* Notre Dame, IN: University of Notre Dame Press.

Polanyi, M. (1962). *Personal knowledge: Towards a post-critical philosophy.* Chicago: University of Chicago Press.

Polkinghorne, J. C. (1990). A revived natural theology. In J. Fennema & I. Paul (Eds.), *Science and religion: One world-changing perspectives on reality* (pp. 87–97). Norwell, MA: Kluwer Academic.

Poloma, M. M., & Pendleton, B. F. (1991). The effects of prayer and prayer experiences on measures of general well-being. *Journal of Psychology and Theology, 19,* 71–83.

Ponterotto, J. G., Casas, J. P., Suzuki, L. A., & Alexander, C. M. (Eds.) (1995). *Handbook of multicultural counseling.* Thousand Oaks, CA: Sage.

Ponterotto, J. G., Suzuki, L. A., Mellor, P. J. (Eds.). (1996). *Handbook of multicultural assessment.* San Francisco: Jossey-Bass.

Pope, E. (1989, October). [Letter to the editor]. *Central Washington University Observer,* p. 2.

Pope, K. S. (1985). Dual relationships: A violation of ethical, legal, and clinical standards. *California State Psychologist, 20,* 3–5.

Popper, K. R. (Ed.). (1972). *Objective knowledge.* Oxford, England: Clarendon Press.

Popper, K. R., & Eccles, J. C. (1977). *The self and its brain.* New York: Springer.

Powell, L. H., & Thoresen, C. E. (1987). Modifying the Type A behavior pattern: A small group treatment approach. In J. A. Blumenthal & D. C. McKee (Eds.), *Applications in behavioral medicine and health psychology: A clinician's source book* (pp. 171–207). Sarasota, FL: Professional Resource Exchange.

Preece, J. E. (1994). *An ethnographic study into the concerns and issues of participants attending a therapy group for individuals with chronic pain and/or illness.* Unpublished doctoral dissertation, Brigham Young University, Provo, UT.

Princeton Religious Research Center. (1990). *Religion in America 1990.* Princeton, NJ: Gallup Organization.

Propst, L. R. (1980). The comparative efficacy of religious and nonreligious imagery for the treatment of mild depression in religious individuals. *Cognitive Therapy and Research, 4,* 167–178.

Propst, L. R. (1988). *Psychotherapy in a religious framework: Spirituality in the emotional healing process.* New York: Human Sciences Press.

Propst, L. R. (1996). Cognitive–behavioral therapy and the religious person. In E. P. Shafranske (Ed.), *Religion and the clinical practice of psychology* (pp. 391–407). Washington, DC: American Psychological Association.

Propst, L. R., Ostrom, R., Watkins, P., Dean, T., & Mashburn, D. (1992). Comparative efficacy of religious and nonreligious cognitive–behavioral therapy for the treatment of clinical depression in religious individuals. *Journal of Consulting and Clinical Psychology, 60,* 94–103.

Pruyser, P. (1971). Assessment of the patient's religious attitudes in the psychiatric case study. *Bulletin of the Menninger Clinic, 35,* 272–291.

Randour, M. L. (1987). *Women's psyche women's spirit.* New York: Columbia University Press.

Ray, W. J., & Ravizza, R. (1988). *Methods: Toward a science of behavior and experience* (3rd ed.). Belmont, CA: Wadsworth.

Rayburn, C. A. (1985). Some ethical considerations in psychotherapy with religious women. *Psychotherapy, 22,* 803–812.

Rayburn, C. A. (1997). *Inventory on religiousness.* Silver Spring, MD: Author.

Rayburn, C. A., & Richmond, L. J. (1996). *Inventory on spirituality.* Silver Spring, MD: Authors.

Redfield, J. (1993). *The celestine prophecy: An adventure.* New York: Warner Books.

Reichardt, C. S., & Cook, T. D. (1979). Beyond qualitative versus quantitative methods. In T. D. Cook & C. S. Reichardt (Eds.), *Qualitative and quantitative methods in evaluation research* (pp. 7–32). Beverly Hills, CA: Sage.

Report on trends. (1993). *Gallup Poll Monthly, 331* (4), 36–38.

Rice, L. N., & Greenberg, L. S. (1984). *Patterns of change: Intensive analysis of psychotherapy process.* New York: Guilford Press.

Richards, D. G. (1991). The phenomenology and psychological correlates of verbal prayer. *Journal of Psychology and Theology, 19,* 354–363.

Richards, P. S. (1991). Religious devoutness in college students: Relations with emotional adjustment and psychological separation from parents. *Journal of Counseling Psychology, 38,* 189–196.

Richards, P. S. (1995). [Therapist critical incident case reports]. Unpublished raw data, Department of Educational Psychology, Brigham Young University.

Richards, P. S., & Davison, M. L. (1989). The effects of theistic and atheistic counselor values on client trust: A multidimensional scaling analysis. *Counseling and Values, 33,* 109–120.

Richards, P. S., Owen, L., & Stein, S. (1993). A religiously oriented group counseling intervention for self-defeating perfectionism: A pilot study. *Counseling and Values, 37,* 96–104.

Richards, P. S., & Potts, R. W. (1995a). Using spiritual interventions in psychotherapy: Practices, successes, failures, and ethical concerns of Mormon psychotherapists. *Professional Psychology: Research and Practice, 26,* 163–170.

Richards, P. S., & Potts, R. (1995b). Spiritual interventions in psychotherapy: A survey of the practices and beliefs of AMCAP members. *Association of Mormon Counselors and Psychotherapists Journal, 21,* 39–68.

Richards, P. S., Rector, J., & Tjeltveit, A. C. (in press). Values and psychotherapy. In W. R. Miller (Ed.), *Integrating spirituality in treatment: Resources for practitioners.* Washington, DC: American Psychological Association.

Richards, P. S., Smith, S. A., & Davis, L. F. (1989). Healthy and unhealthy forms of religiousness manifested by psychotherapy clients: An empirical investigation. *Journal of Research in Personality, 23,* 506–524.

Rickman, H. P. (Ed.). (1976). *W. Dilthey selected writings.* New York: Cambridge University Press.

Rickman, H. P. (1979). *Wilhelm Dilthey: Pioneer of the human studies.* London: Paul Elek.

Ring, K. (1980). *Life at death: A scientific investigation of the near-death experience.* New York: Coward, McCann & Geoghegan.

Ring, K. (1995, August). Near-death experiences in the blind: Can they really see? Paper presented at the International Association for Near-Death Studies, West Hartford, CT.

Roberts, K. A. (1990). *Religion in sociological perspective.* (2nd ed.) Belmont, CA: Wadsworth.

Robinson, J. P., & Shaver, P. R. (1973). *Measures of social psychological attitudes* (Rev. ed.). Ann Arbor, MI: Survey Research Center, Institute for Social Research.

Rodegast, P., & Stanton, J. (1985). *Emmanuel's book: A manual for living comfortably in the cosmos.* New York: Bantam Books.

Rogers, C. R. (1951). *Client-centered therapy.* Boston: Houghton Mifflin.

Rogers, C. R. (1957). The necessary and sufficient conditions of therapeutic personality change. *Journal of Consulting Psychology, 21,* 95–103.

Rogers, C. R. (1959). A theory of therapy, personality, and interpersonal relationships, as developed in the client-centered framework. In S. Koch (Ed.), *Psychology: A study of a science* (Vol. 3, pp. 184–256). New York: Basic Books.

Rogers, C. R. (1961). *On becoming a person.* Boston: Houghton Mifflin.

Rogers, C. R. (1973). Some new challenges. *American Psychologist, 28,* 379–387.

Rogers, C. R. (1980). *A way of being.* Boston: Houghton Mifflin.

Ronan, C. A. (1982). *Science: Its history and development among the world's cultures.* New York: Hamlyn Publishing.

Rychlak, J. F. (1981). *Introduction to personality and psychotherapy: A theory-construction approach (2nd ed.)*. Boston: Houghton Mifflin.

Sagan, C. (1995). *The demon-haunted world: Science as a candle in the dark*. New York: Random House.

Sanua, V. D. (1969). Religion, mental health, and personality: A review of empirical studies. *American Journal of Psychiatry, 125*, 1203–1213.

Sarason, S. B. (1981). *Psychology misdirected*. New York: Free Press.

Scharman, J. S. (1994). Relationship issues in LDS blended families. *Association of Mormon Counselors and Psychotherapists Journal, 20*, 15–38.

Scott, W. G., & Hart, D. K. (1989). *Organizational values in America*. New Brunswick, NJ: Transaction Books.

Seligman, L. (1988). Invited commentary: Three contributions of a spiritual perspective to counseling, psychotherapy, and behavior change. *Counseling and Values, 33*, 55–56.

Seligman, M. E. P. (1995). The effectiveness of psychotherapy: The *Consumer Report* study. *American Psychologist, 50*, 965–974.

Shafranske, E. P. (Ed.). (1996). *Religion and the clinical practice of psychology*. Washington, DC: American Psychological Association.

Shafranske, E. P., & Malony, H. N. (1990). Clinical psychologists' religious and spiritual orientations and their practice of psychotherapy. *Psychotherapy, 27*, 72–78.

Shafranske, E. P., & Malony, H. N. (1996). Religion and the clinical practice of psychology: A case for inclusion. In E. P. Shafranske (Ed.), *Religion and the clinical practice of psychology* (pp. 561–586). Washington, DC: American Psychological Association.

Shine, J. (1996, February 9–11). Religious revival on campus. *USA Weekend*, pp. 8–9.

Shrock, D. A. (1984). Suppression of women by religion. *Counseling and Values, 29*, 49–58.

Siegel, B. S. (1986). *Love, medicine & miracles: Lessons learned about self-healing from a surgeon's experience with exceptional patients*. New York: Harper & Row.

Siegel, R. K. (1980). The psychology of life after death. *American Psychologist, 35*, 911–931.

Siegelman, E. (1990). *Metaphor and meaning in psychotherapy*. New York: Guilford Press.

Silverman, W. H., Pargament, K. I., Johnson, S. M., Echemendia, R. J., & Snyder, S. (1983). Measuring member satisfaction with the church. *Journal of Applied Psychology, 68*, 664–677.

Sire, J. W. (1976). *The universe next door*. Downers Grove, IL: InterVarsity Press.

Slife, B. D. (1993). *Time and psychological explanation*. Albany: State University of New York Press.

Slife, B. D., & Williams, R. N. (1995). *What's behind the research? Discovering hidden assumptions in the behavioral sciences*. Thousand Oaks, CA: Sage.

Slife, B., Hope, C., & Nebeker, S. (1996, August). *Examining the relationship between religious spirituality and psychological science.* Paper presented at the 104th Annual Convention of the American Psychological Association, Toronto, Ontario.

Smart, N. (1983). *Worldviews: Crosscultural explorations of human beliefs.* New York: Scribner.

Smart, N. (1993). *Religions of Asia.* Englewood Cliffs, NJ: Prentice Hall.

Smart, N. (1994). *Religions of the West.* Englewood Cliffs, NJ: Prentice Hall.

Smith, J. C. (1975). Meditation as psychotherapy: A review of the literature. *Psychological Bulletin, 82,* 558–564.

Smith, L. M. (1994). Biographical method. In N. K. Denzin & Y. S. Lincoln (Eds.), *Handbook of qualitative research* (pp. 286–305). Thousand Oaks, CA: Sage.

Solomon, R. C. (1990). *The big questions: A short introduction to philosophy* (3rd ed.). San Diego, CA: Harcourt Brace Jovanovich.

Sorokin, P. A. (1957). *Social and cultural dynamics: A study of art, truth, ethics, law, and social relationships* (Rev. and abridged). Boston: Extending Horizons Books.

Speight, S. L., Myers, L. J., Cox, C. I., & Highlen, P. S. (1991). A redefinition of multicultural counseling. *Journal of Counseling and Development, 70,* 29–36.

Spendlove, D. C., West, D. W., & Danish, W. W. (1984). Risk factors and the prevalence of depression in Mormon women. *Social Science and Medicine, 18,* 491–495.

Spero, M. H. (Ed.). (1985). *Psychotherapy of the religious patient.* Springfield, IL: Charles C Thomas.

Spero, M. H. (1992). *Religious objects as psychological structures.* Chicago: University of Chicago Press.

Sperry, L., & Giblin, P. (1996). Marital and family therapy with religious persons. In E. P. Shafranske (Ed.), *Religion and the clinical practice of psychology* (pp. 511–532). Washington, DC: American Psychological Association.

Sperry, R. W. (1988). Psychology's mentalist paradigm and the religion/science tension. *American Psychologist, 43,* 607–613.

Sperry, R. W. (1995). The riddle of consciousness and the changing scientific worldview. *Journal of Humanistic Psychology, 35,* 7–33.

Spiegel, D., Bloom, J. R., Kraemer, H. C., & Gottheil, E. (1989). Effect of psychosocial treatment on survival of patients with metastatic breast cancer. *The Lancet, 2,* 888–891.

Spilka, B., Comp, G., & Goldsmith, W. M. (1981). Faith and behavior: Religion in introductory psychology texts of the 1950's and 1970's. *Teaching of Psychology, 8,* 158–160.

Spilka, B., Hood, R. W., Jr., & Gorsuch, R. L. (1985). *The psychology of religion: An empirical approach.* Englewood Cliffs, NJ: Prentice Hall.

Spilka, B., Shaver, P., & Kirkpatrick, L. (1985). General attribution theory for the psychology of religion. *Journal for the Scientific Study of Religion, 24,* 1–20.

Stake, R. E. (1994). Case studies. In N. K. Denzin & Y. S. Lincoln (Eds.), *Handbook of qualitative research* (pp. 236–247). Thousand Oaks, CA: Sage.

Stark, R. (1971). Psychopathology and religious commitment. *Review of Religious Research, 12,* 165–176.

Stark, R., & Glock, C. Y. (1968). *American piety: The nature of religious commitment.* Berkeley: University of California Press.

Staver, M. D. (1995). *Faith and freedom: A complete handbook for defending your religious rights.* Wheaton, IL: Crossway Books.

Stern, E. M. (Ed.). (1985). *Psychotherapy and the religiously committed patient.* New York: Haworth Press.

Stricker, G., & Gold, J. R. (Eds.). (1993). *Comprehensive handbook of psychotherapy integration.* New York: Plenum.

Strommen, M. P. (Ed.). (1971). *Research on religious development: A comprehensive handbook.* New York: Hawthorn.

Strommen, M. P. (1984). Psychology's blind spot: A religious faith. *Counseling and Values, 28,* 150–161.

Strunk, O., Jr. (1970). Humanistic religious psychology: A new chapter in the psychology of religion. *Journal of Pastoral Care, 24,* 90–97.

Stuart, R. B. (1980). *Helping couples change: A social learning approach to marital therapy.* New York: Guilford Press.

Sue, D. W. (1978). Eliminating cultural oppression in counseling: A conceptual analysis. *Personnel and Guidance Journal, 55,* 422–424.

Sue, D. W. (1981). *Counseling the culturally different.* New York: Wiley.

Sue, D. W., & Sue, D. (1977). Barriers to effective cross-cultural counseling. *Journal of Counseling Psychology, 24,* 420–429.

Sue, D. W., & Sue, D. (1990). *Counseling the culturally different: Theory and practice* (2nd ed.). New York: Wiley.

Sue, D. W., Bergnier, J. E., Duran, A., Feinberg, L., Pedersen, P., Smith, E., & Vasquez-Nuttall, E. (1982). Position paper: Cross-cultural counseling competencies. *The Counseling Psychologist, 10,* 45–52.

Sue, S., Zane, N., & Young, K. (1994). Research on psychotherapy with culturally diverse populations. In A. E. Bergin & S. L. Garfield (Eds.), *Handbook of psychotherapy and behavior change* (4th ed., pp. 783–817). New York: Wiley.

Sutherland, C. (1992). *Reborn in the light: Life after near-death experiences.* New York: Bantam Books.

Sweet, M. J., & Johnson, C. G. (1990). Enhancing empathy: The interpersonal implications of a Buddhist meditation technique. *Psychotherapy, 27,* 19–29.

Tamminen, K. (1991). *Religious development in children and youth: An empirical study.* Helsinki, Finland: Suomalinen Tiedeakatemia.

Tan, S. Y. (1987). Cognitive-behavior therapy: A biblical approach and critique. *Journal of Psychology and Theology, 15,* 103–112.

Tan, S. Y. (1993, January). *Training in professional psychology: Diversity includes religion.* Paper presented at the National Council of Schools of Professional Psychology midwinter conference, La Jolla, CA.

Tan, S. Y. (1994). Ethical considerations in religious psychotherapy: Potential pitfalls and unique resources. *Journal of Psychology and Theology, 22,* 389–394.

Tan, S. Y. (1996). Religion in clinical practice: Implicit and explicit integration. In E. Shafranske (Ed.), *Religion and the clinical practice of psychology* (pp. 365–387). Washington, DC: American Psychological Association.

Taylor, E. (1994, November–December). Desperately seeking spirituality. *Psychology Today,* pp. 54–68.

Templeton, J. M., & Herrmann, R. L. (1994). *Is God the only reality? Science points to a deeper meaning of the universe.* New York: Continuum.

Tipler, F. J. (1994). *The physics of immortality: Modern cosmology, God and the resurrection of the dead.* New York: Doubleday.

Tjeltveit, A. C. (1986). The ethics of value conversion in psychotherapy: Appropriate and inappropriate therapist influence on client values. *Clinical Psychology Review, 6,* 515–537.

Toulmin, S. (1962). *Foresight and understanding.* San Francisco: Harper.

Trzepacz, P. T., & Baker, R. W. (1993). *The psychiatric mental status examination.* New York: Oxford University Press.

Uzoka, A. F. (1979). The myth of the nuclear family. *American Psychologist, 34,* 1095–1106.

Vande Kemp, H. (1996). Historical perspective: Religion and clinical psychology in America. In E. P. Shafranske (Ed.), *Religion and the clinical practice of psychology* (pp. 71–112). Washington, DC: American Psychological Association.

Vaughan, F., Wittine, B., & Walsh, R. (1996). Transpersonal psychology and the religious person. In E. Shafranske (Ed.), *Religion and the clinical practice of psychology* (pp. 483–509). Washington, DC: American Psychological Association.

Vernon, A. (Ed.). (1993). *Counseling children and adolescents.* Denver, CO: Love.

Vitz, P. C. (1990). The use of stories in moral development: New psychological reasons for an old education method. *American Psychologist, 45,* 709–720.

Vitz, P. C. (1992a). Narratives and counseling: Part 1. From analysis of past to stories about it. *Journal of Psychology and Theology, 20,* 11–19.

Vitz, P. C. (1992b). Narratives and counseling: Part 2. From stories of the past to stories for the future. *Journal of Psychology and Theology, 20,* 20–27.

Wagar, W. W. (1977). *World views: A study in comparative history.* New York: Holt, Rinehart & Winston.

Wallas, G. (1926). *The art of thought.* New York: Harcourt, Brace.

Wallis, C. (1996, June 24). Faith and healing. *Time,* pp. 58–64.

Wann, T. W. (1964). *Behaviorism and phenomenology.* Chicago: University of Chicago Press.

Warner, C. T. (1986). What we are. *Brigham Young University Studies, 26,* 39–63.

Warner, C. T. (1995). *Bonds of anguish, bonds of love.* Salt Lake City, UT: Arbinger.

Warner, C. T., & Olson, T. D. (1984). Another view of family conflict and family wholeness. *Association of Mormon Counselors and Psychotherapists Journal, 10,* 15–20.

Watson, J. B. (1983). *Psychology from the standpoint of a behaviorist.* Dover, NH: Frances Pinter. (Original work published 1924).

Weber, P. J. (Ed.). (1990). *Equal separation: Understanding the religion clauses of the first amendment.* Westport, CT: Greenwood Press.

Weidlich, W. (1990). Reconciling concepts between natural science and theology. In J. Fennema & I. Paul (Eds.), *Science and religion: One world-changing perspectives on reality* (pp. 73–86). Norwell, MA: Kluwer Academic.

Wells, G. W. (in press). The context of religion in clinical child psychology. In W. K. Sliverman & T. N. Ollendick (Eds.), *Developmental issues in the clinical treatment of children.* Boston: Allyn & Bacon.

Wertheimer, M. (1970). *A brief history of psychology.* New York: Holt, Rinehart & Winston.

Whiting, J. R. S. (1983). *Religions of man.* Leckhampton, England: Stanley Thornes.

Wicks, R. J., Parsons, R. D., & Capps, D. (Eds.). (1985). *Clinical handbook of pastoral counseling.* New York: Paulist Press.

Woodward, K. L., & Underwood, A. (1993, December 27). Angels. *Newsweek,* pp. 52–57.

Worthington, E. L., Jr. (1986). Religious counseling: A review of published empirical research. *Journal of Counseling and Development, 64,* 421–431.

Worthington, E. L., Jr. (1988). Understanding the values of religious clients: A model and its application to counseling. *Journal of Counseling Psychology, 35,* 166–174.

Worthington, E. L., Jr. (1989a). Religious faith across the life span: Implications for counseling and research. *The Counseling Psychologist, 17,* 555–612.

Worthington, E. L., Jr. (1989b). *Marriage counseling: A Christian approach to counseling couples.* Downers Grove, IL: InterVarsity Press.

Worthington, E. L., Jr. (1990). Marriage counseling: A Christian approach to counseling couples. *Counseling and Values, 35,* 3–15.

Worthington, E. L., Jr. (Ed.). (1993). *Psychotherapy and religious values.* Grand Rapids, MI: Baker Book House.

Worthington, E. L., Jr., & DiBlasio, F. A. (1990). Promoting mutual forgiveness within the fractured relationship. *Psychotherapy, 27,* 219–223.

Worthington, E. L., Jr., Dupont, P. D., Berry, J. T., & Duncan, L. A. (1988). Christian therapists' and clients' perceptions of religious psychotherapy in private and agency settings. *Journal of Psychology and Theology, 16,* 282–293.

Worthington, E. L., Jr., Kurusu, T. A., McCullough, M. E., & Sanders, S. J. (1996). Empirical research on religion and psychotherapeutic processes and outcomes: A ten-year review and research prospectus. *Psychological Bulletin, 119*, 448–487.

Worthington, E. L., Jr., & Scott, G. G. (1983). Goal selection for counseling with potentially religious clients by professional and student counselors in explicitly Christian or secular settings. *Journal of Psychology and Theology, 11*, 318–319.

Wright, L. M., Watson, W. L., & Bell, J. M. (1996). *Beliefs: The heart of healing in families and illness.* New York: Basic Books.

Wulff, D. M. (1991). *Psychology of religion: Classic and contemporary views.* New York: Wiley.

Wulff, D. M. (1997). *Psychology of religion: Classic and contemporary views* (2nd ed.). New York: Wiley.

Yalom, I. D. (1980). *Existential psychotherapy.* New York: Basic Books.

Younggren, J. N. (1993). Ethical issues in religious psychotherapy. *Register Report, 19*, 7–8.

AUTHOR INDEX

SUBJECT INDEX

implementation of meta-empathy,
136–137
significance of, 88–89
sources, 259
spiritual psychodynamic intervention, 261–267
Catholic (Roman), 97, 212, 260, 261,
267
Children and adolescents
parental consent for therapy, 252
spiritual intervention with,
162–163, 249–252
Christian, 55–56, 153, 165, 207, 213,
238, 244, 250, 260, 286
Christians, 8, 56, 123, 232
Christianity, 17, 23, 54–58, 59–61, 215
orthodox, 8, 238
Church-state separation, 159–163
Classical realism, 26, 28
decline of, in science, 36–37
vs. critical realism, 38
vs. theistic realism, 89, 316
Client perspective
mistrust of psychotherapy, 122–124
therapeutic significance, 50–53
treatment packages and sensitivity
to, 247
Cognitive processes
assessment of religious problem-solving style, 177–178
ways of knowing, 310–313
Cognitive psychology
early development, 31–32, 43
early research, 39–40
religious cognitive therapy, 242–244
spiritual interventions, 240, 260
use of sacred writings, 210, 211
Community psychology, 340–341
Confession, 212
Confidentiality
reporting client's unhealthy behaviors, 154–156
therapy with associates, 145–147
Confucianism, 62, 65
Consciousness
assumptions of modernist science, 26
psychological conceptualizations of,
27, 39–40
spiritual implications of, 40
Consultations and referrals
case report, 260
with client's religious leader,
148–149, 151–152, 174–175
211, 220–222, 227
with pastoral counselors, 341

Contemplation and meditation
defined, 205
requirements for, 205–206
spiritual compatibility, 207
therapeutic indications, 206–207
types of, 205
utilization in psychotherapy, 206
Conversion experiences, 84, 109
Coping style
religious problem-solving style,
177–178
spiritual identity and, 179
Crisis intervention, case report, 260
Critical realism, 38

Death-related visions, 92–99
Definitions, 12–13
Denominational practice, 15–16
advantages, 122
assessment for, 121–122, 194,
195–198
characteristics, 238
client's doctrinal knowledge,
181–182
contemplation and meditation techniques in, 207
ethical considerations, 168–169
interventions, 238
therapeutic stance for, 121
use of prayer in, 204
use of ritual and worship, 217–218
values-related interventions,
226–227
Depression
case report, 268–271
religiosity correlated with, 84
religious cognitive therapy for,
242–244
Determinism
as basis of modernist science, 25
conflict with religious philosophy,
29
decline of, in science, 36–37
in development of psychological science, 27
Diversity, 45

Eastern spiritual tradition
assessment instruments, 198
meditation practices, 205

historical development of Western civilization, 23
role of forgiveness in, 212
sacred texts, 208
worldview, 54–58, 208

Legal issues, church-state separation, 159–163
Locus of control/locus of responsibility, 52
Lutheran, 286

Marital therapy
    assessment, 252
    case report, 260, 274–275
    spiritual practice, 249
Marriage
    faithful intimacy in, 106–107
    in theistic spiritual worldview, 107
Marxism, 53
Materialism, 25, 28
    conflict with religious philosophy, 29
Measurement of spirituality, 77–78, 85
    for Christians, 195–196
    for non-Christians, 196–198
    for outcome research, 331
Mechanistic beliefs, 25
    conflict with religious philosophy, 29
    decline of, in science, 36–37
    in early development of psychological science, 27, 28, 32
Meditation. See Contemplation and meditation
Mental health and dysfunction
    alienation from eternal identity in, 101–102, 175, 179
    altruistic service and, 219
    categories of, 79–80
    conceptualizations of religion in, 41–42
    enmeshed religious factors, 84, 172–173, 175
    family relations and, 107–108
    healing process, 213
    importance of social relations, 109
    individual worldview as determinant of, 51–52
    models of religious-spiritual well-being, 182–185

pathological forms of religiosity, 183–185
    personal agency and, 104–105
    protective role of spirituality, 9, 52, 172–173
    self-deception and, 105–106
    severity of illness and treatment design, 128–129
    spiritually integrative personality theory, 110–111
    studies of spiritual/religious factors in, 78–84
    use/abuse of power and, 108–109
    value systems and, 109–110, 131, 223
Mental health professions
    conceptual developments compatible with spirituality, 44 45, 47–48, 76
    historical scientific development, 23–24
    tradition of excluding spiritual content, 6, 10, 17 21–23, 33
    trends towards spirituality, 3, 6, 9, 17, 48
    value systems in, 110
    See also Psychology; Psychotherapy
Mental imagery, 205, 206
Meta-empathy
    assessment and, 198–199
    defined, 102, 136
    implementation, 136–138
    rationale, 137
    therapist preparation for, 136
Metaphysics
    client assessment, 176
    major types of worldviews, 53
    of modernist science, 24–25
    in shaping worldviews, 50–51
Methodological pluralism, 14, 318–322
Middle Ages, 23
Modeling
    ethical values, in therapy, 131
    for faithful intimacy, 106
Modernism
    conflicts with religious tradition, 28–29
    in historical development of psychology, 26–28
    philosophical assumptions of, 24–26
    rejection of spirituality in, 10

Mormon, 97, 137, 212, 224, 232, 233, 237, 238, 291
Mormonism, 208
Multicultural practice
    historical development, 44–45
    therapeutic stance for, 118–119
    therapist skills for, 119
    training for, 338
    worldview sensitivity in, 52–53
Muslim, 153, 165, 208, 223
Muslims, 8, 15, 57–58, 238

Naturalism
    assumptions of, 318–319
    as basis of modernist science, 24–25
    in historical development of psychology, 26, 32
    reconsideration of, in psychology, 47–48
    spiritual worldviews and, 66–67
    as worldview, 4, 53
Near-death experiences, 96–99
Neurosis, religious belief as, 41–42
Newtonian science, 23–24, 36, 317

Obsessive-compulsive disorder, case report, 288–291
Opening Your Heart program, 246–247
Orthodoxy, 177, 209
Outcome factors
    client's perceptions of God, 180
    research on spirituality, 323, 330–331
    in spiritual therapy, 252–253
    therapeutic relationship, 122, 172

Pantheism, 63
Pastoral counseling, 341
    dual relationship concerns, 144–145
Perfectionism, 244
Personality development
    concept of good and evil in, 111
    contributions of spiritual strategy, 339–340
    eternal identity, 101–104
    family kinship for, 107–108
    free agency for, 104–105
    intimate relationships for, 106
    perceptions of God and, 179–180
    personal integrity and, 105–106

    social relations for, 109, 112
    spiritual identity, 178–179
    spiritual interventions with children and adolescents 249–251
    spiritually integrative theory, 99–101, 110–111, 112
    theistic spiritual view, 17
    use/abuse of power and, 108–109
    value systems for, 109–110, 223
    values-lifestyle congruence, 180–181
Pharmacotherapy, 260
Phenomenology
    death-related visions, 92–99
    measurement of spiritual experience, 77–78
    religious, 13, 29
    spiritual, 13
    studies of spirituality, 327
Physical health
    altruistic service and, 219
    heart disease, 246–247
    spirituality and, 78
    studies of religiosity and, 86–88
Physics, 36–37
Polytheism, 63
Positivism
    assumptions of, 318–319
    in conceptual basis of modernist science, 26
    decline of, in science, 36–37
    in early psychological science, 28
    postmodernist rejection of, 38
Postmodernism
    compatibility with spiritual strategy, 76, 322
    conceptual basis, 37–38
    contextuality of, 319–322
    as philosophy of science, 38, 318
Power relations, 108–109
    usurping religious authority in therapy, 148–150, 151–153 227
Prayer
    on behalf of others, 202
    case report, 261–267
    with client during session, 204
    defined, 202
    in denominational practice, 204
    positive effects of, 202–203
    therapeutic considerations, 203–205
    varieties of, 202
Premonitions of death, 94–95
Protective role of spirituality, 9, 52, 172, 173

altruistic service, 219
assessment for, 173–174
in mental health, 85–86
personality theory, 110–111
in physical health, 86–88
religious community, 148–149,
173–174, 270
Protestant, 233
Protestantism, 55
Protestants, 8, 15, 56
Psychoanalytic theory/practice
early dissenters from, 42–43
historical development of, 26–28
receptivity to spiritual concepts, 44
rejection of religious issues, 33
Psychology
assumptions of modernist science in
development of, 26–28
cognitive theories in development
of, 31–32, 43
conceptual conflicts with religious
tradition, 28–29
conceptualizations of mentality,
39–40
humanistic beliefs in development
of, 31, 43
multicultural counseling movement,
44–45
reconsideration of naturalist basis,
47–48
research on religion, 41–42
spiritual thinkers in development of,
32
systemic approach, 43
traditional rejection of religion/spirit-
uality in, 33 41–42
value systems in, 45–47
Psychotherapy
case reports, 259–306
challenges to modernist project,
35–36, 43–44
difficulty of excluding spiritual issues, 10
early dissenters from scientific modernism, 32, 42–44
eclectic practice, 44
goals, 230
goals of theistic spiritual strategy,
116
major conceptual traditions, 43, 44.
See also specific tradition
methodological pluralism for,
318–322

multicultural sensitivity, 44–45
religious client with reservations
about, 122–124
significance of individual worldview,
51–53
significance of theistic spiritual strategy, 11–12, 91–92 142
spiritual practice in, 10–11, 18
value systems in, 45–47, 131–135
See also Mental health professions
Public opinion/understanding
hopes for science, 40–41
interest in spiritual matters, 5, 41

Quantum change
religious conversion, 84
therapeutic use, 109

Rational-emotive therapy, 244, 260,
283–285
Rationalism, 312
Redemption, 213
Reductionism, 25
conflict with religious philosophy,
29
decline of, in science, 36–37
in development of psychological science, 27, 28
Relativism
ethical, 26, 28, 29, 46–47, 129–131
moral, vs. spiritual values, 110
in postmodernism, 37, 76
Relaxation techniques, 205, 206
See also Contemplation and meditation
Religious
defined, 12, 13
interventions, 236–237
Religious institutions
assessment of client affiliation,
176–177
authoritarianism in, 108–109
church-state separation issues in practice, 159–163
client-therapist participation in worship, 217
client's doctrinal knowledge,
181–182
common features, 67
common moral values, 223
conflicts among worldviews, 67–74

treatment manuals, 247
treatment packages, 241–242,
247–249
trivialization of sacred matters in
spiritual practice 167–168,
247–249
twelve-step programs, 244–245
use of fellowship community service
activities, 219–220
use of forgiveness, 211–214
use of sacred writings, 209–211
use of worship and ritual, 214–218
values clarification, 225–226
values correction, 226–227
values instruction, 227
Theistic, spiritual strategy
assessment, 127–128, 187–199
basic assumptions, 76–78
challenges to, from traditional psychology, 16
client's role, 138
clinical practice, 17–18
concept of God in, 11, 16, 17,
76–77
contraindications, 252–253
denominationally specific practice,
15–16
as eclectic practice, 14
as ecumenical practice, 15
epistemological assumptions, 313
ethical practice, 17
foundations of, 16–17
future prospects, 18
implementing interventions,
128–129
meaning of spiritual in, 77
moral framework, 132
need for empirical research, 13–14
postmodernism and, 76
potential ethical challenges, 143
qualities for viability of, 13–16
research designs for, 322–330
research needs, 18, 256–257, 309,
333–335
significance for psychotherapy,
11–12, 91–92, 142, 230
therapeutic goals, 115–118, 230
therapeutic stance, 118–122
therapeutic valuing, 129–135
therapist's spiritual preparation for,
135–138

therapy relationship, 122–126,
138–142
Theistic realism, 88–92, 316–317
Theistic spiritual strategy
church-state separation issues,
159–163
Theistic worldview
conceptual conflicts with modernist
psychology, 28–29
Eastern religious tradition, 54,
62–66
implications for psychotherapy practice, 49–50
major monotheist religions, 11–12,
54–62
role of forgiveness in, 212
science in, 313–316
use of ritual and worship, 215
values of, 129
Therapeutic change, 111
client's spiritual beliefs and,
117–118
conversion experiences for, 109
family relations as factor in,
107–108
goals of theistic spiritual strategy,
116–118, 128
multidimensional conceptualization,
115–116
as restoration of eternal identity,
102–104, 116–117, 175
by restoring capacity for intimacy,
106–107
role of forgiveness for, 212
spiritual identity and, 179
spirituality as source of, 6
theistic spiritual strategy for, 111
through enhancement of personal
agency, 104–105
through inspired integrity, 105–106
unique feature of theistic spiritual
strategy, 116
use of power as target of, 109
use of sacred writings for, 210
Therapeutic relationship
appropriate value style of therapists,
132–135
building, 124–126
challenges to, 139–142
confronting client's unhealthy values, 154–156

ABOUT THE AUTHORS

P. Scott Richards received his PhD in counseling psychology in 1988 from the University of Minnesota. He is currently an associate professor in the Department of Counseling and Special Education at Brigham Young University, where he is the director of the PhD program in counseling psychology. He was given the dissertation of the year award in 1990 from Division 5 (Evaluation, Statistics, and Measurement) of the American Psychological Association for his psychometric investigation of religious bias in moral development research. Dr. Richards has a long-standing interest in research on religion, spirituality, mental health, and psychological measurement and has published a large number of scholarly articles on these topics. He is a licensed psychologist and maintains a small private psychotherapy practice at the Center for Change, in Orem, Utah.

Allen E. Bergin received his PhD in Clinical Psychology in 1960 from Stanford University. He was a faculty member at Teachers College, Columbia University, from 1961 to 1972. He has been a professor of psychology at Brigham Young University since 1972, where he has served as director of the Values Institute (1976–1978) and director of the PhD program in clinical psychology (1989–1993). Dr. Bergin is past-president of the Society for Psychotherapy Research and coeditor of the classic *Handbook of Psychotherapy and Behavior Change*. In 1989 he received an Award for Distinguished Professional Contributions to Knowledge from the American Psychological Association (APA). In 1990, Division 36 (Psychology of Religion) of APA presented him with the William James Award for Psychology of Religion Research. He is a licensed psychologist and maintains a small consultation practice.